The New
England League

ALSO BY CHARLIE BEVIS

*Sunday Baseball: The Major Leagues' Struggle to Play
Baseball on the Lord's Day, 1876–1934* (McFarland, 2003)

*Mickey Cochrane: The Life of a Baseball Hall
of Fame Catcher* (McFarland, 1998)

The New England League

A Baseball History, 1885–1949

CHARLIE BEVIS

McFarland & Company, Inc., Publishers
Jefferson, North Carolina, and London

LIBRARY OF CONGRESS CATALOGUING-IN-PUBLICATION DATA

Bevis, Charle, 1954–
    The New England League : a baseball history, 1885–1949 /
Charlie Bevis.
      p.   cm.
    Includes bibliographical references and index.

    ISBN 978-0-7864-3159-5
    softcover : 50# alkaline paper ∞

    1. New England League — History.   2. Minor league baseball —
United States — History.   I. Title.
GV875.N49 B48   2007
796.357'640974 — dc22   2007048128

British Library cataloguing data are available

On the cover: The championship 1903 Lowell (Massachusetts) ball
club (National Baseball Hall of Fame Library, Cooperstown, New
York); a map of the New England states (Clipart.com); and a postcard
of the Amoskeag Mills in Manchester, New Hampshire (New Hampshire Historical Society)

Manufactured in the United States of America

*McFarland & Company, Inc., Publishers
  Box 611, Jefferson, North Carolina 28640
    www.mcfarlandpub.com*

To Claude Davidson and
Jake Morse, two long-forgotten,
unsung heroes in the making of minor
league baseball in New England

Table of Contents

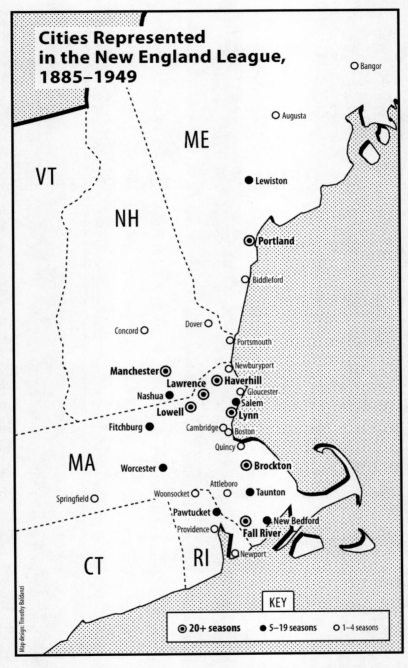

Cities Represented in the New England League, 1885–1949

ME

VT

NH

○ Bangor

○ Augusta

● Lewiston

◉ **Portland**

○ Biddleford

Concord ○

Dover ○

○ Portsmouth

Newburyport ○

Manchester ◉

Lawrence ◉ ◉ **Haverhill**

Nashua ●

○ Gloucester

Lowell ◉

◉ **Salem**
◉ **Lynn**

Fitchburg ●

Cambridge ○

○ Boston

Quincy ○

MA

Worcester ●

◉ **Brockton**

Attleboro ○

Woonsocket ○

● **Taunton**

Springfield ○

Pawtucket ●

Providence ○

◉ ● **New Bedford**

Fall River

Newport ○

CT

RI

KEY

◉ **20+ seasons**   ● **5–19 seasons**   ○ **1–4 seasons**

Map design: Timothy Baldanzi

Map of New England showing the location of all cities that fielded ball clubs in the New England League throughout its minor league history (Timothy Baldanzi).

Preface

The confluence of baseball history, economic history, and the geography of my upbringing fostered my urge to unearth the rich history of the New England League, which lay buried within a mountain of newspaper microfilm lying undisturbed in filing cabinets in libraries across the region.

My research for this book began in 1998, but was interrupted as I pursued a major topic that affected the development of the New England League: Sunday baseball. Coping with the strictures against playing baseball on Sunday was the dominant theme of the history of the New England League, from its formal inception in 1885 until Sunday baseball was made legal in Massachusetts for the 1929 season.

This legal prohibition in the New England states constrained ball clubs from attracting workers from the region's textile mills and shoe factories on their one day off during the work week. Further constraining the New England League was an enclave of permissiveness for Sunday baseball in Rhode Island, where the Providence club of the Eastern League played Sabbath contests at the Rocky Point resort on Narragansett Bay. Crowds flocked to the Sunday games at Rocky Point, and minor league executives ruthlessly protected the money-making franchise in Providence from incursion by the New England League.

Despite the importance of the subject, very little research on Sunday baseball existed in sports literature. My book *Sunday Baseball: The Major Leagues' Struggle to Play Baseball on the Lord's Day, 1876–1934* was published in 2003 to fill that void. After my manuscript for that book was finished, my research continued on the history of the New England League. Portions of Chapter 1 appeared earlier in the article "The Last Days of the New England

1

League" in the 2000 edition of *The National Pastime*, published by the Society for American Baseball Research.

Assembling this history of the New England League was no easy task. I had to depend primarily on newspaper microfilm, since there was no battery of compiled secondary research and precious little primary research related to the league's history (much the same situation I had found earlier with the Sunday baseball topic). Fortunately, several good resources were available to make my research possible. The Boston Public Library, which is a repository for microfilm of many old and forgotten Massachusetts newspapers, was an excellent resource. The Maine State Library in Augusta houses microfilm of newspapers from the state's larger cities, as does the New Hampshire State Library in Concord.

The Pollard Memorial Library in Lowell, Massachusetts, was a treasure trove of obscure, long-forgotten local newspapers, which provided not only insight on the Lowell teams but also information about New England League happenings and baseball gossip from other cities. The *Lowell Daily News*, which ceased printing about 1910, was an invaluable resource for nineteenth century research on the league. Who would have thought that the McArthur Public Library in Biddeford, Maine, would have been an essential stop in learning about the league's formation and initial year of play in 1885? Of all the reporters in New England, the baseball writer for the *Biddeford Journal* had the best grasp of what transpired during the league's first three months. Too bad the Biddeford team disbanded in July 1885 and never again fielded a team in the league.

The history of the New England League is rich in characters, stories, and oddities that occurred on the playing field, which was extensively covered by contemporary newspapers. This book would have taken many more years to produce, and consumed as many pages as Edward Gibbon's *The History of the Decline and Fall of the Roman Empire*, had I tried to include all these aspects of the league's history.

Therefore, I chose to focus on the cultural aspects and the primary people that shaped results in that area. In addition to contributing to Sunday baseball history, the New England League was a minor league pioneer in postseason playoffs, evening baseball (twilight and night), and the use of black players.

Hidden far beneath the surface of New England League history is exactly how Nashua, New Hampshire, came to be the site for the Brooklyn Dodgers to develop its first wave of black players after the signing of Jackie Robinson. I was always troubled by the explanation of how Roy Campanella and Don Newcombe "accidentally" wound up playing at Nashua in 1946. Having dug deep, I'm highly confident that Branch Rickey had in fact researched the situation, planned to use Nashua as the base for black players, and then created a fable to disguise this fact from the public. Support for this conclusion was "hidden in plain sight," as they say, buried in obscure newspapers around New England and even in the *Nashua Telegraph* itself. Few, if any, previous researchers looked at its editions published in 1945, which contained a cornucopia of information before the club's formal creation in January 1946. Articles in the *Boston Guardian*, a little-remembered newspaper in Boston's black community, also lent support to this thesis.

For the early decades of the league's history, it was hard to ferret out the truth, as the league's two administrators both wrote baseball articles for the major sporting publications. Tim Murnane, league president from 1892 to 1915, wrote for the *Boston Globe* and the *Sporting News*. Jake Morse, league secretary from 1892 to 1912, wrote for the *Boston Herald* and *Sporting Life* until 1907. Both individuals obviously put their own spin on events affecting the league.

Additionally, few newspapers in New England League cities opposed Murnane, since most were trying to win approbation for their local teams. This is exhibited in an interesting contrast in the reporting of Morse's exit as league secretary in 1913, where the *Boston Globe* reported that Morse "resigned" while the *Haverhill Evening Gazette* reported that Morse "retired" and intimated that he was forced out of the job.

Newspaper coverage of the several periods where Claude Davidson was league president from the 1920s to the 1940s was more objective, in some cases even cynical about the league's future. Davidson, whom I characterize as the Don Quixote of New England minor league baseball, had much less control of the press than did Murnane during his presidency and needed to curry favor with the baseball writers.

An undercurrent to this baseball history is the economic history of New England's textile and shoe industries, which indirectly supplied the spectator base that attended ball games and often the ownership of the ball clubs themselves.

The aging textile mills of Lowell have far more meaning to me today than in 1986 when I moved to Chelmsford, a Lowell suburb. To many current residents, the mills are simply gentrified condominium developments; to me, they exude baseball's past in Lowell. The mills provided the economic base for small businessmen to earn a living and attend ball games in the late afternoon, while the mill workers got to go to an occasional game on holidays and on Saturday once the half-holiday on that day became part of the standard work week. In 1929 and 1933, mill workers could finally attend ball games on Sunday.

My maternal grandfather, an immigrant from Poland, and two of his children (my aunt and uncle) worked in the textile mills in Lowell during World War I. The 1918 *Lowell City Directory* indicates that Michal and Anna Karasiewicz and their four children boarded at 15 Winter Street, and that Michal and son Aleksander were textile operatives while daughter Stefania was a weaver. The family left the grit of urban Lowell in October 1920 when my grandfather bought a small farm in rural Bridgewater.

My connection to the shoe industry is very deeply ingrained, since I grew up in Bridgewater, which is ten miles south of Brockton, renowned as the Shoe City. There were several shoe factories in Bridgewater, which employed many members of my family, most notably my Uncle Sam and Aunt Didi. I even worked in a shoe factory during my summers while in college in the 1970s, at the Lucey Shoe Company. Charlie, the foreman of the Making Room, made sure I understood that my goal was college, not forty years in a shoe factory.

My father, Harold Bevis, worked thirty years at the Jenkins Mill in Bridgewater, as did many of my uncles (including Uncle Alec, the Aleksander who worked in the textile mills). The mill manufactured leatherboard, which was used in the making of shoes. My dad also played semipro baseball in 1933, a third baseman for the Bridgewater Town Team, which I discovered in the 1980s while researching my family tree. This was where I whetted my appetite to know more about the New England League. It seemed to me that the local newspapers were more interested in covering the games of the Bridgewater Town Team than they were in reporting the New England League games of the Brockton team. Why was this? I asked myself. The journey had just begun.

Jenkins Mill, the shoe factories, and the textile mills were just parts of the landscape to me, until I understood that the textile and shoe industries had shaped the development of a regional minor league baseball organization, the New England League.

While many of the textile mills and shoe factories still stand today to remind us of their pasts, few physical manifestations remain to signify that the New England League ever existed. Any ballpark used in the 1940s, e.g., McCoy Stadium and Holman Stadium, has been refurbished well beyond what spectators from that earlier era could recognize. While baseball is still played at the same location as it was in 1902 at Varick Park in Manchester and Spalding Park in Lowell, the grounds used today by local amateur teams have been converted to Gill Stadium and Alumni Stadium, respectively.

A plaque at the Boys and Girls Club in Fall River announces that Napoleon Lajoie played there in the New England League in 1896. A similar plaque in Taunton, remembering the 1899 exploits of Christy Mathewson in the New England League, has been removed from the field where it was originally installed and is gathering dust in the back room of a recreation department building.

In Nashua, there is Campanella Way, a road near Holman Stadium. Far removed from the stadium on West Hollis Street in downtown Nashua, there is a mural painted on the side of a building depicting Campanella and Newcombe in 1946. There are no signs pointing the way there. You either know where to look or you encounter it accidentally while driving around the city.

The history of the New England League, with its twists and turns through many epochs of baseball and economic history, provides a microcosm of a changing America.

1

Final Days,
September 1949

Bᴏʙ Pᴜɢᴀᴛᴄʜ ᴡᴀs ᴛʜᴇ ʟᴀsᴛ ʙᴀᴛᴛᴇʀ to face a pitch in the long, storied history of the New England League.

On September 18, 1949, at about 4:30 P.M. in Portland, Maine, Pugatch hit an infield fly off the serve of pitcher Charley Dyke to end a Sunday afternoon game. With that pop out, the Portland Pilots defeated the Springfield Cubs to capture the 1949 New England League title.

"What a way to be remembered," Pugatch recalled from his home in Delray Beach, Florida, in 1999. "I thought all I had left of my baseball career was my autograph," he joked of his baseball playing days that ended in the Texas League in 1953 without having made the major leagues. "It was so long ago, I can't remember a thing about the game," Pugatch sheepishly admitted about that last bat-swing of New England League play.[1]

Pugatch, along with the other Springfield players on the losing end of that seven-game playoff series with Portland, didn't receive a dime for playing for the league title.

"League President Claude Davidson presented the $1,200 for which the team played — winner take all — to Manager Skeeter Newsome, whom the Pilots lugged off the field to his obvious embarrassment," the *Portland Press-Herald* reported of the celebration following the final New England League game.[2]

Hank Nasternak, the Springfield shortstop, had no regrets about being on the loser's end of the winner-take-all deal, since he had pushed for it.

"The winner of the game was supposed to get seventy-five percent and the loser twenty-five percent," Nasternak recalled from his home in Buffalo,

New York, in 1999. "We had a choice to vote one hundred percent winner and zero percent loser. I was surprised that a lot of our players voted for the first option. I was very annoyed and spoke up for the hundred percent winner's share. After a little debate, our manager Bob Peterson finally agreed to the winner-take-all. The sad fact about it was we got clobbered in the last game."[3]

In 1949, the New England League was a Class B minor league, four rungs down from the major leagues. While the league's history dated back to 1877 during the earliest days of professional baseball, by August 1949 the league was on its last legs with just four teams remaining among the eight teams that had started the season.

The Providence Grays were the first New England League team to fold in 1949, disbanding on June 21. The league had run the team since early June, when the Grays failed to meet the team's payroll. Hurting the club's fortunes was the fact that Providence was an independent team, not a farm team of a major league team, and played its games at Cranston Stadium in a suburb of Providence.

"Providence became the largest city in the United States not represented in organized baseball at midnight last night," the *Providence Journal* glumly reported, "when the New England League decided to close out the franchise of the Providence Grays and continue as a seven-club circuit."[4]

Four weeks later, on July 19, three more New England League teams succumbed to economic distress: Fall River, Lynn, and Manchester. League president Davidson blamed the franchise collapses on local unemployment and redrew the schedule to handle the four remaining clubs: Nashua, Pawtucket, Portland, and Springfield. But larger forces were at work as the New England League spiraled into permanent demise.

"Several factors were instrumental in the death knell of organized baseball in this city," the *Manchester Union* explained about the failure of the Manchester Yankees. The proximity of the Boston Red Sox and the Boston Braves and televised night games played important roles. "Another item which must not be overlooked was the tag of 78 cents for admission to the local bailiwick. It must be remembered that this is a mill town and there aren't too many people who could afford to dish out that kind of cold cash three or four times a week."[5]

"Night baseball in the majors has killed all interest in the minor cities of the New England League," said the *Lynn Evening Item*, pinpointing the reason that the Lynn franchise failed. "Sunday baseball here for the last few years has proven a dud as fans flocked to Fenway Park and Braves Field or went on weekend motor excursions to summer camps or to the many beaches.

Against these outside interests, Lynn hasn't a chance to retain organized baseball here and the attendance at Fraser Field has been pitiful to behold."[6]

Fans were not only more interested in the Red Sox and Braves, but also more inclined to support local amateur teams. For example, in the *Fall River Herald*, CYO League baseball and Girls Playground League softball had higher status in the "Sports Schedule" than the New England League games of the Fall River Indians.[7]

To cope with only four remaining teams in the league, Davidson essentially canceled the first half of the season. He declared Nashua the winner of the first half, and announced that the postseason playoffs would match the top three teams of the second half of the season. Brooklyn immediately advanced the best players on its Nashua farm club to higher-classification teams in its farm system, causing Nashua to drop to last place in the second half and thus miss the playoffs.

The Pawtucket Slaters captured first place in the second half, clinching the crown with nine games to go. Portland finished in second place and made the standings look closer than the race actually was by sweeping the season-ending, four-game series with Pawtucket. Springfield finished in third place.

Somewhat illogically, Davidson retained the standard playoff format even with only three teams participating. The league's standard playoff format matched the first- and third-place teams in one series and the second- and fourth-place teams in the other series, with the winners meeting for the league championship.

Pawtucket, by virtue of its first-place finish, did not earn a bye for the first round of the playoffs to watch the second- and third-place teams square off, but rather was matched against the third-place finisher. "The New England League playoffs will open at McCoy Stadium Sept. 7 with the Pawtucket Slaters playing the third place club in the final second half standings, probably Springfield, it was announced today by League President Claude Davidson," the *Pawtucket Times* reported. "The second place team will meet the winner of the Pawtucket-third place team series in a best of seven-game championship series."[8]

Although this arrangement seems unfair to Pawtucket, at least the club would gain some additional revenue by playing another round of playoffs. However, only 721 fans showed up at McCoy Stadium for the first game of the playoffs, on a Wednesday night. Worse, the Slaters blew an 8–2 lead and lost 11–9 to Springfield, a team that Pawtucket had defeated in seven of its last eight meetings during the regular season. After the opening game loss, Pawtucket seemed to fold up in the second game, as Springfield scored seven runs in the first inning to cruise to a 10–6 victory.

With first-place Pawtucket out of the playoffs, Portland and Springfield met in a best-of-seven-games series for the Governor's Cup. In many ways, it was a fitting end to the New England League, illustrating how the league had changed since its formative years in the nineteenth century.

Portland and Springfield led the league in attendance in 1949, Springfield attracting 102,387 paying customers and Portland 83,100. The two most successful franchises in drawing fans were located the farthest distance from Boston among the eight teams that began the season. Portland and Springfield were not dependent on the textile industry, as were Pawtucket and Nashua. Springfield was renowned for firearms manufacturing and Portland for shipping (the nickname Pilots referred to the pilot boats that led larger ships into the harbor).

It looked to be a quick series. Portland demolished Springfield in the first game, 20–4, as the Cubs had to get by without second baseman Ed McDade, who had returned to his college studies at Notre Dame. Although Portland won three of the first four games, Springfield battled back in a bid for the winner-take-all payoff by winning the fifth and sixth games.

The Cubs needed to win the fifth game without center fielder Pugatch, another education-minded Springfield player, who missed the game because he was registering for classes at Boston University. "I promised my dad when I signed for $5,000 to play baseball that I'd finish school," Pugatch noted about his baseball career. "It took me seven years or so to finish school. I started playing pro ball and college in 1946. I finished playing pro ball and college in 1953."[9]

As if to symbolize the league's problems, the sixth game of the series at Portland Stadium was delayed a day to Saturday in order that a high school football game could be played there on Friday night. The match between Deering High and Portland High on Friday drew 6,000 fans; the Portland-Springfield game on Sunday attracted just 1,800 fans to see the seventh and deciding game for the New England League championship.

Portland thwarted the Springfield comeback attempt by erupting for eight runs in the first inning to coast to the 11–0 victory and gleefully split the $1,200 winner-take-all pot.

One happy recipient on the Portland team was outfielder Royce "Pinky" Watson, who had married South Portland resident Barbara DePeter right after the last game of the regular season. There was no time for a honeymoon, though, since the playoffs started just a few days later.

Watson, a North Carolina native, stayed in Maine following the end of his baseball career in 1951. He and Barbara lived in the Portland area, where they raised five children and he kept his hand in baseball by coaching Little League and American Legion teams.

Barbara and Royce "Pinky" Watson, an outfielder for the Portland Pilots, at their wedding in 1949 that occurred between the end of the regular season and the beginning of the New England League playoffs (courtesy of Barbara Watson).

"Pinky played baseball for the love of the game, certainly not for the money back then," Barbara Watson explained in 2000. "Pinky stayed in Maine because there was more opportunity here. He got a job working in the Warren Paper Mill. Back in his hometown of Mount Airy, there weren't many jobs. They had a big quarry, and most people worked there, but that was about it. The town was much smaller than it is now. Back then, it was a lot like Mayberry in the *Andy Griffith Show*."[10]

Barbara Watson was a big baseball fan when Pinky played in the New England League. "I went to a lot of Pilots games. South Portland, where I grew up, was only about five miles from the ball park," she remembered. As for television destroying the minor leagues, Barbara, a dyed-in-the-wool baseball fan, remarked, "Why would anyone stay home to watch a game on TV when you can see one in person?"[11]

Pinky Watson died of cancer just before his induction into the Maine Baseball Hall of Fame in 1979. By then, winning the New England League championship in 1949 had become a distant memory.

The failure of the New England League was a precursor to the general decline of the minor leagues following World War II. In 1949, forty-two million people paid to see four hundred and fifty teams play in fifty-nine leagues. By 1954, attendance at minor league games had declined by fifty percent, dropping to nineteen million, and the number of leagues had declined to thirty-six.[12]

In the post-war period of 1946–1949, the New England League gave players such as Pugatch, Nasternak, and Watson a chance to play the game in front of appreciative fans as the era of hometown minor league play began to dissolve. The opportunity to make it to the major leagues was slim. Of the eighteen players that started the seventh game of the Governor's Cup series in 1949, just two — Billy Klaus and Jim Rhodes of Springfield — progressed to play in the major leagues. Even the league's best hitter in 1949, Bob Montag of Pawtucket with a .428 average, never set foot in a major league game.

And, of course, the irony that the last-ever New England League game was played on a Sunday was, no doubt, lost on all the spectators and players at that September 18 game, with the possible exception of league president Davidson.

The legal inability to play Sunday baseball had been a persistent obstacle that inhibited the success of the New England League, not only in the nineteenth century when Sunday laws were widespread, but also well into the twentieth century. Davidson had helped to secure legal sanction for Sunday baseball in Massachusetts for the 1929 season, but by then it was too late for the New England League to flourish.

Before its life was extinguished shortly after that last game on September 18, 1949, the New England League had experienced many ups and downs during its thirty-nine seasons of operation as a minor league. The league had endured a half-dozen potentially fatal stoppages over a seven-decade span, only to be resuscitated for another foray at survival.

Nearly three-quarters of a century before the box score of the league's final game was published, the roots of the venerable New England League were established through a consortium of baseball clubs that had formed a loose confederation in 1877.

2

Roots of the League, 1877

SEVENTY-TWO YEARS BEFORE ITS DEMISE in 1949, the New England League had venerable roots in 1877.

"From a historical viewpoint the story of the minor leagues begins in 1877 with the formation of three different minor league circuits: the International Association, the League Alliance, and the New England League," Robert Obojski wrote in his 1975 book, *Bush League: A History of Minor League Baseball.* Several decades earlier, the *Sporting News* arrived at the same conclusion in its 1905 article "First Minor League; There Were Three in Existence During the Season of 1877."[1]

While this would certainly be an honor to boast about, there were, in fact, no "minor" leagues in 1877, just one "national" and a few "regional" leagues. The labels major and minor wouldn't enter baseball lexicon until several years later after the first National Agreement was formed in 1883.

Reality was that the 1877 version of the New England League, known at the time as the New England Association, was just a loose confederation of five professional teams representing the cities of Fall River, Lowell, Lynn, Manchester, and Providence, which happened to play each other fairly often. The New England Association didn't resemble a league structure in today's vernacular, and was simply a collection of five independent teams. Given that independence, the New England League "neither challenged the National League directly as the International Association had, nor did it try to accommodate the League through the League Alliance."[2]

The *Spalding Guide* in its recap of the 1877 season didn't consider the New England aggregation to be a league. "The game in 1877, so far as figures of any degree of trustworthiness can be obtained, was played in America by six [National] League clubs, thirteen League Alliance clubs, sixteen International Association clubs, [and] thirteen clubs partly or wholly professional but belonging to no organization."[3]

Baseball was still undergoing a transition in 1877, the second year of National League operation. Teams in regional associations like the one in New England had their roots in amateur clubs designed to exhibit, or in some cases to establish, the status of their cities in the post–Civil War industrial economy. In New England, the economy was shaped by the textile and shoe industries. Gradually, teams shifted from purely non-paid players to paying a few of the best players to, by 1877, a complete roster of paid players.

New England had a deep involvement in the development of baseball as a sport, dating back to the game's strictly amateur roots in the mid-nineteenth century. The region's early amateur clubs such as the Olympic Club of Boston, organized in 1854, played a distinct brand of ball called the Massachusetts Game, which differed from the New York Game that eventually became the foundation for the rules of today. The Tri-Mountain Club of Boston, organized in 1857, initiated the adoption of the New York Game within New England, and by 1860, every team was playing this version of baseball.[4]

"Baseball clubs of the 1850s and 1860s often bore a greater resemblance to social clubs and fraternal orders than to athletic teams," Troy Soos wrote in *Before the Curse: The Glory Days of New England Baseball, 1858–1918.* "Ball games were almost incidental; the rituals that surrounded them were what mattered, not the scores." The post-game dinner was often a larger portion of the event than the baseball game itself. "The Lowells, like other New England ball clubs, played for fun and for the fellowship of good sport," another historian wrote. "Clubs entertained visiting players after the game with a reception and often a dinner at which toasts were drunk, speeches made."[5]

After the Civil War, though, athletics began to take precedence over dining. The pinnacle of New England amateur play had been the awarding of a silver baseball for the Championship of New England, a competition dominated by the Tri-Mountain Club and the Lowell Club of Boston. Squabbling and fights ensued over the Silver Ball competition, as recruiting of skilled players and secret payments to some players created a hypocritical atmosphere of "amateur" play. The competition ended in 1868, ushering in the era of pure professional play.

In 1870, the touring professional Cincinnati Red Stockings, undefeated in their coast-to-coast tour in 1869, changed the complexion of top-flight baseball in New England. During the New England segment of its 1870 tour, Cincinnati vanquished the Tri-Mountain Club, 30–6, in Boston, and the

Clippers of Lowell by a 32–5 score. The Cincinnati victories made it quite obvious that the social clubs that drove New England baseball to its prominence could not compete with the paid-player clubs emerging on the national scene.[6]

"Amateur baseball clubs struggled to survive in the 1870s," Soos wrote. "It became a matter of civic pride that a city could afford to acquire and support a professional nine; home-grown teams that played simply for the love of the game were relegated to a lesser status."[7]

In 1871, the Boston Base Ball Association represented the city in the National Association of Professional Base Ball Players, the first nationwide league of professional teams. The Bostons imported talented players from the Cincinnati team (including manager Harry Wright) and several others from Midwestern teams, rather than use local players as the club looked to emulate the success of the Cincinnati ball club.

Many cities and towns throughout New England formed teams, initially paying just a few players but gradually shifting to a complete roster of paid players. These cities sought to exhibit, or in some cases to establish, their status in the burgeoning industrial economy that focused on the textile and shoe industries. But only those clubs with strong financial backing and a dedicated spectator base could afford to pay top players to compete at the highest level. By 1877, just five cities fielded teams in the New England Association.

At this time, locale displaced social club affiliation as the identity of a baseball team. Before the success of the 1869 Cincinnati Red Stockings, nearly all baseball teams were known by a club name (i.e., a nickname) rather than by their home location. As the halo of professional baseball success glowed on a city, baseball teams began adopting their city affiliation as their sole means of recognition. New England Association teams were known exclusively by their home city names; there were no team nicknames. For instance, the team from Lowell was called "the Lowells," the team from Fall River was known as "the Fall Rivers," and the Providence team was called the "Rhode Islands." The one exception was the Live Oaks team based in Lynn, which clung to its amateur roots of a player-oriented club that happened to play its home games in the city of Lynn.

The five 1877 teams were stock companies — owned by stockholders who contributed capital and run by a board of directors, which appointed a president and other officers. The stock companies paid salaries to the players and took the financial risk of making or losing money, as opposed to co-operative ventures that were the scourge of other league operations. Co-operative teams paid players a share of gate receipts after expenses, and were therefore far less stable than their stockholder-owned brethren.

While the 1877 New England Association teams were stock companies, their stockholders during that time leaned more toward the civic aspect of the team's reason d'etre rather than displaying a ruthless business interest in the enterprise. Most stockholders were local businessmen with a vested interest in enhancing the image of their city through the baseball team. "The club has been fostered by the leading citizens of Lowell, who properly have pride in the personnel and morale of the members, and have encouraged these by contributions and, what is as necessary, by attendance and notable interest in their play," one writer said in describing the foundation of the Lowell club in 1877.[8]

Despite the civic leanings of their stockholders, clubs in the New England Association were in the business of making money, or at least not losing money, as the scheduling of numerous games indicates. Games labeled "championship" served to increase attendance, and as such were more promotional in nature to create a premium offering, rather than staged in a quest to capture a league title.

Like future renditions of the New England League that would suffer indiscriminate franchise disbanding when rough economic times hit, the 1877 precursor did not escape such ills. Of the five teams that began the 1877 season, only four teams survived through the end of the season, as the Live Oaks from Lynn disbanded in mid–September. Rampant franchise changes would mar the New England League until a degree of stability was achieved in 1908, when for a second consecutive year all the teams that began the season also completed the campaign without any franchise shifts.

The fact that the New England Association was a regional league didn't mean its players were necessarily inferior to those on the National League clubs. There was no automatic aspiration to play in the National League since many players were more interested in simply collecting a steady paycheck. At the time, the National League was by no means assured to remain in existence past 1877, nor was it necessarily seen as superior despite its insistence that it be called "the League."

Many of the 1877 New England Association teams were stocked with players that had played in the National League a year earlier, in 1876. For instance, Lowell outfielder Frank Whitney played for Boston in 1876, while Providence shortstop Dickey Pearce played for St. Louis and Live Oak pitcher Candy Cummings for Hartford. Other players had the talent to eventually play in the National League in the years to come, such as Lowell pitcher Curry Foley. Some went on to manage National League teams, among them Fall River shortstop Jim Mutrie.

"There were plenty of clubs outside the League as good or better than those who were members," baseball historian Harold Seymour wrote in his seminal work, *Baseball: The Early Years*. "In 1877, for example, about fifty professional non–League clubs were in action, and they succeeded in beating League teams no fewer than seventy-two times. Many games between clubs outside the League were just as well played as those in it."[9]

Indeed, in head-to-head competition, New England Association teams often defeated National League teams. For instance, Lowell had an 11–7 record versus National League competition in 1877, including four victories over Boston, the eventual National League champion.[10]

On June 20 before a thousand spectators, Lowell defeated St. Louis "by the humiliating score of 3–0," as the *Lowell Courier* referred to the outcome. "The joy of the spectators knew no bounds, and the home players were heartily congratulated. The St. Louis nine crept into their wagon and were quietly driven away."[11]

Nine days later on June 29, Lowell defeated Louisville, 7–1. "The Kentucky League men made but a sorry show with the Lowell boys in the game at Lowell, Mass.," the *New York Clipper* reported. "The Louisvilles were overmatched at every point and the way the home team 'thumped' Devlin's swift delivery was enough to turn the head of a man with more control over his temper. The Louisvilles played a first class muffin game."[12]

Since these were avowed exhibition contests, many of which were played on the grounds of the New England Association teams, they were designed to attract as many spectators as possible to produce a financial gain for both teams and not necessarily display the relative skill of each team. Therefore, the results of these New England Association matches with National League opponents need to be viewed with a certain degree of skepticism. It is entirely possible that the National League teams weren't trying as hard as they might otherwise in order to please the crowd. There is also the distinct possibility, albeit unseemly, that the National League teams worked hard *not* to win these exhibition games.

There is evidence that at least one such game, between Lowell and Louisville, was not on the up-and-up. Louisville player George Hall admitted in November 1877 that he and Al Nichols intentionally threw the game to allow Lowell to win. Their admissions of guilt in that game as well as several other National League matches resulted in the banishment of Hall and Nichols, as well as two other players, from the National League.

"Since last night I have thought of another game Nichols and I threw," Hall told Louisville club officials. "It was with the Lowell Club, of Lowell, Massachusetts. He and I agreed to throw it. He did all the telegraphy. Never got a cent from Nichols for the games he and I threw."[13]

Although Hall did not identify the date of the thrown game, it almost certainly was the August 29 game between the two teams rather than the June 29 game, in which Louisville performed so badly that observers should have been suspicious of ill doings on the part of some of the National Leaguers. In the August 29 contest, Louisville masked a fix very well by edging out to a 2–0 lead after five innings before allowing Lowell to score seven runs to go on to win, 7–4. The *Lowell Courier* did, in retrospect, provide a hint of a fix when it reported, "In the seventh the Louisvilles seemed to get badly rattled, and the Lowells scored four runs on errors and a fine three-base hit of Piggott. In this inning, the Lowells crept out of a bad box very luckily," when a Louisville rally fizzled without garnering a run to narrow the deficit.[14]

While the National League played a fixed schedule of games, its teams normally played just three League games each week, creating space for numerous exhibition matches. When National League teams came to Boston, they often also scheduled games with New England Association teams. The westernmost National League teams of Chicago and St. Louis were particularly interested in exhibition games to help defray their extensive travel expenses.

For two weeks, from September 6 to September 20, Chicago played almost as many games with New England Association teams (five) as it did National League matches (six). Between games with Boston on September 8 and 11, Chicago lost to Lowell on September 10, then defeated Fall River twice on September 12 and 13, before playing League rival Hartford on September 14 and 15. Between its games with Boston on September 17 and 20, Chicago lost to Rhode Island on September 18 and a morning game on September 20 at Manchester, which lasted just six innings to allow Chicago to catch a train to Boston for its afternoon game there.

New England Association teams could play so many exhibition games with the National League in 1877 because there was no fixed schedule of New England Association games. A team was supposed to play each of the other four teams ten times during the year. Other than that, the actual dates of the games were left for the teams to decide. Teams could also determine whether matches were "championship" games that counted in the New England Association standings or were simply other games. For instance, Manchester played Lowell fourteen times in 1877, ten championship games and four other contests. There also easily could be confusion over whether a particular game was deemed to be championship caliber, such as the June 22 game between Fall River and Rhode Island at Providence.

The Rhode Islands considered it to be a championship game, as the *Providence Journal* reported that "the first championship game between these clubs will be played here Friday the 22nd." When Fall River lost the game, 3–1, in ten innings, there were some sour grapes. "Believing that a defeat is a defeat, yet to say that the Rhode Islands won a game yesterday would not be the truth," the *Fall River Herald* opined. "To say that the umpire's decision defeated the Fall Rivers would be the truth." Later the *Lynn City Item* weighed in with the thought, "Before many more games are played in the New England championship series, steps should be taken to ascertain what is and what is not a championship game. The Fall River and Rhode Island clubs have played a number of so-called 'exhibition' games together, and both clubs refuse to consider certain games lost to other clubs championship games."[15]

Because New England Association teams often played just one or two championship games a week — only forty such games were required all season — the rest of the week was filled with other games. Competition varied from National League and independent professional teams down to college squads and amateur teams. A typical week for a New England Association team is illustrated by the following summary of Lowell's mid–June slate of games:

> Monday, June 18 — Buckeyes of Columbus, Ohio (lost 6–5)
> Tuesday, June 19 — Buckeyes of Columbus, Ohio (won 11–7)
> Wednesday, June 20— St. Louis, National League (won 3–0)
> Thursday, June 21— at Live Oaks, New England Association (won 15–5)
> Friday, June 22 — no game
> Saturday, June 23 — at Manchester, New England Association (lost 4–2)
> Sunday, June 24 — no game
> Monday, June 25 — Boston, National League (won 7–6)

Laws in all New England states prohibited sporting activities on Sunday. Nearly all activities in 1877, for that matter, were not allowed to take place on Sundays due to the Puritan mandate to strictly observe the Sabbath as the Biblically designated "day of rest." The intense debate over whether "rest" included leisure and recreation would hound the New England League for decades and thus hamper its ability to successfully compete as a minor league operation.

Black teams also provided competition for New England Association teams in 1877. These games between Caucasian and black teams helped to establish a black-friendly attitude in the New England League, which extended into the late 1880s, several years after the color line was established in the major leagues, and subsequently reappeared with the 1946 revival of the league to assist in the integration of professional baseball. On August 10, Lowell played the Mutuals, a team of blacks from Washington, D.C. Before about 600 spectators at the fairgrounds, Lowell defeated the Mutuals, 7–0. The Live Oaks later defeated the Mutuals 10–2 on August 20.[16]

Four of the five cities that fielded baseball teams in the 1877 New England Association had economies formed by the textile industry, the dominant industry in the region. Eighty percent of the national cotton textile output at the time came from mills in New England. The cities of Lowell, Fall River, Manchester, and Providence had grown prosperous due to the textile mills that lined the waterways of their cities. The fifth city in the league, Lynn, had achieved prosperity through a leading position in the New England region's other predominant industry — shoemaking. Two-thirds of the national output of shoes and boots came from New England shoe factories.[17]

Mills in New England had produced cotton yarn by machine since Samuel Slater had perfected the process in Pawtucket, Rhode Island, in the 1790s. The yarn still needed to be turned into cloth, though, which was done by weavers working on hand looms in their homes or small workshops run by enterprising middlemen. This was known as the "put out" system, which was inefficient and led to finished material that lacked consistent quality.

In 1813, the Boston Manufacturing Company instituted the power loom, at a mill in Waltham, Massachusetts, on the Charles River. The power loom dominated the cotton factories in England. Francis Cabot Lowell had expropriated the power loom technology from England by memorizing the fundamental workings of the power loom while visiting the cotton mills of Manchester in 1811 on an excursion to improve his health. Lowell evaded English law that prohibited export of such plans by leaving the jurisdiction with the details embedded only in his brain and not on paper. Lowell and his family and friends, dubbed by historians as the Boston Associates, then established the Boston Manufacturing Company plant in Waltham.[18]

After Lowell died in 1817, the Waltham factory soon outgrew its waterpower supply on the Charles River. In 1821, Nathan Appleton and Patrick Tracy Jackson, relatives of Lowell, selected a site for a new factory in East Chelmsford, which was near the Pawtucket Falls on the Merrimack River. East Chelmsford was also the terminus of the Middlesex Canal, which provided a direct connection to the port of Boston in those pre-railroad days. Appleton and Jackson named the new site Lowell after their decreased relative who had been instrumental in bringing the power loom technology to this country.[19]

Canals built off the little-used Pawtucket Canal provided the waterpower supply for many mills in Lowell, starting with the Merrimack Manufacturing Company in 1823. Within the next five years, sixteen more mills were constructed. In 1826, the town of Lowell was established, and ten years later, in 1836, Lowell became a city. By 1850, Lowell was the second largest city in the state of Massachusetts.

Manchester, New Hampshire, was also located on the Merrimack River, about twenty-five miles north of Lowell. Originally known as the town of Derryfield, the area became known as Manchester in 1810, with promoters hoping that more mills would be built so that the area would resemble the world's largest textile city, Manchester, England. The city began to grow after the Amoskeag Manufacturing Company was founded in 1837 by the Boston Associates. Over time, Amoskeag and Manchester would become virtually synonymous because the textile industry so dominated activity in the city.[20]

Fall River was a late comer to the textile industry. Originally just a village in the town of Troy on the Quequechan Stream, Fall River became the town name in 1834 after several manufacturing concerns built mills on the stream. The small town grew into a city on steam power rather than water power. Jefferson Borden built a steam-powered textile mill in 1852, and the new technology spawned more than forty textile mills since raw material such as coal could easily be delivered by sea through the port of Fall River near the Atlantic Ocean.[21]

"The flexibility of coal-fueled steam power enabled a southern Massachusetts port, Fall River, to replace Lowell as the center of American cotton textile manufacture after the Civil War," wrote author Stephen Yafa, who described how the new technology impacted New England in his book *Big Cotton: How a Humble Fiber Created Fortunes.* By 1876, Fall River was producing one-sixth of the total cotton production in New England and was the second largest producer in the world, ranking second only to Manchester, England.[22]

Providence, Rhode Island, situated at the head of Narragansett Bay, where several rivers converged, was home to many textile mills. Yet unlike Lowell, Manchester, and Fall River, Providence developed a diversified economy in jewelry manufacturing, banking, and perhaps most importantly, as a center of trade. "Providence was the place where middlemen served as agents or factors for all imports and exports — handled the raw cotton and the fuel that entered the state, as well as distributing the various kinds of textiles, jewelry, and machinery exported from it," historian William McLoughlin wrote in his book *Rhode Island: A History.* Providence was the second largest city (behind Boston) in the four eastern New England states of Massachusetts, Rhode Island, New Hampshire, and Maine — the territory that the New England League operated within over the next seven decades.[23]

Lynn was New England's center for manufacturing women's shoes. The city had a history of shoemaking dating to the mid-eighteenth century, when skilled craftsmen, using traditional tools and ancient methods, made whole shoes by working in their homes. The shoe artisans eventually moved their

Textile mills, like the Amoskeag Mills in Manchester, New Hampshire, were important in the development of the New England League. In addition to Manchester, the textile industry powered the economies of several cities in the league, including Fall River, Lowell, and Lawrence (New Hampshire Historical Society).

small operations outside the home to work from "ten-footers," or small shops attached to, but separated from, the household. By 1820, small manufacturing operations emerged. Shopkeepers controlled some functions, such as leather cutting, and "put out" the other functions to the artisans while serving as middlemen for retail sales.

"During the 1850s and '60s, shoe manufacturing experienced the profound impact of mechanization. Machines, factories, and industrial regimentation replaced hand-work, small shops, and informality," Keith Melder wrote in *Life and Times in Shoe City: The Shoe Workers of Lynn.* "One of the early crucial machines, an adaptation of the sewing machine, replaced hand stitching in the making of shoe uppers. Introduced in Lynn in 1852, stitching machines gradually removed the domestic work of shoe binders from the home to the factory. Another device, the McKay stitcher, was first used in Lynn in 1862. It helped to mechanize the stitching of shoe soles to uppers."[24]

Much as the power loom had revolutionized the textile industry, the introduction of machinery completely changed the shoe industry, signaling the demise of the cordwainer, or shoe artisan, and the conversion to complete factory operations. "Lynn's part in revolutionizing the production of shoes was crucial: it was the first to manufacture large numbers of wholesale shoes, was usually ahead of its nearest rival, Philadelphia, as the world's largest producer of ladies shoes, and was the first to adopt the sewing machine and the factory system on a large scale," Alan Dawley wrote in *Class and Community: The Industrial Revolution in Lynn*. Lynn became a center of shoe commerce, featuring a dense commercial and manufacturing district that developed around the Central Square area. By 1870, Lynn was among the six largest cities in Massachusetts.[25]

The spectator base for the New England Association's clubs was not the ownership of the textile mills and shoe factories in these five cities. The owners often were absentee landlords, and the purpose of many mills was not to serve as a primary source of income. While Lowell is considered to be "the cradle of the Industrial Revolution," the city's namesake didn't intend to start a revolution at all. Francis Cabot Lowell's intent in bringing the English technology to this country and building textile mills was simply to preserve his copious wealth rather than to make more money. The mantra of the Boston Associates was "security, steady income, and effective control over management at the expense of higher rates of return on invested capital," according to historian Robert F. Dalzell Jr., author of *Enterprising Elite: The Boston Associates and the World They Made*. This fundamental principle of the textile mills founded by the Boston Associates would foster growth for several decades, but would eventually result in declining economies for the many cities that became dependent on textiles.[26]

The baseball clubs also didn't look toward the workers in the mills and factories as potential spectators; the workers had neither the time nor the income to attend an afternoon ball game. Mill workers labored long hours in the 1870s. In 1874 a new law in Massachusetts shortened the maximum work week to sixty hours, from the previous sixty-six hour standard, making it plausible that a tired mill worker might be able to see the last part of a Saturday afternoon game. As an example of the typical work week, in 1868 workers in the Lowell Mills worked sixty-six hours over six days. On Monday through Friday, workers spent twelve hours a day at the mill, beginning work at 6:30 A.M. and ending work at 6:30 P.M., with a forty-five minute lunch break at noon. On Saturday, the work day began at 6:30 A.M. and lasted until 5:00 P.M.[27]

Even if their work week permitted the time to attend a ball game, mill workers hardly had the extra money to afford the twenty-five cent admission to the game. In 1875, the average annual wages of a cotton mill worker ranged from $337 to $474, according to statistics compiled by the Massachusetts Bureau of the Statistics of Labor. Since the poverty-line annual income at that time for a family of four to six members was $585, this meant that other members of a household, including children, needed to work just so the family could get by minimally. At the low end of the wage scale, the twenty-five cent admission to a ball game represented about one-quarter of a day's pay.

The spectators sought by the baseball clubs were the merchants, small manufacturers, and professionals that populated the cities to deliver products and services to support the textile mills and shoe factories as well as their workers. There were numerous suppliers, machine shops, lawyers, and bakers in each city, the owners of which the baseball clubs counted on to attend games. Economists call this is an agglomeration economy, which arises when a number of businesses involved in a similar trade cluster in one place. "Because of information sharing, the availability of specialized inputs, and/or the concentration of workers with specialized skills or knowledge, manufacturers may find it desirable to locate near each other," wrote Joshua Rosenbloom while explaining the reason for agglomeration economies in an essay in *Engines of Enterprise: An Economic History of New England*. For textile mills, the water power supplied through the canal system in each city was ample reason for the clustering of textile mills.[28]

The respectability that this middle-class spectator base brought to baseball clubs helped to paint the sport as an "acceptable" entertainment venue, which the ball clubs craved in order to sustain the economic viability of their teams and enhance the perception of their cities. The drawing of spectators from an agglomeration economy also had a longer lasting impact. "Where this is true it is possible for patterns of industrial concentration to arise even when the location itself offers no special advantage," Rosenbloom wrote. "Because of their self-reinforcing nature, agglomeration economies are capable of sustaining industrial concentrations long after the reasons that produced them in the first place have vanished."[29]

While small-business owners were the prime target audience for ball game attendance, mill workers did have an occasional chance to attend a ball game even with their long working hours. In 1877, the one viable opportunity for mill workers to attend a baseball game was on the Fourth of July holiday, since neither Decoration Day nor Labor Day had yet been established as a state holiday in the region. Lowell and Manchester played a home-and-home set of two games on July 4, as did the Fall River and Rhode Island teams. The games seemed to be a popular attraction. At the morning game of the two Lowell-Manchester matches, "There was a grand rush for the depots and long trains on both roads were completely filled. The game did not commence till quarter-past ten, when there were between 2500 and 3000 people on the grounds," the *Lowell Courier* reported. In order to get to Manchester on time for the afternoon game, the morning game ended after eight innings. At the afternoon game, the *Manchester Union* reported "a crowd numbering from three to four thousand gathered on the association grounds." Many of the holiday game patrons were no doubt mill workers and others who could not get to a game during the week. The attendance generally reported for most weekday games numbered in the hundreds, at most one thousand or so.[30]

The ball clubs' reluctance to court working class patrons would dampen the success of the New England League for many years. In the 1920s, the league finally scheduled early-evening games in an effort to accommodate the average worker in attending a New England League baseball game. At the same time, the league also battled the loosening of the Sunday laws and experimented with night baseball.

Although Lowell finished in first place in 1877 when the results of the championship games were tabulated, there was no great fanfare over having won a New England Association title. The *Lowell Courier* printed a simple headline in mid–October, stating, "Base Ball — The New England Championship Won by the Lowells." Ten years later, the newspaper rejoiced over the team winning a title in a retrospective article about the 1877 team. Times had changed by 1887 in the New England League, as the circuit had become highly competitive and numerous arguments transpired over which team had won the league championship.[31]

There was also no dash by Lowell to try to move up into the National League, which had two openings due to the departure of the St. Louis and Hartford teams. While the Lowell stockholders considered applying for membership in the National League, the *New York Clipper* summarized in one sentence the feeling of the ball club's investors: "The Lowell Club, by a nearly unanimous vote, has declined to join the League."[32]

The arguments for joining the National League were greatly overshadowed by the reasons against joining. In the "for" column were the ability to attract a consistent flow of first class teams to Lowell, the protection of Lowell's territorial rights to the local market, and Harry Wright's belief that "it is impractical for a first-class club to earn its living and to travel thousands of miles to play games unless it has something to play for of more interest than a local or state championship."[33]

Lowell stockholders were understandably skeptical of the benefits of National League membership. In the "against" column were the large expenditures to travel to Chicago and other western cities in the league, as well as the necessity of increasing admission prices at home from twenty-five cents to fifty cents. Additionally, under the new League rules to curb its embarrassing 1877 exhibition-game record, National League clubs wouldn't be able to play nearly as many exhibition games with non-league clubs during the

1878 season. This scenario would have dramatically curtailed revenue for Lowell.

A lengthy article entitled "Shall the Lowells Join the League?" in the *Lowell Courier* in January 1878 amply laid out the reasoning why Lowell should decline the opportunity to join the National League. "There wouldn't be much left of the Lowell nine in two or three months after the price of admission had been raised from 25 cents to 50 cents. The club barely paid its way last year and the increase in price would, it is perfectly safe to say, diminish audiences in this city more than one-half, taking the season as a whole, so that the receipts would be less than at the lower rate." The article went on to exhort, "The Lowell club should be managed for the pleasure of Lowell People, who would be glad to maintain it if rates are reasonable."[34]

Since the Lowell ball club existed primarily to raise the stature of the city within the regional economy, the ability to accommodate that principle and still make money as a member of the National League was in significant doubt. The Lowell stockholders lost money in 1877 and undoubtedly would have lost even more money in 1878 had Lowell joined the National League.

If the Lowell club had elected to join the National League for the 1878 season, it likely would have been a short one-year stay, based on the experience of two teams that attempted to make the jump to the National League. Few people remember the Milwaukee and Indianapolis teams that competed in the National League in 1878, as both teams suffered significant financial problems and lasted just that one season.

Lowell did move on to the International Association, though, joining that aggregation in February 1878. This move effectively scuttled competition in the New England Association for the 1878 season. Life in the International Association was no less financially precarious, however, as the Lowell club dropped out of competition in September after forfeiting road games in August rather than incur travel expenses that would have exacerbated the club's $1,300 deficit for the season.[35]

One city in the New England Association of 1877, however, did make the leap to the National League. Providence joined the National League for the 1878 season after Louisville dropped out of the league in early 1878. Providence competed at the national level for eight years, winning National League titles in 1879 and 1884, before dropping out of the league following the 1885 season.

The move by Providence into the National League in 1878 proved to be the ultimate obstacle that prevented the New England League from becoming completely successful as a minor league. If the better team in 1877, Lowell rather than Providence, had joined the National League in 1878, it is likely the future of the New England League would have been vastly different.

Not only was Providence the second-largest city in New England behind Boston, Providence more importantly acquired access to a Sunday-only ball grounds fifteen miles south of the city at Rocky Point, a site that Rhode Island officials implicitly sanctioned as a permissible exception to the state's Sunday laws.[36]

In 1891, when Providence organizers sought to have a minor league team, they did not select the geographically proximate New England League but rather the more distant Eastern League, which was comprised of mostly New York-based teams, with cities such as Albany and Rochester having access to grounds for Sunday games. Providence was a prominent member of the Eastern League for twenty-five years, helping the circuit transform into the International League in 1912, largely on the strength of its ability to play Sunday games at Rocky Point and thus draw larger crowds than other non–Sunday-playing clubs. The New England League tried sporadically to play some Sunday games in Rhode Island, but it could never garner enough spectator interest to rival the crowds at Rocky Point for Providence games.

As a result of Providence playing Sunday baseball in the Eastern League, the larger New England cities tended to desire Eastern League membership rather than join the New England League. Springfield, Massachusetts, joined the Eastern League in 1893, Worcester, Massachusetts, in 1899 (after three failed attempts in the New England League), and Hartford, Connecticut, in 1899. At the turn of the century, half of the Eastern League clubs were some of the largest cities in New England.

By having the region's second-largest city consistently outside the orbit of its franchises, the New England League was forced to accept second-class status as a minor league while operating so perilously close to the region's most populous city, Boston. Even Worcester, the third-largest city in the region, was never a consistent member of the New England League after the city's brief, three-year stint in the National League from 1880 to 1882. The other four members of the 1877 New England Association — Fall River, Lowell, Lynn, and Manchester — became long-term members of the New England League.

As minor leagues changed character during the first half of the twentieth century, the New England League never could settle into a viable niche in the baseball hierarchy of New England, which had the major leagues' Boston Red Sox and Boston Braves at the top. New England League franchises were overly dependent on the urban economies that the textile and shoe industries provided New England's second-tier cities, which by the 1920s had shattered in Lawrence, Fall River, Brockton, and Haverhill. When Sunday baseball became legally available to Massachusetts-based teams for the 1929 season, the Great Depression struck just months later and ushered in a final round of deaths and rebirths of the New England League.

Providence did eventually field a team in the New England League in 1946, but by then the city's influence could not salvage the circuit from a final funeral. As the first New England League franchise to disband during the league's final season in 1949, Providence ironically set in motion the events that led to the New England League's final days as active minor league institution.

With Worcester, Providence, and Boston all in the National League in the early 1880s, there was little momentum to organize a regional league to play lower-caliber baseball. However, in 1885, some ambitious promoters were able to organize a top-flight baseball league in the region.

3

Initial Years,
1885–1888

IF THE EARLY SETTLERS FROM EUROPE TO New England in the 1620s could scratch a living from farming the region's rocky soil and otherwise inhospitable terrain, then the ingenuity of independent-minded businessmen in the 1880s could tame the challenging economics of conducting professional baseball on the region's ball grounds.

The mixed ideals espoused by owners of the 1877 New England Association clubs, those of civic promotion with just a mild desire for economic gain, needed tempering with a heavy dose of financial buttressing to make an 1885 incarnation of minor league baseball in New England feasible. Indeed, the five clubs that fielded teams in 1885, the true initial year of what would become the venerable New England League, borrowed management principles that had developed over time by firms engaged in the region's highly successful textile and footwear industries.

While large factories dominated the 1885 landscape of Lowell and Lynn, giants in the region's textile and footwear industry, respectively, small operations manned by skilled craftsmen who controlled the production process initially established the region's dominance in these two industries. In time, however, operational efficiencies such as the Draper loom in textiles and the McKay stitcher in footwear were introduced into the production process, which lessened the need for skilled labor and decreased its value for success in cloth or shoe making. Mass production trumped individual craftsmanship due to the financial ramifications.

A similar transition was needed for professional baseball to thrive economically in New England. Club finances would need to come before individual player skills, and strong management would be needed to keep the players in line to meet ownership goals.

Conditions were certainly favorable in 1885 for this transition to take place. There was a surplus of professional baseball players seeking continued employment on the nation's ball grounds. There were only sixteen major league teams in 1885, down from the twenty-eight teams that had operated in 1884, due to the collapse of the Union Association and the downsizing of the American Association from twelve to eight teams.

Uncertainty over the future of the Northwestern League, the first recognized minor league, also contributed to the player surplus. This was an important consideration for New England baseball proponents. Many of the best players from the New England states had left the region in 1883 and 1884 to play baseball at a higher competitive level since there were scant opportunities to play for pay in New England. Boston and Providence, the region's two most populous cities, boasted clubs in the National League, but it was a long drop in skill level (and monetary reward) to the remaining clubs affiliated with the small cities in the region.

In addition to a general over-supply of ball players nationally, a regional glut existed in New England. Boston-area players such as Jim Cudworth and George Bignell, who had gone west in 1884 to play for Bay City in the Northwestern League and later had found spots in the Union Association after the Northwestern League disbanded, faced uncertain prospects for baseball employment in 1885. The Boston club in the ill-fated Union Association was stocked with some local players, which contributed to the number of players seeking a baseball paycheck in New England in 1885.

With a surplus of available ball players to stock teams, ball clubs only needed to create and sustain spectator demand to make a professional baseball league economically viable in New England.

The Eastern New England League was officially organized on March 21, 1885, at the Essex Hotel in Lawrence, Massachusetts. William Moody, president of the league, presided over the meeting in which six teams agreed to compete for a championship over a sixty-game season.

The 1885 rendition of the New England League was technically called the Eastern New England League to distinguish the circuit from the Connecticut-based Southern New England League. The naming convention of the two leagues was not just semantic; the names reflected the division of the New England region into two historically distinct economies that developed separately, rather than as one economy that developed uniformly throughout the six-state region. This historical difference in economic development would thwart several attempts over the ensuing decades to form one unified New

England League with ball clubs located in both Massachusetts and Connecticut.

In Colonial days where water transportation was essential to transact commerce, Connecticut was isolated from eastern Massachusetts and Rhode Island. The major rivers in Connecticut all drained into Long Island Sound; the Connecticut, Housatonic, Naugatuck, and Thames Rivers and their tributaries all flowed south away from the major ports in Massachusetts and Rhode Island. The 400-mile long Connecticut River, which rises near the Canadian border in northern New Hampshire, did provide a connection to Springfield and other cities in western Massachusetts.

Other than a few mills in the northeastern part of the state, Connecticut did not share a similar industrial development as Massachusetts and Rhode Island did with its textile mills and shoe factories. Instead, Connecticut residents developed a number of industries related to metalworking. Waterbury emerged as a center of brass works, Meriden in silver works, and Hartford in firearms. Clockmaking was also a widespread industry in Connecticut.[1]

Even the advent of the railroad in the mid-nineteenth century failed to facilitate a transportation connection between Connecticut and eastern Massachusetts and Rhode Island. Rail lines connected the major Connecticut cities, but outside the state ran mostly north to western Massachusetts instead of northeast into central Massachusetts. With no convenient transportation means between the larger Connecticut cities of Hartford and New Haven with Worcester and Lowell in Massachusetts, no basic foundation to form an all-encompassing New England League that would engage Connecticut cities existed.

Even the moniker "New England League" was not strictly applicable to baseball. The baseball club owners in 1885 borrowed the name from a league that played a very popular indoor sport during the winters of 1884 and 1885. That winter sport was roller polo, which today is largely a forgotten sport. In the latter part of the nineteenth century, before basketball and ice hockey were popularized, roller polo was THE professional sport during the winter season in New England.

Roller polo was similar to today's game of street hockey, but played in an indoor arena. Players used sticks similar to those used by field hockey players today. As historian Stephen Hardy described the basics of roller polo:

> The stick had a maximum length of four feet and diameter of one inch. The ball was three inches in diameter. The game started with each team forming an inverted wedge. At the referee's signal, opponents rushed the ball placed at center ice. The game was on. There was no rule about offsides, but attackers could not stop within a 5-foot radius around the goal. Two or three team fouls, depending on location,

equaled a goal for the opponent. Matches were best-of-three or best-of-five "goals." There was no "intentional" striking, kicking, or tripping, but newspaper stories graphically described the slashing sticks, whirling fists, cracked bones, and bloodied heads.[2]

The budding baseball entrepreneurs that met at the Essex Hotel in March 1885 to form the Eastern New England League hoped that the popularity of roller polo would spill over to the baseball version of the league.

League president Moody was a thirty-one-year-old lawyer who practiced law in Haverhill. Described in later years as a "real baseball fan" and "a great lover of outdoor sports," Moody formed the league not only as an outlet for the region's burgeoning interest in baseball, but also to generate increased recognition of his own name as a lawyer and civic-minded citizen.[3]

Moody used his two-year stint as league president as a springboard for his legal and political career. In 1888, Moody secured the position of Haverhill city solicitor before becoming district attorney for the eastern district of Massachusetts in 1890. In his role as district attorney, Moody gained ever-lasting acclaim as the prosecutor that failed to obtain a guilty verdict in the

William H. Moody was the first president of the New England League. Moody went on to later fame as the prosecutor in the trial of alleged ax murder Lizzie Borden and also served as a justice on the U.S. Supreme Court (Trustees of Haverhill Public Library).

highly publicized trial of alleged ax murder Lizzie Borden. Moody was elected three times to the U.S. Congress before President Teddy Roosevelt appointed him as secretary of the navy and later as attorney general of the United States. Roosevelt then appointed Moody to the U.S. Supreme Court, where he served from December 1906 until June 1910.[4]

Not a bad career for a lawyer that responded to the "general interest in the diamond sport" and "suggested the formation of a league" to create the Eastern New England League in 1885.[5]

Had it not been for the personal ambitions of many of its founders, the New England League would not have been established. Besides the motivations of Moody, the drive of Walter Burnham also fueled the development of the New England League. Burnham, a twenty-five-year-old native of Portland, Maine, was the manager of the Lawrence, Massachusetts, team in 1885. He honed his skills as a baseball promoter in Portland in 1884, where he single-handedly built a ball grounds and established a top-drawing ball club.

In Portland, Burnham astutely located the ball grounds near the local trolley line, an important consideration for nineteenth century baseball facilities. "Manager Burnham has taken a five years' lease of that part of Lang's pasture just this side of the circus grounds, and evidently intends to begin work immediately," the *Eastern Argus*, a Portland newspaper, reported in June 1884. "The site selected is splendidly situated for the purpose, the distance from the city being just enough for a pleasant walk, while the horse cars pass directly by."[6]

Burnham also arranged for several exhibition games with National League teams, no doubt offering generous guarantees to the teams to journey up to Portland from their stops in Boston. "The year 1884 was an especially rewarding one for Portland-area baseball enthusiasts. Not one, not two, but six major league teams came to town to put on exhibition games before delighted audiences," Will Anderson wrote in his book *Was Baseball Really Invented in Maine?* The visiting National League teams generally thumped the Portland team. When the Boston team visited Portland on July 22, a crowd of 2,000 watched Boston pummel Portland, 29–3. But the important point, to Burnham, was that people came to the ball grounds to pay to watch the games despite the lopsided scores.[7]

Burnham brought his "hustle, enterprise and general management ability" to Lawrence, where he "secured a lease of grounds in Lawrence, put a team in and won the championship," as one writer later described Burnham's debut in the league in a biographical sketch in the *Brockton Enterprise*. In October 1885, the *Boston Globe* described his talents in the face of adversity that first year. "Mr. Burnham pluckily overcame many obstacles and adhered in his determination to create a lively interest in base ball among the Lawrence people and he has succeeded in doing so in a great measure."[8]

The Eastern New England League of 1885, where Burnham applied his skills at baseball promotion, had a different composition of cities than its predecessor, the 1877 New England Association, which had focused on the region's larger cities. The rendition of the New England League in 1885 had teams representing five smaller cities — Lawrence, Brockton, and Haverhill in Massachusetts, and Portland and Biddeford in Maine.

With the motivation of the organizers of the New England League in 1885 centered on personal ambition, the organizers sought financial backing for their teams from businessmen in cities that also had the desire to be known in the same sphere as the leading cities in their industries.

Lawrence, Massachusetts, and Biddeford, Maine, were budding textile cities hoping to be seen in the same class as Lowell and Fall River. The Massachusetts cities of Haverhill and Brockton were shoe cities focused on the manufacturer of men's shoes and boots that longed to ascend into the same stature as Lynn with its shoe factories churning out women's shoes. Portland, Maine, had a diversified industrial economy to support its role as a shipping port, looking to emulate perhaps Providence.

Lawrence was a city created by the Boston Associates in 1845, when Bodwell's Falls was dammed on the Merrimack River about ten miles below Lowell to create a water power source for the Essex Manufacturing Company. Two years later, the Massachusetts legislature set off seven square miles of land from the towns of Andover and Methuen to create Lawrence, named after Abbott and Amos Lawrence, who had established the Middlesex Mills in Lowell in 1830. Soon the Great Stone Dam across the Merrimack River spawned numerous textile mills, including the Bay State, Atlantic, Pacific, and Pemberton Mills.[9]

Biddeford, on the Saco River in southern Maine, was another textile city created by the Boston Associates. "By 1850, a village based on lumbering, farming, and fishing had been remade into a city of brick, machines, and cotton cloth," Richard Judd wrote in *Maine: The Pine Tree State from Prehistory to the Present*. The Pepperell Manufacturing Company opened in the early 1850s and by 1885 Biddeford, along with sister city Saco, was considered a premier manufacturing center in Maine. The city would become renowned for the Lady Pepperell brand of cloth produced at its Pepperell Mills.[10]

Haverhill, once a trading nexus for New Hampshire towns due to its favorable location on the Merrimack River, shifted to shoe manufacturing after the railroads eliminated the location advantage of Haverhill. Dozens of shoe manufacturers that specialized in men's shoes (to differentiate from Lynn, which dominated women's shoe manufacturing) established shops within reach of the Boston & Maine Railroad depot in Haverhill center.

Brockton was another up-and-coming city. Focused on the shoe industry, Brockton had been incorporated as a city only four years earlier, in 1881, forsaking its agrarian roots as the town of North Bridgewater. Unlike Lynn that made its name in women's shoes, Brockton was renowned for manufacturing men's shoes. Bill McGunnigle, who grew up in the Brockton area, was tapped to run the Brockton club.

Portland converted from a merchant port to an industrial hub in the nineteenth century. The city's growth was assisted by serving as a winter port for ice-bound Montreal and Quebec City due to the rail connection between cities on the Grand Trunk Railroad. The Portland Company began in the 1840s as a foundry to build locomotives for the railroad and adapted over the years into other metal areas, such as cannons during the Civil War and later machinery for the burgeoning paper and pulp industry. Located one hundred miles north of Boston, Portland owned a distinct advantage of having a captive audience for professional baseball since it was not convenient for residents to take the train to Boston to see the National League team and return home the same day.

Portland's out-of-the-way nexus to the rest of the New England League cities created a need for a "companion" club to be part of the league to make the economics of traveling to Portland viable for other league teams. This was the role that Biddeford, Maine, played in the 1885 schedule. While Biddeford was a textile center on a much smaller scale than Lowell or Manchester, Biddeford was not attractive on its own as a New England League city. As a stop for Lawrence, Haverhill, and Brockton on the way to Portland, though, Biddeford served the purpose of making the long trip from Massachusetts more worthwhile.

Portland always drew crowds to its home games, thus making it a profitable city in the New England League. Overcoming travel costs incurred by the other New England League clubs was always an issue with Portland and other Maine cities in earning their keep in the league.

The league had its organizing challenges from the beginning. Although six teams had agreed at the March 21 meeting to compete during the 1885 season, only four of them actually fielded teams on the first day of the campaign. Newburyport, Massachusetts, dropped out of the league one week later when the league wouldn't countenance the club's plan to charge fifteen cents for admission to games, a toll that was ten cents less than the twenty-five cent fare to be charged by the other teams.

The Newburyport club believed that it needed the lower admission price to attract spectators to its games since the city's economy was in decline and to restore its image. Newburyport had been the third-largest town in Massachusetts in 1810 due to its location at the mouth of the Merrimack River, which empties into the Atlantic Ocean. The city had been a trading nexus during the eighteenth century, with firms exchanging goods produced inland (and carted to, and floated down, the Merrimack River) with goods transported across the Atlantic Ocean from Europe. Fishing had also been a major industry. However, the Middlesex Canal along with the railroads that were completed in the 1830s, resulted in a steady decline of trade along the Merrimack River in favor of more convenient means of transportation to Boston.

While Newburyport's case may have had some financial merit, President Moody and the owners were concerned about the league being viewed as respectable entertainment by the middle-class businessmen, whom they wanted as patrons at the ball games. "Early promoters of professional baseball sought to create a lofty moral image, shrouded in Christian propriety, as a means of selling their enterprise to the middle-class spectators," one historian wrote. "The notion of an acceptable moral image was vital to the success of a commercialized amusement. It had to possess and advocate values that appealed to a 'respectable' class of citizens who judged this product not only on its merit but also on the perceived quality of the individuals who endorsed it."[11]

At the league meeting on March 28, Brockton was selected to replace Newburyport. On March 31, the *Boston Globe* published the league's first playing schedule, which matched up the six teams Moody thought would comprise the season. Each team would play the other five teams twelve times over the season, featuring six games at home and six games on the road.

However, there was another original club that failed to reach the starting line — Gloucester, Massachusetts, a city located on the shore of the Atlantic Ocean whose economy was based on the fishing industry. The club's organizer, Gloucester native A.G. "Fred" Doe, had to withdraw the team from the league just as the season began in early May, presumably due to a lack of financial backing from the town's business leaders. At a league meeting on May 11, the club owners expressed their wrath at Doe, who had saddled the league with an awkward five-club status that created an unbalanced schedule of games, leaving one team without an opponent on any given day. The owners voted "that Mr. A.G. Doe of Gloucester be expelled for dishonorable conduct."[12]

Doe thus became the first person blacklisted by the New England League. The club owners borrowed a technique often utilized by mill owners in the region to deal with recalcitrant employees. Doe's misdeed was accepting the schedule with Gloucester on it "in writing, and as a man whose word is to be relied on, everything is supposed to be all right," said the *Sporting Life*, castigating the budding sports promoter.[13]

Doe, a top player in roller polo, was reinstated in January 1886. "An important piece of business accomplished by the meeting was the reinstatement of A.G. Doe of last season's Gloucester club, who was blacklisted for apparently no cause," said the *Boston Globe*, reporting on the league's change of heart regarding Doe.[14]

Years later, Doe said he learned a valuable lesson from that blacklisting:

> There was so little baseball interest in Gloucester that spring that it was not wise to continue so I withdrew the club but forgot to notify the league that the city would not be represented, thinking the judge [William Moody, the league president] would attend to it. We started off on a polo tour at this time and when I got back home found that I had been blacklisted for not fulfilling my obligations to the New England League. I couldn't understand why the league would impose such a penalty as it was unintentional on my part to cause any inconvenience in making up the league.... [After playing in one game for Portland], realizing what a mistake I had made I apologized to the league. They forgave and reinstated me but said I had better take a vacation for a year. It immediately dawned upon me that one must keep obligations and do as agreed.[15]

With only five teams, the Eastern New England League was set to open its inaugural season, beginning with two games to be played on Saturday, May 2, with Biddeford at Lawrence and Portland at Haverhill. Rain, however, spoiled the league's opening, canceling both games. The first official game in the Eastern New England League season was played at Haverhill on Monday, May 4, when Haverhill defeated Biddeford, 3–1. "It is probable that the base ball public of Haverhill will not see a prettier exhibition of the game then was played on the Haverhill grounds yesterday, in the presence of five hundred spectators," reported the *Biddeford Journal* on the league's inaugural game.[16]

While the league's five-team field made scheduling awkward, the lack of a sixth team wasn't overly detrimental to league play. The teams were only slated to play three or four league games each week. On the other two to three days each week when league games were not scheduled (never on Sunday, of course), teams often played exhibition matches with independent teams if they didn't need the extra time to make train connections while traveling from one league site to another. The Boston Resolutes, a black team, played several games with league clubs, including a mid–June game in Biddeford. "Yesterday afternoon the home team toyed with Boston's colored nine, the Resolutes, before a small audience," the *Biddeford Journal* reported of the 26–4 victory by Biddeford.[17]

The primary benefit of league affiliation was guaranteed scheduling of several games per week against competitive teams. Independent teams had to endure the time delays and hassle to schedule games via letter or telegram, and then publicize the games to attract patrons. League teams, conversely, could cherry-pick the teams to play on their open dates and supplement revenue from league games. Burnham, for instance, had his Lawrence team play twenty-two exhibition games in addition to its league contests.[18]

Where the five-team setup was devastating to league play was on the two holiday dates on the 1885 schedule, Decoration Day on May 30 and Independence Day on July 4, when only four of the five teams could schedule a league game. Holiday attendance was a critical component of a team's finances since crowds at holiday contests were typically at least double the size of a crowd at a weekday game. Business was generally not conducted at all on a holiday, so the potential audience for a holiday game was the entire population of the surrounding area. The holidays also served as the only days that many workers could attend a game since a six-day workweek was generally in effect throughout New England at that time, especially in the textile mills and shoe factories.

With the expected large crowds at holiday games, two games would be scheduled for each holiday. Teams usually played a home-and-home twin bill, with two teams playing a morning game (then referred to as the forenoon game) at one team's site and an afternoon game at the other team's site. This enabled equitable scheduling of holiday home games, with teams having a morning home game on one holiday and an afternoon home game on the other.

On Decoration Day in 1885, Brockton and Haverhill played a home-and-home series as did Portland and Biddeford. Lawrence was left out of the holiday mix since it had originally been slated to play Gloucester, which had dropped out of the league before the season began. Instead, Lawrence played a holiday match with the team sponsored by the firm of John L. Whiting & Sons.

Brockton hosted and won the forenoon game with Haverhill, 10–0, as "the game was called in the eighth inning to allow the teams to catch the train for Haverhill." A crowd of 1,600 saw the morning game, while 2,000 spectators attended the afternoon game in Haverhill, which resulted in another Brockton victory.[19]

Biddeford won both holiday games with Portland. A crowd of 1,000 saw the forenoon game in Biddeford, while 3,700 jammed the stands in Portland for the afternoon contest. Only 800 people attended Lawrence's 17–4 thrashing of the industrial team at the South Lawrence grounds.

The availability of Decoration Day as a second holiday, in addition to the Fourth of July, was another basis for the establishment of the league in 1885. Decoration Day did not become a state holiday in Massachusetts until 1881. By having a holiday on the playing schedule just a few weeks into the season, risks were substantially mitigated for the financial backers of New England League teams.

While working-class patrons helped to swell attendance on holiday dates, the ball clubs focused on small-business owners as their primary customers for ball games during the workweek. While a seated-liberty quarter from a well-heeled patron or five Indian-head pennies and four liberty-head nickels from a mill worker would allow a person to enter the ball grounds, twenty-five cents only provided for a possible seat on the bleaching boards along the first and third base lines.

For an additional seated-liberty dime, a patron could enter the grand-stand, where seats would be available in an area separated from the bleaching boards and covered by a roof to provide protection from the sun's rays. These were the preferred customers, the respected independent businessmen and their guests, especially female ones. At the grounds in Brockton, the wire netting in front of the grandstand went all the way to the roof "in order that the ladies may be better protected from foul tips."[20]

To facilitate purchases by these patrons, tickets were often sold at down-town locations. Or a season ticket could be purchased, which completely avoided the use of coins at the gate.

Location of the ball grounds was critical to financial success of the ball clubs. A location near the trolley line was preferable so that businessmen could leave their offices in mid-afternoon, board a horse-drawn trolley to go to the ball game, and then either return to the office after the game or pro-ceed home on the trolley. More prominent people could travel to the ball grounds in their own horse-drawn carriages, or those of lesser means could walk if the ball grounds were within a reasonable proximity of the downtown business district.

Haverhill played its games in 1885 at the new riverside grounds near downtown in order to be closer to businessmen instead of forcing potential customers to travel to the more remote Kenoza Park, where previous ball teams had played their games. In Lawrence, Burnham leased grounds in South Lawrence, on the other side of the Merrimack River from the textile mills. While the grounds in South Lawrence were more pastoral than the urban landscape near the downtown district, the required traveling distance did impinge upon attendance.

In Brockton, the ball club built new grounds in the Campello district of southern Brockton, at the corner of Main and Grove streets, near the horse-car trolley line. In Biddeford, the ball club initially played its games at a trotting park before switching to the Granite Street grounds that were closer to the city center.

The playing areas used by the ball clubs generally didn't have formal names at this time, such as Fenway Park, and were simply called "grounds." This term, though, had a beneficial connotation, since "grounds" was the term used to describe the surroundings of a country home, "the acreage devoted to kitchen gardens and ornamental trees, greensward and flower beds." The term was meant to evoke a feeling in a ball game patron of agrarian splendor while escaping the ugly conditions of the local mills.[21]

Colorful uniforms also were designed for spectator approval. Brockton had uniforms consisting of maroon pants, caps, and shirts, with old gold belts and stockings. Lawrence wore blood red jerseys and stockings, with brownish gray pants, coats, and caps. Biddeford wore uniforms the color of Providence gray with navy blue trimming.[22]

After the big crowds for the games on the Fourth of July holiday, the future of the Eastern New England League was cloudy as to whether the league would survive for another three months, until its scheduled terminus on September 30.

Things did not look optimistic for Biddeford to finish out the remaining weeks of the season. The ball club played its July 10 game with Haverhill in Boston, at the South End Grounds, where the Boston club in the National League played its games, hoping to capitalize on the larger population of Boston. Only 300 people attended.

The Biddeford club disbanded in late July, spawning the genesis of the derisive term "Fourth of July League," which was often applied to future editions of the New England League. The term epitomizes the frequent franchise shifts, and occasional league failures, that occurred in July and August after the gate receipts from the Fourth of July game had been deposited in the bank. Biddeford was the victim of the unforgiving business model of professional baseball clubs, especially a minor league one, where game attendance was highly correlated with winning games.

The business model of these 1885 ball clubs was quite simple from an economic perspective: revenue less expenses equaled profit. Revenue consisted of gate receipts and season ticket sales. Expenses were primarily salaries for players and a manager, rent for the ball grounds, travel to road games, and guarantees paid to the visiting teams if attendance was low.

Revenue was highly dependent on the number of spectators in attendance, which was somewhat correlated with the ease of getting to the ball grounds but much more highly correlated with the rate that the team won its games. Sociologists today refer to this principle of sports spectatorship as "basking in reflected glory." In order to field a consistently winning team, ball clubs had to recruit talented ball players, which often meant spending lavishly on salaries. But salary is a fixed expense, while spectator revenue is a variable element. As many ball clubs found out, consistently winning teams did not necessarily attract enough spectators to produce a profit, no matter what size the player payroll. Ball clubs often overspent on player salaries in an attempt to field a winning team.[23]

Newburyport replaced Biddeford, with the league relenting on the fifteen cents admission charge that had kept the club from joining the league in the first place. The league modified its schedule for the remainder of the season, listing games through October 1 and voting "to lengthen the playing season till October 3." Exactly when the season ended would become a bone of contention in the determination of the 1885 league champion and result in the first of several disputed pennant winners in the history of the New England League.[24]

When attendance at ball games began waning in the late summer, some clubs experimented with playing games at neutral sites. Lawrence played several games in Manchester, New Hampshire, hoping to capitalize on the businesses in the city that thrived due to the success of the Amoskeag Mills. Newburyport played some September games at nearby Salisbury Beach. One game at Salisbury Beach, the September 18 contest with Lawrence, became part of another controversy in the 1885 pennant dispute.

John Flynn, a pitcher recently signed by Lawrence after his Meriden, Connecticut, team in the Southern New England League had disbanded, pitched for Lawrence on September 18 in a 13–2 victory over Newburyport. There was, however, some question whether Flynn was actually eligible to play for Lawrence due to his playing time in Connecticut. "Flynn and Moolic, late of the Meridans, were on the base ball grounds at the beach yesterday," the *Newburyport Herald* reported the day before, announcing their arrival in the area. Flynn continued to pitch for Lawrence, but lost most of his games until the last week of the season when he won several contests, including the October 1 game that was a makeup of a postponed game during the season.[25]

Brockton and Lawrence were neck and neck in the standings at the end of September. However, due to a series of protests, there was serious doubt as to which team earned the pennant. Lawrence complained about a doubleheader that Brockton played with Portland on September 26, and Brockton complained about Lawrence's use of pitcher Flynn as well as the league secretary's mandate to play postponed games on dates after the regular season had concluded. Brockton still had two games to play against Lawrence and refused to play one of them on October 2, resulting in a forfeit and an apparent victory for Lawrence.

"The Brocktons have won the pennant. Whether they will get it or not is quite another question," the *Brockton Weekly Gazette* commented. The paper suggested that the victories gained by Lawrence at the end of the season "were 'won' by Secretary Wiggin with the pen and not by players with the bat."[26]

The *Eastern Argus* in Portland laid blame on both teams, remarking: "The wrangling over the pennant in the Eastern New England League still continues and from the present condition of affairs it would seem that both Lawrence and Brockton would prefer to win the championship by bluff and bluster rather than by base hits and earned runs."[27]

Instead of continuing to argue over the merits of the individual protests, a league meeting "voted that in order to settle the question concerning the championship, two games be played, one at Brockton October 10 and the other at Lawrence October 13, with a third game if necessary October 15 at Haverhill or Boston."[28]

In the first playoff series in minor league history, Lawrence easily won the first two games to cop the pennant. Flynn pitched both games for Lawrence. In the 11–4 victory in the second game, "Flynn pitched a magnificent game," according to the *Lawrence Eagle*. "A wonderful one-hand catch by Flynn in the third inning of a liner, which whirled him around like a top, was one of the principal features of the game."[29]

Moody, the league president, received some excellent training as a judge while presiding over the arguments that erupted about the pennant dispute. The arguments continued at the league's October 28 meeting at the Eagle Hotel in Haverhill, where the league formally awarded Lawrence the league pennant, despite protestations from Brockton and a voluminous amount of legal wrangling between lawyers for Lawrence and Brockton. After much debate, the league determined that "Flynn was eligible to sign with the Lawrence club on the 17th day of September, 1885, and that no game played subsequently by the Lawrence club should be considered illegal because of Flynn's participation in the game."[30]

The city of Brockton harbored resentment over the disputed pennant for many years. A decade later, when Burnham was managing the Brockton team in the New England League, the *Brockton Enterprise* wrote, "The old-time ball cranks of the town will remember very vividly Mr. Burnham's Lawrence aggregation of 1885, which was the year when Brockton had a team which its supporters firmly believed rightfully won the pennant themselves."[31]

The league also moved quickly to add a sixth team for the 1886 season to ensure that it would have an evenly balanced schedule. At the October 28 meeting, there were two applicants for the sixth spot: Deering, Maine, and Boston. Although Deering, a town just outside of Portland (and now part of Portland), would have made an excellent companion club for the trek to Maine, the league awarded the sixth spot to J.F. Mullen of Boston. While seemingly unusual by today's standards to have both major and minor league teams in the same city, such an occurrence was not that uncommon in the 1880s.

By adding a Boston club to the New England League for the 1886 season, the owners tried to duplicate the success of a similar arrangement in 1884 when the Boston Reserves competed in the Massachusetts State Association. As the name implies, the Reserves team was essentially the B team of the Boston National League team, which today would be called a farm team. The Reserves vanquished much of the competition in 1884, so much so that many teams dropped out of the league before the season concluded, rendering the Reserves' first-place finish a Pyrrhic victory. The Reserves drew well at the gate due to its victories on the field and not because the team played its home games at the South End Grounds in populous Boston when the National League team was on the road.

Interestingly, the New England League owners didn't wait for the dissolution of the National League's Providence team to try to coax a Providence club into joining the New England League. Providence was forced out of the National League to make room for a Washington, D.C., franchise, and the handwriting had been on the wall for Providence by the end of the 1885 National League season. In mid–December, the stockholders of the Providence club held a meeting where "the advisability of organizing a club to enter either the Eastern League or New England League was discussed." This was the best shot the New England League had at latching onto the Providence territory and apparently did nothing to pursue it, smug in its decision to add a ball club in Boston. Providence joined the Eastern League for the 1886 season.[32]

The newest New England League team was known as the Boston Blues, one of the first professional baseball teams to be known by an official nickname in addition to its home locale. The reasoning for the dual naming centered on the ability to distinguish the New England League team from the National League team in newspaper reports. The nickname stemmed from the team's uniforms. "The nine will have two uniforms to a man," the *Boston Globe* reported. "They will be of a very dark blue flannel, with white stockings, belt and hat, which will have a blue band."[33]

Tim Murnane, who played major league ball with Boston and Providence in the National League in the 1870s, was manager of the Blues. He also became the club's owner for a brief time, making Murnane the first former ball player openly acknowledged as the owner of a ball club in the New England League. Murnane possessed a sharp eye for baseball talent and had a way with words, as future events would attest to, but he apparently lacked a similar acumen for the business of baseball.

The Blues expected to play their games at the Union Grounds on Dartmouth Street, which was owned by the Union Athletic Exhibition Company. The directors of the Boston Blues had a rental arrangement with Frank Winslow of the Union Athletic Exhibition Company. "Mr. Winslow made a verbal agreement with the directors to let them have the grounds for half the net profits," the *Boston Globe* reported. After garnering meager payments from the first few games in May, Winslow changed his mind and "wanted to receive half of the net receipts instead of half the net profits." When the Blues refused to accede to Winslow's demand, Winslow locked the gates of the Union Grounds for the May 10 game and refused to let in the ball players or spectators.[34]

The Blues quickly struck an agreement with President Soden of the Boston National League team to use the team's South End Grounds for the May 10 game since the National League team was on the road. "Manager Murnan (sic) had found President Soden in the crowd, hustled him into a hack, started in the same direction, while most of the crowd cut across lots and filling all the horse cars, headed toward the home of the League nine," the *Boston Globe* reported while recounting the scene. Soden eventually agreed to lease the South End Grounds to the Blues for all their games while the National League team was on the road.[35]

Three weeks later, the owners of the Blues sold out to Murnane, who assumed full control of the club. "It is understood that Mr. Murnane has behind him several well-to-do gentlemen who are ready to put up any money that may be required and have given him carte blanche both in the management of the players and of the business of the club," the *Globe* reported.[36]

Apparently, Murnane's backers lost faith in him, because one month later Murnane sold the club to Walter Burnham. "The complications surrounding the existence of the Boston Blues have finally been cleared away by the sale of the club and its franchise by T.H. Murnan to W.H. Burnham of Portland," the *Globe* reported. "Mr. Burnham assumes all the obligations of the club and will at once take possession and file the bond required by the League that he will play out the season."[37]

Burnham went on to a lengthy career in baseball management, while Murnane focused on his new career as a baseball writer for the *Boston Globe*.

Although he managed the Lawrence club that won the 1885 pennant, Burnham parted ways with the Lawrence organization, likely over a move to lower expenses. Burnham became manager of the Meriden club in the Eastern League while Lawrence hired Frank Cox, former third baseman for the Detroit club in the National League, to be its player-manager. Burnham, who had resigned as manager of the Meriden club in early June, jumped at the opportunity to move into ownership in the New England League, although the Boston Blues finished dead last in the 1886 league standings.

Without the managerial experience of Burnham, the Lawrence club descended into turmoil by July under the leadership of club president William Knox. Upset at the lackluster play of the Lawrence team, Knox suspended Gorman on July 12 and fined him $75. Knox also fined O'Connell $40, Clayton $25, and Burns and Burke $10 each. When a good salary for a ball player was $100 a month, which is what O'Connell earned, these fines were substantial amounts.[38]

On Saturday, July 17, with 1,000 people in the stands in Lawrence for its game with Newburyport, the Lawrence team went on strike to protest the fines. "Lawrence players notified the directors that they declined to play unless the fines recently imposed on four of the club were remitted," the *Lawrence Eagle* reported. After the game was forfeited to Newburyport, "President Knox immediately took away the uniforms of the Lawrence players and notified them that they would be blacklisted."[39]

At a special meeting of the New England League owners that evening at the Parker House in Boston, President Moody presided over a lengthy discussion of the merits of each Lawrence player's action. The owners then voted on the punishment for each player. Both Cox, the team's manager, and Gorman were blacklisted at the outset of the meeting. "Mr. J.F. Gorman was next called and attempted a successful explanation of the alleged misdemeanors," the *Boston Globe* reported on the proceedings. "His excuses were not accepted, and on motion of Mr. Withington [of Newburyport], seconded by Mr. Nason [of Haverhill], Mr. Gorman was placed upon the blacklist."[40]

Next up on the docket was Dick Conway, who hadn't been fined by Knox, but had participated in the player mutiny.

> R.B. Conway had no explanations to make, neither had he excuses or apologies for the claimed misconduct. He stated that although he was not one of the members who was fined he stood by those who were, inasmuch as it was claimed that should any of those fines be allowed by the members of the club and paid, similar fines would be imposed without restraint. He refused to pay any fine to the New England League, as proposed by President Moody, but on motion of Mr. Withington, which had apparently the endorsement of all the League managers present, his case was laid upon the table.[41]

With no contrition coming forth from the Lawrence players, the club owners needed a new tack since the threat of blacklisting wasn't working. They finally convinced one player, Dick Conway's brother Bill, who had initially admitted no responsibility, of the severity of their collective action:

> William Conway was then called and practically admitted the charges made by the League and was equally hearty in his assertion that should the League reinstate him he would make such reparations as was reasonably demanded by the New England League. He was fined $20 and reinstated to the League, as was Richard B. Conway with whom a similar settlement was made.[42]

The Conways were reinstated after answering three questions posed to them: "Do you think, on the whole, that you were acting right to your employers? Will you play to the best of your ability, and will you submit to such punishment as you may think reasonable?"[43]

Knox had other plans for the Conway brothers, a pitcher/catcher combination, that he couldn't execute if they were blacklisted. Knox sold the Conways to Billy Barnie, manager of the Baltimore team in the American Association, for a reported price tag of $1,800.[44]

Dick Conway was not ready for the major leagues, as he compiled a dismal 2–7 record over the six weeks he was with the last-place Baltimore team. "Judging by the way Dick Conway was batted at Baltimore yesterday, it will not be long before he will wish he had remained at Lawrence," the *Lawrence Daily American* remarked soon after he left the team. Perhaps it was Knox's odd way to exact retribution from Conway, by having him pummeled at the major league level.[45]

Conway's last game with Baltimore was on August 29, when he pitched against Brooklyn in a Sunday game held at the team's Sunday grounds at Ridgewood Park in Queens. The Brooklyn team in the American Association played ball games on Sunday, which was considered a heretical act in Puritan New England, where the law required Sunday to be observed as a day of rest; no ball playing of any sort was permitted on the Sabbath, amateur or professional. Sunday games were also prohibited in the National League. The American Association, though, sanctioned Sunday games since that league appealed more to working class patrons, who worked six-day workweeks and could only attend games on their Sunday day off.

Sunday baseball was also a heretical act within the borders of Kings County, where the city of Brooklyn was located. Brooklyn president Charlie Byrne, however, arranged for games to be staged at Ridgewood Park in neighboring Queens County, where the constabulary was more tolerant of Sunday activities. Throngs of city dwellers traveled to then-rural Queens on Sundays to regale in the fresh air during the summer and fill the coffers of local businessmen. Crowds at ball games held at Ridgewood Park on Sunday routinely were triple the size of the crowds during the week for Brooklyn's games played at Washington Park, thereby generating bountiful gate receipts for Byrne.

The excitement of pitching on a Sunday before a large crowd didn't help Conway. "Barnie's new phenomenon, Conway, was put in the box for the first time against the Brooklyn batsmen, and his exhibition in the box as a pitcher was such as to make it an advantage for Barnie to send him down East again," the *Brooklyn Eagle* reported, panning his pitching performance. "He lacks judgment, command of the ball, and in fact all the elements of a first class pitcher, as far as his work yesterday showed."[46]

Portland of the New England League paid $600 to Baltimore to obtain the services of the Conway brothers. Conway pitched several shutouts for Portland, leading the team to the 1886 league pennant. Conway must have had a good laugh at the expense of Knox, whose Lawrence team finished next-to-last in the league standings.

By September, teams were not happy to travel to Portland. Newbury-port, the interim stop before heading to Portland, had transferred its club to Lynn for the balance of the 1886 season, thus making for a long haul to Portland.

Brockton also had its problems in 1886 as McGunnigle tried another run at the pennant. "Dissatisfied with its performance, the directors asked Mac to impose a fine," a McGunnigle biographer wrote. "He refused. The directors then fined the entire team. McGunnigle responded by asking for his release and joining John Irwin's Haverhill team."[47]

The directors of the Brockton ball club ran an ad in the *Brockton Enterprise* seeking buyers:

FOR SALE

The Property and Franchise of the Brockton Base Ball Association. The receipts on the home grounds for 1886 were $11,096. If no satisfactory bids received by Nov. 1st, fence and grand stand to be removed. Address, H.S. Bicknell, Secretary[48]

Apparently, the newspaper advertisement didn't help attract a qualified buyer, as the Brockton team disbanded in early 1887.

After two years as league president, Moody stepped down to focus on his legal career. William Knox, renowned for his tough stance to quell the mutiny of the Lawrence team in 1886, was elected president at a league meeting in November 1886. Like Moody, Knox was an ambitious lawyer. He went on to become the city solicitor in Lawrence and then, beginning in 1895, served four successive terms as a U.S. Congressman.[49]

Knox expanded the league to eight teams for the 1887 season by adding the textile cities of Manchester, New Hampshire, and Lowell, Massachusetts. The two cities had been baseball stalwarts ten years earlier during the 1877 season of the New England Association. When Brockton dropped out of the league, Knox and the league opted for Salem, Massachusetts, to be the eighth ball club.

Salem, like Newburyport, was seeking better days from its decline as one of the premier seaports in Massachusetts. Salem had been the second-largest town in Massachusetts in 1810, with a population about one-third that of Boston, having overcome its notoriety as the location of witchcraft trials in the seventeenth century. With canals and railroads making Boston a more convenient destination and shipping point, the fortunes of Salem plummeted in the nineteenth century.

The addition of Lowell to the league in 1887 signaled changing dynamics on two fronts related to attracting more spectators to the ball grounds — the integration of transportation in the location for grounds and the initial foray to actively court mill workers as spectators. The influence of these two factors, plus a strong team led by ex-Brockton manager McGunnigle, led to relative success for the Lowell ball club both on the field and in the treasury.

Lowell played its games in 1887 at the new River Street grounds, located across the Merrimack River from the city center of Lowell. The Lowell and Dracut Street Railway Company laid a new horse car line on Bridge Street to cross the river and extend to the Dracut navy yard. The new trolley line provided better access to ball grounds for downtown businessmen than they had to the more remote fair grounds located far outside the city center on Gorham Street.

On May 5, Lowell defeated Lawrence in the first game played on the River Street grounds, before an audience of 2,000 spectators. The proprietors of the Lowell ball club were very spectator friendly for those that used private transportation as well as those that used the public trolley line. "A gate will be cut through the fence to let the wagons in," the *Lowell Courier* reported. "There is a spare lot outside the grounds, just behind the grand stand. On this lot the management will place hitching rails, and two men in the pay of the club will be on hand to take care of teams. The Lowell and Dracut Street Railway Company ran two cars on their River Street route for the first time. The cars were overflowing."[50]

The evolution of the workweek for mill workers produced a Saturday half holiday in Lowell in 1887, which created far greater access to ball games than was the case with the six full-day workweek. The term "half holiday" referred to workers having an afternoon off from work (a pejorative phrase, as if workers by divine rule should always work six full days each week). Saturday afternoon games became a big attendance day for Lowell. "Now that the mill operatives have, through the agitation of The News, obtained the Saturday half-holiday, the games on that day will be largely attended," the *Lowell Daily News* declared. Indeed, a crowd of 1,500 attended the game on Saturday, May 14, in contrast to the 500 people that saw the game in Lowell on Monday, May 16.[51]

Shoe factories in Haverhill began to observe a Saturday half holiday in 1886, closing on Saturdays at noon during the summer months. "By granting the request we will not lose very much, for there is very little work done in the factories after dinner on Saturdays," the *Haverhill Evening Gazette* quoted one factory owner. "We always shut down our shops at 5 o'clock Saturdays and only four hours intervene between dinner and that time. I have little doubt but what my cutters will turn out just as many shoes by giving them a half holiday as they do at present working full time."[52]

Brockton had tried to accommodate shoe workers getting to ball games by scheduling the ball club's games for a 4:00 P.M. start, "in order not to interfere with manufacturers by drawing men from the shops early in the afternoon."[53]

While the half holiday on Saturday was becoming more accepted in many manufacturing work places, and thus allowed mill workers to attend ball games on Saturday afternoons, Walter Burnham was making progress on the ultimate solution to get mill workers to ball games — staging games on Sunday.

In April of 1887, Burnham arranged a spring trip for the Boston Blues to play a few games in the New York area, where the spring conditions were milder than back in Boston. Ostensibly, the trip was to prepare the squad for the upcoming season; however, the trip also permitted Burnham to check out a new arrangement for playing baseball games that was making its initial headway in the Eastern states — Sunday games.

Burnham's stop in Brooklyn during the spring of 1887 impacted the future of the New England League more than he could have imagined. As an inveterate baseball man, Burnham was no doubt aware of the Sunday baseball policy in the American Association and its economic impact on teams that could stage Sabbath games. On Sunday, April 10, 1887, Brooklyn defeated Burnham's Boston Blues, 21–5, as "fully 6,000 people visited Wallace's Ridgewood Park yesterday afternoon," the *Brooklyn Eagle* reported. "It was made evident by the vast attendance of yesterday that double the seating facilities are needed, and arrangements have been made for the erection of a new grand stand to the west of the new one [just built] ... so as to seat 10,000 people, for it is plain that that number will frequently be present."[54]

Scorecard from the May 28, 1887, game between Lowell and Lawrence. Lowell won the game, 15–7, which was played in Lawrence (Lawrence Public Library, Special Collections).

The large number of spectators at this Sunday game was roughly ten times the number that Burnham saw at an average New England League game, and was four times the typical attendance at a holiday game on Decoration Day or the Fourth of July. After witnessing the crowds that day at Ridgewood Park, Burnham was clearly hooked on Sunday baseball as the path to economic success in professional baseball. The only problem was how to engage in such an activity in a legal manner within reasonable proximity of a major city in New England. Within five years, Burnham would solve the vexing challenge of where to play Sunday baseball in New England.

Since holiday games were a key component to the financial solvency of the New England League, having just two holidays, Decoration Day and Independence Day, was limiting. By fielding a team in Lynn in 1887, though, the league gained an additional holiday twin bill, since the city of Lynn celebrated Bunker Hill Day on June 17 each year. While only 300 people attended the 10:00 A.M. game between Lynn and Lowell, the *Lynn Item* reported that the afternoon game at 4:00 P.M. drew 1,000 to Bicycle Park to see the Boston Blues defeat Lynn, 17–12.

Another holiday found its way into the New England League schedule in 1887 when Labor Day was first celebrated as a Massachusetts state holiday on Monday, September 5, 1887. "Monday was a proud day for labor as on that day for the first time in the annals of Massachusetts was celebrated a holiday distinctively set apart to labor," the *Lynn Bee* reported, yet declined to print an attendance figure for the forenoon game with Manchester.[55]

Salem also staged a holiday game when "about 1200 persons attended the base ball game at the Bridge Street grounds in the morning" against Lowell. The two teams played an afternoon game before a small audience since the holiday was not generally celebrated that year in Lowell.[56]

In 1888, Labor Day was incorporated as a third holiday date for all teams in the New England League.

Despite the ability to increase ball game attendance with Saturday half holidays and the addition of Bunker Hill Day and Labor Day as regular holiday dates, many ball clubs experienced financial difficulties just six weeks into the 1887 season. Clubs had spent lavishly to attract top playing talent in their quest for the pennant, and attendance levels didn't justify those expenditures in several cities. And in cities with good prospects for attendance, such as Haverhill and Salem, even the lavish spending for ball players failed to put a quality team on the field.

On July 1, Haverhill and Salem were mired at the bottom of the league standings. Both teams had dismal won-lost records, Haverhill at 13–35 and Salem at 7–40. There was talk of combining teams in a league consolidation if four teams could agree to merge into two teams. "The proposed scheme was, since the Lawrences have been drawing poor audiences with a fairly good team, and Haverhill has been drawing well with a poor team, to consolidate the two," the *Boston Globe* reported in late June. "This was all arranged, providing that two other teams in the league do the same to make an even number of teams." However, negotiations to consolidate the Boston Blues and Salem broke down when Burnham, manager of the Blues, wanted an ownership interest in the combined Salem club.[57]

The league met several times in early July to talk about the financial situation, including discussions to reduce player salaries. In a tense atmosphere, there were radical ideas posed, such as Lynn manager Murphy wanting "the N.E. League to pass a law to reduce all players' salaries to $75 per month."[58]

With no league action taken on player salaries, the Salem ball club owners sold the club. "Two Peabody men are understood to be the purchasers and the price paid is somewhere about $400," the *Salem Evening News* reported. However, when the new owners were jilted on the apparent promise that Salem would get first pick of players from the disbanding Haverhill and Lawrence clubs, they "decided rather than to remain in with the present club, to dispose of their newly acquired right and retiree altogether."[59]

Haverhill reorganized its ownership and purchased Burnham's Boston Blues club, with the Blues moving to Haverhill and retaining its league record (instead of the Haverhill club's wretched record). With the Salem and Boston clubs out of the league, Lawrence remained to maintain a six-club setup, despite the club's extreme financial difficulties. (The bridge over the Merrimack River between the city and the ball grounds had burned down, making the grounds nearly inaccessible.)

One of the bright spots on the Salem team was shortstop Hugh Duffy, who routinely garnered two or three hits for the team each game while the team lost four of every five games it played. "Duffy is a splendid batter and shortstop," the *Salem Evening News* remarked about the future Hall of Fame ball player upon the disbanding of the Salem team and Duffy's transfer to the Lowell club.[60]

Two weeks after the Boston club relocated to Haverhill, the Lawrence club moved to Salem. With two clubs now representing cities of disbanded franchises, the league standings carried in newspapers usually contained won-lost records of all eight clubs, with "New Salems," the original Lawrence club, contrasted with "Old Salems," the defunct club. Similarly, the "Old Haverhills" were contrasted with "New Haverhills" or sometimes "Haverhill Blues" to denote the connection to Burnham's team.

Burnham's club in Haverhill didn't make it to Labor Day, disbanding on August 31, just as labor strikes, fomented by the Knights of Labor union, descended on the city's shoe factories. Burnham likely was already negotiating for the next stop in his baseball management career (now totaling four cities in three years), as Worcester applied for a franchise at the August 31 meeting of the league's club owners.

Lowell and Portland were the class of the league during the 1887 season. Lowell, in particular, seemed to have an inside track on getting choice ball players from the league's disbanded franchises that season. Duffy, by one historian's count, hit safely in forty-eight of the fifty-two games he played for Lowell in 1887 (albeit a walk counted as a hit in 1887), as Lowell was victorious, or tied, thirty-nine of those fifty-two games.[61]

In his first game for Lowell on July 12, Duffy collected two hits in four at-bats. "Duffy, one of the new men taken by Lowell from the Salems, and who played shortstop with that club, was placed at third [base] yesterday, Shinnick going to right field," the *Lowell Courier* reported. "Duffy played a fine game. He made a put out, four assists, no errors, a single and a three-base hit."[62]

Lowell battled with Portland through September for the New England League pennant. When Portland defeated Lowell twice in the last two games of the season, the two teams wound up in a tie for first place. That was before the protests began. For the second time in three years, the New England League had to confront a disputed championship.

While the league debated the disputed pennant race, Lowell played two exhibition games with the Cuban Giants, one of the best black teams of the 1880s. The Cuban Giants, based in Trenton, New Jersey, employed highly skilled players and often defeated teams from both the National League and the American Association. The skill of the light-skinned mulattos that dominated the roster made the Cuban Giants an attractive draw for Caucasian teams.

"Black clubs benefited from the instability of the white clubs," historian Michael Lomax wrote in his book *Black Baseball Entrepreneurs, 1860–1901.* "As the Cuban Giants and the Gorhams exhibited their ability to draw large crowds, one exhibition game with these clubs could possibly meet the weekly payroll and expenses of these struggling white teams."[63]

However, the attractiveness of the Cuban Giants to Caucasian teams began to wane in early September when the St. Browns of the American Association refused to play a Sunday exhibition game with the Cuban Giants in New Jersey due to a boycott by the St. Louis players. The *Boston Globe* publicized the boycott with an article on September 12 that was headlined "Color Line in Base Ball; Refusal of the St. Louis Browns to Play With the Cuban Giants." The *Globe* even printed the letter the St. Louis players wrote to St. Louis owner Chris Von der Ahe:

> Dear Sir — We, the undersigned, members of the St. Louis Base Ball Club, do not agree to play against negroes tomorrow. We will cheerfully play against white players at any time, and think, by refusing to play we are only doing what is right, taking everything into consideration, and the shape the team is in at present.[64]

This work stoppage by the St. Louis Browns reflected the growing hostility toward black players among Caucasian players, as soon "the prejudice of white players gaining wider acceptance in the baseball world" trumped the economic benefit of staging the inter-racial games. This racial prejudice had earlier manifested itself in the International League, when in July the league banned new player contracts with black players even though the league employed several black players.[65]

Two weeks following the St. Louis Browns' boycott, the Cuban Giants barnstormed through the Boston area. Although Lowell officials no doubt expected a big day at the gate, attendance was sparse at the two games with the Cuban Giants on September 26 and 27. Publicity about the "color line" being established in professional baseball likely kept attendance down.

Lowell defeated the Cuban Giants on September 26 before an unspecified "crowd of fair size at the grounds." The next day Lowell lost to the Cuban Giants before a "small attendance," as the visitors "made more fun yesterday than Monday, and played better ball, as well."[66]

At a league meeting at the Parker House in Boston on September 27, the club owners tried to settle the pennant dispute between Lowell and Portland. The Lowell club had engaged William Moody, former league president, to represent its interests at the meeting. Moody offered "two ways to settle the championship question. One was for the two clubs to waive their protests and decide to play a series of games. The other was to take up the protests, consider them on their merits and decide the championship accordingly."[67]

The club owners decided to debate the protests, one of which was the vexing question regarding the legality of two six-inning games Portland had played with Lynn on September 9. Portland concurred with Moody's analysis that the games were illegal — they should have been one nine-inning game with the second played for as many innings as possible before darkness — but said it was an unintentional act. Portland offered the pennant to Lowell if the club wanted to claim it on this "technicality," but Lowell demurred.

"After a long and animated discussion, the two clubs were unable to come to any agreement, and the league took the matter in hand," the *Boston Globe* reported. "On the motion of Mr. Murphy it was ordered that the clubs play a series of five games, to settle the ownership of the pennant. The schedule was made up as follows: Sept. 29 at Portland, Sept. 30 at Lowell, Oct. 1 at Boston, Oct. 3 at Lynn, Oct. 4 at Haverhill."[68]

Believing the club had been robbed of the pennant, Lowell proved on the ball field that it was the better team. Lowell won the first two games of the post-season series, including a narrow 5–4 victory in ten innings in the second game. After rain washed out the next three scheduled game dates, the third game was played in Boston on October 5. After Lowell shut out Portland, 7–0, in the third game to secure the championship, a celebration erupted in Lowell.

> Tonight hundreds of young men assembled in Merrimack and Central streets, armed with brooms and loaded with fireworks of all descriptions. They marched through Central and Merrimack streets to the northern station, where barouches awaited the arrival of the winning team. When the train arrived at 8 o'clock it was almost impossible for the passengers to get through the Middlesex street station, owing to the crowd. On the players leaving the train they were given an enthusiastic welcome, and some of the more excited in the crowd grabbed Shinnick, Duffy and McGunnigle and almost carried them to the barouches [for the parade]. Cudworth, who was seated in one of the barouches, was not forgotten by the people, and many inquiries were made regarding the manner and how badly he was injured in today's game. The barouches were adorned with brooms to be indicative of the sweeping victory over the Portlands. At the head of the procession were banners borne by young men bearing the inscription: "Lowells, Champions New England League."[69]

This 1887 championship was very meaningful to Jim Cudworth, who was injured in a pre-game collision while getting ready for the third game.

In the Clark Cemetery in Lakeville, Massachusetts, the 1887 championship is memorialized on Cudworth's gravestone by a diagram of crossed bats surrounded by baseballs, with the inscription "N.E. League" to the left and "Lowell 1887" to the right.[70]

By the time of the Lowell championship celebration, it was obvious that twenty-year-old Hugh Duffy would likely not return to Lowell for the 1888 season. "All in all, Duffy is a star player, and in all probability, he will go up higher in the profession," wrote the *Lowell Courier* in a special supplement focused on the Lowell ball club in its October 8 edition. Duffy led the team with a .437 "actual" average, the *Courier* noted, and a .484 "legal" average when counting walks as hits as was the convention in 1887.[71]

Tim Murnane quietly assumed an unofficial role in the New England League, beyond his official role as baseball writer for the *Boston Globe* (and indirect publicist for the league). With Murnane's connections with the major league teams through his position with the *Globe*, he had an arrangement with Cap Anson of the National League's Chicago club to scout for players to send Anson's way. Murnane's first signing was Marty Sullivan, catcher for the Boston Blues, who signed with Anson after the 1886 season. Duffy became his most famous signing.

At the time, New England League teams had until October 20 to resign their players for the 1888 season, or the players were free to sign with other teams. By September, the *Lowell Courier* was already reporting that Murnane had recommended Duffy to Anson to play in Chicago. Murnane told the story in a bylined article in the *Boston Globe* during the winter of 1889:

> This kind of playing was sure to attract the attention of the older organizations, and the young man who a few months before, was glad to pick up $75 for his services, was sought after by league and association clubs. He signed a personal agreement to go to Chicago for $1200, in August. A few weeks after the Boston club had an agent looking for him, and he was offered as high as $2250 to come to the Hub. He finally went to Chicago for $2000, $300 of which was advance money.[72]

Murnane, a great storyteller, embellished on the event as the years went on. In 1916, at a meeting of the Bunting Club in Lowell, Murnane told the audience:

> I got Duffy to sign an agreement to the effect that when he signed to go up to the big show, he would sign with Chicago. The day before the time limit for signing, I got Duffy to Boston and entertained him a whole day while other scouts were up in Lowell looking for him. I told him I would give him $2000 to sign with Chicago with $500 additional the moment he signed. I put out the money in two dollar bills, and it formed a most impressive looking bundle. Duffy signed immediately.[73]

Following the postseason series for the 1887 pennant, Duffy wasn't the only one in the New England League to move up in his career.

The managers of the Lowell and Portland teams both parlayed their roles in the tight 1887 pennant race into managerial jobs at the major league level in 1888. Harry Spence, manager of the Portland team, piloted Indianapolis of the National League, while Bill McGunnigle, manager of the Lowell team, directed the Brooklyn team in the American Association.

Knox, the league president, stepped down to pursue his legal career. The club owners elected Edward Cheney of the Lowell club to be the league president for the 1888 season. Cheney, who helped run his family's bobbin factory in Lowell, was a secondary member of the 1887 club management, which was headed by Frank Howe.

Burnham convinced backers in Worcester to support a team in the New England League under his direction. The move to Worcester was another step in Burnham's ambitions to operate a top-flight minor league team in the New England region.

Unlike most cities that had baseball clubs in the New England League, Worcester developed a diversified economy rather than one having a one-industry dependence. Worcester became a center for metal trades after the opening of the Blackstone Canal in 1828 and the introduction of railroad lines in the 1830s that connected the city with Boston, Providence, and points north. The city became a supplier of machine parts and other metal goods needed by the textile and shoe industries. Worcester generally had a stable economy, making the city a sought-after location for minor league teams.

"A wide variety of immigrants, in addition to diversity of industries, meant that workers tended to be isolated from one another, living in ethnic ghettos," historians wrote in describing the development of Worcester. "Consequently they were unable to organize and were easily manipulated by the more unified business classes. The result was that Worcester never developed a radical labor consciousness and had very few strikes."[74]

The infamous Blizzard of 1888, which hit the region in mid–March, was a setback to the New England League since teams had less opportunity to prepare for the 1888 season. The blizzard was particularly detrimental to Portland, which was hit hard by the storm. In an article entitled "The Great Storm," the *Eastern Argus* described the snow storm in a dispatch received from Biddeford: "It has been snowing hard since noon and to-night the wind is blowing almost a blizzard. The snow is piled into huge drifts. All the night trains over both divisions of the Boston & Maine are behind time. Telegraphic communication between here [Biddeford] and Boston has been cut off since noon."[75]

Snow on the ball grounds in Portland prevented the ball club from getting in any practice until the third week in April. With the season opening on April 28, the Portland ball club got off to a rocky start, losing sixteen of its first seventeen games before defeating Lynn on May 23 for its second victory of the season. On June 9, carrying a 5–28 record, Portland disbanded.

> The Portlands finished the miserable existence that they have been dragging out the past week ... the game winds up the affairs of the Portland club. Notwithstanding the fact that the Portland people want a team and are making so much fuss about it, the franchise which has been laying around as a free gift, finds no takers.[76]

The New England League, at its June 11 meeting, decided to count only the first four games that each team played against Portland, so the club's official won-lost tally was downsized to 2–18. With just five teams left in the league after Portland's disbanding, the fortunes of the league in 1888 didn't look good.

Worcester, under the direction of Burnham, experienced limited success on the city's new ball grounds at the corner of Grove Street and Park Avenue. Burnham decided to experiment with new ways to try to win baseball games. In June, Burnham hired black pitcher George Stovey to face the all-Caucasian batters in the New England League, in contravention of the "color line" that was in its formative stages in mid–1888.

Worcester's new pitcher wasn't just any black pitcher. Baseball history has linked Stovey, who had recorded more than thirty wins in 1887 with Newark of the International League, to the commencement of the unofficial "color line" that excluded black players from organized baseball until 1946. On July 14, 1887, Stovey had been advertised to pitch an exhibition game for Newark against the National League's Chicago team, managed by Cap Anson.

> Stovey's fine 1887 season was marred in mid–July when he was placed in the glare of unwarranted controversy. Newark scheduled an exhibition game against Anson's great White Stockings. It promised to be a rare opportunity for Stovey to showcase his abilities against the very best that baseball had to offer. Tragically, Jim Crow in the person of Cap Anson intervened to keep Stovey and his batterymate Walker from showing their talent.[77]

When Anson insisted that Stovey not pitch the exhibition game in Newark, the Chicago manager's racist views and influence among the National League clubs instigated baseball's color line, which was manifested more publicly in the St. Louis Browns' boycott of the game with the Cuban Giants in September 1887. "The *Newark Evening News* attributed Stovey's absence to illness, but the *Toronto World* got it right in reporting that 'Hackett intended putting Stovey in the box against the Chicagos, but Anson objected to his playing on account of his color,'" historian Jerry Malloy wrote.[78]

The ostracism of black players apparently didn't concern Burnham, who was trying to win a pennant for Worcester in the New England League.

Burnham knew of Stovey's pitching talent, having seen him pitch for Jersey City in 1886 when Burnham managed the Meriden team in the Eastern League. At the spring exhibition game between Worcester and Newark prior to the 1888 season, the topic of Stovey surely surfaced. One contemporary writer wrote that Stovey had a "bewildering array of hard breaking pitches" and "the brunette fellow with the sinister fin and the demonic delivery ... has such a knack of tossing up balls that appear to be as large as an alderman's opinion of himself, but you cannot hit 'em with a cellar door."[79]

While he recognized Stovey's talent in the pitcher's box, Burnham, though, probably wasn't totally aware of his personal nature, which one writer described as "unbearably petulant, willful and explosively temperamental." Stovey's Jersey City manager Pat Powers once said of the black pitcher, "I consider him to be one of the greatest pitchers in the country, but ... he is head strong and obstinate, and, consequently, hard to manage."[80]

The *Worcester Telegram* heralded Stovey's arrival with an article headlined, "At Last! The Colored Pitcher Arrives and Will Exorcise the Demon This Afternoon." The *Telegram* had hopes for the new pitcher. "Stovey, the new colored gentleman from Trenton, who is expected to change the luck for Worcester's baseball nine, arrived in the city last evening at 9:25 o'clock, over the Boston and Albany railroad. The chances are that Stovey will try and twirl a very small ball on the Grove Street grounds this afternoon at 3:30 o'clock."[81]

The mercurial Stovey debuted with Worcester on June 9 in an 8–7 victory over Lowell at the Grove Street grounds. "When the team first came out on the field there was an inclination to applaud him, but it took quite a minute to pick him out, as his color is not so dark as many had anticipated," the *Worcester Spy* reported.[82]

Stovey lasted just a few weeks in the New England League, though. Burnham released Stovey in mid–July, a few days after he pitched Worcester to a victory against Manchester on July 12. His skin color does not seem to have been the problem. "Stovey and Dowd are to be released," the *Worcester Spy* reported on July 16. "Stovey has done the club good service, but has not been proved entirely trustworthy."[83]

Flying in the face of the *Spy*'s explanation for Stovey's release was more pointed commentary by the *Lowell Daily News*, which wrote, "We blush to be compelled to say it, but it may as well be said: Stovey is an A No. 1 pitcher, but his color, over which he had no control, barred him from receiving the proper support of his so-called 'white' associates. And this is civilization."[84]

"This is sentimental, but is not true," said the *Spy*, responding to the *Daily News*' charge. "Stovey's trouble was not in his support but in himself. If Lowell wants to try and keep him in shape to play ball, let them sign him."[85]

At the time Burnham released Stovey (probably for reasons due to both his personal habits and non-support by the other players, rather than his skin color, since Burnham was in the business of winning baseball games), the New England League began to crumble and fall apart. The league had operated as a five-team circuit for several weeks after Portland had disbanded in June. It briefly operated as a six-team circuit in mid–July when Portsmouth, New Hampshire, joined the league, but soon contracted to four teams when Lynn and Salem both disbanded by early August.

The loss of Lynn and Salem was crushing to the hopes of the remaining clubs in the league. The financial situation was so bad that Lynn dropped out when the team was in first place in the standings; Salem had been in second place when that club disbanded.

"Matters are at a crisis with the Lynn base ball team, the leaders in the New England League," the *Boston Herald* reported on July 25. "At 11:30 it was uncertain whether the nine would play its scheduled game with Lowell." Lynn lost 11–1 to Lowell, and the next day, Lynn sold Larougue to the Detroit club of the National League for $500 to reduce some of its debt before going out of business.[86]

Portsmouth transferred to the New England League from the defunct New England Interstate League, where the ball club managed by Frank Leonard had dominated competition among the New Hampshire cities of Dover, Nashua, and Rochester along with a club from Haverhill, Massachusetts. Portsmouth won its first New England League game on July 21 against Lynn at the Portsmouth ball grounds at the corner of Newcastle Avenue and South Street. "The Portsmouth club, by winning the first game played in the New England League in this city on Friday, took the head of the list, and remained there till Saturday, when the Worcester club beat them on the Worcesters' grounds," the *Portsmouth Chronicle* declared.[87]

Worcester and Lowell basically battled for the pennant over the last few weeks of the 1888 season, with Manchester and Portsmouth providing some alternative competition as the two New Hampshire teams played out the schedule. After the Labor Day games on September 3, the league shortened the season by two weeks to have it end on September 15, but to play only postponed games after September 8.

Lowell defeated Worcester on September 7 at the River Street grounds in Lowell to edge into first place. When the game the next day between Lowell and Worcester was rained out after one inning (with Lowell ahead 4–0), Worcester had to pin its hopes for a first-place finish on the outcome of two postponed games that Lowell was to play against Portsmouth on Monday, September 10. If Lowell lost at least one game, then the rained out game of September 8 would be played on September 11 to determine the championship.

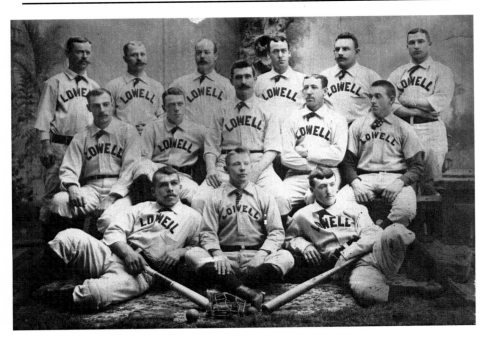

Team picture of the 1888 Lowell ball club that won the New England League championship (National Baseball Hall of Fame Library, Cooperstown, N.Y.).

Lowell backed into the pennant, though, when the Portsmouth team failed to show up for the two games on September 10. Portsmouth "did not appear and sent no notice to Lowell that they did not intend to come until afternoon," the *Worcester Spy* reported. "Such a piece of business as this at a time when the championship hinged on those games, providing they were fairly played, is contemptuous and should bar the Portsmouth team from ever joining any honest league again."[88]

There was no rejoicing in Lowell for the second consecutive pennant. Whereas in 1887 "the town turned out royally," in 1888 "everything was as doleful as a Quaker funeral," the *Lowell Courier* remarked. "The pennant thus belongs to Lowell, though the way the deciding games were won gives the triumph an unsatisfactory cast," the *Courier* continued. "The spectators on the grounds were so disheartened and sad that they did not even cheer for the victors of the contest, and their sorrow was transformed into irritation and resentment when they learned that they could realize nothing on their tickets, no money being paid back."[89]

Burnham, who was a spectator at the ball grounds in Lowell when Portsmouth failed to show up for its game with Lowell, was no doubt disappointed that his Worcester club had lost the pennant. Burnham likely expressed no remorse, since he had already prepared to move on from the New England League, an organization he no doubt began to consider as a backwater of baseball.

In early August, the *Worcester Spy* printed an item, likely planted by Burnham, suggesting that a league expanding beyond the New England borders would be beneficial. "It is thought by some knowing ones that a league composed of four New England cities and four in the vicinity of New York City would make a paying league for next season. Manchester, Lowell, Worcester, and Providence should be good enough for this part of the country." Added the *Spy*, "It doesn't cost much more to go to Jersey City or Newark than to Manchester or Portsmouth, and there is a good deal more money to be got in return."[90]

The New Jersey cities were especially attractive to Burnham since the game's survival no longer relied solely on attendance by middle class businessmen as it did in New England. Jersey City and Newark favored games on Sunday, when the laboring class swelled attendance and produced ample gate receipts to offset meager crowds that often showed up during the workweek. Both teams had experimented with Sunday baseball in 1888. Newark used the Ridgewood Park grounds for a July 15 game when the Brooklyn team was on the road in Kansas City. Jersey City played an exhibition game on August 5 with Louisville of the American Association at the ball grounds in Weehawken, New Jersey.

Nowhere in New England could professional baseball be played on Sunday; even ball games played by amateur players were barred in many locales. For instance, in May of 1887, police arrested nine players on charges of playing ball on Sunday along with seven others just for being present at the game played in South Boston.

"The commandment to keep holy the Sabbath seemed to have escaped the memory of a number of the residents of Crescent place yesterday," the *Boston Herald* reported in an article entitled "Ball Tossers Arrested; South Boston Young Men Locked Up for Playing on Sunday." The article went on to say, "Their love of the national game so absorbed their attention that Sergeant Foster and Patrolman Wyman of the third police precinct managed to get into their midst before the players were aware of their approach."[91]

The New England League made a feeble attempt to organize for the 1889 season at the league's annual meeting on November 9. At the meeting, which was attended by representatives from Worcester and Lowell, "the situation regarding the prospects of the league for next season was thoroughly discussed." The situation didn't look good. "Not much encouragement was set forth in that direction, but it was deemed best not to dissolve the organization at this time but to continue it for the present in the hope that during the winter several cities would arouse interest enough in the national game to organize teams and join the league."[92]

Two weeks later, the *Boston Globe* printed remarks from National League president Nick Young on what it would take for the New England League to become a viable minor league. Young didn't mince his words, saying, "To attempt to establish or continue the New England League upon the same basis upon which it was established last season would be fallacy." He went on to suggest:

> A league composed of cities within a radius of 50 miles might be established and placed on a sound financial footing, but the players will not be given any Dan Brothers or Mike Kelly salary. The league of last season was a remarkably strong one. All the teams represented had players in their ranks who were well known throughout the country as good ball players. There were men who have established reputations and who sought and obtained good salaries. This was one cause which led to the failure of the league of the past season. What is wanted is young players who seek a training. The sooner managers recognize this the better.[93]

Young's comments set the stage for a decades-long argument over the role of minor league teams within organized baseball. Should the teams serve as a feeder system for the major leagues or operate as independent ball clubs functioning as part of the local community?

4

Burnham Thwarts League, 1890–1891

WITH THE INEVITABLE COLLAPSE OF THE New England League after the 1888 season, Walter Burnham's ambition to be a baseball "magnate" drove him to the new Atlantic Association for the 1889 baseball season.

To Burnham, the Atlantic Association was a significant step-up from the New England League. The Atlantic Association was comprised of larger cities throughout the Northeast, which included the two surviving New England League clubs (Worcester and Lowell) as well as Hartford and New Haven in Connecticut, Newark and Jersey City in New Jersey, and Wilkes-Barre and Easton in Pennsylvania.

In addition to covering a larger area of the Northeast and being closer to the country's largest city, New York, the Atlantic Association had several ball clubs with ambitions to play Sunday baseball. Since Burnham wasn't going to be playing home games on Sunday any time soon in New England, he could at least get a visitor's share of the gate receipts for Sunday games played in northern New Jersey.

During April 1889, both Newark and Jersey City played Sunday exhibition games against the Brooklyn team of the American Association at Ridgewood Park, the team's Sunday grounds in Queens. The experience bolstered the belief that both clubs could hold Sunday games at their own ball grounds that season.

At the April 7 game between Jersey City and Brooklyn, the weather "was totally unfit for ball playing, a cold northeasterly wind making it exceedingly unpleasant for players and spectators alike and yet 3,040 people paid their way into Ridgewood Park to see the Jersey City team play the Brooklyns on the occasion," the *Brooklyn Eagle* reported. The following Sunday, April 14, better weather for the Newark game with Brooklyn attracted 8,409 people, an attendance figure the *Brooklyn Eagle* described as one of "the best on record known in the annals of any Spring exhibition campaign," and testified "to the great public interest taken in the game this season."[1]

Newark and Jersey City first tested the mettle of New Jersey officials to enforce that state's law prohibiting Sunday ball games when the two clubs arranged exhibition games to be played on Sunday, June 9, with Worcester and Lowell. Proceeds from the games went to the Johnstown Relief Fund to help victims of the devastating flood in that Pennsylvania city. One of the flood victims was former Newark manager Chris Meisel, who was traveling from Ohio to New Jersey when the flood swept his train off its tracks.[2]

The unstated purpose of the Sunday games, though, was to validate the level of patronage for Sunday games held at each ball club's regular playing grounds.

Burnham probably couldn't believe his eyes when he saw 10,000 people at the Newark grounds to witness the ball game with Worcester that Sunday. That attendance was nearly twice the size of the Sunday crowd he saw at the April 1887 game at Ridgewood Park, which itself was beyond belief to Burnham. The Jersey City game reportedly netted $835 for the flood relief effort, indicating that several thousand fans viewed the contest with Lowell if admission were the standard twenty-five cents.[3]

On the following Sunday, Burnham attempted to have Worcester play a regular-season game in Jersey City. "The Jersey City Base Ball Club played a game last Sunday for the Johnstown sufferers. They propose playing a game next Sunday for the suffering stockholders," the *Worcester Spy* quipped. "A lively row is promised. The First Presbyterian Church trustees held a meeting and signed a protest 'against such desecrations of the Sabbath day' and then requested the police commissioner to interfere." Authorities did step in to prevent the Sunday game on June 16.[4]

Burnham had a willing accomplice for his Sunday game desires in Denny Sullivan, a director of the Lowell team and champion of the working class as editor of the city's Democratic-leaning newspaper, the *Lowell Daily News*. On the next road trip to New Jersey in July, Lowell played a regular Atlantic Association game on Sunday, July 14, at Newark. Four thousand spectators showed up for the Sunday game to see Newark pummel Lowell, 17–4.[5]

"The Lowells can lose on a Sunday as well as any other day," the *Lowell Daily News* remarked regarding the fortunes of the next-to-last-place Lowell club. "Who are those new names we see in Sunday's game in the Lowell column? Smith and Jones strike us as somewhat familiar but somewhat out of company in the Lowells' list," as some of the Lowell players hid behind an alias to shield their participation in a Sunday ball game. The *Daily News* also reported, "Sunday ball playing is allowed in Rhode Island and 5,000 people attended an amateur game at Rocky Point Sunday."[6]

The following Sunday, July 21, Burnham had his first taste of championship baseball on a Sunday. As the *Boston Globe* recounted the next day, "The Jersey City and Worcester base ball teams decided to violate the vice and immorality law of the State of New Jersey yesterday afternoon by playing a game on the Oakland Avenue grounds." After the victory by Worcester, the players on both teams were arrested and fined $2 each.[7]

Burnham and his team participated in a ball game conducted in eerie solitude, according to the *New York Tribune* report on the Jersey City game with Worcester:

Sunday baseball was inaugurated at Oakland Park, Jersey City, yesterday in a decidedly unique and interesting way... Everything was as quiet as a Quaker meeting, a buzzing Jersey mosquito around little 'Chic' Hofford's head causing the only atmospheric disturbance. Umpire Hopkins called 'Play!' in a subdued stage whisper, dropping his usual wild and defiant yell. The peanut man took a seat in the rear of the grand-stand and swapped sympathy with the tutti-frutti peddler, the pie-man and the head barkeeper. They had all failed to get permission to retail their wares... Manager Powers sat demurely in a corner, with one eye on the fat policeman who had both eyes on 'Pat' Powers. Everything was quiet, but the game went on steadily.[8]

Walter Burnham, shown in a line drawing from the *Brockton Enterprise* in 1896, applied his skills as a baseball promoter for minor league ball clubs throughout New England. In 1890, though, Burnham attempted to derail the New England League by preventing the league from locating a team in Worcester.

After the game, witnessed by "1,597 people [who]

had paid 25 cents each to see the game and about 200 women [who] had been admitted free," all eighteen ball players were arrested and "marched down before Justice Norton, who, with great dignity, fined each player $1 and costs."[9]

Burnham was so encouraged by the Sunday crowds seen in New Jersey that he began to investigate ways to play on Sunday closer to home. The only place in New England with any experience at the time with Sunday games was the Rocky Point resort in Rhode Island, about fifteen miles down Narragansett Bay from Providence. Rocky Point had been cast as "a tiny island of illicit professional baseball on Sunday within the vast New England ocean of strict Puritan observance of a Sunday day of rest."[10]

"The New England descendants of the Puritans looked down upon little state of Rhode Island as a sort of annex to Satan's hideout, because the lax officials of that state made it possible for the baseball fans of Providence and vicinity to revel in professional games on Sundays by traveling on crowded excursion boats down the river to an isolated resort called Rocky Point," one commentator claimed in describing the nature of the Sunday baseball haven.[11]

Randall Harrington, the proprietor of the Rocky Point resort for many years, began leasing the grounds of the resort in 1888 from its owner, the American Steamship Company. Harrington initiated Sunday baseball at Rocky Point in 1889, when amateur teams played Sunday games there with legal impunity. "Two Sunday base ball games were played at Rocky Point yesterday and witnessed by large crowds," the *New Bedford Evening Standard* reported in July. "The police there say in regard to Sunday base ball games that 'as they allow most anything in Warwick now, we don't propose to interfere with the games Sundays as long as they are conducted in an orderly manner and the spectators behave themselves.'"[12]

"The Atlantic Association is seriously agitating the question of playing Sunday games at Rocky Point, R.I., where there is a commodious ground, with a grand stand capable of holding several thousand people," the *Worcester Spy* reported on July 23 in an article entitled "Plan Proposed for Sunday Games at Rocky Point." In early August, the *Spy* reported, "An effort has been made to get an entering wedge into Providence. If Sunday games could be played at Rocky Point, the Atlantic Association would put the Wilkes-Barre team into Providence on its own responsibility."[13]

When putting a ball club in Providence for the balance of the 1889 season turned out to be unworkable, Burnham arranged for Worcester to play a Rhode Island amateur team at Rocky Point on Sunday, August 4, to test Sunday play for himself. The next Sunday, August 11, Worcester played the Athletics of Providence in one game of a four-game extravaganza at Rocky Point before a crowd of 1,500.

After a successful test run at Sunday baseball against amateur teams at Rocky Point, Worcester and Lowell played an exhibition game there on August 18. As the *Boston Globe* recounted in an article entitled "Rocky Time at Rocky Point," the two teams engaged in an exhibition amid more frivolity on a Sunday than anyone on those two teams had ever witnessed.

> As it was reported that the ball games would be prevented by the police, a big crowd was on hand to see the attempt made. So many fights took place about the Point, however, between drunken men and women that the police had their hands full and the sports went merrily on while rum was sold openly from a dozen unlicensed bars in the vicinity. It was the wildest and most riotous time ever seen at a shore resort in these plantations on a Sabbath. As the county jail is six miles away from the Point, no arrests were made.[14]

Lowell defeated Worcester, 8–5, before 1,300 spectators in the last game played by both teams that season at Rocky Point.

While Worcester copped the pennant in the Atlantic Association in 1889, the season was anything but a financial success. Burnham said the club lost $2,500 in 1889, more than twice what the club lost in 1888. The visitor's share of gate receipts from a few Sunday games wasn't enough for Worcester to offset the expenses associated with traveling to the far-flung cities in New Jersey and Pennsylvania to play its Atlantic Association games. Compounding the economics was the lack of spectator interest in home games with these distant entities. "You must figure on clubs making their money at home, as there is 65 per cent of the gate and grand stand profits, with no traveling or hotel bills, against a $75 guarantee, or 35 per cent, away with traveling and hotel bills to deduct," Burnham told the *Worcester Spy*.[15]

Since only five clubs remained in business by season's end, a committee consisting of Burnham, Sullivan, and Sam Trott of the Newark club was appointed in October to consider new cities to increase the Atlantic Association to six or eight teams. That list included Providence, no doubt at the urging of Burnham based on his Sunday game experiences at Rocky Point during the summer.

By December, though, the directors of both the Lowell and Worcester clubs and the owners of the team based in Hartford, Connecticut had a change of heart about staying in the Atlantic Association. Their big concern was the addition of a Baltimore club to the Atlantic Association, which would add an even longer, and expensive, road trip for their teams. The Baltimore team would be managed by Billie Barnie.

On December 26, a meeting was held in Worcester among representatives from Lowell, Springfield, and Hartford to revive the New England League for the 1890 season. No one from Worcester attended this meeting; by this time Burnham was no longer associated with the Worcester club. The directors of the Worcester club, though, seemed to be leaning toward rejoining the New England League.

"Now is the time to organize a New England League," the *Boston Globe* opined. "Baltimore is too big a jump for clubs from Lowell and Worcester, and is a poor paying city in the bargain. Brockton, Portland and Providence would do well next year [in a New England League]."[16]

"It was voted to form a New England League of eight clubs, with a monthly salary list not to exceed $1500," the *Lowell Courier* reported. The working group formed a committee to draw up a constitution and authorized Sullivan to apply for protected status under the National Agreement. Other cities under consideration included Holyoke, Brockton, and Manchester.[17]

The New England League effort was led by Frank Bancroft, the Springfield team representative and former manager of the major league clubs in Worcester and Providence in the early 1880s. For a brief period in January 1890, Bancroft served as president of the New England League. The Springfield–Hartford nexus would have been a dramatic shift compared to the New England League setup during its four-year run from 1885 to 1888, when its base was firmly established in the eastern cities of New England.

There was some question, though, whether Worcester, Lowell, and Hartford could transfer the reserved players on their Atlantic Association clubs to their teams in the New England League. Burnham, firmly in the Atlantic Association camp, argued that the players belonged to the league when a club left. E.S. Pierce, a director of the Worcester club, argued that players belonged to the club, regardless of whether it stayed in the league or joined another circuit. The issue was presented to the Board of Arbitration of the National Commission, which consisted of six team presidents from the major leagues — three from the National League and three from the American Association.

As the Board of Arbitration pondered the player-transfer issue during January 1890, the fight between the Atlantic Association and the New England League turned nasty as the two leagues clashed over which circuit Providence would join.

Representatives from Providence had requested admission to the New England League at the league's meeting at the end of December. At a meeting in Providence on January 11, Bancroft met with the team's financial backers and left believing the New England League held the stronger position in the battle. The *Boston Globe* even ran a headline, "Providence to Have a Team in N. E. League."[18]

However, on January 13, the Atlantic Association formally admitted

Providence without any application for membership. "This action of the Atlantic Association will entirely overthrow the plans discussed by the representatives from the New England League, who met at the City Hotel in this city last Saturday afternoon," the *Providence Journal* reported. "The admission of Providence to the Atlantic Association will, it is claimed, prevent the New England League from placing a team here. The National Agreement fully protects the Atlantic Association on that ground, as the New England League is not yet a party to that agreement."[19]

The *Worcester Spy* considered the admission of Providence "simply a ruse to ruin the chances of reservation by the cities of the New England League." On January 16, Pierce of the Worcester club and Sullivan of the Lowell club met with New England League secretary Jacob Morse to discuss the reformation of the league. "The prospects of the new league were thoroughly discussed, and the underhanded methods of those who are trying to build up the Atlantic Association and ruin the New England League received due attention," the *Spy* reported. "The despicable methods used to throw them overboard have aroused their ire" along with "the double dealing of the 'B's' [Barnie and Burnham]."[20]

Pierce was even more emphatic in comments published by the *Spy* the next day. "Has it come to this, that a couple of skylarking managers, wholly irresponsible, are to be given the same consideration as the gentlemen who are behind the clubs of the New England Association and who have their clubs formed and their money invested?"[21]

According to the men from the Atlantic Association, it was all about strength of play. The financial backers of the Providence club in the Atlantic Association "believe that Providence people want to see the best ball game that it can get, and they are not of the opinion that the kind of team they want would be provided by the New England League." As George Brackett, the manager of that club, said, "The New England League is too small fry for Providence and it is quite likely that a salary limit will be adopted which will not attract the best players."[22]

Lowell, Worcester, and Hartford withdrew from the Atlantic Association in mid–January, even before the Board of Arbitration ruling was released. "There is a very bitter feeling among the backers of these clubs against Burnham, Braden and Barnie, who, they claim, have been working against their interests."[23]

The Board of Arbitration sided with the New England League. In a decision released on January 29, the board ruled that teams could switch leagues and still retain their reserved players. To memorialize its decision, the board adopted the following resolution:

Resolved, that the New England League, consisting of the Hartford, Lowell, Worcester and Springfield clubs, be admitted to protection under the qualified articles to the national agreement, upon the tendering of the resignations to the Atlantic Association of the Lowell, Worcester and Hartford clubs; proof of the same to be furnished to the chairman of the board of arbitration.[24]

The Board of Arbitration, though, demurred on the Providence issue. "The question of admission of the Providence club to the New England League is held in abeyance," the *Boston Globe* reported, "pending inquiries into the status of the Providence club, recently admitted to the Atlantic Association."[25]

While the *Worcester Spy* heralded the news with the headline, "Score One For us; The New England League Is Recognized," the ruling turned out to be only a Pyrrhic victory.[26]

It seems that the Worcester owners were more interested in immediately eliminating their debt from the 1889 Atlantic Association season rather than trying to turn a profit during an 1890 New England League season and reverse their financial situation. Comments from Secretary Pierce of the Worcester club, published in the *Worcester Spy* on February 1, were very telling:

Secretary Pierce is sick of base ball, and said last evening: "Don't come to me after tomorrow for any more base ball news, as I am going to quit. I have had enough of it, and now that I have gained my point in the Atlantic Association-New England League fight, I am going to get out, as my business demands my entire attention."[27]

On February 1, the stockholders of the Worcester club approved its sale for $2,000 to a consortium of Atlantic Association owners led by Burnham and Barnie. The deal had been in the works for three days, beginning the minute the Board of Arbitration decision was released. At that meeting Pierce had asked several Atlantic Association owners, "If you want the Worcester club in the Atlantic Association, why don't you buy the stock?" Seemingly startled, they asked, "Can it be bought?" Pierce replied, "Yes, any time before Saturday [February 1]."[28]

It was a stunning conclusion to an acrimonious feud between the Atlantic Association and the New England League, and demonstrated the length that Burnham would go in order to advance his own ambitions. There was no lack of ill will directed toward Burnham.

"Walter Burnham is gloating over what he considers a great victory for the Atlantic Association," the *Lowell Daily News* wrote after the sale of the Worcester club. "In a taunting, insulting letter to a Lowell director he shows more forcibly than ever his total lack of all manly qualities and the venom and cussedness that forms the greater part of his composition. He is not out of the woods yet and his laugh is likely to have a hollow echo."[29]

Sullivan also took the Worcester owners to task for their actions. "They seemed to forget that, in deserting their associates in the New England League and playing into the hands of their enemies, they gave a serious blow to the new enterprise," the *Worcester Spy* reported. "Had the backers of the Worcester club signified their intention of selling out, the New England people would have purchased the franchise and players rather than have their opponents become the purchasers." Sullivan added, "The sentiment of the best people in Worcester is decidedly against the Atlantic Association, for the reasons that the organization cannot live without Sunday games, which are very repugnant to the religious convictions of New England people."[30]

Immediately following the sale of the Worcester club, Providence announced that it would join the Atlantic Association, not the New England League. However, Providence never fielded a team for the 1890 season.

Burnham seemed to be so sure that Providence, with Sunday baseball at Rocky Point, was the future of minor league baseball in New England that he was willing to burn bridges with the remaining New England League owners and the cities they represented. That is, if Burnham even thought it possible that the league could ever resurrect itself again.

Bancroft resigned as president of the New England League in early February. Tom Lovell, proprietor of the Lovell Arms Company, filled the leadership void and attempted to revive the New England League without either a Worcester or Providence entry. Lovell visited Manchester, New Hampshire, and Portland, Maine, "to feel the baseball pulse," but "the pulse didn't beat at all."[31]

Lovell kept at it and eventually had an organizing meeting at the Parker House in Boston on March 31, where representatives from Cambridge, Waltham, Salem, Lynn, Lawrence, and Brockton attended. After another meeting on April 10, Lovell gave up on a league revival for the 1890 season.

It was just as well that the New England League couldn't re-establish itself for the 1890 season; otherwise, the idea of a regional minor league might have been forever shelved.

The Atlantic Association hobbled through the 1890 season under intense pressure presented by the now three major leagues: National League, American Association, and Players League. With twenty-four major league teams, there was not much talent left to stock minor league teams. New Haven, managed by Burnham, had the best record that year in the Atlantic Association, but there weren't many teams left in the league by the end of August. Worcester, the subject of heated debate over the winter by two leagues that coveted the city, lost its team in July when the franchise relocated to Lebanon, Pennsylvania. The failure of the Worcester baseball club left Burnham's New Haven team as the sole minor league team in New England, in one of its farthest reaches in southwestern Connecticut, nowhere near the central focus of the New England League.

Back in Boston, there were renewed rumblings to revive the New England League again for the 1891 season, despite the aborted attempt the previous winter. In a December 1890 interview with Tim Murnane of the *Boston Globe*, former New England League manager Bill McGunnigle suggested an approach that would help make the New England League successful.

> I think a 10 or 12-club circuit would be best for New England. It might be made up from these cities: Portland and either Lewiston or Bangor, Lowell and Manchester, Lynn and Salem, Fall River and New Bedford, Providence and Worcester, Hartford and New Haven. A league like this would make matters lively all over New England, and if some of the weak clubs wanted to drop out along about the middle of the season, the league could go right on by pairing the cities off. My object would be to get up a local rivalry.[32]

Inter-city rivalry did become a key ingredient in sustaining the New England League in its many incarnations over the coming years. Murnane, who had given the New England League extensive coverage in the sports pages of the *Boston Globe* during the last two years of the league's four-year tenure that ended in 1888, became the key person to keep the league alive when he was elected its president in 1892.

When the Players League collapsed after the 1890 season, creating a surplus of unemployed ball players, serious thought was once again devoted to crafting a plan to engage the largest cities in eastern New England into one minor league.

At the center of discussion was Providence, the second-largest city in the region and centrally located relative to the larger urban areas in Massachusetts. An organization called "New England League" didn't make a whole lot of sense without the inclusion of the largest city available to field a team (excepting Boston, of course, which had its major league teams). Inclusion of the western New England cities of Springfield and Hartford was a secondary priority.

New England League advocates thought that more favorable economics, if not regional loyalty, should compel Providence to be part of the New England League. Being a member of the New England League would entail shorter travel distances, and thus lower expenses, than those of a larger endeavor, such as one involving teams based in New York (the Eastern Association organization, which Burnham was drumming up). Attendance would be more favorable for local city rivalries, as McGunnigle advocated in his 1890 comments, compared to games with teams from distant locales.

Tom Lovell did the stomping for a New England League revival in 1891.

Lovell had high hopes for a grander New England League than its 1888 incarnation. In March he visited Providence and Springfield, hoping to entice clubs to represent these larger New England cities. Lovell's March 26 visit to Providence seemed promising, based on the *Providence Journal's* account of his remarks at the New England League meeting on March 28:

> The statement was made that Providence was still a base ball city, and that with the right kind of work there could be plenty of money obtained. The old stockholders had not lost their love for the national game, and they could be induced to subscribe once more, providing the stock was made non-assessable.... Suitable grounds could be secured on Broad Street, the Davis estate, which were easy of access by horse car and private carriages. One year lease only could be had, but the prospects were that it will be several years before the land will be cut up for residential purposes.[33]

At the league's meeting the following week, optimism reigned that Providence would join the New England League. "A very favorable report was received from Mr. J. L. Bacon of Providence, as to the outlook in that city, and financial arrangements depend upon the acquisition of suitable grounds," the *Lowell Daily News* reported. "Of all the cities mentioned as desiring to enter the league, Providence is much the best. Providence will make the best city in the New England League."[34]

But ten days later, Providence had entered the Eastern Association, a league formed by clubs representing cities mostly in upstate New York (Buffalo, Rochester, Syracuse, and Albany) with a club located in New Haven, Connecticut, managed by Burnham. Lack of an appropriate playing facility was the public reason. "Owing to the inability to secure suitable grounds in Providence, that city will not enter the New England League," the *Lowell Daily News* reported. "There are but two sites at all conveniently located and the parties who control them will not let them for base ball purposes."[35]

The real reason for the Providence decision was the persuasive power of Walter Burnham. "Providence people were about willing to go into the New England League until Walter Burnham came along with a lot of Eastern Association capital," the *Daily News* railed, "and will put in a club there for that league, in which no Providence man will have any money."[36]

Ever since Burnham sabotaged the New England League revival effort in February 1890, there was no love lost between Burnham and the *Lowell Daily News*, whose editor was Denny Sullivan, a former director of the Lowell ball club. Earlier in 1891, the *Daily News* had described Burnham in these words: "He is a most gullible talker, and can serve a mean trick on a man with all the polish of a French courtier."[37]

Lovell and the other New England League organizers were focused on the regional merits of having Providence in the New England League. Burnham, on the other hand, was squarely focused on the Sunday baseball prospects at Rocky Point, down river from Providence.

The playing grounds within the city of Providence didn't matter to Burnham; striking a deal with Harrington, the proprietor of Rocky Point, for Sunday games was far more important. While Lovell scouted for a playing area within the city limits in order to draw spectators from the city, Burnham picked an isolated site because attendance during the week didn't matter.

Burnham's pitch for a Providence club had two Sunday baseball aspects: the home games on Sunday at Rocky Point and the visitor's receipts from Sunday games slated to be played in the New York cities of Albany and Rochester. Thus, while on the surface it seemed crazy for Providence to enter the Eastern Association, where travel expenses to Connecticut and New York venues would be wildly expensive compared to the short hops in the New England League, the prospect of Sunday gate receipts many weeks on the road made the economics work better than those associated with the New England League.

The clincher was that McGunnigle, having been deposed as Brooklyn manager despite having won two consecutive pennants, was available to be manager of the Providence team. McGunnigle was ousted due to the politics of the consolidation of the Brooklyn National League club with the Brooklyn club of the Players League. John Montgomery Ward, the manager of the Players League club, was installed as manager of the consolidated club.

Unfortunately for Burnham and the Eastern Association, the Sunday home games at Rocky Point didn't work out until later in the 1891 season. Harrington struck a deal with the new Boston team in the American Association to play exhibition games at Rocky Point in June and July. Harrington thought more spectators would attend matches between major league clubs instead of the Providence team in minor league games.[38]

Not getting Providence in the league was just one of many tribulations that confronted the New England League in 1891.

Lovell was not able to lure a big-name candidate to serve as league president. It was becoming preferable in the minor leagues to have a league president be someone without an ownership interest in one of the league's ball clubs in order to have the most effective league operations. The choice of Frank Bancroft for president in 1890 was the right move, but the timing was off. In 1891, the New England League had to settle for E. B. Fuller of Haverhill as its president; Lovell was elected as vice president.

After Providence dropped out as a potential club, the Lovell-Fuller coalition cobbled together a six-club circuit at the April 11 league meeting. The six cities to represent the league were Lowell, Manchester, Haverhill, Portland, Worcester, and Lynn.

Portland had already caused a stir among league organizers in late March, when team manager Frank Leonard announced that he would employ a black team — the Cuban Giants — to represent Portland in the New England League. The decision to employ the Cuban Giants was reached at a meeting of the Portland Base Ball Association on March 25 at the United States Hotel in Portland. As reported the next day in the *Eastern Argus*: "Mr. Leonard submitted a report of the arrangements made with the Cuban Giants which was ratified by the meeting and he was instructed to represent the Portland Association at the New England [League] meeting to be held in Boston next Saturday."[39]

Portland's decision to use a black-based team was not well received by others in the league, reflecting a growing racial bias throughout organized baseball. "The idea of putting the Cuban Giants in Portland as members of the New England League is preposterous," said the *Lowell Daily News*, after the idea was panned at the March 27 league meeting. "It would simply mean the breaking up of the league."[40]

It's unclear what Leonard's motivations were in negotiating with the Cuban Giants to play in Portland, Maine. Did he really wish to use black players? Or was there a hidden agenda? The motives of the Cuban Giants were clear; with barnstorming opportunities drying up due to increased hesitation by Caucasian teams to schedule the team, the Cuban Giants sought to obtain scheduling stability by joining an organized league.

Based on the following excerpt from the *Eastern Argus* article "Cuban Giants Dropped; Portland Will Not Be Represented by a Colored Team," Leonard may well have used the Cuban Giants simply as a ploy to generate better financing for the Portland ball club:

Ever since it was announced that Manager Leonard had secured the Cuban Giants, a team composed of colored young men, to represent this city in the New England League, there has been much complaint by patrons of the game here, who have freely expressed their preference for a club of white players. After considering the matter in all its phases Mr. Leonard has concluded to abandon the project, as will be seen by the following telegram received last night:

Lynn, March 27

To satisfy everyone I have concluded to drop the Cuban Giants and will sign a white team.

F. J. Leonard

There is little doubt about this being a wise move on the part of Mr. Leonard, and is an illustration of his good judgment and his intention to do that which will be most satisfactory to lovers of the sport in Portland and productive of the best results to those financially interested. The novel idea of having the city represented by a colored team has caused a general discussion and consequent increased interest, and if any further financial backing is necessary it ought to be readily secured now.[41]

After the New England League nixed the entry of the Cuban Giants, the team convinced the Connecticut League to allow it to represent the city of Ansonia. But after playing to miniscule crowds, the Cuban Giants had a short stay in the Connecticut League, which itself dissolved before the end of June. According to noted black baseball historian Jerry Malloy, with the departure of the Cuban Giants from the Connecticut League, "for all intents and purposes, baseball's Color Curtain had closed in 1891, not to be parted again for another 55 years." While the New England League had just a bit part in the curtain closing, the league would play a prominent role, albeit unsung, in its reopening more than half a century later.[42]

The league certainly had the backing of the *Boston Globe* and baseball writer Tim Murnane. In late March, the *Globe* published three columns of material on the prospects for various cities in the New England League, including the elusive Providence. The series of short articles concluded: "With a compact circuit and the salary limit $1500 per month, there is no reason why the New England League cannot be put on paying and permanent footing this season. The gentlemen now at the head of the organization have the confidence of the lovers of the game, and The Globe will encourage a league of this kind."[43]

Less than two weeks before opening day in the New England League, on April 30, the Haverhill club dropped out of the league and was replaced by Salem. Since league president Fuller was associated with the Haverhill club, he resigned his position several weeks later, leaving the league in a leadership lurch. Lovell stepped in to assume the top job as league president.

There was action on several fronts in 1891 to improve the economics of running ball clubs in the league.

At the league level, rules were established to rein in spending by club owners. This was most visible through a salary limit on the player payroll, at $1,500 per month. There was also a rule to police the salary limit, since in the past many league rules were routinely ignored if they interfered with attempts to win the league championship. Any manager found exceeding the salary limit was barred from serving in any league capacity — essentially blacklisted — and the ball club would be fined $300. There were also rules providing for a more equitable distribution of gate receipts. The visitor guarantee was lowered to $50, from $75 in 1888, although the optional percentage take was increased to forty percent from thirty-five percent in 1888. Holiday gates were to be split fifty-fifty.[44]

This nineteenth century business practice of blaming the high wages of workers for unprofitable business conditions rather than the lack of owner foresight to expand markets and customer bases was short-sighted and nearly killed off the New England League.

In this latter regard, some clubs in 1891 attempted to lure spectators at a lower end of the economic spectrum than the patrons the clubs marketed to in the 1880s. In addition to the traditional season ticket, which sold for $10 in Lowell, the Lowell club decided to sell ticket books in smaller lots. "The idea is to issue four tickets, good for admission to any games during the season, and sell them for $1," the *Lowell Daily News* reported on the opportunity for those that "are anxious to have a team here and cannot afford to purchase a $10 book." The ball club wasn't yet targeting textile mill workers, but was taking a step in the right direction by encouraging businessmen of smaller enterprises to make a small level of commitment to baseball in Lowell.[45]

The league also passed a resolution that "each club was authorized to issue 150 complimentary tickets to the opening game," hoping to create an interest to purchase tickets to future games. Many clubs also more frequently employed, and actively promoted, "ladies day" where female patrons (presumably accompanied by a paying male patron) were admitted free.[46]

Although Lynn experienced low attendance with its previous New England League clubs, a new innovation was expected to expand patronage. Home to the Thomson-Houston Electric Company, Lynn was one of the first cities in New England to have an electric trolley line. The firm would become world famous after it merged in 1892 with the Edison Electric Company to form the General Electric Company, known worldwide as GE. However, the electric trolley was not immediately successful. "The Lynn grounds are three miles from the centre of the city and it takes 35 minutes to reach them on the electric cars," said the *Sporting Life* in May.[47]

Attendance was strong in Portland on opening day, featuring 1,200 spectators, but was weak in other cities, such as in Lynn and Lowell, where only about 500 people showed up for each game. Despite persistent low attendance levels throughout the league, one of Lovell's first acts as league president was to expand the league to eight teams. In early June, Lovell added ball clubs in Lewiston, Maine, and Woonsocket, Rhode Island.

While Lewiston and Woonsocket may have had strong state-league clubs, neither team was any match for the minor-league caliber of play in the New England League. Both clubs lost their first nine games. In a battle of the two winless clubs on June 23, Lewiston defeated Woonsocket, 6–5, before a "crowd" of 300 at Agricultural Park in Woonsocket.[48]

Tepid attendance like the tiny throng in Woonsocket on June 23 occurred throughout the league. Well before the Fourth of July holiday, the league was in precarious shape and not much better than it had been in 1888 when the league last operated.

"Another handful of spectators assembled at the Fair Grounds yesterday," the *Lowell Morning Mail* bemoaned in early July, "the attendance not being sufficient to pay the visiting club's guarantee, let alone increasing the surplus of the Lowells' treasury." The *Morning Mail* cited the average crowd in Lowell to be 500 during the early part of the season, but "now it has dwindled down in the neighborhood of 150 and 200." The paper also noted that recent games in Portland and Manchester, which had the better winning records in the league, each attracted only 250 spectators.[49]

Trouble surfaced when several clubs, keeping a close watch on expenses to try to remain afloat economically, couldn't supply enough baseballs to continue a game and were thus forced to forfeit.

On July 10, Worcester was forced to forfeit to Woonsocket when the Worcester club couldn't produce a new ball at the game played at Worcester's Grove Street grounds. Manager Greenleaf had brought only four balls with him. Two balls ripped early in the game, and in the seventh inning, with Worcester ahead, 4–3, Woonsocket batter "Allen fouled two balls over the grand stand." While Greenleaf sent a messenger downtown to get new balls, umpire Mahoney waited only two minutes before forfeiting the game to Woonsocket. "A crowd of 300 left disgusted," the *Worcester Spy* reported.[50]

Mahoney's patience was short because he, like all the league umpires, was owed back wages, since the league treasury was bereft of funds. The *Lowell Morning Mail* reported in mid–July that "umpire Mahoney claims he's owed $272," while umpire Callahan was short $125.[51]

Expecting at least one ball club to go under before the season ended in September, President Lovell lined up a team in Dover, New Hampshire, to serve as a replacement team. One or two replacement teams, however, weren't going to be sufficient.

By the third week in July, the league began to implode due to the expanding debt being compiled by nearly all of the league's eight clubs. Lowell, Salem, Manchester, and Lynn were reported to be in debt for amounts ranging from $500 to $1,000. Players openly complained about playing without being paid. When Lynn disbanded in mid–July, the ball club owed John Corcoran, catcher and team captain, $92.50; Reynolds and Condroff $90 each; Niland $75; and the remaining players $45–$55 each.[52]

Like vultures circled a dying carcass, agents for major league clubs began attending games in preparation of raiding player talent once the collapse of clubs, or the league itself, occurred. Murnane, the *Boston Globe* baseball writer, played a dual role at this time, reporting on the games but also scouting the players. After the Lowell club disbanded, one of its top players, outfielder Joe Kelley, joined the Boston team in the National League. Kelley went on to become an integral part of the Baltimore Orioles machine in the 1890s and eventually was enshrined in the Baseball Hall of Fame in Cooperstown. Murnane likely had a part in arranging that transfer.

After Lynn, Salem, and Lowell disbanded in July, the five remaining teams chugged forward, but it was clear that Lovell could not keep the league operating. There was no money in it for the owners and little spectator interest to suggest the situation might turn around over the remaining eight weeks of the season. The *Lewiston Evening Journal* printed a blunt assessment of the local ball club's financial situation from an interview with one of the club's directors:

> I don't care to continue in the business any longer. There are many vexations, very little money, and while we have drawn as well as any of the teams in the league and while we have paid more money to other teams than was ever paid to us in guarantees, we have made no money. While away, we can barely make traveling expenses. At home, we must make the salaries of the players. They are over $1,000 a month, almost $1,300, and we have only about a dozen games a month at home. If we had 800 people a game (which we do not) we would get $200 at the gate, of which we would get $120 and the visitors $80. The grand stand would amount to perhaps $30, or $150 in all. At that rate we could pay expenses, but as a matter of fact the average tickets at the gate is less than 400. Upon that basis we take $100, pay the visitors $50 [guarantee], pick up $20 at the grand stand and a rainy day or two at home would leave us in the hole.[53]

Worcester took drastic measures to supplement its revenue from New England League games by playing a Sunday exhibition game on July 26. "At Rocky Point, R.I., the Worcesters defeated the Clyde team of the State League, 5 to 3," the *Worcester Spy* reported in barely acknowledging the existence of the ball game the next day.[54]

By August 1, the Worcester players "seemed to think that it was their last game and with few exceptions, played listlessly" in a win over Manchester before a publicized crowd of 250 spectators at the Grove Street grounds. There was no money to pay the players, with the club in debt to the tune of $1,200. As an example of the team's financial difficulties, the *Spy* printed an account of the previous weekend, from an interview with club secretary Morway, about the disposition of funds from the Sunday game at Rocky Point and $57 as the visitor's share of the gate receipts from the day before in Manchester:

> The Sunday game at Rocky Point gave the club $96.10, making the receipts for two games $153.10, yet when the team got back, Secretary Morway went down to his

pocket and brought out over $6 to make the receipts meet the expenses. He said it was about time to quit.[55]

The last games in the league were played on August 1, although the Portland victory over Lewiston at the Sabatis Street grounds in that city was a farce because Lewiston fielded a team of local players rather than its usual team. With all the questions over what constituted a valid league game in the last few weeks of the season, it was difficult to determine whether Worcester or Portland, which had the best won-loss records, was the actual league champion.

At the August 6 windup meeting of the league, the championship was awarded to Portland on economic merits. "Portland paid all its assessments, and was the only club to pay the $500 to the board of protection, which was the amount insisted upon by the managers of the Worcester club... The Worcester club owes the league $160."[56]

After his one-year stint as league president, Lovell focused on running the retail business of the Boston-based firm founded by his father fifty years earlier, the John P. Lovell Arms Company, and supporting the company-sponsored baseball team. Lovell died in April 1899 at the age of fifty in Jacksonville, Florida, where he had gone to recuperate from an illness that had afflicted him for several years. The company fell into financial difficulties during Lovell's illness, and seven months after his death, the Lovell Arms Company, which had expanded well beyond guns into many types of sporting goods, went into bankruptcy.[57]

Over in the Eastern Association, Providence didn't have a much better experience. After finally scheduling its first Sunday game at Rocky Point for August 9, only 1,000 spectators attended the match with Burnham's New Haven team. Less than a week later, Providence exited the league.[58]

While this created one last opportunity for the New England League to entice Providence into accepting membership in the league, the instability of the New England League made this possibility far more theoretical than a practical reality. And with Burnham determined to make a Providence franchise successful through Sunday baseball at Rocky Point, there was no chance that Providence would not be in the Eastern League for the 1892 season.

Not taking any chances for the 1892 season, Burnham moved to lock up the Providence franchise for himself in the Eastern League before the New England League could successfully reorganize itself. In mid–March, Burnham had used a combination of philosophical and secular arguments, the latter perhaps being more convincing, to persuade the Eastern League owners that Providence was a worthy candidate for readmission to the league. According to the *Sporting Life* account of that Eastern League meeting:

Those fickle damsels from Yankeeland — New Haven and Providence — remembering that it is leap year, came again and proposed to the [Eastern] League; but this time they brought their dowry with them in the shape of $1000 guarantee and $4000 subscribed and paid-up stock. This kind of an appeal could not be resisted and they are now members of the League household in good standing.[59]

The New Haven correspondent wrote, "Providence, with Walter Burnham at the head, is sure to have good ball. I anticipate great rivalry between them and us, and the result will be fine and interesting ball for the patrons of the game." The writer did not divulge exactly where the patrons would witness the games, but Burnham surely had regular Sunday dates at Rocky Point on the agenda for the 1892 season.[60]

After a disastrous 1891 season, the New England League could only hope for a revival in 1892. However, the American Association merged with the National League after the 1891 season to make a twelve-team National League, creating another four dozen unemployed major league ball players. With an additional surplus of ball players waiting in the wings, the New England League could dream once more about minor league prosperity. This time, though, the New England League owners selected an outsider as league president, rather than one of its own club owners, to help make that dream a reality.

5

Murnane Saves League, 1892–1899

AT THE MARCH 30, 1892, MEETING OF THE New England League at the Tremont House in Boston, the future of the league was assured with the election of a new president and secretary. "The first business was the appointment of a committee ... to bring in a list of officers, and the following were elected unanimously: President, T. H. Murnane of the *Boston Globe*; vice-president, Gilbert M. Soule of Portland; secretary, J. C. Morse of the *Boston Herald*."[1]

Lost to history is the person who conceived the idea of hiring baseball writers Tim Murnane and Jake Morse to be president and secretary, respectively, of the New England League. Perhaps it was Tom Lovell, who presided over the March 30 meeting until Murnane was officially elected. But the hiring of Murnane and Morse was a brilliant idea. The team of "Me 'n Jake," as Murnane often referred to the two newspapermen, turned out to be a formidable administrative duo that oversaw the New England League for two decades.

"President Murnane's tact and Secretary Morse's executive ability proved a double asset to the New England organization, which as time passed encountered some pretty rough spots, financially and otherwise," the *Lowell Courier-Citizen* commented years later on their working relationship.[2]

Morse was a strong Mr. Inside to Murnane's Mr. Outside. Morse was the man that made the administrative wheels turn efficiently within the New England League, while Murnane was the league's public face. The two sports journalists brought needed objectivity to league administration, and with Morse a strong dose of rational business sense. For all that Murnane and

Morse did to keep the league operating over the years, the inability to play Sunday baseball (which Providence could do at Rocky Point) held the league back from achieving maximum success.

Murnane brought two critical elements to the New England League. As a newspaperman, Murnane could deliver publicity to attract spectators, through both the *Boston Globe* as well as his correspondent's position with the *Sporting News*. (Additionally, Morse wrote for the *Boston Herald* and contributed to *Sporting Life*.) Murnane's newspaper background probably contributed another motivating factor for his taking the job as league president—journalism didn't pay much. With his children maturing, Murnane needed the additional income.

Perhaps more importantly, Murnane had connections with the major league owners. He could secure for the New England League owners better financial compensation for player sales (or at least protect the players from being poached by the major league teams) as well marshal their concerns about their relationship with the major leagues.

As a first-generation Irish-American, Murnane had player interests at heart as well. Murnane had been instrumental in securing major league employment for several New England League players, such as Hugh Duffy in 1887. Although the minor leagues agreed in 1892 to a limited player draft by the major leagues teams, the New England League club owners didn't agree with this provision of the National Agreement and instead hired Murnane to watch over their concerns.

"There was a time when the New England League relied almost wholly on the influence of the Boston press for protection of their players," the *Boston Globe* reported several years after 1892. "Clubs under the protection of the National Agreement were anxious to take the promising players, but were not unmindful of the elegant 'roast' they were sure to receive from the press of Boston, and it was this alone that allowed the New England League to live for two years."[3]

Murnane essentially added another revenue element to the business model for New England League club owners, one consisting of money from player sales. It was this aspect of operating a minor league team that created financial viability for many owners.

Murnane also had contacts with many ball players. His contacts provided the impetus for several former major league players to become player-managers in the league; several went on to invest in New England League franchises and become an owner, not just an employee. This became a vital element to the continued existence of the New England League, as the decline of the textile and footwear industries, and the resulting impact on supporting businesses, reduced the pool of potential owners among local businesspeople. This became an established pattern for many minor leagues.

"Minor league baseball in the late nineteenth century was a different game from that we have come to know," Neil Sullivan wrote in *The Minors.* "Organized baseball was so volatile during this period that it makes more sense to refer to non–League rather than minor league teams. Many excellent ball players performed for teams and leagues in an era that was too unstable to permit comparisons of the quality of different leagues."[4]

Tim Murnane was president of the New England League from 1892 through 1915. Murnane handled his administrative duties while also serving as baseball editor of the *Boston Globe* (National Baseball Hall of Fame Library, Cooperstown, N.Y.).

Murnane's influence led to the New England League establishing its office in Boston and keeping it there for many years after Murnane's presidency ended. Murnane's place of employment, the *Boston Globe*, was strategically located in the capital city of Massachusetts, making him a well-connected individual. "In Boston, one can walk from the waterfront to the State House. From Newspaper Row [on Washington Street] to the State House, moreover, was only a two-minute stroll, and the walk took one past the front door of City Hall," Herbert Kenny wrote in *Newspaper Row: Journalism in the Pre–Television Era.* "The result was that representatives, senators, commissioners, attorneys general, and other state officials mingled daily with the throng in Newspaper Row."[5]

Murnane understood the challenge associated with his assignment. At the March 30 meeting, "there was a general discussion in answer to the chairman's call for cities, relevant to the best way of organizing the league on a paying basis and with the necessary stamina to last a full season."[6]

Three months later, Murnane still struggled to have the league run under sound business principles. "The New England League is trying hard to keep together, but it is a difficult task," the *Sporting Life* wrote. "Here is a league with a salary limit of $900 which cannot make it pay. The average salary is $75. Even with this low figure the players get more than comes in the gate. Why? Expenses are heavy." Few clubs paid more than the $50 guarantee and the only big attendance days were Saturdays and holidays.[7]

Murnane focused the league on cities where spectators would attend ball games, which were not necessarily the largest cities in the region. Woonsocket and Lewiston, the two teams added by Lovell in mid–season 1891, were key components of the 1892 version of the New England League. Both cities were heavily populated by French-Canadian residents.

In Woonsocket, French-Canadian immigrants from Quebec were drawn to work in the textile mills of the Blackstone River Valley. In Lewiston, the French-Canadians could work in the textile mills on the east side of the Androscoggin River, like the Bates Manufacturing Company, or work in the shoe factories on the west side of the river in the city of Auburn. Lewiston was more industrial, while Auburn more rural. "Although Auburn's population doubled between 1870 and 1890, the shoe industry did not foster the massive changes that characterized Lewiston," historian Richard Judd wrote in *Maine: The Pine Tree State from Prehistory to the Present*. "Auburn retained an atmosphere more typical of a quiet, church-going New England town. On the nearby hills, business leaders and professionals built cozy, sometimes sumptuous residences and summer cottages, giving the community a resort-like atmosphere."[8]

Pawtucket, Rhode Island, was another city added by Murnane in 1892 with spectator potential. Pawtucket was the original cradle of the industrial revolution in the United States, where Moses Brown and Samuel Slater established the country's first successful cotton spinning mill in 1790. "Pawtucket provided an ideal site for water-powered mills," one historian wrote. "Here the waters of the Blackstone River descended through a series of rapids and cascaded into Narragansett Bay. Vessels passing from the bay, through Providence, could reach the head of tide at the base of Pawtucket Falls."[9]

Woonsocket introduced the New England League to its first taste of Sunday baseball, playing an exhibition game at Rocky Point on July 10 against Brockton. "Woonsocket was unfortunate in playing a Sunday game yesterday at Rocky Point, for it succeeded in dropping the game to the Brocktons," the *Woonsocket Call* reported. "It was a good game of ball and was enjoyed by about 1,000 people." Fred Doe pitched Brockton to victory, in one of the many Sunday games Doe would participate in during his playing days in the New England League. Doe later became a high-profile proponent of changing the Sunday baseball law in Massachusetts.[10]

Woonsocket played its weekday games at 3:30 P.M. at Agricultural Park. An advertisement for the July 11 game with Brockton said "street cars leave Market Square at 2 P.M. and every fifteen minutes for the ball grounds." Regarding the cost to attend the ball game, the advertisement read: "Admission 25c. Boys under 15 years, 15c. Grand Stand 10. Ladies Free."[11]

The electric trolley helped Murnane to rescue the New England League by making it easier for spectators to get to the ball grounds than they could in the old horse-drawn trolleys. After the first electric railway in Massachusetts was constructed in 1887, the concept quickly spread to Boston and other cities within New England such as Lowell and Brockton.

"During the decade between 1890 and 1900, not only was practically all the existing horse railroad mileage converted to trolley, but the total street railway mileage was tripled," one historian wrote in describing the impact of the electric trolley.[12]

This increased efficiency of transportation and wider service area created by the electric trolley did enlarge the potential patronage for ball games. But the greater impact was the investment by railway companies in New England League ball clubs, or active support in some cases, as a way to stimulate increased demand for the trolley service.

Woonsocket finished in first place in the 1892 standings amid widespread allegations that the club's talent level was acquired by having exceeded the league's salary limit. "Those at all conversant with the state of affairs know that they obtained the flag by not over and above-based methods," the *Sporting Life* remarked in the spring of 1893.[13]

When the Woonsocket club expressed a lukewarm attitude toward forming for the 1893 season, the league at its April 5 meeting declared the Woonsocket club "to have forfeited membership in the association because of non–compliance with the terms of the constitution." Symbolically, the league thus striped Woonsocket of its 1892 pennant.[14]

One rule change for 1893 was designed to stimulate increased interest among spectators. The league adopted the new National League pitching rules, which called for the pitcher to move back five feet from where he had delivered his pitches in 1892. Due to the increased pitching distance, more hitting was expected to occur during the game.

Fall River, Massachusetts, and Dover, New Hampshire, were admitted to the league for the 1893 season. Both cities were textile mill hubs in their sections of New England. With the street railway company in Dover running the ball club, attendance at games was expected to be enhanced by timely, efficient, and well-advertised means of transportation to get to the ball grounds. In Fall River, the electric railway was anticipated to transport spectators from the outlying sections of the city to the Bedford Street grounds.

Fall River had a fabulous season in 1893. Mike McDermott, who pitched at the major league level briefly in 1889, managed the Fall River team to the league championship in its initial year in the New England League. More importantly, the ball club turned a profit, as *the Fall River Globe* reported, "The Fall River club will close the season with fully $4000 in the treasury."[15]

However, the foundation for the league's future was not all that solid. A national economic depression began in 1893 that undermined the business prospects for textile mills and shoe factories in New England. By mid–summer, the Anawan and Metacomet textile mills were shutting down in Fall River. "These mills have enough cloth on hand to fill all their contracts, and do not care to pile up any more, considering the present state of the market and the poor prospect of disposing of goods," the *Fall River Globe* glumly noted.[16]

The depression of the 1890s was one of the worst in American history. Many historians consider the four-year economic depression from 1893 to 1897 to have been more devastating than the more famous Great Depression of the 1930s.

In 1893, the depression sneaked up on most Americans, as "no frantic newspaper headlines announcing the failure of a great bank or the sudden collapse of stock-market prices signaled the beginning of the Panic of 1893." Dozens of railroads went bankrupt, crippling not only their investors but also businessmen that relied on this mode of transportation to ship goods or simply travel from one location to another. "For the year ending June 30, 1894, over 125 railroad companies went into receivership ... involving about one-fourth of all railroad mileage and capitalization," economist Charles Hoffman wrote in *The Depression of the Nineties*. "Railroad reorganization on such a grand scale was one dimension of the intensity of the depression." Violent strikes were another dimension of this depression, most notably evidenced by the Pullman Strike of 1894.[17]

Economic turmoil made Murnane's job as league president all the more difficult.

The real key to Fall River's financial success was not necessarily the crowds at its league games, but rather the crowds that attended its exhibition games, particularly those with the independent ball club from New Bedford. The two cities had a natural rivalry, located just ten miles apart on the southern coast of Massachusetts.

New Bedford had transformed itself from a city that lived and breathed whaling to one dependent on textile mills after the discovery of petroleum in 1859 destroyed the market for whale oil. Although the Wamsutta Mill opened in 1847, textile mills did not come in great numbers until 1880, when mills could be operated on an all-steam basis. New Bedford's textile specialty was sheets, which was illustrated by the renown of the Percale sheets of Wamsutta.[18]

The close proximity of Fall River and New Bedford easily facilitated spectators traveling from one city to the other to watch the road games of its local club. "The Fall River team, accompanied by 400 admirers, went over to the Whale City to show the ambitious ball tossers of that town how the national game is played," the *Fall River Globe* wrote in jest regarding the rivalry. About 2,000 spectators attended the exhibition game between Fall River and New Bedford on a Wednesday afternoon in early August. In contrast, attendance was a mere 800 people at a Friday afternoon league game between Fall River and Portland.[19]

Another crack in the league's foundation was Morse's resignation as league secretary after the 1893 season concluded. Murnane was elected to fulfill three important constitutional offices of the league — president, secretary, and treasurer. After just two years as league president, Murnane had ascended to virtually an omnipotent position.

Murnane looked for economic stability for league clubs in Maine, where the burgeoning paper industry continued to prosper while the textile and shoe industries were ravaged by the economic depression.

Bangor, located in central Maine about two hundred and fifty miles north of Boston, was one target. Bangor had thrived on lumber trade in the early nineteenth century. The city facilitated the transfer of logs cut in the northern Maine woods, which were floated down the Penobscot River to saw mills in Bangor and loaded onto ships for transport to markets down the Atlantic seaboard.

"That lumbering was the core of Bangor's economy was unmistakable to travelers," one historian wrote. "The huge brick warehouses near the river, the saloons and bawdy houses along Exchange and Harlow streets, the scream of the mills below the town, the smell of pine in the air, and the rows of elegant Federal-style mansions testified to the fortunes made in owning, cutting, [river] driving, milling, or speculating in timber."[20]

Although competition from western timberlands and railroad transportation diminished Bangor's lumber economy, the rise of the pulp and paper industry in the 1880s brought new life to Bangor. When rising demand for paper in the nation's industrial economy soon outgrew the available supply of cloth rags needed to produce paper, papermakers searched for new sources of fiber — which they found in the abundant supply of spruce trees in northern Maine. In the 1880s, paper mills sprouted on the Penobscot, re–energizing Bangor's economy.[21]

When the economic depression swept the nation in 1893, Bangor and other Maine cities tied to the paper industry were more insulated from the depression's devastating effects than other New England cities dependent on the textile and shoe industries. Thus in 1894, the New England League located a ball club in a third Maine city — Bangor — in addition to Portland and Lewiston. Although attendance for games at Maplewood Park in Bangor was respectable, the expense of traveling to Bangor, and the extended time period for the entire road trip to the Maine cities, created significant concern for the five ball clubs located in Massachusetts and Rhode Island whose economies were driven by textile mills or shoe factories.

A new holiday was decreed in Massachusetts in 1894 (and also adopted in Maine), celebrated on April 19 as Patriots Day. The holiday replaced Fast Day, a flexible-date holiday usually celebrated during the first week of April. While the Boston National League team typically played an exhibition game on Fast Day, the holiday was too early for New England League teams. Patriots Day, two-thirds the way into the month of April, was a better date for a ball game. Haverhill took advantage of the new holiday by scheduling a game with Boston Law School. In Lewiston, the New England League team played Bates College on the college grounds in Lewiston.

Pawtucket, Rhode Island, returned to the league for the 1894 season. To counteract the effects of the depression that crippled the traditional spectator base of small businessmen, the Pawtucket club turned to Sunday baseball to attract mill workers on their one day off from work during the week. When the Providence club in the Eastern League was on the road and not using the Rocky Point grounds on Sunday, Pawtucket scheduled games.

On July 1, Pawtucket hosted Haverhill at Rocky Point, as Haverhill player-manager Fred Doe led the visiting team to victory. Pawtucket began to use the bicycle grounds at Crescent Park in nearby East Providence on Sundays rather than the more remote Rocky Point since mill workers could use the trolley to more easily get to Crescent Park. Pawtucket hosted Haverhill there for two more Sunday games in August, when 2,000 spectators attended each game, according to reports in the *Pawtucket Times*. In contrast, only hundreds attended weekday games at the Dexter Street grounds in Pawtucket.

Early in the season, Pawtucket also employed a black pitcher, "a colored youth" by the name of Fred Robinson. "Robinson, the colored twirler, enlivened the game by his coaching," said the *Haverhill Evening Gazette* of the black's appearance at the city's new Athletic Park facility, located along an electric trolley line. Robinson, though, saw only limited action in the pitcher's box. The *Evening Gazette* reported that "Robinson pitched two innings for Pawtucket" in a mop-up relief appearance on May 5 when Worcester crushed Pawtucket by a 23–15 score.[22]

Basking in the success of its 1893 season, Fall River rolled to a second straight pennant before immense crowds at the Bedford Street grounds. On opening day, "Just 3307 persons paid admission and the 200 ladies who attended [for free] swelled the number up to 3500. Two hundred stood along the east foul line, and more stood out in right field."[23]

Exhibition games with the New Bedford ball club drew thousands as well. On July 18, another crowd of 3,000 people jammed the Fall River ball field. One of the spectators was Murnane, who came to witness the spectacle for himself. "Long before time for the game the grand stand and bleachers were packed solid with a crowd pruned for the outdoor event of the season in this section of the country," Murnane wrote. "The noise was greater than at a Harvard–Yale game, and went through without a let up. On the left field bleachers every one had either a fish horn or a pair of cymbals. Down in the right field was a small cannon which went booming for every run made by the home team."[24]

New Bedford was definitely a candidate to join the New England League for the 1895 season. Murnane needed the new franchise since the Wilson–Gorham Tariff passed by Congress during the summer of 1894 demolished the recovery hopes for textile mills trying to escape the effects of the depression. The new law removed the tariff on woolen cloth, which allowed inexpensive foreign cloth to flood the U.S. market. This precipitated the building of new textile mills in the South, where they'd be closer to the raw material and experience lower costs of production than in New England, in order to compete with the cheaper foreign goods.

While Maine-based teams kept the New England League alive in 1894, the expense of traveling to Maine and long road trips that zapped interest at home led the Haverhill ball club to abandon the New England League in favor of a new minor league being established for the 1895 season.

Jake Morse, the former secretary of the New England League, was the man behind the New England Association, which was formed in January 1895. To counter the situation in the New England League, Morse sought to have a compact circuit in order to reduce travel and hotel expenses and to have each team play three home games each week. Six cities — Manchester,

Lowell, Haverhill, Lawrence, Salem, and Brockton — initially signed on to field teams in the new league.

"I think the rivalry will be double what it was in the New England League," said Haverhill's John Irwin, who was openly critical of the long trips to Bangor in 1894. "Lawrence and Haverhill were always anxious to see their teams play ball. Manchester and Lowell were always rivals, and Salem almost as big a rival as any when playing good ball. Brockton has two baseball grounds and under new management and a strong team I am sure they will make money next year."[25]

Morse, the president of the new league, took care to emphasize that the new league wasn't out to compete with the existing New England League. "Mr. Morse said that his association could in no way interfere with the New England League, and that he anticipated an exchange of games, especially in the fall when the leagues could play off for the championship of New England," the *Boston Globe* noted.[26]

An inter-league playoff series in the minor leagues was a novel idea at the time, as no such postseason series between league champions had ever been conducted between minor leagues. Morse no doubt recalled the spectator enthusiasm at the intra-league playoff series in the New England League to settle the first-place tie in 1887 and to a lesser degree a similar playoff series to settle the tie in 1885.

The new league seemed to be off to an auspicious start. Morse secured the participation of several leading baseball promoters in New England, including Frank Leonard, who was organizing a ball club in Salem, Walter Burnham in Manchester (who was available, having been let go from the Providence club), and Fred Doe in Lowell. Morse had founded the league on sound business practices, as "its sole purpose was to conduct the game on a successful basis, especially financially, as was impossible with any but a compact circuit and by the rigid enforcement of the salary limit agreed upon."[27]

Morse, though, didn't count on baseball politics disrupting his new league.

By March, Horace Keith, president of the Brockton club, was negotiating with the New England League to affiliate his club with that circuit rather than with the New England Association. Brockton was interested in furthering the rivalry with nearby Fall River since no clubs in the new league were close to Brockton to pursue a rivalry. Keith had tried in vain to convince Fall River, which also despised the long trips to Maine, to switch from the New England League to the New England Association. On March 16, Keith sent a telegram to Morse to resign Brockton's membership in the New England Association and another telegram to Murnane to apply for membership in the New England League.

Burnham, now representing Lowell, "after finding out that Brockton really meant to make the change was not long in figuring out that Lowell should be with the best New England could afford, and decided to make out the same papers that Mr. Keith had," the *Globe* reported. With the two ball clubs shifting leagues, the future of the New England Association was in peril. "Mr. Morse was frank enough to say that without Lowell the New England Association was a dead cock in the pit and had no show to start in the business," the *Globe* said of the league's prospects.[28]

Morse could have taken the laborious and lengthy approach of appealing through the baseball hierarchy to debate the merits of Brockton and Lowell leaving one league for another. Instead, Morse chose to take the shorter route of having Arthur Soden, president of the Boston club in the National League and a member of the arbitration board, decide the situation.

On March 23, Soden employed the wisdom of Solomon and commanded that Brockton go to the New England League and Lowell go to the New England Association. He then handed out cards that indicated the makeup of the two leagues, with seven clubs in each. Soden then further commanded that the leagues could take in an eighth club, but that none of the seven clubs named in each league could jump to the other league during the current season.

Some thought Soden made his decision based solely on his contempt for the ambitious Burnham, who was organizing the Lowell club. "Mr. Burnham is personally attacked by his late associates in a way to disgust many of his friends of the game in the association cities," the *Globe* commented. "It was by wholly misrepresenting this manager that the association gained a point, and the Lowell case was settled on that basis." To some, it was just redemption for what Burnham did to undermine the attempted revival of the New England League in January 1890, when the Worcester ball club sought to shift from the Atlantic Association to the New England League.[29]

While the dislike of Burnham may have played a part, Soden's decision made perfect sense from a geographic perspective. By designating Lowell to be in the New England Association, the ball club could pursue rivalries with the nearby Merrimack River Valley cities of Lawrence, Haverhill, and Nashua. Similarly, in southeastern Massachusetts, Brockton had the potential for rivalries with Fall River and New Bedford as well as with Pawtucket, Rhode Island.

Still, the New England League had cities with established spectator bases and teams with strong players, while the New England Association had to start from scratch and use mostly young, untested ball players. Morse's new league was doomed from the beginning. Despite support from the local street railway companies, the league barely lasted through the Fourth of July holiday, and collapsed soon thereafter.

Burnham, still yearning to build a baseball enterprise, joined forces with the New England League to run the team in Augusta, Maine, the eighth team added to the league for the 1895 season. "A franchise was granted to the association in Augusta, known as the Kennebec Valley Company, which controls the grounds in Augusta and will have games at Gardiner and other neighboring towns," the *Kennebec Journal* reported in early April on Burnham's return to his native Maine.[30]

Burnham created a regional team known as the "Kennebecs" that was centered in Augusta, the state's capital city. By promising to play games in nearby cities in central Maine, Burnham expanded not only the potential spectator base for the ball club, but also its ownership base. Businessmen in Waterville were far more likely to subscribe to stock in the new ball club if a number of the team's games were played there. By adopting a team nickname that was regional in nature and not identified with just one city — a tactic he borrowed from his days as manager of the Boston Blues — Burnham also stimulated interest in the fledging ball club. And he struck a deal for cheap rail fares to get to the games, as "very liberal arrangements will be made on the Maine Central for patrons of the game from other towns."[31]

When not playing at the Augusta Driving Park, Burnham staged games in Gardiner and at the Colby College field in Waterville. However, the team was not very good and quickly plunged into last place in the league standings, where it remained throughout the season. Interest naturally dampened in the regional team to the point where the *Kennebec Journal* had to admit "the attendance at the games on the Gardiner grounds to date has not been very promising."[32]

Conditions were better for the other new team in the league, the New Bedford ball club managed by Fred Doe. New Bedford supplied the competition to stoke a hugely popular rivalry with Fall River only ten miles away.

While the Fall River–New Bedford nexus was encouraging news on the financial front for the league, the addition of Augusta as a fourth Maine team only added to the expense woes of the four non–Maine teams in the league. While Augusta did provide a stop on the way to Bangor to alleviate the long hop from Lewiston, teams were obligated to incur an eight-game road trip four times a year to go to Maine. On each road trip, a team would play each of the Maine teams twice.

Brockton apparently had received some financial inducements to lower its cost of traveling to Maine before Keith committed to joining the New England League. New Bedford officials leveraged this to negotiate their own lower costs, the concessions being "of such a nature that the argument of long and expensive jumps is virtually silenced," the *New Bedford Morning Mercury* reported. Whereas it had cost $8 a man to take the train from Portland to Bangor, it would now cost just $3, a savings of $5 a man. The $1.50 cost to board for a day was reduced to $1.00 through lower hotel rates.[33]

Limited Sunday baseball experiments continued at Crescent Park in East Providence, Rhode Island, when the Providence club of the Eastern League was not using the grounds. This created a means of increasing revenue since the economic depression continued to pummel the New England economy. Lewiston and Augusta tried to play an exhibition game at Crescent Park on July 14, but got in only two innings before rain halted play. About one thousand spectators were on hand to watch the game. Two weeks later, Doe arranged for his New Bedford team to play Providence, where a crowd of 1,500 attended the match.[34]

Fall River won its third consecutive pennant in 1895, rolling over the other seven clubs in the league on the strength of its pitchers, Fred Klobedanz and Ezra Lincoln. After the regular season was over, Fall River and three other teams conducted a postseason series among themselves to help replenish a depleted club treasury. Fall River's superiority on the field helped induce spectators to the Bedford Street grounds to see the team play, but on the road attendance was low since the visiting team was expected to win instead of the home team.

The series was played among three local clubs — Fall River, New Bedford, and Newport — and the barnstorming Cuban Giants, a team of black players. The Cuban Giants of 1895, though, were not nearly on par with the talent exhibited by the touring Cuban Giants of the 1880s. On September 20, Fall River annihilated the Cuban Giants, 20–3.

After wining the four-club series, Fall River then tested itself against Springfield, the champion of the Eastern League, in an informal inter–league series like the one Morse had envisioned between his ill-fated New England Association and the New England League. Fall River easily bested Springfield in a three-game series to claim an all-New England title and fuel the club's claim that it deserved a spot in the Eastern League.

The games with Springfield were Mike McDermott's last for the Fall River club. After managing Fall River to three consecutive pennants in the New England League, McDermott left the team to manage the Scranton club in the Eastern League for the 1896 season.

Morse returned as league secretary for the 1896 season to assist Murnane in navigating the New England League through the turbulent minor league waters of the late 1890s. The National League, meanwhile, increasingly took actions to ensure that the minor leagues were subservient to the sole remaining major league.

Murnane took a prominent role in a nascent minor league organization that began forming during the winter of 1896 to challenge the authority of the National League and retain some power within the minor leagues. Ban Johnson, president of the Western League, was the head of the unnamed organization of the minor leagues, with Murnane an outspoken proponent of independent minor league baseball.

"Tim Murnane said the big league was squeezing and wrenching the minors and predicted the game would be crushed out of existence in the minor league cities unless the national agreement is framed on more liberal lines," the *Chicago Tribune* reported on Murnane's position before a National League meeting in Washington in March 1896.[35]

The new minor league body didn't get very far with the National League owners that March, but the unified position of the minor leagues built the foundation for a stronger negotiating position in future battles with the major leagues.

The same eight clubs began the 1896 season that finished the 1895 season, an accomplishment in itself given the dismal financials of the previous season where all ball clubs in the league lost money. Burnham moved on to manage the Brockton club in 1896, hooking up with Horace Keith, who had encouraged Burnham to leap with him from the formative New England Association to the more established New England League. Charlie Marston took over for Mike McDermott in Fall River.

By the Fourth of July holiday, Fall River was once again leading the league standings. Marston had signed a player off the sandlots of Woonsocket, Rhode Island, to play outfield for Fall River during the 1896 season, a young man by the name of Napoleon Lajoie. Marston signed the 21-year-old livery stable employee to a $100-a-month contract to play baseball, more than three times the $7.50 a week that Lajoie made delivering coal, wood, and hay.[36]

Before Fall River sold Lajoie's contract in early August to the Philadelphia club of the National League, Lajoie compiled a .429 batting average for Fall River, collecting 163 hits in 380 at-bats. His batting prowess was best displayed in the July 2 game between Fall River and Pawtucket, when Lajoie had six hits in seven at-bats in a 31–5 Fall River victory. Lajoie went on to a Hall of Fame career in the major leagues after less than one season in the minor leagues. One hundred years later, in 1996, a plaque to honor Lajoie was dedicated at the Boys' and Girls' Club located on the site where the Bedford Street grounds once stood.[37]

With Lajoie's bat leading the team to victory, Fall River was cruising to a fourth straight pennant. However, after Lajoie's departure to the big leagues, Bangor came on strong to challenge Fall River despite the lengthy travel conditions the team faced even to play its in-state opponents. For example, after playing in Pawtucket on July 14, "the Bangors returned home yesterday morning sleepy and tired. They had been on the [train] cars all night and had been obliged to sit up, owing to the fact that all the berths were engaged in the Pullman cars."[38]

One advantage that Bangor had over Fall River was its new manager, Mike McDermott, the former manager of Fall River who was hired in June. McDermott knew the Fall River team, which showed when Bangor shut out Fall River twice in a row in mid–August at the Bedford Street grounds in Fall River. Those two victories propelled Bangor to first place in the standings, a position the club held for much of the remaining season.

Some would say Bangor remained in first place for the rest of the season, contradicting the league's edict that Fall River had won the 1896 pennant. The disputed championship of 1896 was the beginning of the ugly years of the New England League, a time when the rancor and secret deals reduced the club owners to the status of feuding clansmen.

Both clubs stumbled down the stretch, losing most of their games in early September, including two games each on the Labor Day holiday. After Bangor played its last game on Tuesday, September 8, and defeated Brockton, the *Bangor Whig and Courier* ran the headline: "Champion Bangors Win From the Brocktons."[39]

However, the season wasn't over. Fall River, which had the same number of victories as Bangor but two additional losses, decided to play some postponed games during the remaining four days of the official season in an attempt to overtake Bangor for first place. Where Fall River couldn't win on the field, the club resorted to deception to claim victory.

On Friday, September 11, Fall River intended to play three games. In the first morning game, Fall River defeated Pawtucket. The second game with Pawtucket was stopped after four innings when Fall River claimed Pawtucket needed to catch a train. Fall River was losing the second game when the train schedule suddenly loomed important.

That afternoon, Fall River lost a game with New Bedford, although Fall River was later declared the winner by forfeit when it claimed the home team couldn't produce enough new balls according to league rules. Apparently, the old balls used during the game had been good enough to satisfy the crowd. The *Fall River Globe* gave this account of the missing balls:

> There were six new balls on the grounds. These were all remaining of the association's supply and no more were ordered, as under ordinary circumstances that number would be enough for three games. All six of these balls were used in Thursday's game, and Manager Doe was not aware that there were no more at the grounds

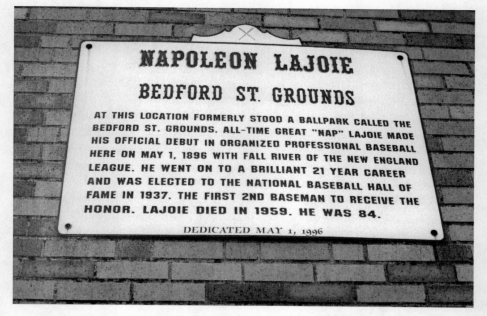

NAPOLEON LAJOIE
BEDFORD ST. GROUNDS
AT THIS LOCATION FORMERLY STOOD A BALLPARK CALLED THE
BEDFORD ST. GROUNDS. ALL-TIME GREAT "NAP" LAJOIE MADE
HIS OFFICIAL DEBUT IN ORGANIZED PROFESSIONAL BASEBALL
HERE ON MAY 1, 1896 WITH FALL RIVER OF THE NEW ENGLAND
LEAGUE. HE WENT ON TO A BRILLIANT 21 YEAR CAREER
AND WAS ELECTED TO THE NATIONAL BASEBALL HALL OF
FAME IN 1937. THE FIRST 2ND BASEMAN TO RECEIVE THE
HONOR. LAJOIE DIED IN 1959. HE WAS 84.

DEDICATED MAY 1, 1996

Plaque honoring Nap Lajoie's early years in the New England League. Lajoie played for Fall River in 1896, when Fall River won its fourth consecutive league championship (courtesy of Kerry Keene).

Friday. Then messengers were sent scouring the city, but no official balls could be found. The Fall River captain was duly informed of the circumstances. He saw fit to claim the game, and it afterwards turned out the umpire gave it to him.[40]

Fall River then defeated New Bedford on Saturday, September 12, with perhaps little competitive fire on the part of Doe's men, to claim the pennant by a thin margin over Bangor. The Maine teams smelled a rat. "The information is received with feelings of surprise mixed with regret that methods open to such justifiable suspicion should be resorted to in accomplishing an end which is certainly without honor if the trophy is awarded the Massachusetts city," the *Eastern Argus* told its readers in Portland. "We do not know that this was the result of connivance, but we do know that a job could not have been better put up."[41]

Feelings against the Maine teams, especially Bangor, were running high at the time. At the league meeting on September 24, Keith said, "There was not a club in the circuit that has not lost money this season." Doe put the blame squarely on the men from Maine, saying, "The people in Bangor and Augusta were pleasant, but the trips to Maine could not be made to pay."[42]

Bangor protested the league's decision to award Fall River the pennant. The appeal was taken up at the league meeting on January 13, 1897, at the Parker House in Boston, but the decision was a foregone conclusion. "The board of directors in the forenoon considered the protest of Bangor against the Fall River club for the championship on account of games played illegally last season," the *Bangor Whig and Courier* reported. "The board found that the Fall River club had taken no undue advantage of its rival; that there had simply been an exchange of dates, which was perfectly legal." The headline on the article quite accurately read: "Base Ball Robbers: They Refused Bangor the Pennant Fairly Won."[43]

After formally awarding the pennant to Fall River, the league proceeded to disenfranchise the Maine teams despite protests from the representatives of Bangor and Augusta regarding the legality of such action.

It was probably just as well that Bangor dropped out of the New England League after the 1896 season. The next year a major change occurred in the paper industry that would change Bangor's economy and thus lessen its prospects to support a minor league baseball team. In 1897, several paper company owners banded together to merge their companies to form the International Paper Company, a colossus that controlled two-thirds of the paper production in the country. A year later the Great Northern Paper Company was founded by Boston capitalists, who funded the building of a huge paper plant in Millinocket, north of Bangor.[44]

With the dumping of the Maine clubs, the league retrenched to a six-club league for the 1897 season by adding clubs in Taunton, Massachusetts, and Newport, Rhode Island.

Taunton was a small city in southeastern Massachusetts, 15 miles southwest of Brockton, with an economy based on the metals industry. Newport, at the foot of Narragansett Bay, was once an important maritime port, but in the 1890s gained everlasting fame as a summer resort for the extremely wealthy. "Newport became the most palatial, extravagant, and expensive summer resort the world had seen since the days of the Roman Empire," William McLoughlin wrote in his book *Rhode Island: A History*. Immense granite and marble palaces were erected on the southern tip of Newport away from the old harbor area, epitomized by The Breakers "cottage" built by Cornelius Vanderbilt at a cost of several millions of dollars.[45]

It was not the Astors or Vanderbilts that the New England League sought to attract as spectators to its games played by the Newport club, but rather the shop owners and contractors of Newport that built the opulence and helped to sustain it through the many social events held there each summer. The Rhode Island legislature at the time also rotated its sessions between the dual capitals of Providence and Newport, adding another economic dynamic to having a baseball team play in Newport.

The 1897 edition of the New England League was on par with what Morse had envisioned for the New England Association back in 1895, a compact circuit with minimal travel expenses and no overnight stays. The six clubs pared up well for rivalry purposes: Fall River with New Bedford, Brockton with Taunton, and Pawtucket with Newport. However, most of the games did not inspire a flurry of attendance since the New England economy needed some time to recover from the depression of the previous four years.

The nature of spectators at New England League ball games began to change during the late 1890s when the electric streetcar created major modifications to transportation patterns as well as to housing and work conventions. Downtown areas changed dramatically and, suddenly, the small businessman was not as likely to attend a ball game.

"For the first time in the history of the world, middle-class families in the late nineteenth century could reasonably expect to buy a detached home on an accessible lot in a safe and sanitary environment" outside the city center as the result of expanding streetcar lines, Kenneth Jackson wrote in *Crabgrass Frontier: The Suburbanization of the United States*.[46]

"The growth of downtown drove middle- and upper-middle class families from the center to the periphery... More and more property owners paid taxes not to the cities in which they worked but to the suburbs in which they lived," Robert Fogelson wrote in *Downtown: Its Rise and Fall, 1880–1950*. "For professionals and businessmen the suburbs offered a haven from the workplace, an idyllic setting in which they would do a little gardening in the morning and, after returning from a hard day downtown, dine with the family and maybe sit outdoors, reading a paper and smoking a cigar under their own semi-rustic vine and fig tree."[47]

These exiting citizens had been the core of ball game attendance: working in the city, going to the game in the late afternoon, and returning to their home in the city for dinner. When these plant managers, small-business owners, and lawyers moved to the suburbs due to inexpensive home prices and cheap, convenient streetcar service, they stopped attending ball games as often.

In his book *Streetcar Suburbs*, author Sam Warner estimated that fifteen percent of the urban population was comprised of the central middle class — the typical spectators at a ball game. Warner believed five percent were wealthy and twenty to thirty percent were associated with the lower middle class. This latter group was the new source of spectators for weekday ball games, with the increasingly available half holiday on Saturday attracting spectators from the fifty to sixty percent of the population that were common laborers.[48]

Ball club owners were slow to either recognize or target this larger but less prosperous pool of spectators for ball games. As consolidation of many industries began to occur in the latter part of the decade, the small business-man became less of a factor in the economies of small cities. "Advancement no longer required opening a business," Charles Morris wrote in *The Tycoons: How Andrew Carnegie, John D. Rockefeller, Jay Gould, and J.P. Morgan Invented the American Supereconomy.* "Exponential growth in the range and reach of white-collar occupations meant that an ambitious young man could often achieve status, power, and a good income over the course of a career with a single firm."[49]

Pawtucket was one ball club that did target the broadest segment of the population. In 1897, Pawtucket began to focus on staging exhibition games on Sunday at Crescent Park against National League teams as a primary means of generating revenue instead of its weekday ball games. Providence was now play-ing its Sunday games again at Rocky Point, making the grounds at Crescent Park available every weekend. Thousands of mill workers came to the Sunday games in contrast to the few hundred businessmen that went to the weekday games.

On Sunday, June 13, Pawtucket hosted the National League's Cincin-nati team at Crescent Park. "There were nearly 3,000 persons within the grounds and these saw an exhibition of the game which was at the same time creditable to the home team and not at all to the discredit of the National Leaguers," the *Pawtucket Times* reported. It was "a splendid crowd and the Pawtucket management has every reason to feel flattered with the success of the venture."[50]

The following Sunday, Pawtucket tried an exhibition game with Taunton at Crescent Park, but only 500 people attended on a rainy day. Even good weather on Sunday, July 4, enticed just 600 people to see another Paw-tucket–Taunton match. With meager attendance at Sunday games between New England League foes, Pawtucket concentrated on scheduling Sunday contests with other competition. After a game with Hartford of the Eastern League on Sunday, July 18, attracted 2,000 spectators, Pawtucket tried one more time to make Sunday ball games with New England League rivals work.

On Sunday, August 1, Pawtucket defeated Taunton in a regular-season game at Crescent Park before an audience of just 1,200 people. "The atten-dance should have been larger but there was no excursion from Taunton as was expected," the *Pawtucket Times* explained. "There was a crowd of about 50 who came over on a yacht and a number of others come on their wheels but there was no railroad excursion."[51]

Pawtucket learned that the caliber of play in the New England League wasn't good enough to entice mill workers to go to Crescent Park for a ball game on a Sunday afternoon. The mill workers would pay to see skilled play-ers, regardless of whether it was an exhibition game or a championship game.

On Sunday, August 8, Pawtucket played the Baltimore team of the National League and thousands streamed to the Crescent Park ball grounds. "The grand stand and bleachers were crowded with a mass of humanity and a goodly sum of money was realized by the Pawtucket club after the guarantee of the Baltimore team had been paid," the *Pawtucket Times* reported. "There were nearly 5,000 people inside the grounds."[52]

Later in August, Pawtucket pulled in crowds of the same size for Sunday games with Louisville and Cleveland of the National League.

Sunday baseball posed a conundrum for New England League clubs. Attendance at weekday games was flagging, as the depression economy hurt most small businesses, many of which closed, and curtailed operations in many textile mills and shoe factories. Sunday was the one day when mill workers could attend ball games in droves, but they preferred to watch high-caliber games on that day. Club owners couldn't afford to pay higher salaries to attract better talent. It was a vicious circle.

Tensions remained high among the money-losing New England League owners, who hoped that at least a pennant would lift hopes for a better season in 1898.

Newport and Brockton battled for first place down the stretch. After the games of Thursday, September 9, both teams were tied for first place with just two days remaining in the regular season. Newport, seeking an edge for the pennant, scheduled a second game for Saturday morning, September 11, against Taunton, to makeup a postponed game from July. Brockton, managed by shrewd negotiator Burnham, countered Newport's move.

"Manager Burnham, anticipating this move, telephoned last night to President Marston of the Fall River club, and arranged with that gentleman in case of need, to play off at Fall River tomorrow morning the Brockton–Fall River postponed game of May 14," the *Brockton Enterprise* reported. "He was given until tonight by Mr. Marston to decide whether he would go there to play or not. Should Newport lose today and Brockton win it would not be necessary for Brockton to play to-morrow morning."[53]

When Newport lost to Fall River on Friday, and Brockton defeated New Bedford, Brockton seemingly had the pennant wrapped up. Burnham telegraphed Marston "thanking the latter and notifying him that he shouldn't be obliged to call on his players to meet the Brocktons this morning," the *Enterprise* reported on Saturday. However, Marston and Fall River didn't have the same understanding about not playing the game.[54]

Murnane awarded Fall River a forfeit victory over Brockton when Burnham's team failed to show up at Fall River on Saturday morning. Combined with Brockton's loss to Taunton in the afternoon, that forfeit loss created a tie for first place with Newport, which had won a farcical game against Taunton in the morning (an amateur pitched for Taunton) and lost to Pawtucket in the afternoon.

Brockton's case seemed to be bolstered by league secretary Morse's cancellation of the umpire assignment for the Saturday morning game, indicating that Morse believed Burnham had canceled the conditional game on time. However, Marston said he wanted a decision by noon, not night, which was ridiculous since the results of the afternoon games wouldn't have been known by noon time. Murnane seemed steadfast in denying Burnham an outright championship.

When the two teams failed to agree to a playoff to settle the tie (which the league's constitution called for), the league postponed a decision on the championship until its annual meeting in January 1898.

"Out of a league of six clubs, there are two champions," the *Brockton Enterprise* reported after the January meeting. "President Tim Murnane, the universal encyclopedia of all base ball wisdom, said so at the close of the season and he said so again yesterday. By the force of his magic words the board of directors agree with him, and Brockton and Newport are the champions of 1897."[55]

The dual championship of 1897 was the last natural ending to a New England League season in the nineteenth century.

Shoe factories, like the George E. Keith Company facility in Brockton, drove the economy of Brockton in the 1890s. The city weathered the depression of 1893 to support the New England League ball club in 1897 in its quest for the disputed championship that year (Stonehill College, Archives and Special Collections).

The New England League ball clubs were losing money, not unlike most of the textile mills and many other manufacturers. The textile mills, with a virtually captive audience of unskilled workers, could afford to slash wages and still retain the bulk of their workforce. The only weapon that mill workers had at their disposal to forestall wage cuts was the threat of a strike.

When the Wamsutta Mill, the largest textile mill in New Bedford, and the city's other textile mills cut wages by ten percent in January 1898, textile workers went on strike. Many stayed on strike into April, causing a massive disruption to the New Bedford economy. The strike impacted not just the mill owners but also the grocers, butchers, and other stores that served the needs of the average mill worker. In turn, the economic downturn for these small businessmen impacted the New Bedford ball club since the store owners attended ball games.

"Local tradesmen offered credit and specially low-priced groceries to strikers, some landlords refused to evict their tenants, and fish dealers contributed five hundred pounds of fresh cod each week," historian Mary Blewitt stated in describing how ordinary storekeepers tried to help the struggling strikers. "A soup kitchen, set up by a sympathetic storekeeper and former operative, distributed quarts of soup each day to families and pints to individuals not too ashamed to be seen in public with empty pails and cans."[56]

Although the textile strike ended by early spring, its resultant impact did not bode well for the New Bedford ball club. When the season began, attendance at ball games was often a hundred or so spectators. The 25-cent admission just wasn't in the budget for many businessmen rocked by the three-month-long strike.

Luckily, every club in the league was either located in Rhode Island or was proximate to the state so that it could play Sunday baseball at a Rhode Island location. New Bedford quickly tried to take advantage of the quirk in the enforcement of the Sunday laws in Rhode Island.

On Sunday, May 29, Pawtucket played New Bedford at Crescent Park before a crowd of 1,200. The following Sunday, June 5, Fall River inaugurated Sunday baseball at Mount Hope Park in Tiverton, Rhode Island, with a game against New Bedford. However, only about 1,000 people attended the game at Mount Hope Park.

The receipts from the Sunday games were not enough to keep the New Bedford ball club in business. In mid–June, only six of thirty-two stockholders in the New Bedford ball club attended a meeting on the financial situation of the club. The low attendance indicated a disinterest in the affairs of the club if not a fear that the stockholders would be tapped for an assessment to buy more stock to keep the club afloat. The club gave the team to the New Bedford players.

"The local team are in business for themselves now," the *New Bedford Morning Mercury* reported of the transition to a cooperative arrangement from a stockholder-funded organization. However, only 135 people paid to see the game on June 14, with receipts totaling about $40. "The expenses of the game amounted to about $60, and it is easy to calculate that if they were all paid, the players ran the game at an expense of about $2 a man." The cooperative team lasted about a week before the New Bedford team disbanded. At the end of June, a team from Grafton, Massachusetts, took its place, playing the team's games in Worcester.[57]

Sunday games continued through June at both Crescent Park and Mount Hope Park, but the crowds were not enough to offset the dismally low attendance at weekday games. After the Fourth of July holiday games, Brockton disbanded and "though ahead financially and artistically, not only withdrew, but induced other clubs to do so to kill the league." Burnham exacted retribution on Murnane for having denied Brockton the championship in the disputed 1897 pennant race.[58]

The Spanish–American War is usually cited as the reason why minor leagues failed in 1898. But in the case of the New England League, it was simply the repercussions of the economic depression of 1893–1896 that did in the league. A dash of revenge on the part of Burnham only hastened the league's demise in 1898.

If the Sunday baseball experiment at the two sites in Rhode Island could have been continued through the summer of 1898, there's no telling how successful the New England League might have become. By ceding Sunday baseball to Rocky Point and the Providence club of the Eastern League, though, the New England League saddled itself with a confining Monday-to-Saturday schedule over the next two decades, requiring the league to find other ways to remain financially solvent. The Eastern League, on the other hand, thrived on Sunday baseball at Rocky Point and other locations in New York and New Jersey and captured most of the larger cities in the region as franchises.

Without the New Bedford rivalry, Fall River dropped out of the league for the 1899 season. Murnane did convince four (Brockton, Pawtucket, Newport and Taunton) of the six cities in the league at the end of the shortened 1898 season to field teams for the resumption of the league in 1899. He also persuaded Portland and Manchester to re-establish teams, and enticed two cities — Cambridge and Fitchburg — to test the minor league waters for the first time to create the highly desired eight-team circuit.

Besides his love of minor league baseball, Murnane also had an ulterior motive to revive the league for 1899. Quite simply, he needed the money from the stipend as league president to support his expanding family. At age 41, Murnane fathered a son, Horace Greeley Murnane, who was born on February 15, 1899, and named him after the famous journalist. The son was the fruit of Murnane's second marriage, one in which he wed Mary Agnes Dowling in February 1898. Murnane already had two daughters from his first marriage in 1878 to Frances Manning, who had died at age 35 in August 1895.

Adding Cambridge and Fitchburg to the New England League was quickly exposed as a mistake. Fitchburg lasted two weeks, and won only three of its ten games, before the team was transferred to Lawrence (where it promptly lost seven straight games). Cambridge didn't have much more success on the field than Fitchburg did, first playing its games at Charles River Park before using a field in South Boston for its games. Both clubs disbanded right after Decoration Day.

Down to six teams by early June, the New England League lumbered through the summer with attendance only in the hundreds at nearly all league encounters. Bickering and infighting among club owners turned nasty in August. As club owners faced dismal prospects for financial gain in the 1899 season, a faction of the strongest clubs turned on the weakest one and summarily ejected the club from the league.

After Brockton disbanded in early August, just five teams were left in the league. The owners of the Newport, Taunton, Manchester, and Portland teams met in Taunton to revoke Pawtucket's membership in the league and curtail the league to four teams. At the time, there was little uproar about this business practice, since industrial magnates like Rockefeller and Carnagie exercised ruthless actions like this all the time to enhance the value of their organizations.

The *Pawtucket Times* called this a "despicable action" on the part of the other four clubs, and a "spectacular display of ungratefulness" since the Pawtucket club had advanced money to several teams early in the season to tide them over until gate receipts improved once the weather improved.[59]

Since Pawtucket was the league's biggest proponent of Sunday baseball, the club's departure from the league created a huge obstacle in its future efforts to play on Sunday. Without a Pawtucket club in the league, the Providence team in the Eastern League had no competition for its Sunday games at Rocky Point. Pawtucket did not field another club in the New England League until the league's semi-pro years during World War II, when the legal acceptability of Sunday baseball was clear and games were mostly played either at night during the work week or on Sundays.

The last Sunday game in the New England League in the 1890s was played on July 23, 1899, when Portland defeated Pawtucket at Mount Hope

Park. The condition of the field was indicative of the low prospects for Sunday baseball outside of the games at Rocky Point. "The diamond at Mount Hope Park is certainly the worst that ever happened," the *Pawtucket Times* reported. "The infield would remind one of a ploughed potato patch, while the grass was knee deep in the outfield. Under such conditions, a good exhibition is entirely out of the question."[60]

With the ouster of Pawtucket and departure of Brockton, Murnane executed a radical idea by declaring the season through August 8 to be a first half (with Portland in first place) and beginning a second half on August 9 with the remaining four teams.

A split-season format had been used in 1892 by the National League and several minor leagues after the National League expanded to 12 teams upon its merger with the American Association. But the split-season concept was abandoned thereafter since it proved unpopular. While it made the second half more exciting for teams that didn't have a good showing in the first half, it lowered the value of the results in the first half. Determining the league champion through a playoff of first and second half winners went against the accepted standard of proving a team's worthiness over the entire season.

Among the four remaining clubs, Taunton was the weak link in the league lineup. This created the opportunity for a young, college-educated pitcher from Pennsylvania to test out a newly learned pitch that would become his trademark as a major leaguer. Christy Mathewson pitched in seventeen games for Taunton in 1899 and received the chance to experiment with and refine his fade-away pitch that helped to eventually land him in the Baseball Hall of Fame in Cooperstown.

Mathewson exhibited little in 1899 to indicate his future fame. "Matty pitched well at times, but he was unable to overcome the caliber of his mates," one author wrote in describing Mathewson's pitching days in Taunton. He compiled a 2–13 record, including a 1–7 mark over the woeful second half for Taunton. Apparently, his fade-away, or screwball, didn't phase New England League batters.[61]

He also pitched one game of a tripleheader loss to Newport on Labor Day, September 4, a three-game set that was one part of a circus ending to the 1899 New England League season.

Coming into the finale of the second half on Labor Day, Newport was in first place and Manchester in second place. Newport had two more victories than Manchester did since Newport had played doubleheaders on both the Friday and Saturday before Labor Day, while Manchester had played just one game each day.

Instead of the traditional twin bill on the holiday, Newport added one

Plaque honoring Christy Mathewson's early years in the New England League, when he played for Taunton in 1899 (Courtesy of Kerry Keene).

more game that day against lowly Taunton, looking to secure the championship. Manchester went even further than Newport in its quest for the second half championship by cramming in six games against Portland, which rolled over to play a willing victim. Newport won all three games of its tripleheader against Taunton (4–0, 12–4, 11–1), while Manchester won all six games of its sextupleheader against Portland (14–7, 12–6, 12–2, 8–4, 9–4, 9–0).

Most newspapers immediately decried the Labor Day results. "The howling farce which marked the close of the supplementary series in the New England League is something which cannot help disgusting every true lover of base ball," the *Eastern Argus* remarked to its Portland readers.[62]

President Soden of the Boston National League club put it bluntly: "The whole affair at Manchester last Monday, when Portland gave away six games in one day, was a black eye for the sport, as the public is no fool and the matter should be looked into further."[63]

Newport was awarded the championship of the second half since only two victories were counted for each team on Labor Day, with the other games being disregarded. Newport, though, never returned to play in the New England League.

The turmoil sent New England League players and managers scurrying elsewhere for the 1900 season. Mathewson played with Norfolk of the Virginia League. Doe managed Norwich in the Connecticut League. Burnham went to the Atlantic League.

The New England League might have entered oblivion if not for the rise of a competitor to the National League in 1901 that placed one of its franchises in Boston. The entity that saved the New England League was known as the American League.

6

Heyday of the League, 1901–1912

AFTER HIBERNATING DURING THE 1900 SEASON, the New England League returned to action in 1901.

"A season's rest for minor league base ball has undoubtedly whetted the appetite for another season of pleasant summer sport," Murnane wrote in the *Sporting News* in December 1900. "Next year would be a good time for the New England Leaguers to try it again, as there will doubtless be quite a revival of the game in New England thanks in great measure to the new interest bound to be created by [the] Boston Club of the new [American League]."[1]

The upstart American League, with Ban Johnson as its president, was just the tonic needed for a catalyst to revive the New England League. The Boston ball club played at a new ball grounds on Huntington Avenue, and was managed by popular Jimmy Collins, who had jumped from Boston's National League team to manage the new American League team. The second major league team in Boston generated significant interest in baseball throughout the region, and the New England League collected that spillover of enthusiasm.

Since Murnane had to rely on old friends to assist him in reviving the New England League, he needed to make certain compromises in the league structure. The biggest one was locating teams in the dreaded baseball territory of Maine, where both Walter Burnham and Fred Doe wanted to run their teams. Burnham, a native of Maine, wanted his team to be in Bangor. However, in Bangor's last time in the league, the club was a lightning rod for criticism from ball club owners south of Boston over the expense of traveling to central Maine. Doe, a Massachusetts native, had found success running a roller polo team in Lewiston, Maine, during the winter of 1901 and desired to start a ball club in that city.

With his key allies seeking to locate ball clubs in central Maine, Murnane had to have stopover cities in southern Maine to soften the long excursion to Lewiston and Bangor by locating other franchises as north as possible to keep overall travel expenses down. For stopover cities, Murnane rounded up Portland, Maine, and Dover, New Hampshire, just a short hop from the Maine state line, where the street railway company was going to sponsor the team. As for the other four cities to complement the Maine-oriented clubs, Murnane was able to recruit four cities in the Merrimack River valley. Murnane was able to convince backers to form clubs in Lowell and Haverhill in Massachusetts and in Manchester and Nashua in New Hampshire. Travel among those four cities involved just short train hops and travel to Maine was not an extensive undertaking.

However, Dover backed out at the last minute, forcing Murnane to scramble to find a replacement for an eighth club. Burnham, using his Maine connections, was able to place a team in Augusta, Maine. The 1901 edition of the New England League started with half its teams located in Maine, something the league had found to be wholly intolerable just five years earlier in 1896. But that was the price of restarting the league.

Not surprisingly, Augusta and Bangor quickly fell out of favor with the other club owners early in the 1901 season, and both clubs were ejected from the league in late June.

Attendance at Bangor was meager, as the club averaged less than 300 paid admissions per game at Maplewood Park. "As it requires 266 paid admissions to pay the guarantee of $50 to the visiting team, the cost of police officers, ticket sellers and ground keepers, it can be seen that there was very little left with which to pay advertising bills and salaries of players," said the *Bangor Daily News* on the club's finances.[2]

When Augusta, then in last place in the league standings, couldn't pay the guarantee to Lowell for a late June game, the non–Maine teams in the league moved to oust both Augusta and Bangor. Although in second place in the standings, Bangor got the boot because "the Massachusetts teams refused to come here unless there was a chance to play one day on the jump from Lewiston to this city."[3]

Both teams were transferred to sites in Massachusetts, Augusta to Lynn and Bangor to Brockton. These shifts were short lived, though, as the clubs shut down after their games on the Fourth of July holiday. The league voted to downsize to six clubs and to go with a split-season format, with Portland declared the winner of the first half. Two weeks later, though, perhaps remembering the fiasco of the 1899 split-season adventure, the league reverted to the conventional full-season format.

Burnham cut a deal with Lowell player-owner Fred Lake to join the Lowell club, provided Burnham brought with him a couple of pitchers from the Bangor/Brockton team. Whether Lake lied to Burnham simply to get the players or Burnham truly misunderstood the conversation is not known. Burnham thought his role was to manage the Lowell team, which was clearly at odds with Lake's intent. Burnham lasted only a few days in Lowell.

"Walter Burnham, who was given a clerical position by Manager Lake in consideration of the acquisition of three of the Brockton players, has tendered his resignation," said the *Lowell Courier* on the conflict. "It seems that Mr. Burnham came to Lowell under a misapprehension. He had the impression that he was to manage the team and Lake was to have the position of captain."[4]

That was the last straw for Burnham with the New England League. After he had invested so much energy to assist Murnane in reviving the league, Burnham devoted the rest of his baseball career to the Eastern League, helping Pat Powers to develop that league into a Sunday-playing, minor league heavyweight.

With an almost xenophobic attitude toward ball clubs in Maine, the New England League owners of clubs in Massachusetts and New Hampshire moved to consolidate the league within those two states for the 1902 season after Portland won the 1901 pennant. Murnane likely had a hand in this action as well. While he needed the Maine locations to restart the league for 1901 in order to appease top promoters Burnham and Doe, as Murnane's stature in baseball increased he no longer needed to make as many concessions to achieve his goals.

As the National League and American League waged war in 1901, the nation's minor leagues were left in an unsettled position. In September, the presidents of the more prominent minor leagues met in Chicago to create an organized front in dealing with the two sparring major leagues. Murnane went to Chicago to help shape the formation of the National Association of Professional Baseball Leagues, known today as the minor leagues rather than the NAPBL. Eastern League head Powers was chosen president of the new body that would represent the interests of all the minor leagues, thereby ushering in a new direction for minor league baseball.

Murnane was so confident of the success of the New England League following the formation of the NAPBL that he convinced the New England League club owners to enter into a ten-year agreement to continue the league's operations.[5]

This ten-year agreement was an explicit manifestation of what modern-day sociologist Kenneth Land calls "structured mutualism." In his paper "Organizing the Boys of Summer: The Evolution of Minor-League Baseball, 1883–1990," Land discussed how this concept was essential to the development of minor league baseball:

> By "structured mutualism" we mean the type of direct mutualism or cooperation that occurs among the teams within a league to the benefit of each. This type of mutualism, promoted by league membership, works through both of the distinct bases for mutualism defined by [A.H.] Hawley: commensalism, defined as positive interdependence among organizations based on supplementary similarities, and symbiosis, which is positive interdependence based on complementary differences. Commensalism among minor-league teams is found in their participation in a particular minor league for the purpose of arranging schedules, playing games, paying the game officials and referees, participating in joint advertising efforts, and so forth. Symbiosis occurs most evidently in the transactions that occur when one team plays another for the purpose of deciding a contest and entertaining fans.[6]

There was a twofold impetus for Murnane to engage in this type of activity with the New England League club owners. He had observed Ban Johnson organize the American League by stringing together eight strong franchises, often with the league taking the lead to secure a prime location rather than wait for someone in that city to step forward to back a club. This was a different approach than the New England League had experienced. In the mid–1890s, strong clubs forced out weaker clubs, only to then feast on other weaker clubs that were waiting in the wings to join the league. By the late 1890s, though, there were no more clubs desiring to join the league to replace the exiting ball clubs.

"Minor-league baseball teams cannot be successful unless they have other existing minor-league teams to play," Land stated in his paper. "That is to say that there is an intrinsic structural force that impels teams to cooperate with other teams within a league. This situation differs from that of other populations of business organizations in which, say, one firm may profit from the demise of another through increased sales."[7]

Murnane had also witnessed the success of the Eastern League, one of the few minor leagues to hold together throughout the 1890s. Sunday baseball at Rocky Point was a unifying force to keep Pat Powers and the club owners (independent businessmen) focused on somewhat banding together for a common good (perpetuation of the league, which created profits for the clubs).

Analogous to today's difficult task of "herding cats," it was nearly impossible for Murnane to get the independent owners of New England League ball clubs to focus on a common good. Even Powers in the Eastern League, with its availability of Sunday baseball, was challenged to keep those club owners focused. The best Murnane could do was to have several club owners of a common ilk that, as independent businessmen, would by nature share a common goal that had community-minded extensions. He was able to accomplish this in two ways: by appealing to the electric interurban trolley companies and to former major league ball players with ties to the region.

For the 1902 season, Murnane arranged to transfer the Portland and Lewiston clubs to more southern locations, Lewiston to Dover, New Hampshire, and Portland to Fall River, Massachusetts. Two new clubs were also granted to represent Concord, New Hampshire, and Lawrence, Massachusetts, in order to expand the league to the preferred eight-club format.

These four new clubs relied a great deal on the advent of the interurban trolley lines, which extended the transportation network away from the city center that the electric trolley lines had initiated in the 1890s. Interurban trolley lines connected cities and towns throughout the region, enabling businessmen and residents to easily travel from one city to another to conduct business or shop. Baseball fans in one city could conveniently travel to another city to attend a ball game. This transportation system was a major reason the New England League was able to survive through the entire first decade of the twentieth century.

"The small leagues, as well as the large ones, have been materially benefited by the trolley roads, as the public can get to the ball parks much quicker than in years past," Murnane wrote in the *Boston Globe* in 1903. "In many of the smaller leagues, the teams go from town to town in this way, the roads often helping out in a financial way."[8]

These trolley lines allowed ball grounds to be built in rural areas instead of urban areas of the textile-dominated cities, which were increasingly less desirable locations. Neighborhoods of tenement buildings now surrounded deteriorating textile mills, as owners reduced their investment in northern manufacturing plants and increased their investment in southern plants. Similar effects occurred in shoe-oriented cities, but in that industry owners transferred their investment farther north to facilities in New Hampshire and Maine.

In 1901, the Lewiston team played at the new Thompson Park, built in the Perryville section of neighboring Auburn. Although the ball park was remote, an electric trolley transported spectators from both the textile city of Lewiston and the shoe city of Auburn. The *Lewiston Evening Journal* reported that the games attracted "not only the Campbells, but the Jones's and the Browns and the Snyders and the McIverneys and the Flahertys and the Belliveaus and the Bosiverts," encompassing a cross section of English, Irish, and French-Canadian spectators.[9]

Glen Forest was another of the first ball grounds to be situated outside of the city center and connected by an electric trolley line. Located just west of the Lawrence city line in the town of Methuen, Glen Forest hosted ball games beginning in the mid–1890s. When Lawrence resumed play in the New England League in 1902, forging a partnership with the trolley company that owned the Glen Forest grounds was critical to the ball club's success.

In 1902, Lowell also played in a non-urban venue that spectators reached via electric trolley. Lowell played at the new Spalding Park, built just over the Lowell city line in neighboring Tewksbury, where trolley service connected spectators with the city center. In 1906, the city of Lowell annexed Wigginsville, the section of Tewksbury where Spalding Park was located. "The people of Wigginsville are our people, they work in our mills and expend their money in Lowell," said A.G. Walsh, president of the Lowell Board of Trade, in the spring of 1906. "Tewksbury voters have expressed their willingness to have this territory joined to Lowell. I want a larger, a better and a lovelier Lowell."[10]

On April 30, the governor of Massachusetts signed into law a bill providing for the annexation by Lowell of the Wigginsville section of Tewksbury. On May 1, 1906, after playing four years at Spalding Park when it was located in Tewksbury, the Lowell ball club began playing its home games within the city limits of Lowell.

The new franchise in Concord, New Hampshire, was a perfect example of a partnership between trolley company and ball club. John Carney, owner of the club, knew the Boston & Maine Railroad was in the final stages of completing an interurban trolley line between Manchester and Concord (which began service on August 11 that year). For the 1903 season, the B&M built a new ball grounds, Rumford Field, to create demand for passengers to use the Concord & Manchester line. At the opening game at Rumford Field on May 15, 1903, the *Concord Evening Monitor* reported that "the total attendance was fully 3,500, a special from Manchester bringing up 500 and as many more being present from other out of town points."[11]

The success that the New England League derived from the interurban trolley lines was ephemeral, however. "Few industries have risen so rapidly or declined so quickly and no industry of its size has had a worse financial record," George Hilton and John Due concluded in their book, *The Electric Interurban Railways in America.* "The interurbans were a rare example of an industry that never enjoyed a period of prolonged prosperity; accordingly, they played out their life cycle in a shorter period than any other important American industry."[12]

The interurban trolley systems had the misfortune of being developed

Electric interurban trolleys, like the Concord & Manchester line, were a key element in the revival of the New England League in the early 1900s. Interurban trolleys allowed baseball fans to travel more easily to road games to watch their team
play (New Hampshire Historical Society).

just before the advent of the automobile, so that both transportation methods came of age at the same time. By 1912, the interurban trolleys had reached
their peak of success. Thereafter, the automobile, the bus, and the "jitney"
would seriously impede interurban trolley operations.

Murnane's second application of the structured mutualism concept was
club management in the hands of former major league ball players. After the
1901 season, the next nine New England League pennants were won by teams
piloted by player-managers who were former major league players. These five
players — John "Phenomenal" Smith, Fred Lake, Billy Hamilton, Frank
Eustace, and Jesse Burkett — brought not only high caliber playing skills (even
at an older age) and understanding of big league strategy, but also used their
status to establish a connection with local fans. These former major leaguers
attracted numerous spectators to the ball grounds to enhance the all-impor-
tant revenue element in minor league economics.

Although Smith was thirty-eight years old in 1902, he could still rap out
base hits at a prodigious pace to draw spectators to Varick Park in Manchester as well as the league's other playing sites. Smith, who now played in the
outfield, had been a pitcher at the major league level from 1884 to 1891. He
acquired the nickname "Phenomenal" early in his career when he struck out
sixteen batters in a minor league game in Newark, New Jersey. Rather than
continuing to toil in the major leagues, Smith discovered that he could make
nearly as much money in the minor leagues and not have to travel as much.

He joined the Pawtucket team in the New England League in the mid–1890s and then moved on to Manchester a few years later.

Smith, like Hamilton and Burkett, was a left-handed batter, which may have given him an advantage against his younger right-handed-hitting peers in the league since he faced mostly right-handed pitching. Smith led the league in batting in 1902, as Manchester captured the pennant in the first year of Murnane's refurbishing of the New England League.

One enhancement that Smith brought to the New England League was playing exhibition games on Fast Day, a New Hampshire holiday that was celebrated in April. Fast Day had no specific date, as the day for the holiday was determined annually by the governor. In combination with the Massachusetts holiday of Patriots Day on April 19, Fast Day games played in New Hampshire gave New England League teams a head start on financial stability for the coming season.

Part of the reason that Concord and Dover were added to the league for the 1902 season, to augment the New Hampshire contingent of Manchester and Nashua, was to capture a holiday gate on Fast Day. On April 17, 1902, all four cities attracted large crowds for games on the Fast Day holiday: Haverhill at Nashua, Lowell at Concord, Lawrence at Dover, and a twin bill at Manchester with Worcester of the Eastern League in the morning and Dartmouth College in the afternoon.

The crowd for the Dover-Lawrence game inundated the trolley cars headed to Central Park for the game. "There were about 2500 spectators present and the attendance would have been much larger but the service on the electric railway was not sufficient to accommodate them," said the Dover newspaper, *Foster's Daily Democrat.* "There were nearly five hundred people who were unable to get transportation to the park and they turned back and went home." After the game was over, "some waited for three-quarters of an hour before they could get transportation home. Many walked [back to the city]."[13]

In 1903, Fred Lake led Lowell to the league pennant. Lake had a sporadic major league career, playing in forty-five games as a catcher during the 1890s. At Lowell in 1903, the thirty-six-year-old Lake alternated catching duties with Billy Merritt to help pitcher Lem Cross propel the team to the championship. Cross also was a former major leaguer, having pitched eleven games in the early 1890s for Cincinnati. Cross won twenty-seven games for Lowell in 1903, including both ends of a season-ending doubleheader on September 12 to clinch the pennant.

Lake introduced to the New England League the concept of playing a postseason series against another league. In 1903, Lake's Lowell team played the Connecticut League pennant-winner in a postseason duel to determine the "Championship of New England." This was the first time that two minor leagues had contested a formal inter-league, postseason match. There had been intra-league postseason series before, like the Steinert Cup in the Eastern League, but those series between teams from the same league proved as unpopular as the Temple Cup series had in the National League during the 1890s.

Lowell played Holyoke, Massachusetts, one of two Massachusetts-based clubs in the Connecticut League. Lake and Dan O'Neil, manager of the Holyoke club, almost certainly patterned the Lowell-Holyoke series after the upcoming Boston-Pittsburgh matchup for bragging rights at the major league level (which would soon be known as the World Series).

Contrary to the musings of the *Holyoke Transcript* that "there has already been aroused much interest in the games, and they are sure to draw large crowds if the weather is fine," interest in Lowell was very tepid. Capturing the New England League title was the paramount accomplishment in the

The 1903 Lowell ball club that won the New England League pennant, and then contested a postseason series with Holyoke, champion of the Connecticut League. Fred Lake, a former major leaguer who was owner-manager-player of the team, is seated in the back row, fourth from the left (National Baseball Hall of Fame Library, Cooperstown, N.Y.).

minds of both players and spectators, who considered the postseason series strictly as a secondary exhibition.[14]

Attendance in Lowell at each of the first three games of the seven-game series never exceeded 500 people, as the home team dropped two of the three games. "The local team went out to Spalding Park expecting to face a lot of young farmers who catch without gloves and play three strikes out on first bounces," said the *Lowell Sun* on the Lowell club's underestimation of the Holyoke club. "They found to their sorrow that the papermakers had the goods in all their pockets and up their sleeves, and were just as good as anything in the New England League."[15]

Interest in Holyoke was much more intense than in Lowell, since Holyoke saw the series as an opportunity to improve the lowly Connecticut League's stature within New England (at the time, the Connecticut League was in Class D, two rungs below the Class B New England League). Nearly a thousand spectators attended the fourth game on September 18 to see Rube Vickers pitch a 1–0 shutout to defeat Lowell. Holyoke copped the championship the following day when the two teams split a doubleheader as 5,000 people jammed Holyoke's Hampden Park (3,547 men paid; 1,000 women admitted free; hundreds of boys snuck in).[16]

Holyoke's victory over Lowell, four games to two, was the first step forward by the Connecticut League in its quest to overtake the New England League as the region's top minor league.

Lake also may have had a hand in shaping league policy to help counter the legal prohibition against Sunday baseball. For the 1903 season, the league voted to split gate receipts evenly between home and road teams for Saturday games.

This allowed the scheduling of Saturday games at the locations that would generate the largest crowds, rather than try to balance the schedule so that teams would receive a proportionate share of Saturday dates. With the Saturday half-holiday now fairly standard across the region, mill workers helped swell attendance at Saturday games, making this day by far the most lucrative among the six days of the workweek. The new league policy basically put Concord and Nashua on the road every Saturday, as neither team had any Saturday home games.

Even with the new Saturday policy, Fall River attempted a few Sunday games. Having rival New Bedford with Doe as owner-manager back in the league in 1903 apparently was not enough of a gate attraction to obviate the need for additional revenue.

Fall River played several exhibition games on Sunday in Rhode Island in 1903 and 1904. On September 13, 1903, the Boston team of the American

League provided the opposition in a match at Crescent Park attended by 10,000 spectators, according to the *Fall River Globe*. Most were there to see the American League champions, though, not the fifth-place Fall River team.

In 1904, Fall River used nearby Mount Hope Park for a few Sunday exhibitions. Attendance was mediocre, though, as most baseball fans preferred to watch Sunday games at Rocky Point, where Providence of the Eastern League provided the competition. On August 21, 1904, Fall River enticed 2,000 spectators to a Sunday game against New Bedford at Mount Hope Park, but the greater attraction that day was to raise funds for local strikers in the textile mills.[17]

With no trolley line to Mount Hope Park, it wasn't easy for spectators to get to the Sunday ball grounds. The facility also deteriorated over time. "Fall River could play Sunday ball across the river in Rhode Island, but the accommodations are not satisfactory for seating the spectators," one writer noted. Since the playing field also suffered from lack of upkeep, Fall River abandoned the Sunday baseball experiment after the 1904 season.[18]

Because Murnane was opposed to the concept of Sunday baseball, there was no explicit encouragement to try to expand the league schedule to include Sunday games. As a matter of fact, Murnane actually reveled in the fact that the New England League existed despite not being able to play Sunday baseball. "The New England and Connecticut Leagues are the only baseball organizations to live without Sunday ball playing," he wrote in the *Boston Globe* after the 1904 season.[19]

Murnane discouraged league expansion into Rhode Island, which would have actively encouraged Sunday baseball. "Woonsocket, having tired of exhibition games, would like to see the league expand to a 10-club circuit, taking in Pawtucket and Woonsocket," Murnane wrote in the *Globe* after the 1904 season. "This, however, is out of the question," he concluded, without further elaboration.[20]

During the 1904 season, Billy Hamilton joined the Haverhill club after playing with the Boston Nationals for the previous six years, and led Haverhill to its one and only championship during the city's twenty-two years of play over the course of New England League history.

Hamilton, who was enshrined in Cooperstown in 1961, played nearly as many full years in the minor leagues (ten) as he did in the major leagues (thirteen) over his professional baseball career that spanned from 1887 to 1910. "Sliding Billy" Hamilton brought to Haverhill his batting and base-running skills that had made him a fan favorite with the Boston Nationals. Hamilton compiled a .344 lifetime batting average in the major leagues, and was credited with 912 stolen bases (some of which, under the rules of the day, came by taking an extra base on an out or hit).

In 1904, Hamilton led his Haverhill team on the field by leading the New England League in hitting and stolen bases. In the latter category, he eclipsed Manchester's Archie "Moonlight" Graham, who is now more renowned for playing one game with the New York Giants in 1905, as popularized by the movie *Field of Dreams*.

"At the age of thirty-eight — unaided by any antiquated rules — Hamilton, as manager of the New England League's Haverhill squad, still was able to pace that league with 74 stolen sacks (in just 113 games). And at age forty-two he would purloin 39 in a mere 85 contests," a Hamilton biographer wrote, describing his base-running exploits at an advanced age in the New England League.[21]

There was no postseason series in 1904, as Lowell had played with Holyoke of the Connecticut League a year earlier. "We haven't heard from the Connecticut League teams as yet, but, then, there is such a close race there, that the winner will probably not be settled until the last days of the race," the *Haverhill Evening Gazette* reported in early September. Just as there was no postseason series for the champion Boston team in the American League, since the New York Giants of the National League refused to play Boston, there was no similar minor league series in New England.[22]

Concord, New Hampshire, won the 1905 New England League pennant in its fourth and final year in the league. The team was owned in 1905 by the Boston & Maine Railroad, which had taken over the team from local ownership after the 1904 season to preserve the railroad's investment in Rumfield Field, where the Concord team played its games.[23]

Concord is best known in New England League lore as the team that used a nine-year-old player to avoid a forfeit in a game at Lowell on June 25, 1904.

"Concord's failure to carry along a sufficient number of men Saturday afternoon made the Lowell-Concord game a farce at Spalding Park," the *Lowell Courier* reported. "Diggins retired voluntarily, and Clark was benched by the umpire, upon which the Concord manager sent his mascot, a boy nine years old, into right field." The desperation move to use a young boy, the catcher's son, in the game did not result in victory for Concord, as Lowell won the game 5–4.[24]

The *Concord Daily Patriot* provided some detail about why the Concord players had prematurely departed the game. George Diggins, the Concord catcher, "was overcome by the heat and compelled to retire" in the early innings, leaving Concord with the bare minimum nine players on the field. "Shortly afterwards Clark protested against the act of [umpire] McCloud in calling him out at first when Lake had deliberately forced his foot from the bag, and was sent to the bench."[25]

BASE BALL.
New England League.

FORENOON GAME,
Concord vs. Manchester.

Reduced Rates.

The Boston & Maine Railroad will place on sale round trip tickets good going August 20, and good for return passage August 20 and 21, at the following rates:

Penacook,	$ .30	E. Lebanon,	$1.85	Newbury,	$1.05
Boscawen,	.40	Lebanon,	1.95	Lake Sunapee,	1.05
No. Boscawen,	.60	W. Lebanon,	2.10	Mt. Sunapee,	1.15
Franklin,	.80	White River Jct.,	2.10	Sunapee,	1.20
E. Andover,	1.00	Franklin Falls,	.80	Newport, N. H.,	1.30
Andover, N. H.,	1.00	Hill,	1.00	Claremont,	1.65
Potter Place,	1.00	Bristol,	1.00	Claremont Jct.,	1.75
W. Andover,	1.00	W. Concord,	.20	Henniker,	.80
So. Danbury,	1.05	Mast Yard,	.35	W. Henniker,	.90
Danbury,	1.20	Contoocook,	.50	Hillsboro,	1.00
Grafton,	1.35	Warner,	.80	Antrim,	1.05
Grafton Centre,	1.40	Waterloo,	.85	Bennington,	1.10
Canaan,	1.60	Roby,	.95	Elmwood,	1.15
W. Canaan,	1.70	Bradford, N. H.,	1.00	Peterboro,	1.35
Enfield,	1.80				

D. J. FLANDERS, G. P. & T. A.

Ira C. Evans Co., Printers, Concord, N. H.

This lower portion of a six-foot-high broadside advertisement shows the cost for train fare from various locales in New Hampshire to travel to Concord to see the August 20, 1903, ball game with Manchester. The game was being staged as part of Concord's semicentennial celebration (New Hampshire Historical Society).

"It looked as though the game must be forfeited, when young George Diggins, 9 years of age, stalked forth in his miniature mascot's uniform and offered to stop the gap," the *Concord Evening Monitor* reported. "George is a clever kid and some day will be a great ball player, but of course it made a farce of the game for him to play. But in he went and the nine innings were played out. He had no chances in the field and a strike out was registered against him the only time he came to the bat."[26]

"Little Georgie received a salary of one dollar for his brief professional service with the Concord club," the *Lowell Sun* commented decades later in a retrospective on the game, when the younger Diggins became one of the youngest players ever to appear in a minor league ball game. "That was the beginning and the end of the professional baseball career of George Diggins. He later became a pipe-fitter in Philadelphia and played on various athletic teams sponsored by the company for which he worked."[27]

The 1905 edition of the Concord club was managed by Frank Eustace, who had played a couple dozen games in 1896 for the Louisville club of the National League. Concord won the pennant in a neck-and-neck race with Fall River for the championship. Both teams participated in the postseason series with the Connecticut League, which was resumed that year and expanded to include the top two teams from each league rather than only the pennant winners.

The four-team format seemed to be a trial run for an integrated league, combining the best teams of the New England League and the Connecticut League. After the series was over, Tommy McDermott, manager of the Fall River club, proposed a New England League consisting of Fall River, New Bedford, Lynn, Worcester, Springfield, Holyoke, Hartford, and either Bridgeport or New Haven. "He says that there is a possibility of a pow-wow between the magnates of the Connecticut and New England Leagues to talk over the pairing," the *Concord Evening Monitor* reported. Such a merger would also give the Boston & Maine Railroad an out for its interest in the Concord ball club.[28]

Holyoke repeated its 1903 accomplishment and easily won the 1905 post-season series to claim the minor league championship of New England. Few people showed up to watch the games (only 700 came for the doubleheader on Saturday, September 16, at Holyoke) and even fewer read about the action; the *Concord Evening Monitor* virtually ignored coverage of the postseason series and the *Fall River Globe* only ran sporadic accounts.

The championship of New England series did not attain nearly the same level of regional acclaim as the national World Series, which was just coming into its own in 1905 as a serious test of supremacy between the National League and the American League.

The only beneficiary of the New England postseason series was the Connecticut League, which in 1905 began its ascension from the lowest levels of the minor league ranks by moving up to Class B status, equivalent in rank to the New England League. Sunday baseball was the Connecticut League's currency to gain success, just as it had been for the Eastern League with Providence's use of Rocky Point for Sunday games. The Connecticut League soon would overshadow the New England League, and it had little to do with Holyoke winning the first two postseason series between the two leagues.

In July 1905, Jim O'Rourke's Bridgeport club started to play Sunday games at Steeplechase Park, beginning with the inaugural Sunday game on July 23 against Hartford. Waterbury joined the league in 1906, and the liberal mores of the citizens of the Brass City overlooked the law to permit Sunday ball in that city, thereby giving the Connecticut League two Sunday-playing sites.

While the Connecticut League was definitely moving up in 1905, the New England League was still sorting itself out. Only Haverhill and Manchester provided any continuity from the 1901 inaugural season of the latest league revival, even though both Hamilton and Smith had departed the league (Hamilton to another league and Smith to retirement from baseball). Without Smith, attendance dwindled in Manchester and the club was transferred to Lawrence in midseason. Lake sold out in Lowell, bought the Nashua franchise and transferred it to Lynn. Lake later sold the club in midseason to Lynn interests. The new Lowell owners were inept at running the team, and the club reverted to the league midseason and was transferred to Taunton in August.

Murnane needed another former major leaguer as a crowd attraction for the 1906 season, and during the winter he found one in Jesse Burkett. After completing his last year in the major leagues in 1905 with the Boston Americans, Burkett purchased the Concord franchise and moved it to Worcester, Massachusetts, where he had resided since his days in 1889 playing for Burnham's Worcester club in the Atlantic Association. "On the field he enjoyed a great season, winning 39 games," a Burkett biographer wrote. "Off the field he fell in love with Ellen G. McGrath. They were married the following year, and made Worcester their home for the rest of their lives."[29]

Burkett had invested his baseball earnings wisely during his fifteen years in the major leagues, playing outfield for Cleveland and St. Louis in the National League and St. Louis and Boston in the American League. Inducted into the Hall of Fame in 1946, Burkett compiled a lifetime batting average of .338. He was also well known as a tough-nosed ball player.

"He was known as a colorful hustler, a good team man, fast and rough on base paths, and a steady, if not brilliant fielder," the *Worcester Telegram* reported in describing Burkett upon his death in 1953. "He was given the nickname of 'The Crab' by his Cleveland teammates because of his serious disposition during the game. 'Once the bell rang,' he once said, 'I had no friends on the other team. Of course, it was natural to resume friendship after a game, but never on the playing field.'"[30]

"Burkett wants to win. Whether playing a game of baseball that decides the championship for a season or sitting down to a game of whist with Kitty Bransfield and other players during the winter, *Burkett is striving with all his might to win*," wrote one writer while describing Burkett in a 1909 profile in *Baseball Magazine*. "He fights every inch of the way and never gives up, even for an instant."[31]

Burkett brought his tenacity to Boulevard Park, which he had constructed on Shrewsbury Street in Worcester, near the intersection with Casco Street. The new ball grounds were near Union Station, enabling spectators to easily get to games by train from locations outside the city. The facility had a seating capacity of 4,500 spectators. "Worcester now has one of the finest baseball plants in the country, situated within easy walking distance of the railroad station," *Baseball Magazine* said of Burkett's ball yard.[32]

Burkett was legendary for his outbursts in the New England League. Murnane generally ignored Burkett's antics since Burkett's edgy attitude was good for business.

On May 17, 1906, Burkett had to be removed by policemen from the Fall River ball grounds after he punched the umpire. "Burkett came tearing up to the plate with his eyes flashing fire and his tongue adding fuel," reported the *Fall River Globe* in describing Burkett's tirade. "He became so abusive in his talk that Umpire Henry ordered him to the bench. Burkett refused to go, then shot out his fist and caught the umpire on the jaw. Quick as a flash the umpire swung his right and landed on Burkett's nose. In a jiffy they were at it hammer and tongs."[33]

One of the most famous incidents, recorded for posterity in a cartoon in the *Lynn Evening Item*, occurred on July 23, 1908, at Ocean Park in Lynn. Worcester lost by forfeit to Lynn "because of alleged abusive remarks to the umpire by manager Burkett over a close decision" made by umpire Connolly in the seventh inning, according to an account in the *Worcester Telegram*. "McCune of Worcester knocked a ball along the third base line, which Connolly declared foul. Burkett insisted that it was not. An altercation followed and Burkett was ordered from the field. He refused to go and a policeman was ordered to eject him, [but] declined to do so." Connolly then declared the game forfeited to Lynn.[34]

Burkett, while often overly vocal and physically intimidating, got results. Worcester captured four consecutive New England League pennants from 1906 to 1909. Burkett was also a good businessman. He had a flair for promotion, and used his extensive connections with major leaguers to arrange numerous exhibition games, which often attracted more spectators than the team's league games.

Burkett sometimes didn't let the league schedule deter his exhibition calendar. On June 13, 1907, Burkett sent a scrub team to Lowell to play the team's scheduled league game (which Worcester lost), while the regulars stayed in Worcester to play an exhibition with the St. Louis Browns of the American League (which pocketed Burkett a good sum of money).

Burkett opened and closed the 1906 season with games against opponents from the Connecticut League. The opening game at Boulevard Park was on April 19, when 4,000 people packed the new ball grounds for a Patriots Day holiday game against Bridgeport.

The two leagues staged one more postseason series in 1906, again featuring the two top teams from each league. Worcester, the New England League champion, won just two of six games against Springfield and Norwich, and failed to demonstrate its prowess exhibited over the regular season. There simply was no incentive for the league champion to perform at a high level in the postseason series. Lynn, the league runner-up, did perform better, winning five of six games and advancing to the new final round to play Springfield in a battle of the second-place teams (Lynn edged Springfield, three games to two). The championship of New England had seemed to run its course, deemed a dismal failure.

Burkett was also no stranger to Sunday baseball, having played on Sundays regularly during his major league days in St. Louis. While with Cleveland, when the club was experimenting with Sunday baseball in contravention of Ohio law, Burkett was arrested during the team's game on May 16, 1897. While with the Boston Americans in 1905, Burkett saw firsthand the crowds at Rocky Point when 7,500 spectators watched Boston play an exhibition game with Providence in early October.

Burkett may have wanted to try to play Sunday baseball at Rocky Point in 1906, but the new owner of the Providence minor league club used the Rocky Point grounds nearly every Sunday that year. Pat Powers, the new owner, felt so strongly about the financial prospects of the Providence club and its Sunday games that he resigned as president of the Eastern League to buy the ball club.

Not content simply to play Sunday games during homestands, Powers routinely had his club return to Providence while on road trips in order to play an exhibition game on Sunday with a major league team. Distance was no deterrent to get in a Sunday game at Rocky Point. For Providence's July 29 game with the Chicago Cubs, the team took the train from Jersey City,

This cartoon from the *Lynn Evening Item* shows the twin sides of Worcester owner-manager-player Jesse Burkett — good-natured fisherman in the morning, and hard-driving ball player in the afternoon. Burkett was ejected from the game for arguing with the umpire.

New Jersey, to Rhode Island and then after the game returned to Newark, New Jersey, to resume the team's road schedule. The following Sunday, August 5, the team traveled from Baltimore on Saturday to Rocky Point for a Sunday game with the Pittsburgh Pirates and then jumped on a train to Montreal.[35]

Powers sold the Providence club after the 1906 season to Fred Doe, the former New England League manager who had been a business partner with Burkett in Worcester in 1906, and Hugh Duffy, a long-time major leaguer who had played in the New England League in 1887. With Doe and Duffy in charge, there were a few open dates at Rocky Point that Burkett could take advantage of in 1907.

Worcester played Fall River in a Sunday game on June 23, as "the absence of the Providence team on its western trip enabled the New England Leaguers to play a game at Rocky Point." The *Worcester Telegram* reported that "the game attracted a crowd of 3,000, the majority coming from Providence. A delegation was present from Fall River, and encouraged its team freely."[36]

In August, Burkett played two exhibition games at Rocky Point. On August 11, Worcester played the Providence club before an audience of 3,000 spectators. On August 18, Worcester battled the Boston team of the National League before a crowd of 2,000 people.[37]

While the attendance for the Worcester games at Rocky Point was respectable, it didn't measure up to the crowds that the Providence club attracted to its Sunday games there. Providence's games usually drew at least 5,000 spectators, and it was not unusual for the crowd to exceed 10,000 for an important league game or high-profile exhibition match against a major league team.

Despite the extra revenue from Sunday games in 1907, the finances of Burkett's club took a tumble after Labor Day when rain washed out most of the team's games. "The rain this week has cost the Worcester club more than $1,500," the *Worcester Telegram* reported. Since the Connecticut League season ran a week longer than the New England League in 1907, Burkett agreed to an intra-league series in order to make up for the lost revenue of the rained-out games.[38]

Worcester, Lynn, and Brockton contested the 1907 postseason series, with each team agreeing to play each other twice. Worcester won the series, but attendance was poor. Only 890 people showed up for a doubleheader at Boulevard Park on September 13 to see Worcester play Lynn in the first game and Brockton in the second game. "After season playing doesn't develop much enthusiasm," the *Worcester Telegram* concluded. "The postseason series hasn't been a money-maker for any of the teams."[39]

Murnane tried to arrange another postseason series with the Connecticut League, but Burkett's lukewarm attitude toward the series scuttled the idea, especially since he had financial gain from another avenue. "Burkett discarded thoughts of games with Connecticut League clubs," the *Worcester Telegram* explained, "partly because he thinks Worcester patrons of the game

Jesse Burkett, who led Worcester to four consecutive New England League championships from 1906 to 1909, is best known today in Worcester as the name of a local Little League.

have had their fill of baseball, and partly because he could not maintain the full strength of his team" after fulfilling his commitment to deliver several players to the Boston club of the National League to get a major league tryout in September.[40]

Burkett also experimented with the novel idea of night baseball in 1907 by playing a game under artificial lights on September 9 in Worcester against a barnstorming team of Cherokee Indians.

"A string of 30 gasoline lamps ran around the diamond, just outside the base lines. There are five poles, only two of which are in the playing field," reported the *Worcester Telegram* in describing the portable lighting system. "The lamps furnish a bright light, being of the mantle kind, and judging by the 2000-candlepower of Worcester arc lights, the lamps easily supply the 50,000-candlepower which the manager of the Indians advertises to furnish."[41]

The actual game played under the lights was a modified version of regular baseball since the lighting system fell short of approximating natural conditions during the day. "The ball used is about once and a half the size of a league ball, and is of soft material, making it well nigh impossible to hit out of the infield," reported one newspaper in describing the modifications to the equipment for night play. "Its surface is coated with a glistening white enamel so that it can be plainly seen. The bat used is very small and light."[42]

"The game brought out a tremendous crowd, considering that the sun didn't show during the entire day and everybody expected rain might fall," reported the *Telegram* on the audience for the 9–7 Cherokee victory over Worcester. "There were 2400 paid admissions and several hundred small boys who worked in by some means other than buying a ticket at the gate." The baseball game at night attracted more than eight times the audience of that afternoon's game with Brockton in the intra-league postseason series. The published attendance for the Worcester-Brockton game was just 381 people.[43]

Burkett abandoned the Sunday baseball experiment after the 1908 season, when the August 23 league game at Rocky Point attracted a mere 800 spectators. "The game did not have much interest as it was too one sided," the *Telegram* reasoned. "Burkett's champions easily showed their right to the title, compared with the New Bedford team."[44]

Rocky Point games for Burkett only paid well when major league teams provided the competition. A Sunday game earlier in the year at Rocky Point, on May 17 between Worcester and the Boston team of the American League, attracted a crowd of 2,000 spectators, more than double the audience for the New Bedford game in August. Even then, the Sunday games weren't a spectacular financial deal. Rocky Point was just too far an excursion for many Worcester patrons in order to benefit Burkett.

Judging by the attendance at the Cherokee exhibition game, ball games played under the lights at night had possibilities for attracting a large number of spectators. However, technology to adequately light ball fields would not be available for another twenty years. Burkett was on to two distinct trends — night games and Sunday baseball — but he was too early to take advantage of them with his Worcester ball club.

Fall River picked up the Sunday baseball cudgel from Worcester in 1909, but also met with little success in attracting crowds. While Burkett was seeking to augment his income from a financially successful venture, Fall River was simply trying to break even. "This financial year has been the poorest for several reasons," the *Fall River Globe* reported on the club's condition in 1909. Fall River planned to use Rocky Point whenever the Providence club wasn't using the grounds, and play in Newport on other Sundays against local competition.[45]

On May 16, Fall River played Brockton at Rocky Point. It was an all-day affair for Brockton to get to Rocky Point, play the game, and return to Brockton. "The team will leave to-morrow morning at 8 on the Taunton short line electric. The team will proceed by rail to Fall River and boat to Rocky Point," reported the *Brockton Enterprise* on the team's itinerary on the Saturday before the game.[46]

Attendance at the May 16 match was scant. "Better weather should help business," the *Fall River Globe* commented, "but the promoters got as heavy a chill yesterday as the fans did from the biting [wind] blasts when they saw the meager attendance."[47]

Fall River played another Sunday game at Rocky Point on August 1, against Lawrence, where "attendance was light" according to the *Fall River Globe*. In contrast, the August 15 Sunday game between Providence and Rochester in the Eastern League attracted 8,000 to the Rocky Point grounds.[48]

Sunday baseball had clearly failed in the New England League. It wasn't unpopular with local citizens, but most fans couldn't afford to travel to the ball grounds in Rhode Island where the Sunday games could be staged. In his twin roles as both president of the minor leagues (NAPBL) and the Eastern League, Pat Powers interpreted the five-mile territorial rights rule under the National Agreement to grant the Providence team in the Eastern League a monopoly in Rhode Island. Thus, the New England League had difficulty locating a ball club in Rhode Island that could take advantage of a tolerant attitude toward that state's Sunday laws. Even if there were a New England League team in Rhode Island, the competition posed by Rocky Point was nearly insurmountable. The Providence ball club had a virtual monopoly on Sunday baseball in eastern New England.

League secretary Morse favored Sunday baseball, while league president Murnane had the opposite attitude on the subject. In an unexpected turn of events, Morse had a larger bully pulpit than Murnane upon which to pontificate about the merits of Sunday baseball.

In 1907, management changes at the *Boston Herald* resulted in the ouster of Morse from his job as sports editor, a position he had held since 1885. "After a connection of twenty-three years with the *Boston Herald*, I naturally expected to die in the harness in that institution, but one can never tell," Morse reported to his Harvard classmates in 1931 upon the 50th anniversary of the Class of 1881. "The unexpected will happen every now and then, and changes in management bring about changes in personnel; so it was a case of pull up your stakes and go at it."[49]

Morse's misfortune at losing his job proved to be a fortunate turn of events for baseball fans (and present-day historians). Needing to augment his stipend as New England League secretary, Morse struck out on his own to start a new publication called *Baseball Magazine*.

A monthly baseball publication was unique for the times. The monthly

The Fall River ball club played an active role in trying to play Sunday baseball games in the New England League by staging games in Rhode Island at Mount Hope Park and Rocky Point. In this 1905 photo, manager Tom McDermott is in street clothes in the second row. Players who played in the major leagues include Ben Bowcock (second row, far right), Bill Carrick (top row, second from the right), and Joe Harris (top row, far right) (National Baseball Hall of Fame Library, Cooperstown, N.Y.).

format of *Baseball Magazine* permitted lengthy examination of baseball issues, which the weekly *Sporting Life* and its competitor, the *Sporting News*, didn't often pursue with their focus on on-the-field results. "Baseball has never had a magazine of its own, while almost every other sport has a high class publication," Morse wrote in the inaugural May 1908 issue. "So, the *Baseball Magazine* is supplying a long-felt need; in substance, the need of a monthly organ filled with the highest thought surrounding the game, well edited, well printed, and filled with first-class illustrations."[50]

Morse was unabashed in *Baseball Magazine*'s editorial focus on the legalization of Sunday baseball. He published numerous essays supporting acceptance of Sunday baseball, including one by his rabbi, Charles Fleischer.

"I believe in one day's rest in seven and preferably on Sunday, the day enshrined in the reverent affection of the vast majority of Americans," Fleischer wrote. "But a day's rest is not idle dilly-dallying in one's room or on one's veranda, but active participation in something healthful and helpful." Fleischer concluded, "Give them the sunshine, and their pleasure of pleasures by throwing aside Colonial narrowness and by making antiquated the law against Sunday baseball."[51]

Murnane was still opposed to Sunday baseball, but he was mellowing a bit on the issue. "Personally I don't care for Sunday ball, as I get all I can stand six days in the week, but that is no good reason why I should deprive others from playing or witnessing others play the game on the first day of the week," Murnane wrote in a *Sporting Life* column in 1908.[52]

However, Murnane continued to expound on the merits of his league not playing on Sundays. "It is the only league of this country where Sunday ball is unknown," Murnane wrote in early 1908, "not because the club owners object to baseball on the Sabbath, but simply because the public is willing to attend the games on the workdays and give the organization liberal support."[53]

In a nod to the power wielded by minor league mogul Pat Powers, Murnane also wouldn't encourage potential placement of a New England League club in a city in Rhode Island, where Sunday baseball might be played on a regular basis. Stephen Flanagan, who ran a ball club in Manchester in 1906 to try the market for a non–John Smith team in the Queen City, considered relocating to Rhode Island during the 1906 season. He looked at both Woonsocket and Pawtucket. According to a report in *Sporting Life*, presumably submitted by Morse, Powers quashed the move to Pawtucket in July.[54]

While Pawtucket was very proximate to Providence, actually bordering the city to the east, Woonsocket was fifteen miles north of Providence and seemingly was a location that Powers couldn't veto on the basis of territorial rights. Flanagan visited Woonsocket in January to check out the city, but ultimately decided to move the Manchester club to Brockton, Massachusetts, for the 1907 season.[55]

In truth, Woonsocket wasn't ready for Sunday baseball. The city had a franchise in the short-lived Atlantic Association in 1908, a minor league organized by Fred Lake. With two clubs based in Rhode Island, Pawtucket and Woonsocket, Lake ostensibly tried to take advantage of Sunday baseball to make the league viable. However, after officials looked askance at a Sunday exhibition game with Brockton held in early May in Woonsocket, the league's Sunday hopes were dashed and the league collapsed less than two weeks later.[56]

New Bedford broke Worcester's string of four straight championships by capturing the 1910 pennant. This was the first, and only, New England

League title won by a team from southeastern Massachusetts during the league's heyday from 1901 to 1912.

It's not that Burkett didn't try his hardest to win a fifth consecutive title. Worcester played a tripleheader on Labor Day against Haverhill in an attempt to gain ground on first-place New Bedford. In the morning, Worcester won the first of three games at Boulevard Park, but then lost two close decisions in the afternoon to scuttle its chance of repeating as champion. Perhaps recollecting the fiasco of the 1899 season when Manchester and Portland attempted to play six games on the last day of the season, the league proceeded to ban the practice of playing more than two games on one day after the 1910 season.

During the winter of 1911, intense opposition surfaced regarding a Sunday baseball bill that had been introduced in the Massachusetts legislature. The Lord's Day League, which had changed its name a few years earlier from the dowdy-sounding New England Sabbath League, led the charge against legalization of Sunday baseball. Because the head of the league was often a former governor of Massachusetts, the organization had access to influential people and substantial political clout.

"We object to professional baseball on the Lord's day," Father Roche said on behalf of Cardinal O'Connell in lobbying against the Sunday baseball bill. "It is a commercial enterprise and if it should be allowed it will be a valid argument for Sunday drama, theatrical performances, prize fights, wrestling matches, football and every other form of entertainment."[57]

The Sunday baseball bill was resoundingly defeated in the House of Representatives in March by nearly a two-to-one margin.

The Lord's Day League had general support from working people. The organization steadfastly opposed work on Sunday, except for items of necessity and charity, and helped lobby for the general acceptance by employers of the Saturday half-holiday. However, the Lord's Day League also lobbied for a ban on serving liquor in hotels on Sunday, and was a proponent of the closing of drug stores on Sunday, the abolition of Sunday political rallies, and a reduction in train service on Sunday. Continuing to prohibit sports on Sunday was a huge issue for the Lord's Day League. In its annual report to membership covering the 1911 calendar year, the Rev. Martin Kneeland, secretary of the Lord's Day League, outlined the organization's position:

One question is pressing upon us which must be settled, and settled right. It is the question of public parks and playgrounds. Opening them to Sunday games and sports is but a step toward a much wider opening of the Lord's day. If the next generation is taught that Sunday morning and afternoon is the proper time to engage in public sports or games, on the property and at the expense of the money of the public, and if this kind of instruction be upheld by public school committees and teachers, the battle for a quiet, sacred Sunday is then lost.[58]

While professional baseball on Sunday was flourishing in parts of Rhode Island and Connecticut, in the Eastern League and Connecticut League, respectively, any baseball on Sunday — whether amateur or professional — continued to be illegal in Massachusetts. By 1912, the Connecticut League played on Sundays in three cities. With New Haven now also staging Sunday baseball, the entire six-team league could play every Sunday.

Lowell captured the 1911 pennant behind the pitching of Red Wolfgang and the hitting of Cuke Barrows. Money from player sales was now an important component of the economic equation for ball clubs. Both Wolfgang and Barrows were sold to the major leagues during the season, scheduled to report after the end of the New England League season. They were just two of eleven such players from the league. Lowell sold four players in all, while the Boston Americans bought four players, two from Brockton and two from New Bedford. "It is estimated that the players brought $25,000 to the New England League clubs," the *Haverhill Evening Gazette* reported. Fall River was the only club that failed to attract a major league offer for one of its players.[59]

With financial woes mounting among the clubs in the league, some owners expressed dissatisfaction with the leadership of league president Murnane. He was not a proponent of Sunday baseball and was "on the record as favoring a continuance of the league as now constituted and opposed to averages with the Connecticut League." Murnane's reluctance to merge with the Connecticut League would be a sticking point with the club owners for the next several years. By 1911, some club owners were already meeting without Murnane to discuss a possible combination with the Connecticut League, which at the very least would allow some teams now in the New England League to play road games on Sunday in those Connecticut cities that tolerated Sunday baseball.[60]

"While there has been a well defined opposition to President Murnane from certain cities, the fact is still recognized that it was he and Secretary Morse that first organized the league," said the *Haverhill Evening Gazette* on league politics. "Furthermore, the prominent position which President Murnane occupies among the leading baseball men of the country makes it unlikely that any change in the leadership will be sought."[61]

Murnane's position in baseball circles was solidified even more when Tom Lynch became president of the National League in 1909. Lynch, who served as an umpire in the New England League in the 1880s, was an old friend of Murnane, which translated into even more power for Murnane than his minor league base of political power would indicate.

One casualty of Murnane's power consolidation was Jake Morse, the league secretary and the other half of the "Me 'n Jake" team. At the September 18 league meeting, Murnane was re-elected president, and owners agreed to extend the present ten-year league agreement, which was set to expire in February 1912, for another five years. There was, however, no vote for league secretary.[62]

Morse's income from the *Baseball Magazine* venture must have been thin. He took a job in 1910 as a clerk at the Field and Fay brokerage, ostensibly to pay the bills while he labored on *Baseball Magazine* during the evening hours. By the January 1912 issue, however, Morse had left the publication, replaced by F.C. Lane, as the magazine moved its offices from Boston to New York. The vigilance on the Sunday baseball issue in *Baseball Magazine* was at an even higher level in 1911, with one article carrying the following disclaimer:

> The following article presents a graphic picture of the present situation in Sunday baseball. The subject is one of much deeper importance than is commonly supposed, and its final settlement strikes deep at the root of all future prosperity in the National Game. Because we believe that such a movement is necessary for the largest measure of success in organized baseball, and because we believe, further, that it answers the needs and merits the support of the great majority throughout the United States, the *Baseball Magazine* wishes to make clear its firm stand in favor of Sunday baseball.[63]

By the January 11, 1912, league meeting, though, Morse used his influence to re-secure the secretary's seat. At this meeting, the club owners voted to open the season on April 18, about a week earlier than the season had opened during the previous several years. This new starting date allowed regular season games to be played on the Patriots Day holiday, which would attract larger crowds to the ball park than the exhibition games with teams from other leagues that were played on the holiday.

With Patriots Day now on the New England League schedule, the Lynn club could host games on five holidays during the season. In addition to the three primary holidays of Decoration Day, Independence Day, and Labor Day, Lynn observed Bunker Hill Day on June 17. Lynn typically played a twin bill at Ocean Park on Bunker Hill Day, playing one team in a morning game and a second team in an afternoon game since the holiday was not celebrated in other New England League cities (although it was celebrated in Boston).

Lynn played its games at Ocean Park, which as its name implies was located right on the water. Naturally, with the sea so close to the ball field, odd weather-related happenings occurred at Ocean Park. For instance, on May 20, 1911, the *Boston Globe* reported that "an east wind blew a thick fog from the ocean across the Lynn baseball park this afternoon, necessitating the calling of the game in the disgust of the Fall River players, who were sent home defeated, 5 to 4, although they supposed the game had been tied." In the top of the seventh inning, with Haight on second base, Weaver "batted out a high fly, but the fog was so thick that the spheroid disappeared from sight." Both Fall River players crossed home plate "while the Lynn outfielders were vainly trying to discover the ball." Was Weaver's swat a home run? Or at least a double? No, the hit was disregarded. "Umpire Walsh called the game, ruling that the score at the end of the sixth must stand as the score for the game."[64]

The year 1912 marked the sixth consecutive season the league hosted teams from the same eight cities, a remarkable accomplishment given the franchise shifts that occurred at a frenetic pace over the league's history. However, this ostensible stability belied the underlying trouble with the textile-based economies that ruled a majority of the New England League cities. As the textile business moved to locations in the South, the neglected mills in the North dampened the economic outlook. Aggravating the situation were new laws that limited worker hours and other laws that added new expenses, such as the worker's compensation law passed in Massachusetts in 1911.

On the day after the New England League meeting that added the Patriots Day holiday to the league schedule, a massive labor strike occurred in Lawrence in reaction to how mill owners implemented a new labor law in Massachusetts. The "Bread & Roses" strike created national headlines, not just local ones, and became an iconic event in labor history.

> The most dramatic strike in American history was sparked by a pay cut of thirty-two cents a week. Yet as management would note again and again, hourly wages had not been cut at all. On January 1, 1912, a new labor law had taken effect in Massachusetts, reducing the work week from fifty-six to fifty-four hours. Workers welcomed the reduction, but only if it came with no cut in pay... The last time the legislature had mandated a cut in hours — in 1909 — weekly pay had remained the same. This time, however, with annual profits having since plummeted forty-four percent, mill owners were not feeling magnanimous.[65]

The strike began on January 12, a frigid day in Lawrence, when workers refused to enter the mills. Governor Eugene Foss sent state militia troops to Lawrence to enforce order among the restless throng of strikers. With martial law virtually in effect in Lawrence, the juxtaposition of newspaper headlines between the news and sports pages was eerie. "Militia Charges Mob With Bayonets Fixed," the *Lawrence Evening Tribune* highlighted in an extra-large font size on page 1 of a mid–January edition. A few pages in, it was business as usual in baseball, with an article headlined, "Says League Will Not Be Changed," which recounted Murnane's views on the lineup in the New England League.[66]

Over the course of the nine-week strike, the workers sought union help from the Industrial Workers of the World. The appearance of IWW personnel seemed to inflame the emotions of the mill owners, and violence erupted on more than one occasion. In late February, police beat women and children at the Lawrence train station when strikers attempted to send their families to safer locations outside the city. The attacks precipitated a congressional investigation in early March, which exposed just how horrible working conditions were in the mills. A fourteen-year-old girl testified that she was scalped when her hair was caught in a machine in one of the mills.[67]

With such adverse national publicity, the mill owners quickly granted a hefty pay increase to end the strike. However, it was a Pyrrhic victory for the workers. "Ethnic solidarity among the working poor had won the day for the Lawrence strikers," stated one history of the strike. "However, owners would later retaliate by moving their plants to the South where unions could be suppressed."[68]

Despite the effects of the strike, baseball went on as usual in Lawrence during the 1912 season and even flourished. Lawrence won the 1912 pennant in the New England League, as the arm of pitcher Ray Keating propelled the team to the title while playing its home games in Riverside Park, a new facility built in 1911 near downtown Lawrence.

The eighteen-year-old Keating won his first nine games of the 1912 season. These initial victories included a one-hitter on May 22 against Lynn at Riverside Park and a no-hitter on May 25 at Worcester's Boulevard Park. For the May 12 game in Lowell, where Keating was to pitch, the Boston & Northern Street Railway Company added "special electrics [to] leave for the Lowell ball grounds this afternoon at 1:20," which went directly to Spalding Park and left for Lawrence after the game. "Fully 1000 fans went up from this city" in eight special electric trolleys the *Evening Tribune* reported after the game.[69]

Major league scouts swarmed to Riverside Park to watch Keating pitch and negotiate with Lawrence owner Louis Pieper, who had acquired the club the previous year. Pieper eventually arranged a deal through Arthur Irwin to sell to the American League's New York Highlanders an option to take Keating's contract. On June 20, the *Lawrence Evening Tribune* announced that New York had exercised its option on Keating, who owned a 12–3 pitching record, to report after the end of the New England League season. Lawrence reportedly received $7,000 for developing Keating. "Arthur Irwin is firm in the belief that Keating will make good in the majors," the *Evening Tribune* remarked. "He has watched him in many games and likes him better today than the first time he saw him work."[70]

Although Keating pitched six years in the major leagues, it was Irwin that became a more famous baseball legend due to his death on board the steamship *Calvin Austin* in July 1921. When Irwin mysteriously disappeared from the ship after it left New York City, he was thought to have committed suicide by jumping off the ship into the ocean. Shortly thereafter, though, it was revealed that Irwin had led a double life for nearly three decades. He had two families, "a legal wife and three grown children in Boston and a common-law wife and a son in New York City."[71]

"The New York wife got all the money," said grandson Ira Harris in a 1990 interview about the distribution of Irwin's estate. The Boston family believed Irwin's death was suicide, discounting a tale that Irwin was murdered and his body thrown overboard. "As far as I know, my grandfather didn't smoke or drink. Having two wives was his only vice. Today, nobody would think twice about it."[72]

Keating wound up with twenty-six victories for Lawrence, culminating in a Labor Day victory over Lowell before one of the largest crowds in New England League history. The attendance at Riverside Park for the morning game of a twin bill with Lowell was reported to be 12,000, which saw the future major leaguer pitch Lawrence closer to the league title. The afternoon game at Spalding Park in Lowell also attracted a big crowd, reported to be 8,000.

The Labor Day crowds in 1912 marked the end of the New England League heyday. Tough times would plague the league during the next three years of its existence.

7

Prelude to Merger,
1913–1915

BENEATH THE VENEER OF SUCCESS IN THE New England League at the end of the 1912 season, there were definite undercurrents of trouble ahead.

"Financially, the season was not satisfactory," said the *Lowell Courier-Citizen* of the situation. "While four of the cities in the circuit got by without loss, the other four went deep in the hole. New Bedford, Fall River, Haverhill and Lynn were the victims. Lowell, Worcester, Lawrence and Brockton made some money, but not in the volume of other years."[1]

Player sales, not gate receipts, were propping up team finances. Lawrence, the 1912 league champion, was a financial success only due to the thousands of dollars the team received from the sale of its star pitcher, Ray Keating.

"Fall River and New Bedford were the conspicuous derelicts of the league," the *Lowell Courier-Citizen* reported. "While New Bedford had the advantage over Fall River in the matter of financial backing, neither city paid substantially more than the guarantees to visiting teams, and the guarantees hardly paid traveling and hotel expenses, to say nothing of salaries." The *Courier-Citizen* closed with the thought, "There is talk of a new lineup in the little old New England circuit."[2]

The club owners were so concerned about the league's future that they decided to mount a frontal attack on the league's most vexing problem — the inability to play Sunday baseball. At the league's annual meeting on November 7, the owners voted "to sanction a movement to secure the passage of a bill allowing the playing of professional baseball in Massachusetts on Sunday."[3]

"Magnates along the circuit have agreed to interview their senators and

representatives and urge upon them their view as to Sunday baseball legislation," described the *Lowell Courier-Citizen* on the practical implication of the
league's Sunday baseball initiative. "Sunday baseball means good wholesome
entertainment, and tends to take young men out of the hotels, thereby decreasing the sale of liquor. Moreover, as most of the parks along the New England
circuit are practically in the country, the point is made that Sunday baseball
is a health measure in that it takes men and women out of the confines of the
city."[4]

To appeal to the religious groups that vigilantly opposed the Sunday
baseball concept, the proposed Sunday baseball bill restricted playing time to
just four hours in the afternoon, between 2:00 P.M. and 6:00 P.M., in order
not to conflict with church services in the morning and evening. The proposed bill also had a "local option" provision, so that cities and towns couldn't
be forced to permit Sunday baseball, but rather allowed each city and town
to explicitly grant approval for Sunday baseball within its borders. This technique was helpful in getting a Sunday baseball law passed in Ohio in 1911.

The New England League initiative attracted strong opposition from the
outset from the Rev. Martin Kneeland, the secretary of the Lord's Day League.
The Rev. Kneeland spoke at two Lowell churches on Sunday, November 10,
on the subject, "The Continental Sunday or the New England Sabbath —
Which?" Kneeland spoke at the 10:30 A.M. service at the Highland Congregational Church and at the 6:30 P.M. service at the Pawtucket Congregational
Church. "At the Pawtucket church in the evening, he took occasion to
denounce in strong terms the movement for Sunday baseball in the New
England League," the *Lowell Courier-Citizen* described Kneeland's speech.
Kneeland also "regretted to see that Lowell had elected to the legislature one
representative who had announced his intention to work and vote for Sunday games."[5]

Despite the optimism of the club owners in 1912, it would take another
sixteen years for Sunday baseball to become legal in Massachusetts due to the
political influence wielded by opposition groups like the Lord's Day League.

Fall River was definitely the number one problem franchise in the league.
The club had failed to meet its payroll at the end of the 1912 season and had
to be rescued by the owners of the Lawrence and Lowell clubs. As agreed to
at the November 7 league meeting, the plan was to auction off the Fall River
franchise in hopes of keeping it in Fall River, where the city had been a mainstay of the league since 1893.

President Murnane had little trouble seeking a buyer for the Fall River
franchise, as three bidders emerged as leading candidates to purchase the club.
Charles McLaughlin, a former ballplayer at Harvard, was an early candidate.

Frank Leonard, the former manager of the Lynn club, seemed to have the edge, given his longstanding relationship with the league, dating back to the 1880s. The third bidder was Hugh Duffy, the former manager of the Chicago White Sox and once co-owner of the Providence minor league club, who was a good friend of Murnane.

In the midst of the Fall River franchise sale, a new minor league started to form in New England, which was called the Northeastern League. The new league had its eyes set on Portland, Maine, a vacancy on the minor league map. Portland had a diversified economy and good prospects for attendance given its hundred-mile distance from Boston.

Murnane thought moving the Fall River club to Portland was essential to quash the fledgling minor league and retain the New England League's dominant position within the region.

Thomas Manning of Binghamton, New York, was organizing the North-eastern League, which expected to have franchises not only in Portland, but also in Bangor, Maine, and St. John, New Brunswick, along with Manches-ter, New Hampshire, and Gloucester, Massachusetts. To firm up the league's claim on Portland for a franchise, George Mills of Portland was elected pres-ident of the league at its January 23 meeting. Mills set out to secure a lease on a ballpark in Portland.

Frank Leonard, bidding for the Fall River franchise in the New England League, also actively sought a lease on a Portland ballpark during the end of January. On January 28, Leonard negotiated a lease on the Forest Avenue grounds. "Leonard is confident that he has the inside track in the matter of landing the Fall River franchise now that he has secured grounds in the city," the *Eastern Argus* reported.[6]

Leonard's action to stave off the Northeastern League from access to an enclosed ball grounds in Portland seemed to clinch the deal for the New England League in Portland and also strike a fatal blow to the fortunes of the Northeastern League.

"The Northeastern League, as arranged, is broken up without Portland and will have to be reorganized on different lines, and will also mean the dropping out of all of the Maine teams as well as St. John," said President Mills on the possibility of the New England League gaining Portland as a fran-chise after hearing about Leonard's lease. "But I cannot see how there can be any decision except in our favor." It was one of the last remarks heard from the Northeastern League as it disappeared from the baseball landscape.[7]

Despite Leonard's heroic effort, the league awarded the franchise to Hugh Duffy at its January 31, 1913, meeting. "After the claims of all had been heard the franchise was awarded to Duffy by a practically unanimous vote, Lynn not voting. Duffy presumably will place the club in Portland," the *Boston Globe* reported, as Lynn abstained in deference to the spurned Leonard. "Duffy is regarded as a very valuable acquisition by the league because of his long experience in the game as a player and manager, as well as for the reputation he enjoys of being one of the squarest men that ever lived."[8]

"In turning down Frank Leonard for Hugh Duffy, as owner of the Fall River franchise, the New England League may have been a trifle harsh to Leonard but it certainly made the preferable selection," the *Lowell Courier-Citizen* remarked. "Without detracting from Mr. Leonard's ability as a baseball man, it is to be said that Duffy has had big league experience that will be of value to the New England League organization, and that he has the money and is willing to spend it for a live outfit."[9]

The *Lynn Evening Item* was candid in reporting Leonard's assessment of the transaction, with its headline: "Leonard States That Deal Was a Raw One." The *Evening Item* revealed that Leonard had offered $1,000 more for the club than Duffy had, and wrote about Leonard's hard feelings.

> Frank J. Leonard stuck to his original offer of $3470, and claimed that he had an option on the club for that amount made by a verbal agreement with Messrs. Gray of Lowell and Pieper of Lawrence at the time they took the Fall River club. Mr. Leonard was naturally incensed over an alleged broken agreement, and expressed himself in rather plain terms. He told Mr. Gray that it was a downright steal. Mr. Leonard today did not wish to say much about it, but did say that he could say something that would make a scandal in baseball, but he would not for fear it would injure the honest men who have their money invested in the sport."[10]

Not surprisingly, Leonard was never again actively associated with the New England League.

Duffy did indeed move the Fall River club to Portland, the first step into Maine by the New England League since 1901, and the team played in a newly built ballpark, Bayside Park. The team's inaugural game at Bayside Park on May 8 drew 9,000 spectators to see Portland lose, 17–9, to Lowell. "There is some balm for the bitter defeat in the fact that the fondest hopes of Portland base ball lovers for many years were realized in the dedication of Bayside Park, a home for the great national game of which any city might justly feel proud," the *Eastern Argus* reported.[11]

The sale of the Fall River franchise to Duffy, and its relocation to Portland, had a more devastating blow to the future of the New England League when its long-time league secretary, Jake Morse, resigned on March 7.

Morse had been the internal glue that held the league together for nearly twenty years, since he and Murnane first assumed their league posts in 1892. "President Murnane's tact and Secretary Morse's executive ability proved a double asset to the New England organization, which as time passed encountered some pretty rough spots, financially and otherwise," said the *Lowell Courier-Citizen* on the working relationship between the two men. Relations between the two men seemingly frayed over the years, as the *Courier-Citizen* reported "rumors that all was not smooth sailing, that friction had developed in the firm of 'Me an' Jake.'"[12]

Several issues may have led to Morse's resignation as league secretary and the dissolution of his decades-long working relationship with Murnane. "Mr. Morse says that he is retiring because of increased business with the brokerage company, of which he is a member," said the *Lynn Evening Item* on the public reason espoused for Morse's departure. "He states that his work there has become onerous, so that he could not attend to the work now required of him as secretary of the league, as this work has been increased the past few years."[13]

There surely were other reasons, though, why Morse abandoned the league secretary post. Morse may have quit in protest of the sale of the Fall River club to Duffy. He could well have felt that the awarding of the franchise to Duffy, a veritable interloper in New England League activities, was an unfair snub of Leonard, who had longstanding roots in the league as a team manager dating to the 1880s.

Money may have also played a part in Morse's departure from the league. A few years later, the *Lowell Courier-Citizen* reported that the league still owed Morse a year's salary. Since Morse had been forced out of his editor position at *Baseball Magazine* in 1911, he needed to take a non-baseball job as a clerk at the Field and Fay brokerage to support his family. Although Morse was by all accounts a caring man, one who supported numerous charitable endeavors in the community, he was no longer in a financial position to conduct the duties of league secretary without compensation.[14]

Murnane may also have soured on Morse and considered him disloyal when it was reported in December 1912 that Morse would be named president of the Northeastern League, the formative minor league that had its eyes set on Portland, Maine, as a franchise.[15]

Morse had also been a bit more outspoken of late, taking a more public profile than he had in the past. Some of his comments may not have gone over well with Murnane, particularly remarks that Morse made regarding the financial situation of the 1912 season. Morse "claimed the weather which gave the clubs no holidays at all and the great work of the Red Sox in winning the American League championship, high cost of living, and tight money were responsible for the slump in attendance in the New England League," reported the *Lowell Courier-Citizen*, paraphrasing Morse's comments. The newspaper continued with a direct quote from Morse: "But the greatest detriment to baseball, in my opinion, is the baseball pools which are so numerous in nearly every city in the New England League. Gambling never helped any sport and I hope to see this evil stamped out for the good of the sport."[16]

Morse may have been prescient about the future of the league, as the *Haverhill Evening Gazette* indicated in its story under the headline, "Retirement of Morse Regarded As Indicator of New England League Death Knell." The newspaper remarked "the rickety old sign will soon be taken down from over the door of the New England League" and "has Jacob with his usual perspicacity deciphered the handwriting on the wall and got

Jake Morse served as secretary of the New England League for most of the years between 1892 and 1912 and was instrumental in helping to keep the league alive. Morse was also the baseball editor for the *Boston Herald* and in 1908 became the first editor of *Baseball Magazine* (courtesy of the Boston Public Library, Print Department. Photograph by Bachrach.).

out from under lest the mighty structure which he and Tim have bolstered up with hot air for so long should fall and bury him beneath the debris."[17]

Arthur Cooper replaced Morse as secretary of the league two days later, which may be the most telling reason why Morse left the league. "Cooper has been a great friend of Murnane, he stands high with Duffy, and is also close to one or two others in the circuit," the *Lowell Courier-Citizen* revealed, "all of which may or may not have a bearing on the question of why Morse resigned."[18]

Morse might have been able to cure the trouble brewing in Haverhill, where a bitter battle erupted between the owners of the ball club, Dan Clohecy and Sherman Marshall, and the Haverhill Base Ball Association, which controlled the lease to use Athletic Park in Haverhill. After fielding a team for twelve consecutive seasons following the league's 1901 revival, Haverhill lost its team when the owners transferred the team to Fall River rather than continue the skirmish in Haverhill. The league ratified the franchise shift at its April 12 meeting, retaining a franchise in the moribund Fall River market, where the decline of the textile industry ravaged prospects for baseball success.

Several factions within the league began to split it apart in the 1913 season. It was a particularly bad time for this to occur; in August 1913 the Federal League announced that it would take on major league status for the 1914 season.

Murnane arranged a postseason series in 1913 between the pennant winners in the New England League and the Eastern Association. He hoped to capitalize on the success of the Boston Red Sox in the 1912 World Series, and to a lesser extent the advent of the Minor League Championship between the American Association and Western League that had been initiated in 1912.

The Eastern Association, formerly the Connecticut League, under the leadership of its president, Jim O'Rourke, signaled that it had larger ambitions that extended beyond the borders of the Nutmeg State and western Massachusetts. When the Eastern League changed its name to the International League for the 1912 season to indicate its broader geographical base, O'Rourke seized upon the opportunity to deploy the "eastern" moniker for his minor league aggregation based in Connecticut. To avoid confusion with the former Eastern League, O'Rourke selected Eastern Association as the new name for the Connecticut League.

In September 1913, Lowell and Hartford engaged in a renewal of the postseason series between the two leagues that had lapsed in 1907. The 1913 version was more successful than the earlier attempts, as attendance was generally good. The largest crowd gathered on Saturday, September 20, at Hartford when 5,000 spectators appeared for the fourth game of the series. Lowell defeated Hartford four games to two to earn bragging rights in the region. Murnane and O'Rourke made the postseason series a permanent fixture of the season over the winter of 1914.

Many New England League patrons and club owners viewed the postseason series in 1913 with the Eastern Association as a first step toward consolidation of the two leagues, the idea of a "complete" New England League that had been eyed since the 1880s. However, both Murnane and O'Rourke maximized their powerful positions by maintaining separate leagues in the region, and neither was a proponent of a merger.

Murnane, once a staunch advocate for the players and local ownership when his term as league president began in 1892, had increasingly come to treat the position as a sinecure and the league as a haven for his friends. Murnane had already dumped long-time league secretary Morse in favor of Cooper, and had steered the winning bid for the Fall River franchise the way of Duffy. In the fall of 1913, another Murnane buddy Fred Lake, who bought the New Bedford club in late October, entered league ownership.

At a league meeting on January 8, 1914, Murnane arranged to jettison the three clubs in southeastern Massachusetts — Brockton, Fall River, and New Bedford — and transfer them to other cities. The good times in the New England League did not extend to these cities, as all three suffered financially from the long trips to the other cities in the league and the small crowds that attended home games. The New Bedford club, recently purchased by Lake, moved to Fitchburg, the Fall River club moved back to Haverhill, and the Brockton club moved to Lewiston, Maine. The lure of all three cities was the building of a new ballpark, or refurbishing of an existing one, where the team could play its games.

"The Chamber of Commerce, Board of Trade, all the newspapers, and, as far as I can find out, every man in Lewiston are in favor of having a New England League club in the city," said Joseph Burns, owner of the Brockton team, on relocating to Lewiston. "They stand ready to build a fine park, and when the league is away the grounds can be used free by the schools."[19]

Tener Park, named after the new National League president John Tener, who had begun his baseball career with Haverhill of the New England League back in the 1880s, was built in Haverhill for the 1914 season. While Haverhill was the birth place of his wife, Tener demurred at having the park named after him and instead suggested it be called Moody Park, after the league's first president, William Moody, who was a native of Haverhill. The naming of Tener Park was clearly designed to curry favor with the National League president.[20]

"Lake has been promised many things in regard to the park," the *Fitchburg Sentinel* reported, including enlargement of the stands and "at least 500 opera chairs will be placed in this stand so that the fans will be assured of nice comfortable seats from which to watch the league contests." The street car company was willing to pay for the improvements as well as "furnish free transportation to the ball teams along the line."[21]

All three cities vacated by the New England League immediately formed the nucleus of the new Colonial League, a Class C minor league being formed in southeastern Massachusetts and eastern Rhode Island. While the New England League abandoned the cities due to low attendance, the organizers of the Colonial League took a different perspective and plotted how to play Sunday baseball in Rhode Island to make the circuit financially viable. "Sunday baseball could be played at Newport, which is also a summer city like Portland, and probably also at Woonsocket," remarked the *New Bedford Morning Mercury* about the future of the Colonial League in the region.[22]

While Newport and Woonsocket did join the three New England League ex-patriots along with Attleboro, Massachusetts, to form the six-team Colonial League, Sunday baseball did not materialize. Murnane didn't worry about the Colonial League making inroads on the New England League, but he did underestimate the impact that the Colonial League would ultimately have on the New England League.

The emergence of the Colonial League, combined with the elevation of the Federal League to major league status, posed serious concerns for the New England League (as well as for its postseason partner, the Eastern Association). New England League club owners, already squeezed for profits, scrambled to cope with the inverse relationship of escalated salary demands and reduced talent levels of available ball players.

The basic financial principle in the New England League — a winning team attracted spectators to the ballpark — was always dicey because it required spending money for salaries on ball players with an uncertain return on the playing field and at the gate. When the principle applied strictly to the city in which the New England League team played, i.e., a closed universe, it was somewhat manageable and businessmen could almost always be enticed to back the clubs. However, in 1914, the movement of minor leaguers to the Federal League, and the demand for minor leaguers to stock teams in the Colonial League, added pressure to the New England League financial equation.

While the Federal League did not compete directly with the New England League since it didn't place a franchise in the region, the Federal League did significantly impact the New England League by initiating a bidding war for talented ballplayers. As players left the higher minor leagues to play in the Federal League, those teams needed to obtain ballplayers from lower classifications in the minors. Compounding the situation for the New England League was the new Colonial League, which was seeking players with local acclaim that would attract spectators to their ballparks.

Further compounding the situation was the success of the two Boston teams at the major league level. Improved rail connections between cities in the New England League and Boston and the spread of automobile owner-ship made getting to Boston to see the Braves or the Red Sox much easier than it had been in the early 1900s. Fenway Park, the new ballpark that the Red Sox played in, was built in 1912 and was a draw for baseball fans in the New England League cities. Fenway Park was a modern facility, made of steel and concrete, in contrast to the old-fashioned wooden ballparks that domi-nated the minor league landscape.

Making matters worse in 1914, the Braves contended for the National League pennant and began to play their games at Fenway Park in mid-sum-mer. "Anticipating that a bigger crowd will turn out for the game between the Cardinals and the Braves on Saturday than can be accommodated at the Walpole St. Grounds, Pres. Gaffney has asked for permission to transfer the game to Fenway Park. Pres. Lannin [of the Red Sox] is quite willing that the Braves have the use of his park," the *Boston Globe* reported on July 31. "Quite a crowd, it is said, will come from Springfield and Windsor Locks, Conn. The special train from Springfield will be made up in three sections and will, it is estimated, bring 2500 persons, about 1500 of whom are expected to attend the game."[23]

An overflow crowd of 16,000 had attended the Braves game on July 25. With part of the crowd lining the field, a ground rule was necessary that turned several sure outs into two-base hits. At the Braves game with the Car-dinals on August 1, the crowd of 20,000 comfortably fit into the seats at Fen-way Park and didn't interrupt the flow of the game by lining the field.

The Braves, mired in last place in early July, surged to win the National League pennant in 1914, while the Red Sox finished in second place in the American League. Both teams led their respective leagues in attendance, with the combined twosome attracting more than three-quarters of a million spec-tators, which siphoned off many spectators that might have attended New England League games.

It was a tough season for the New England League in 1914, as Murnane grappled with the strain of too many minor league teams in New England chasing too few ballplayers and spectators. The weather in 1914 only added to the financial woes of the New England League. Numerous games were postponed due to the effects of Jupiter Pluvis, which the newspapers often referred to the instigator of the rain that cancelled games.

"The unfavorable weather conditions experienced thus far have raised havoc with the financial conditions of the New England League," the *Lynn Evening Item* reported in July. "It is considered extremely doubtful if the receipts of the remainder of the season will be able to wipe out the deficit already faced by the league magnates."[24]

With few open dates in the cramped schedule, many of these rainouts were, by necessity, rescheduled as second games of single-admission doubleheaders. Owners generally lost money on these doubleheaders. The attendance was, at best, only slightly better for a two-game set than it would have been for a single game and much less than attendance combined for two separate dates. Because so many doubleheaders were played in 1914 — playing two doubleheaders during the course of a week was not unusual — many fans no doubt became selective in which games they attended and waited for a two-for-one double bill before heading to the ballpark.

For spectators, the single-admission doubleheader was not necessarily a bonanza, though. The league changed its rule for 1914 that previously required at least two hours of daylight before starting the second game of a doubleheader in order to try to get in a full nine innings. In 1914, the second game could begin within one hour and fifteen minutes of sundown, which would allow time for at least five innings to be completed and the game to count as an official contest. In practicality, it was really a one-and-a-half bill rather than a double bill, with at most seven innings often being played in the second game of a doubleheader.

The financial situation was so acute that Fitchburg transferred to Manchester, New Hampshire, at the end of July. This was the first mid-season franchise shift in the New England League since 1905. The location shift was a foreboding indicator of the future, since previous franchise shifts almost universally equated to an eventual collapse of the league. Murnane, knowing the league history intimately, no doubt reluctantly blessed the transaction requested by the Fitchburg owner, his friend Fred Lake. The shift seemed to be a good move for Lake. The Amoskeag Corporation had fixed up old Varick Park to become the new Textile Field, with an electric scoreboard and dugouts in addition to enhanced seating capacity.

The outbreak of armed conflict in Europe during the summer of 1914 following the assassination of Archduke Ferdinand of Austria-Hungary in June only exacerbated the woes of the New England League. The league's only experience with U.S. wartime was the short-lived Spanish-American War in 1898 — and that year the New England League folded before the Fourth of July holiday. While President Wilson maintained a neutrality stance, the prospect of U.S. entry into a European war, or at least the American economy being impacted by the war, was chilling to the future viability of the league.

After Lawrence won the 1914 pennant in the New England League and defeated New London in the postseason series with the Eastern Association champion, the New England League owners became a restless lot. Several had major investments in the team and a ballpark, and they clamored for a solution to their financial plight, which many believed involved a merger with the Eastern Association. Why they believed this to be a panacea is not obvious.

Prospects for Sunday baseball in Massachusetts were, at best, a few years away. In April 1914, the Massachusetts House of Representatives voted 128 to 84 on a motion to kill a Sunday baseball bill. The owners may have believed that a merger would allow them to share in Sunday gates at Bridgeport, New Haven, and Waterbury, where Sunday games were played in the Eastern Association despite the Connecticut law prohibiting Sunday baseball.[25]

Besides the competition from other baseball leagues, notably the Boston major league teams, the New England League now competed with other enter-

The 1914 Lawrence ball club won the New England League championship and then won a postseason playoff series with New London, the champion of the Eastern Association. Lou Pieper, who was instrumental in forging the merger of the New England League and the Eastern Association after the 1915 season, is pictured in street clothes in the top row (Lawrence Public Library, Special Collections).

tainment options, such as the moving pictures now shown at theaters. More people lived in the suburbs than the center city, and small businesses in general were suffering as textile and footwear industries looked to flee high-cost Massachusetts and its worker compensation laws, restrictions on the hours of work, and its predominately non–English speaking immigrant work force. The ball clubs also focused more on lowering expenses rather than finding new ways to attract spectators, especially those toiling in the mills.

Merger talk reached a fever pitch during the winter of 1915 with the specter of another minor league operating in New England. The Federal League's desire to establish a minor league system in the New England states was the tipping point for not only New England League owners, but also several owners in the Eastern Association.

"The independents have practically decided to branch out to minor league territory this spring," reported the *New York Times* in January on the Federal League's plan. "The outlaws will undoubtedly invade New England and possibly one or two of the Class B and C circuits in the Middle West. The Feds have come to realize that they must have some field to send their surplus players."[26]

Agents for the Federal League reportedly looked into numerous cities in the New England League and Eastern Association for possible locations for its new minor league, including Lynn, Worcester, Springfield, and Hartford. Worcester was a particular target since the city was the third largest in New England behind Boston and Providence, but yet only had a Class B minor league baseball team. In contrast, Boston had teams in the major leagues, and Providence had a club in the Class AA International League, the highest minor league classification.

Several owners openly lobbied for merger, including William Carey, owner of the Springfield team in the Eastern Association. In early January, the *Springfield Republican* reported, "A league composed of Springfield, Hartford, New Haven, and Bridgeport from the Eastern Association and Worcester, Lynn, Lowell, and Lawrence, would make an ideal circuit and one that would please club managers in those eight cities more than their present condition. But just when that ideal league is going to become a fact is another question." Every owner in the Eastern Association was attempting to sell its club. "Nobody wants to buy a club in this league," the *Republican* commented. "That is one reason why some of the club owners would like to see the league wrecked and a merger with the New England League."[27]

Murnane dismissed such merger talk:

I have read in the papers that but for Pres. James O'Rourke of the Eastern Association and the president of the New England League, it would be possible to make a combination of the four best cities in each league, formed into one circuit. The truth of the matter is that not more than three men of the 16 who control conditions in these two Class B leagues would consider the move for a moment. And those three men come from the Eastern Association.[28]

On January 30, the Federal League announced definite plans to launch a minor league in New England after a meeting in New Haven. "The first step in the invasion of Eastern Association and New England League territory by the Federals was taken here today when it was announced that action had been decided upon that would result in clubs being placed in eight cities now in the two leagues," the *Washington Post* reported. "We are going to invade Eastern and New England territory," said league president James Gilmore. "Nothing definite has been decided upon as yet, except that point."[29]

The Federal League announcement created a firestorm of activity and discussion in minor league cities throughout New England. The *Boston Globe*, in an article under the byline of J.C. O'Leary but certainly reflecting Murnane's opinion, lambasted the proposal:

> The dispatch does not state whether or not Mr. Gilmore saw the color of the money spoken of, nor how in the few hours spent in New Haven he made the discovery that conditions for such an organization were so favorable. People who have been in the baseball business much longer than Pres. Gilmore have gone over New England with a fine-toothed comb, trying to develop such conditions as existed, and no very wonderful successes have yet gone on record. It was simply a fight for existence for most of the clubs, and the one thing which kept many of them from going to the wall was the fact that they were able to develop a player which they could sell to the major leagues and thus get enough to tide them over from one season to another. And this was at a time when baseball was, generally speaking, sailing on an even keel and there were no typhoons and tidal waves such as prevailed last season and which have not yet subsided. Men who have real money tied up in baseball at the present time do not know where they are at, and are simply plugging along by dead reckoning.[30]

In an attempt to enhance attendance during the 1915 season, the Eastern Association considered adopting a split-season format favored by O'Rourke, which was a radical departure from the normal full-season format to determine the league champion. "The plans for the double season follow: Start April 28 and close July 4; start the second season July 5 and close Sept. 6; the two winners then to play best three in five games for the championship of the league."[31]

The idea behind the split-season format was to retain spectator interest in games during the summer in those cities not in contention for the pennant. A competitive second half would keep paying customers coming to the ballpark longer through the summer.

A split-season format had been used only sporadically in Organized Baseball. The National League tried the split-season format in 1892, when there were twelve teams following the merger with the American Association, and a few minor leagues tried the approach in the 1890s, including one season in the New England League in 1899. But the format proved unpopular with both ball clubs and their fans. Following the formation of the National Association in 1901, the split-season format was used in the minor leagues mostly by Class D leagues; it was only adopted at a higher classification by the Class C South Atlantic League, which had used it consistently since 1909, and the Class B Three-I League on a trial basis in 1915.

The New England League briefly considered the split-season format at its February 4 meeting, but rejected it with a touch of hubris. "The double season idea was talked over, but passed up as impracticable for an eight-club league," the *Globe* reported. "In fact, it was agreed by all that the present circuit is by all odds the best that the league has ever controlled, and that it would be a foolish move to try any new schemes." As for a possible merger, "The idea of combination of the best cities in the minor leagues in New England was spoken of very lightly, one member remarking that the Eastern Association has only two cities, Springfield and Hartford, that can match up with the New England League standard." Apparently, the New England League owners expected the Eastern Association owners to appear at the meeting and ask for the merger (perhaps plead), but no representatives showed up.[32]

If only matters had been that sound in the New England League.

"The little old league, sometimes called the cradle of baseball, is about the rockiest looking cradle ever viewed by fond parents," the *Lowell Courier-Citizen* commented. "Heavy losses face the New England League team owners the coming season unless a new arrangement is made. It might take the form of a merger under organized baseball, or it might be an arrangement whereby gate receipts in all cities on Saturday and holidays be pooled and apportioned in equal amounts to the eight teams."[33]

Manchester and Haverhill were in unstable condition. Lake sold the Manchester club to Tom Keady, who was having a difficult time negotiating a lease for Textile Field. Haverhill, under new ownership since Clohecy and Marshall sold out the previous summer, eventually transferred to Fitchburg to play the 1915 season. Lowell didn't know where it would play its games since Spalding Park had been damaged in a fire at the end of the 1914 season.

While it passed on the split-season idea, the New England League did adopt a schedule change for 1915, adding fourteen games to the season by scheduling an equal number of doubleheaders. Expanding the schedule by two weeks to add fourteen games would have necessitated the addition of playing dates during cool-weather weeks in mid–April and mid–September, which would not likely attract that many spectators to the games. The scheduling of doubleheaders was a desperation move by the league to attract spectators to its games, since these "synthetic doubleheaders" were generally despised by major league club owners as a cheapening of the game rather than a legitimate promotional technique.

It was a chaotic situation in New England minor league baseball. The Federal League bailed out on its plan to form a minor league in New England after Ed Barrow, president of the International League, made overtures to recruit Springfield, Hartford, and Worcester into the International League during mid–February. Soon thereafter, the Eastern Association failed to form in 1915, as Springfield and Hartford balked at participating in a six-club league after Waterbury and New Britain disbanded operations. Both Springfield and Hartford, along with New Haven, joined the remnants of the Colonial League when the Federal League offered to support that league. Robert Ward, owner of the Brooklyn team in the Federal League, was the Colonial League's financial benefactor.

"The acquisition of the three strongholds of the suspended Eastern Association strengthens the league to a point where it takes second rank to none in the East and in the opinion of many now tops the famous old New England League," *Sporting Life* commented.[34]

Because the Colonial League operated outside of Organized Baseball during 1915, the question of who owned the rights to operate minor league teams in Hartford and Springfield would ultimately determine the future direction of the New England League.

By playing Sunday baseball, the Colonial League, with teams located in the Rhode Island cities of Pawtucket and Woonsocket, could have delivered a knockout blow to both the still-operating New England League as well as the suspended-season Eastern Association. However, "no Sunday baseball will be played by any of the Colonial League clubs in deference to the religious scruples of Mr. R.B. Ward, the Brooklyn Federal League magnate, who is the chief backer of the Colonial League."[35]

The stability of the New England League was shaken during the 1915 season by two huge problems that surfaced in Manchester and Worcester.

Despite playing in the new Textile Field facility, the Manchester team did not draw many spectators. Less than two months into the season, club owner Keady sought to cure his financial ills. Keady used the threat of moving the team to drum up support within the Manchester community. What was unique about Keady's strategy was where he threatened to move the team. Keady did not use the conventional ploy of envy by rekindling interest in a city formerly in the New England League, but instead used embarrassment to stir up the citizens of Manchester. Keady announced that he wanted to move the team to Greenfield, Massachusetts, a city in western Massachusetts that had about one-sixth the population of Manchester.

"A golden opportunity for Greenfield to get on the baseball map was offered yesterday by President Thomas Keady of the Manchester club of the New England League," the *Greenfield Recorder* remarked in a front-page story. "Civic pride, if nothing else, should lead the fans to give every encouragement to the movement. To have Greenfield in the league will advertise the town immensely."[36]

When Greenfield agreed to meet Keady's stipulation for "$1,000 to help defray expenses and the sale of 200 ticket books at $5 each," the city thought it had attained minor league status. "We Get Team: Manchester Franchise Transferred to Greenfield," was the front-page headline in the *Greenfield Recorder* on June 30. Greenfield expected to host its first game on July 1 against Fitchburg.[37]

However, Keady was only using Greenfield to get a better deal in Manchester. On the evening of June 30, Keady organized a meeting at city hall, which raised $3,000 to invest in stock of the club, about a one-half interest in the team. Mayor Harry Spaulding spoke at the gathering and said that without the ball club, "Manchester's claim as a live city" would disappear. Keady had clearly wounded the pride of the city's business leaders by suggesting that tiny Greenfield could support his team while the much larger Manchester could not.[38]

Worcester experienced a deeper rejection of its team due to a growing dislike for irascible owner Jesse Burkett. The team played its last home game on August 24, and played on the road for the remaining two weeks of the season, with the players paid on a cooperative basis based on the team's share of the gate receipts. "The players are behind in their salaries, the club owners have other financial obligations to meet and there is no chance to get any money back at Boulevard Park, because of the slim attendance," described the *Boston Globe* of the team's plight. The team's major asset was the ballpark, which sat on leased land.[39]

Braves Field opened in August, dealing perhaps the knockout blow to the fate of the New England League. The new home of the Braves was "the largest baseball park ever fitted up, with a seating capacity of 45,000." The spacious seating incorporated into the design, as well as the transportation arrangements, made it obvious that the team expected to attract numerous spectators from not only the city of Boston but also its suburbs and outlying cities and towns in Massachusetts.[40]

"The new park is on Babcock St., Allston, on the former site of the Allston Golf Club. The entrances on Babcock St. are only 50 feet from the [street] cars on Commonwealth Av.," stated the *Globe* on the location of Braves Field. "This ball park is the only one which [street] cars will enter; after the game the Elevated will send its cars on the siding, a part of the park, and they can be reached in the park via pre-payment stations." In addition to easy street-car access, the club owners created a parking area for private automobiles. "There will be a large parking space with a frontage of 200 feet and a depth of 150 feet at Commonwealth Av. and Babcock St. for machines."[41]

The parking lot, while at the time a convenience for the team's more well-heeled patrons, would turn out to a decimating factor in the lack of success for New England League revivals when the "machines" changed from automobiles transporting one or two passengers to buses that carried dozens of spectators. The "jitney," a forerunner to today's larger bus, was already making its appearance felt in the New England League. "The jitneys continue to make money between Lowell and Lawrence. Big seven passenger touring cars are now available," the *Lowell Courier-Citizen* reported in 1915. "About 200 Lowell fans took in the game [at Lawrence]. Some came by electrics and some by jitneys. They agreed they got their money's worth."[42]

On August 18, a crowd of 46,000 jammed Braves Field for the inaugural game, with many thousands more turned away at the gate. The Braves invited a vast number of dignitaries to the game, including the mayors of all cities in Massachusetts, who were asked to a celebratory luncheon before the game. Mayors Kane of Lawrence and Solomon of Lynn posed for a pre-game photograph of the mayoral dignitaries, but the mayor of Lowell did not attend. Perhaps he abstained knowing how devastating the impact of Braves Field would be to his city's team in the New England League.

The *Globe* reported that "Billy Peters of Lawrence, statistician of the New England League, came down to report the game for his paper." Rather than attend the doubleheader that Lawrence played that day in Fitchburg, Peters traveled to Boston to watch trains and automobiles ferry thousands of Massachusetts residents to Boston from their homes dozens of miles from the city, all for a mid-season baseball game. Peters had to believe that the future of the New England League, playing to small crowds in old wooden ballparks, was numbered.[43]

Many newspapers conceded the fate of the independent New England League before the end of the 1915 season. "That the much suggested and long sought consolidation of the New England and Eastern Association cities will be put through this winter is the belief of the sports writers," the *Manchester Union* reported in late August.[44]

The 1915 season ended on Labor Day, September 6. Traditional home-

and-home twin bills were played on the holiday by three sets of league clubs; the other two teams played a doubleheader in Lynn since Worcester had reverted to being a road-only team by that point.

It was fitting that a multi-game scheduling squabble would erupt on the last day of the 1915 season. There had been numerous contested pennants over the years resulting from hi-jinks during the final days of the season. These included the game awarded to Lowell in 1888 when Portsmouth failed to show up, the sextuple-header played by Manchester and Portland in 1899, and the tripleheader hastily arranged in 1910 by Worcester and Haverhill.

In 1915, despite a league rule that now prohibited more than two games played on a single date, Manchester tried to squeeze in a third game in its home-and-home twin bill with Lawrence. After the morning game in Manchester, which Lawrence won 8–4, Manchester tried to play a second game before the teams needed to catch their train to be back in Lawrence for the afternoon portion of the twin bill. The two teams squeezed in four-and-a-half innings during the second game in Manchester, as the home team claimed a 3–1 victory to clinch seventh place in the standings. Staying out of last place was the avowed reason for the second game in Manchester. The league disagreed, though, tossing out the results of the second game, especially since Lawrence did not take the second game seriously, using shortstop Larry Mahoney as the pitcher in the game. Even the *Manchester Union* called the second game a "burlesque."[45]

With the Labor Day games in the books and the 1915 season concluded, it was time to focus on the future of the league.

"New England League Will Be Reorganized" was the headline in the *Lawrence Evening Tribune* the day after Labor Day, which foretold the likely fate of the league, especially since Murnane had earlier announced that he would step down as league president after the 1915 season concluded.[46]

Portland, the pennant winner, was the only club that made money during the 1915 season. Even Lawrence, the second-place finisher, was in the hole as the club's internal squabbles and management's economy moves only alienated its fans. The only hope appeared to be a merger with the remnants of the Eastern Association. "There has been some talk of amalgamation, but it is going to be a more difficult job to put through a merger scheme than appears on the face," the *Evening Tribune* astutely commented. "The past season was a financial failure, yet many of those who lost money are willing to keep in the game, hoping that better times and conditions will recoup their 1915 losses."[47]

"It would not be too much to expect in the remapping of the baseball territory, a league that has been wanted for years, the circuit composed of the best cities of the Eastern Association and the New England League," the *Springfield Republican* commented. "The merger is the baseball need for New England and the chances are it will be seen next season. Then Springfield will have a baseball league that it has longed for for years."[48]

When Ward died in October, the Colonial League was destined to pass away as well, since it had been only Ward's money that had kept the league afloat in 1915. If Ward and the Colonial League had lived to see the 1916 season, he might have introduced night baseball to the professional game long before the concept became a mainstay of the minor leagues in the early 1930s. Night baseball in 1916 would have completely changed the complexion of minor league baseball in New England.

The Federal League tried an experimental night game on October 27, at Ward's ballpark in Brooklyn, Washington Park, where Joe Wall's Sixth Ward All-Leaguers played a team of all-leaguers from the Federal League. "With the exception of a few dark spots in the outfield, the diamond was flooded with an excellent light, rivaling day light," reported one newspaper on the playing conditions. The experiment with night baseball was quickly forgotten, though, when the Federal League went out of existence later in the year.[49]

On October 19, the Eastern Association held its annual meeting in Bridgeport. No one from Springfield, Hartford, or New Haven attended; only O'Rourke and representatives from Pittsfield, New London, and Bridgeport were on hand. The *Springfield Republican* reported sarcastically, "One dream of the association involves Springfield, Hartford, New Haven, Bridgeport, New London, and Pittsfield as a working basis for a league that may be even expanded to eight clubs."[50]

On October 28, the New England League club owners met to discuss the anticipated merger and announced a proposed framework for an eight-club circuit. According to the *Lynn Evening Item*, the combined league would consist of five teams from the New England League — Lynn, Portland, Lowell, Lawrence, and Worcester — and three teams from the old Eastern Association — Springfield, Hartford, and New Haven. The owners clearly viewed the combined organization as a continuation of the existing New England League and a simple absorbing of three new teams. "All indications point toward the New England League the coming year to be the strongest ever in the history of the organization," the *Lynn Evening Item* remarked the following day. "Big Baseball Merger Coming to Help N.E. League Baseball," stated a *Lowell Courier-Citizen* headline a few days later.[51]

Since the three new teams had not operated within Organized Baseball the previous year, it seemed to be a relatively easy matter to bring them within the fold of the New England League. However, Jim O'Rourke had placed a bond to reserve the territory of the old Eastern Association for the 1916 season. The fundamental issue to resolve was which league had territorial rights to place teams in Springfield, Hartford, and New Haven. Louis Pieper was appointed the emissary of the New England League to argue the league's case at a meeting of the National Association in San Francisco in early November.

While the club owners seemed aligned to favor a merger, the presidents of the two affected leagues were definitely not in favor of a merger. Both Murnane and O'Rourke remained adamantly opposed to combining the two leagues. The real issue to confront was how to orchestrate a merger without involving both league presidents.

The New England League was increasingly rudderless, though, since the club owners and the league president, who was a lame duck, were at odds with each other over the proposed merger. "Murnane will oppose the merger. Pieper, his old friend, will go the limit to make it effective," reported the *Lowell Courier-Citizen*, summing up the situation. "We only hope the pair won't come to blows in their respective attitudes."[52]

Murnane had suggested that the league elect a new president. However, there was no clear choice for a new president among the club owners. "John H. Donnelly of Lowell was present with at least four votes for the position, but lacked the fifth" that would have given him a majority of the eight votes. If Burkett hadn't already sold the Worcester franchise and were still eligible to vote, Donnelly would have been elected president, absent a filibuster by the other club owners. Among those other owners, though, were Duffy and Pieper, both powerful forces in the league. They favored Steve Flanagan, the secretary of the Providence club in the International League, for president.[53]

The New England League owners surely thought they had the leverage in the merger situation compared to that held by the Eastern Association, or more accurately by its president, Jim O'Rourke, who seemed to be the only one that wanted to continue the Connecticut-based circuit. The New England League had actually conducted a 1915 season with eight teams, whereas the Eastern Association had failed to operate at all in 1915. In addition, the New England League was also bringing back into the fold of Organized Baseball the three largest cities in the 1914 Eastern Association, which had all bolted in 1915 to play in the Colonial League, an outlaw league due to its close association with the Federal League.

The position of the New England League owners seemingly was strengthened when the National Association, the governing body of the minor leagues, named its committee to evaluate the proposed merger. At the National Association's November 12 meeting in San Francisco, Pieper laid out the reasoning for the merger and the proposed composition of the new league's eight clubs, comprised of five cities from the New England League and three cities from the Eastern Association. "A committee of three was created, consisting of Messrs. Barrow, Murnane, and Farrell, to investigate the several claims and report to the Chairman of the Board with the understanding that the Board would accept the report of the committee as final."[54]

It was an interesting cast to determine the fate of the New England League. John Farrell was secretary of the National Association and was motivated to secure the best solution for the minor leagues. Ed Barrow, president of the International League, could be expected to seek the best solution for a lower-level league to support the higher-classification International League and to position the Providence franchise in his league. Barrow also had his eye on the Worcester franchise as a possible International League club.

Murnane was opposed to the merger. He introduced a property rights concept into the negotiation to take care of his friend O'Rourke and possibly prevent the New England League owners from going through with the merger if they had to come up with money to pay off the other owners.

The proposed merger was no sure thing, however. The "several claims" referred to opposition posed by O'Rourke, who was assembling a case to restart the Eastern Association in 1916.

By excluding Bridgeport from the proposed merger lineup, the New England League owners had overplayed their hand. They opened up a hornet's nest by angering O'Rourke, who happened to control the ballpark used by the Bridgeport team and therefore had an economic interest in the merged league. As the president of the Eastern Association (at least on paper), O'Rourke also had a political interest in the merged league. He was obviously being left out of the merger discussions and thus would have no role in the new organization. O'Rourke fought the proposed merger structure.

By mid–December, though, Murnane had gotten religion and began to support the merger. "At present the game is in a bad way in at least three cities in the New England League, while the Eastern Association failed to start at all last year," Murnane was quoted as saying. "The situation is such that the merger seems the only solution of the baseball problem in this part of the country."[55]

Murnane likely changed his stance on the merger when he learned in early December that the owners of the Boston Braves and Providence Grays were planning to sell their ball clubs to new owners at substantial prices. While the value of these two clubs had escalated — especially Providence due to its Sunday games at Rocky Point — the value of New England League clubs had plummeted to the point where there were few, if any, potential buyers.

Only a merger with the Eastern Association clubs could salvage some value to the New England League club owners, and hopefully a merger would inject some enhanced value. Only with increased franchise value could minor league baseball continue in New England outside of Providence.

In early January, James Gaffney, president of the Boston Braves, announced the sale of the club to a syndicate of Boston businessmen. "While Pres. Gaffney would not name the price that he sold out for, he did say that he received much more than he gave for it, and he had made money out of his baseball venture," the *Boston Globe* reported on the transaction.[56]

Two weeks later, Joseph Lannin, president of the Boston Red Sox who also owned the Providence club, announced the sale of the Grays to Providence businessman William Draper. Lannin had owned the club less than two years, having purchased it from Frank Navin, president of the Detroit Tigers, in 1914. Lannin would sell his interest in the Red Sox later in 1916.[57]

Since it appeared to be a seller's market for baseball clubs, Murnane switched his stance on the merger to support the New England League owners. Murnane, however, bemoaned the transition of baseball from a sporting pastime to a business. In "Baseball Is Now a Big Problem in High Finance," Murnane wrote in August 1916, "Thirty years ago, the public was satisfied with the simple grounds and good clean, hustling, up-to-the-hour baseball. As the country grew more populous and the game more popular, men of means came into the business as a good financial proposition."[58]

The three-person National Association committee held hearings on the proposed merger on December 17 in New York City. O'Rourke contended that he had new owners for teams to be located in Springfield, Hartford, and New Haven, cities that arguably were still in the Eastern Association since Organized Baseball did not recognize the Colonial League to which the teams had transferred. But O'Rourke could not produce any documentation to prove that he had secured new owners. Pieper had already submitted documentation to show that the owners of the three existing teams that had gone to the Colonial League — Clarkin of Hartford, Carey of Springfield, and the Cameron estate of New Haven — had more than $50,000 invested in their franchises.

As a guiding principle to the proposed merger, "the committee's first thought would be the protection of property rights and that none of its club members could be ruthlessly dropped without adequate compensation." This principle established a firm foundation for the proposed eight-team merger as desired by the New England League owners. However, it also meant that compensation would need to be made to Eastern Association owners whose franchises weren't absorbed by the merger. That meant O'Rourke in Bridgeport and two other owners, Jack Zeller of Pittsfield and Plant of New London, had to be compensated. The committee gave O'Rourke a month to produce the documentation that he had six clubs lined up to operate the Eastern Association. In reality, it was four weeks for the New England League owners to negotiate with O'Rourke and the other owners.[59]

Over the next two weeks, the New England League owners took care of the three teams that would not go into the merged league — Manchester, Lewiston, and Fitchburg. The Lewiston owners were to become part owners of the Lynn team, as would the Manchester owners become part owners of the Lowell team. A financial reimbursement was to be made for the Fitchburg franchise. These settlements were announced at a New England League meeting held on December 30. The league also announced that the merged league would be expanded to ten clubs, to include five unspecified cities from the Eastern Association.

The resolve of the Lowell club to continue on was strengthened in December when a proposal was floated to build a new stadium near downtown Lowell, as conveyed in the *Courier-Citizen* headline: "Merrimack River Stadium Suggested As Development for First Street Dump." The new stadium was designed for spectators arriving either straight from downtown Lowell or by automobile since it was located next to the proposed state highway to Lawrence and offered a large parking space next to the stadium.[60]

The owners also met separately to elect a new president to succeed Murnane, "who announced that he would not be a candidate for re-election." The favorite for the post was John Donnelly of Lowell, but no election was held since Murnane was not present at the meeting and "his resignation had not been formally received."[61]

On January 10, 1916, the New England League owners came to a vague agreement that Bridgeport would be part of the merged league and that Bridgeport agreed to the merger "provided some $1600 charged as league dues was paid and $8000 was paid to dissolve the Pittsfield franchise." New London also agreed to participate in the new league and not obstruct the merger. When a firmer agreement with O'Rourke and friends couldn't be struck by the date slated for the final committee meeting on January 17, the meeting was postponed a week.[62]

At the January 24 meeting, O'Rourke presented his plan for operating the Eastern Association in six cities in 1916. Investigation disclosed that the options on ballparks in New Haven and Waterbury were only for payments of one dollar, and that options on the ballparks in Hartford and Springfield were held by Zeller, the Pittsfield owner, who would also have a club in the league. It was quite evident that O'Rourke's organization was simply a "paper league" and couldn't match up to the $28,900 invested by Carey in the Springfield club and $29,500 invested by Clarkin in the Hartford club. It looked fairly certain that the New England League proposal, now consisting of ten clubs, would be approved and that it was only a matter of agreeing upon restitution to O'Rourke and Zeller for their Bridgeport and Pittsfield investments, respectively.

The New England League held its final annual meeting on January 31 at the Quincy House in Boston. Under the headline "N.E. League Is Out of Existence," the *Lowell Courier-Citizen* reported, "The New England League of Baseball Clubs passed out of existence tonight, when President Timothy H. Murnane finally adjourned its annual meeting." The adjournment, though, occurred without any action on either the merger, which was still waiting approval from the National Association, or election of a new president, which arguably was moot since the league likely would no longer exist. The latter inaction was not good news for Donnelly, who aspired to the presidency of the merged league. The *Courier-Citizen* reported that Donnelly had four of eight votes for election, but lacked a majority since Burkett, who did support Donnelly, no longer represented Worcester after selling his interest in the club.[63]

The club owners were no doubt searching for a nationally known baseball figure to head the merged league — someone with the stature of Murnane, but who wasn't Murnane himself. A local person like Donnelly, who may well have been capable as an administrator, lacked the political clout needed for the league to adequately deal with the major league club owners and other minor league presidents. One name widely floated for league president was Tom Lynch, the former head of the National League.

The National Association, as expected, voted to approve the merger of the two leagues. In its report released on February 14, the committee reached the following conclusion:

In the last analysis we find that four of the six original club members of the Eastern Association are on record as favoring a merger for the best interests of baseball in the community. We find that seven of the eight New England club owners favor merger. This alliance constitutes an overwhelming majority of club owners with large financial interests in both circuits. The committee is free to express its opinion that it finds a public demand for the merger. These two component interests, viz., invested property rights and a genuine public demand, force the conclusions upon your committee that the best interests of baseball will be conserved by the allowing of the merger requested.[64]

The ruling also granted payments of $3,000 to Zeller and $1,000 to O'Rourke, payable by March 1.

O'Rourke predictably dismissed the report's conclusion and announced that he would appeal the decision. He gave up the fight a week later.

While the two leagues had merged, and there was agreement on which ten clubs would comprise the league, there was no official name for the new league nor were there any elected officials in leadership positions to guide the new league.

At a February 17 meeting, the New England League officially dissolved itself. Immediately thereafter, another meeting was held with representatives from the ten cities in the first meeting of the merged league. With Eugene Fraser presiding over the meeting as temporary chairman, Pieper made a motion to name the merged league the Eastern League. The new name combined words from the names of both predecessor leagues, and it was felt that "Eastern" presented a broader geographical perspective that would benefit the league. The approval of the new name made it easier for baseball fans to forget about the New England League, and for that matter, for the cities from the old Eastern Association to forget about who had pushed for the merger.[65]

Officers of the new Eastern League were announced at a February 24 league meeting in Springfield. The club owners had quickly soured on Lynch as president after he said he wanted an annual salary of $5,000 to take the job. With the losses they'd experienced the past few years, they could ill afford an expensive president to lead them to profitability. They compromised and elected Murnane for a one-year term.

While the retention of Murnane was ostensibly good for the faction of five former New England League clubs, it actually proved horrible. Murnane was strictly the titular head of the league. All the power was wielded by Dan O'Neil, who had been elected vice president and secretary. O'Neil, who was from Holyoke, Massachusetts, had a long affiliation with the old Connecticut League (including leading Holyoke to a postseason victory over Lowell in 1903). Fraser of the Lynn club was elected treasurer of the league.[66]

To the owners' detriment, O'Rourke, aided by Zeller, wound up playing a more prominent role in the eventual reshaping of minor league baseball in New England than the New England League owners had wanted. This error was compounded by two disastrous mistakes in the ten days following the official approval of the merger by the National Association — the adoption of the Eastern League name and the failure to elect a viable league president.

Another strategic error on the part of the New England League owners was not making Sunday baseball a key point to the merger of the two leagues. Both New Haven and Bridgeport had staged home games on Sunday in the Eastern Association during the 1914 season, and did so again in 1916. Surprisingly, Sunday baseball was hardly mentioned in newspaper reports about the proposed merger.

If the New England League owners had openly embraced Bridgeport as a Sunday baseball haven for the merged league, the results of the merger might have turned out differently than they did. The fifty-fifty blend of the ten-team Eastern League — five clubs from the New England League and five clubs from the Eastern Association — lasted just one season. Within six months of the approved merger, the New England League owners were bemoaning the merger. By the 1917 season, former Eastern Association cities dominated the composition of the Eastern League.

The five former New England League clubs did get a taste of Sunday baseball for the first time while playing on the road in Bridgeport and New Haven, generating a visitor's share of the populous gates for the Sabbath games.

For instance, Lowell played its first Sunday game at New Haven on April 30 before 2,200 spectators. Crowds of this size at ball games in Lowell were rarely seen and then most often on holiday dates. However, Sunday baseball in 1916 got off to a rocky start. The *Worcester Evening Post* reported that at the April 30 game played at Savin Rock were police detectives, "who jotted down a list of names of many present, including those of the players and umpires." The presence of police at the April 30 game indicated that further legal action might be planned to stop Sunday games at the New Haven ball grounds. The article entitled "Sunday Games in E.L. May Be Barred" went on to say, "Under the law, Sunday ball is clearly prohibited. The success of the new league lies to a great degree upon its ability to play Sunday games of baseball and the step which has been begun is a serious blow to the team here."[67]

The Sunday game in Bridgeport on April 30 against Portland drew 3,900 spectators. Worcester played its first Sunday game on May 14 in Bridgeport after the Sunday games on May 7 were rained out. Lynn went so far as taking an expensive one-game Sunday road trip to Bridgeport to play on Sunday, May 28, between games on Saturday in Lowell and Monday in Worcester.

However, just like the ill-fated combination that spawned the Atlantic Association back in 1889, the expenses of traveling to Connecticut for lengthy road trips and the meager crowds at home to see the Connecticut-based teams quickly spawned a financial nightmare for the former New England League clubs. The Sunday games in Bridgeport were not enough to offset the losses. Desperation set in after holiday doubleheaders on July 4 were rained out.

"The situation in Lawrence is acute. The future of baseball is at stake," the *Lawrence Evening Tribune* wrote. "The poorest brand of baseball weather on top of experimenting with a new league is proving a costly investment for the men who have their money tied up in franchises." The *Tribune* reported that Lynn had already lost $4,000 that season, with the players having gone without a paycheck since June 1. Lowell similarly was $4,000 in the hole. While the Lawrence players were paid through July 1, the situation appeared bleak for the remainder of the season. "Not a club in the league is ahead," the *Tribune* wrote. "The local losses run pretty high."[68]

By mid-summer, the owners of the Lawrence, Lowell, and Lynn clubs wanted to abandon the Eastern League. Indeed, the Eastern League did need to assume ownership of the Lawrence club to keep a ten-club league operating. O'Neil convinced Lowell and Lynn to stay in the circuit until Labor Day, taking advantage of the loyalty of owners Roach and Fraser.

Following an 11-inning, 4–4 tie ended by darkness in the afternoon game of its Labor Day doubleheader with Worcester, Lowell dropped out of the Eastern League and didn't finish out the season. The *Lowell Courier-Citizen* reported that Roach had lost $20,000 in baseball during his six years owning the Lowell club, including an estimated $7,000 loss in 1916. Had Roach continued the club for the two weeks remaining in the season after Labor Day, he would have lost another $1,500. Contributing to the community spirit had its financial limits, even for a baseball man like Roach.[69]

Lowell never saw the proposed Merrimack River Stadium to be built near downtown, which might have improved patronage at Lowell games from the low levels experienced in 1916 at outlying Spalding Park. Instead, when the Lowell-Haverhill highway was built along the river, now Route 110, the proposed site for the ballpark became an interchange with Route 38.

Facing an untenable nine-club league for the last two weeks of the 1916 season, the Eastern League took the opportunity to drop its support of the Lawrence club and disbanded the team in order to have an eight-club configuration for the remainder of the season. Fraser supported Lynn through the end of the season, with merger-proponent Pieper managing the club, but disbanded the team soon thereafter.

Dan O'Neil ascended to the presidency of the Eastern League on October 17, 1916, taking over from Tim Murnane, who retired from minor league administration. Facing a decimated Massachusetts section of the league, without franchises in Lawrence, Lowell, or Lynn (three of the five teams in the merger from the prior New England League), O'Neil worked to retain at least one of these teams in the league. By spring of 1917, O'Neil had arranged for a team to remain in Lawrence. While the Portland franchise stayed in the league, Hugh Duffy was no longer associated with the team.

Less than one year following a merger that had begun with the New

England League teams expecting to dominate the composition of the two merged leagues, the old Connecticut League faction held five of the eight remaining teams in the league as well as all of the league's constitutional officers. The former New England League clubs, now comprising just three of the eight clubs in the league (but with none of their original owners), held very little negotiation power in their new league and were virtual interlopers in a circuit that they had lobbied so vigorously to establish.

8

Donnelly Revives
League, 1919

With all the ball clubs formerly in the New England League either disbanded or fully absorbed into the Eastern League by the end of the 1916 season, the twenty-eight seasons of New England League play, from 1885 to 1915, quickly faded from the consciousness of baseball fans and were consigned to the baseball history books.

Memories of the New England League's storied past eroded more rapidly when former president Tim Murnane died unexpectedly on February 7, 1917, just four months after yielding the Eastern League presidency to Dan O'Neil. On the evening of February 7, Murnane dropped dead in the foyer of the Shubert Theatre in Boston as he waited to check his coat before attending a performance of *Eileen*, an Irish operetta.

"Thus went away the sunniest man in all the newspaper world, and one of the best-known writers of sporting news in the country," the *Boston Globe* described Murnane in a lengthy obituary that began on the front page. "There is no man who has had anything to do with baseball in the past generation who cannot tell stories of Tim Murnane; there is no man who ever speaks of him except with admiration or with love."[1]

There were many words of tribute devoted to the memory of Murnane, from baseball executives, players, and others whose lives he touched as a journalist. "The death of Mr. Murnane, whom I have known for years, is a great loss to baseball," said Ban Johnson, president of the American League. Former player Fred Tenney said, "The game of baseball has lost, in Mr. Murnane's death, one of its best friends. Mr. Murnane was always a strong advocate for clean tactics in professional baseball, and he did more for the game in that way than any other writer in the country."[2]

169

Cardinal O'Connell of Boston officiated at the funeral mass for Murnane at St. Alden's Catholic Church in Brookline before his burial in the Old Catholic Burial Grounds in Dorchester. Murnane left a widow and four children to be cared for, with meager savings from his long career in baseball. "Despite Murnane's immense popularity, he left very little for his family," explained a 1985 profile of Murnane in *The Pilot*, a publication of the Catholic Archdiocese in Boston.[3]

The American League and the Baseball Writers Association of America established a fund on behalf of Murnane's family. On September 27, 1917, a benefit game for Murnane's family was played at Fenway Park between the Red Sox and an all-star team comprised of many of the game's greats. Babe Ruth pitched for the Red Sox and the outfield combination for the all-star team consisted of Ty Cobb, Joe Jackson, and Tris Speaker. A crowd of 17,000 watched the Red Sox defeat the all-star team, 2–0, and raise $14,000 for Murnane's family.[4]

Receipts from the benefit game also purchased an impressive gravestone, which was erected in 1918 in Calvary Cemetery where Murnane's body was relocated. The inscription on the gravestone reads:

> Pioneer of Baseball
> Champion of Its Integrity
> Gifted and Fearless Writer
> This Monument Erected by the American League[5]

In 1979, Murnane was honored at the Baseball Hall of Fame as a recipient of the J.G. Taylor Spink Award. Murnane's service to the New England League was duly noted on the script honoring him, saying simply, "Was President of New England League for 24 Years."

After the 1917 season, both the Portland and Lawrence clubs, which were under new ownership from their New England League days, were no longer in the Eastern League, leaving Worcester as the last former New England League team in the Eastern League. To keep the circuit at eight teams, O'Neil arranged for Portland to relocate to Providence and Waterbury to join the Eastern League for the 1918 season. Providence, a member of the International League for twenty-five years, had dropped out of the league after the 1917 season due to the uncertainties of the league continuing during the war and several clubs seeking to disband.

The entry of the United States into World War I in 1917 caused an early end to most baseball seasons in 1918, including that of the Eastern League, which by then had shed almost every vestige of its roots in the New England League. "There is no doubt that the Government considers baseball nonessential and we hasten to comply with the Government's wishes in this matter," O'Neil said on

July 20, 1918. "Consequently I have notified the club owners of the Eastern League that the season will suspend next Sunday night, July 21."[6]

While cutting back on the number of actual games played in 1918, the war did spawn two innovations that would enable the New England League to attempt a revival following the end of the war—daylight saving time and legal Sunday baseball played by military personnel.

In March 1918, President Woodrow Wilson signed into law daylight saving time, which required the nation to advance clocks one hour from the last Sunday in March through the last Sunday in October. While the extra hour of daylight after the dinner hour was designed to conserve fuel and electricity during wartime, it also provided an extra hour for outdoor amusement activities in the evening.

The extra hour of daylight was especially helpful to baseball in the New England states, since they were located on the eastern edge of the Eastern Time Zone. From mid–May through July, sunset normally occurred between 7:00 P.M. and 7:30 P.M., which did not provide enough time after supper to get in a full game of baseball. Twilight games in August were nearly impossible to conduct, with sunsets occurring at 6:15 P.M. by the end of the month. With daylight saving time, baseball games could be played in the twilight hours from early May into mid–August, when sunset ranged from 7:30 P.M. to 8:30 P.M.

In April 1918, the Massachusetts legislature passed a law permitting Sunday sports to be played by military personnel, recognizing the sacrifice these men were making in their service to the country. The extent of interest in Sunday baseball by the state's citizens was immediately evident at a game staged by two service teams at Braves Field on April 28. "More than 25,000 persons, mostly men and boys, with officers and enlisted men from the Army and Navy, were at Braves Field yesterday afternoon to see the first baseball game ever played on Sunday in Boston," the *Boston Globe* reported. "The big grandstand, with a seating capacity of about 17,000, was pretty well filled up, and between 8,000 and 10,000 found warm spots in the sunshine on the bleachers on either side." The *Globe* article went on to say, "More women would probably have been in attendance if the weather had been a little warmer, but as it was, the size of the crowd was significant of the interest in baseball and the popularity of Sunday games."[7]

On the following Sunday, a crowd of 40,000 turned out at Braves Field to watch the Boston Navy Yard defeat Camp Devens, 5–1. "The big crowd was orderly and well handled by the ushers and a large detail of police," the *Globe* reported. "There were a number of clergymen present, and the Army and Navy were well represented by officers in uniform, who occupied front boxes. Mayor Peters also occupied a box."[8]

Sunday baseball, without an admission fee, was clearly popular in Massachusetts. Down in Rhode Island, though, Sunday baseball for a price underwent a change.

In 1918, the Providence club in the Eastern League didn't play Sunday baseball at Rocky Point as its International League predecessor had for so many years due to the deteriorating health of Randall Harrington, the owner of the Rocky Point grounds. Harrington died on October 13, 1918. "His second wife Amelia, left with a six-year-old son, was not enamored with running either an amusement park or a baseball diamond," one baseball historian wrote, "thus ending the days that Rocky Point could serve as a Sunday home for the Providence baseball club."[9]

With Rocky Point no longer a viable location for Sunday games, Rhode Island became the first New England state to legalize professional baseball on Sunday. In April 1919, a Sunday baseball bill easily passed through the Rhode Island legislature, even with strong opposition from religious groups. The House of Representatives voted favorably, 71 to 19, while the Senate vote was 26 to 11. On April 10, 1919, Governor R. Livingston Beeckman signed the bill legalizing Sunday baseball in Rhode Island.[10]

Sunday baseball at the professional level debuted within the Providence city limits on May 18, 1919. Providence defeated Hartford, 4–2, before 5,000 fans in "the first Sunday game played by a Providence team in any league other than at Rocky Point or Crescent Park."[11]

Despite having home games scheduled every Sunday on the 1919 Eastern League schedule, the Providence team hobbled through the 1919 season and then disbanded before the 1920 season. "With Sunday games now completely legal and easily accessible, Sunday baseball, nearing its thirty-year anniversary of sanctioned illegality at Rocky Point, was completely routine by the time it was played in Providence. Sunday baseball was no longer unique or special as a promotional element to attract spectators."[12]

Over the winter of 1919, John Donnelly, who had been spurned in his attempt during the winter of 1916 to gain a leadership position in the Eastern League following the merger of the New England League with the Eastern Association, led an effort to revive the New England League.

Donnelly seemed to be oversold on the possibility that Sunday baseball would be legalized in Massachusetts in 1919, his reasoning based on its huge popularity with the citizenry that attended the legally permitted games played by military personnel on Sunday in 1918. Without Sunday baseball, a minor league baseball club based in New England had almost no economic value — and little public relations value as well — a lesson that Donnelly surely had learned from his experience dabbling in league politics in 1916.

Despite the apparent long odds of a successful league revival, Donnelly fronted the money with the National Association to secure franchises in the New England League. He quickly discovered that he couldn't easily resell them. Many people attended Donnelly's organizing meeting on March 27, 1919, at the Franklin Hotel in Lawrence, but demand was not robust for franchises. "The outlook from yesterday's gathering is not a rosy one," the *Lawrence Evening Tribune* reported. "There was no clamoring for franchises even though they may be had for a small figure. Instead the promoters are doing their best to give the franchises away."[13]

Even worse than being saddled with a limited market for team franchises, Donnelly was pillaged by the newspapers as an opportunist whose only motivation in singing the praises of the New England League was financial gain, not love of baseball or civic duty. As early as May 1, Donnelly had to issue denials. "President Donnelly, who has organized the league, told the *Lewiston Journal* that he isn't looking for personal profit," the Lewiston newspaper reported, "and put it squarely on the basis of whether the fans in Lewiston want baseball to the extent of financing the game."[14]

Donnelly couldn't shake the label of carpetbagger, and his resurrection of the New England League lasted all of ten weeks before the league disintegrated in late July. His difficulties were evident from the beginning. "Jack Donnelly sometime may write a story entitled 'The Troubles of a League Organizer' and he won't have to depend on fiction to make it interesting," the *Lewiston Evening Journal* noted in early May. "Three months ago he started to get six clubs under the same roof; now he has five and if he fails to get the sixth, the chain snaps like a thread."[15]

Four franchises were awarded at the Match 27 meeting, to Lowell and Fitchburg in Massachusetts and to Portland and Lewiston in Maine. Donnelly, who would eventually be elected as league president on April 2, also granted options for franchises in Lawrence and Haverhill. Donnelly avoided working with owners from the old New England League cities that had joined in the merger to form the Eastern League, such as Eugene Fraser and Hugh Duffy, and instead sought out new ownership.

While a six-club league was sub-optimal, the clubs were backed by baseball men like Heinie Wagner and Bill Carrigan, both former members of the Red Sox, and Jesse Burkett, the former owner of the Worcester club in the old New England League. While the baseball men provided sound financial footing, they were also steeped in the traditional 3:00 start for ball games. While wartime daylight saving time was still in effect during the summer of 1919, twilight games were not in the operating plan.

Not playing twilight games in 1919 was perhaps the ultimate downfall for this revival of the New England League. Many potential ballpark customers no doubt passed up going to a mid-afternoon ball game that spring in order to pursue other outdoor activities after dinner in the extra hour of daylight available, perhaps even attending a twilight league ball game. Twilight leagues, where teams of local amateur players captured the attention of residents, were in full bloom in many cities and towns throughout New England during the summer of 1919, and were stiff competition for Donnelly's revival of the New England League.

Donnelly's best idea was to shorten the season to 90 games, from the 126 games scheduled in 1915, and to delay the start of the season until May 23. These moves were designed to give the team owners a solid start for financial gain. The late May start avoided the typical cool and rainy weather weeks in early May, and also ensured that several prime attendance dates were contained within the first ten days of the season. Opening day on Friday, May 23, and the Decoration Day holiday a week later, on May 30, would both draw a significant crowd. The two Saturday dates immediately following each of those two days would also be good draws.

"After three years of slumber, the little Old New England League starts on its career anew today," the *Lowell Courier-Citizen* reported on May 23, placing credit for the league revival with Donnelly being "the principal factor," especially for getting Carrigan to take on the Lewiston club.[16]

While Lewiston, Maine, was one of the first franchises awarded in March 1919, the backing for the Lewiston club didn't come together until early May, when Donnelly visited Lewiston to personally argue that "baseball is a good thing for a community." The *Lewiston Evening Journal* reported on May 1 that "it has been proposed that the new Chamber of Commerce take hold of the enterprise and furnish money for the club in the absence of anyone who would invest in baseball."[17]

A writer for the *Evening Journal* laid out the argument for community benefit:

> If Lewiston had a strong team in the league, it would advertise the city far and near. It would help keep us on the map, and it would also give the thousands of baseball fans in Lewiston-Auburn a chance to see the game they love so well. My idea would be to have the games called late enough in the day to allow the people who work in the factories a chance to go, and under the daylight savings plan — many of the workers getting out as early as five o'clock which would be four o'clock by sun time — it could be arranged.[18]

Under the community benefit principle, tempered with a dose of old-fashioned business sense, Donnelly garnered a Lewiston team for the 1919 season. "The four directing heads of the Union Theatre Company — William

P. Gray and William F. Carrigan of Lewiston, Governor Bartlett of New Hampshire and Mayor Hislop of Portsouth — are willing to take hold [of the team]. They are willing to come forward, not through any personal desire but wholly in the interests of Lewiston — to provide this city with clean sport and give it a lot of the very best kind of advertising."[19]

There was every hope that the foursome would have the team play twilight baseball. "Baseball fans in Lewiston and Auburn want twilight baseball," the *Evening Journal* commented several days later. "This writer has heard not only people working in the mills and factories make this request, but professional men who would like to see the game but are held down town as a general rule until later in the afternoon. With an extra hour of the day to spare [due to daylight saving time], fans would have a chance, they say, to see baseball on days other than holidays."[20]

Twilight baseball, though, would cut heavily into the four owners' theater business, giving them every incentive to play the ball games in the afternoon so that spectators could still go to the theater at night. They likely financed the Lewiston ball club to prevent a Chamber of Commerce-minded owner from playing twilight baseball, which certainly would have cut deeply into theater patronage.

Opening day was not a smashing success, as only 1,000 attended the game in Lowell against Lewiston. About six weeks later, the league was clearly in trouble, as reflected in the *Lowell Courier-Citizen* headline on July 11, "The N.E. League Near Collapse." Both Lowell and Lawrence looked to disband their teams. Donnelly waged "as thankless a fight to give New England fans good baseball as a man ever [could]," the *Courier-Citizen* wrote. "He paid for the franchises out of his own pocket and when he tried to give them away for exactly what they cost him, his wares went begging."[21]

When the Lewiston theater owners pulled their financial support of the Lewiston ball club in early July, the end was near for this short-lived revival of the New England League. The owners expected to lose money (which reportedly totaled $1,400), but they anticipated a better community attitude toward the team. What apparently motivated the club owners to stop supporting the team was a riot at the July 4 holiday game.

"At seven minutes past noon we had the score tied and a man on second and only one out when Umps McCarthy called the game and started a riot," the *Evening Journal* reported. The two teams had agreed to a noon ending to the holiday morning game so the teams could catch the train to Portland for the afternoon game of the holiday twin bill. "The crowd surged on the field, sore at the ump, sore at the management and disappointed in getting six and one-third innings of baseball on a holiday."[22]

Facing the prospect of having just three teams in the league — Fitchburg, Haverhill, and Portland — Donnelly arranged for a novel integration of the Lowell and Lewiston teams. Lowell had good players, as evidenced by its first-place position in the league standings, and Lewiston had good fans (generally). The Lowell team transferred to Lewiston on July 14 to play the rest of its home games in Maine.

However, the underpinnings of the league were just not solid enough. When Haverhill disbanded on August 2 after the team's doubleheader at Fitchburg, Donnelly gave up the ship for the 1919 season. That same day, Lewiston split a doubleheader with Portland, winning the second game, 3–1, to finish in first place in the standings. "If there is any such thing as a pennant in the league, we in dear old Lewiston have the right to see it wave over the Lewiston Athletic Park," the *Evening Journal* remarked.[23]

"President Donnelly worked hard to keep things in motion and the harder he worked, the worse things broke, apparently," the *Lowell Courier-Citizen* wrote. "He will make an effort to reserve the territory for next season, when Sunday baseball will make possible an eight-club league more prosperous than any within recent years in this section of the country."[24]

The *Evening Journal* pegged Donnelly's unrecouped out-of-pocket expenses at $8,000. He supported every team in the league at some point, with the sole exception of Fitchburg, "the only paying city in the league."[25]

Donnelly had irrational optimism that Sunday baseball would be legalized in Massachusetts following the experiment with military games on Sunday in 1918. He had postponed the beginning of the 1919 season, hoping that the legislature would approve a Sunday baseball bill. On May 14, though, the Massachusetts House of Representatives voted down a bill to permit amateur games on Sunday. Even with numerous provisos in the bill, there was no loosening of the Puritan shackles on the Sunday day of rest. The bill "would permit amateur baseball and other sports on Sundays between 2 and 8 P.M. provided that the act was accepted by the municipality, that no admission fee be charged, that no other business enterprise or collection be carried on in connection with the sport, and that its conduct should be subject to regulation by the local authorities."[26]

Even after this defeat on amateur games on Sunday, Donnelly held out hope that professional games would be approved for 1920.

"With Sunday baseball tolerated next season, as the magnates and fans look forward to, the ground now barren will take life, and the thousands of dollars lost in the brief six or seven weeks of the present organization's career will come back bearing interest," the *Lowell Courier-Citizen* wrote. "In Connecticut and Rhode Island, baseball crowds are turning out at Sunday games in sufficient volume to pay all expenses and the weekday games are 'velvet.' New England League baseball will pay only when Sunday baseball becomes a reality."[27]

Donnelly's Sunday baseball hopes were dashed, however.

With a Sunday baseball law passed in New York in 1919, Massachusetts appeared clearly behind the times with its Sunday baseball stance. "Does any sane man mean to tell me that the people of Chicago, St. Louis, and Cincinnati are any worse than those of ... Boston and Philadelphia because they sanction Sunday baseball?" Charles Murphy wrote in "The Pros and Cons of Sunday Baseball" in a 1919 issue of *Baseball Magazine*. "Is any moral question involved? No. I say the citizens of Chicago, St. Louis, and Cincinnati are simply a great many steps ahead of their eastern brethren in regard to the doctrine of human rights ... [where] the poor fellow who works hard all week to support his family is denied the most innocent forms of amusement on Sunday."[28]

There was a bit more progress in 1920 as the Massachusetts legislature finally consented to allow amateur play of Sunday sports. The use of the "local option" technique, which was included in both the 1911 Ohio and 1919 New York laws permitting Sunday baseball, was a key to the passage of the new Massachusetts law. Local option allowed each community to decide for itself whether to allow the permitted sports and games on Sunday. A church proximity restriction, which was contained in the 1909 Indiana Sunday baseball law, also helped secure passage.

The Lord's Day League opposed the bill to allow Sunday sports played by amateurs. "Any Nation which keeps the Lord's Day prospers and those that do not keep it do not prosper. You never heard of a man being more holy because he got out and rooted at a baseball game," remarked the Rev. A.Z. Conrad, vice president of the Lord's Day League, in early 1920.[29]

While still influential, the Lord's Day League was losing its political sway due to its extremely conservative view of Sabbath observance. "Sunday baseball, golf, theatrical performances, movies, soda fountains, cigar counters, colored newspaper supplements and all the rest of the Sabbath Day amusements were vigorously denounced at the annual meeting of the Lord's Day League of New England, held at Tremont Temple yesterday afternoon," the *Globe* reported. Because many state legislators liked to play golf on Sunday, the League's inclusion of this sport on its prohibited list began to turn the entire legislature around on the question of Sunday sports for the masses.[30]

In March, the Committee on Legal Affairs reported favorably on a measure to provide for sports or games to take place on public playgrounds, parks, or other places designated by permit. The activities needed to take place between 2:00 and 6:00 in the afternoon, when there were typically few or no church services. There also could be no charge for admission, and the participants had to be people "that are not promised and do not receive, directly or indirectly, any pecuniary reward." Exceptions to the sports and games permitted on Sunday were horse races, automobile races, boxing matches, and hunting with firearms. Permitted sports and games could not take place within 1,000 feet of a church. And, importantly, the law was subject to local option.[31]

The House of Representatives voted overwhelmingly, 146 to 69, for the Sunday sports bill for amateur players. Massachusetts Governor Calvin Coolidge, who later that summer became a candidate for vice president on the Democratic Party ticket, signed the amateur Sunday sports bill on April 2 following a short hearing on the bill in the State Senate. The bill's proponents ensured that religious backing of the bill attended the hearing. In answer to the charge that the law would be a step toward professional baseball on Sunday, the Rev. E.D. Robinson of Holyoke declared that the amateur games on Sundays were part of the "fight against commercialism." The Rev. Robinson then told the Senate hearing, "I'd like to know if it is holier to stand on the street corner Sunday afternoon, criticize the people who are passing and spit tobacco juice, than to take part in a good healthy game of baseball."[32]

Opposition also spoke at the hearing. "Rev. Martin Kneeland of the Lord's Day League protested that Sunday baseball would lower the Sunday ideals of the community," the *Boston Globe* reported. Kneeland assailed the bill as passed by the legislature and declared it to be a "thoroughly bad measure."[33]

Local option and limiting the proximity of games to churches helped the measure to finally break through the Puritan wall of Sunday sports prohibition. In 1920, baseball could finally be played on Sunday in Massachusetts — at least by unpaid players.

A week later Coolidge signed another law that would impact the future of baseball in New England when he approved the bill to enact daylight saving time in Massachusetts. Despite the repeal of nationwide daylight saving time in 1919, which Congress passed via an override of President Wilson's veto, Massachusetts became one of the few states to continue operating on that time schedule.[34]

Daylight saving time set the foundation for the next revival of the New England League through the twilight leagues that sprang up in cities throughout Massachusetts in 1919. Teams of adult ball players in twilight leagues squared off on the diamond in games that began at 6:00 P.M. during the week. Because they were amateurs, twilight league teams could also play on Sunday afternoon (where permitted by local ordinance, which was just about everywhere in the state). Both the twilight games during the week and Sunday afternoon games attracted thousands of spectators, with baseball fans able to see quality play without an admission fee.

"Daylight saving and baseball have become synonymous. Popular interest in the 'twilight' baseball games during the season just coming to a close has been unmatched in the history of the sport," the *Boston Globe* wrote in September 1921. "Sunday baseball has proved to be immensely popular and sectional and intertown and district rivalry has enhanced the interest until it is not unusual for crowds of from 5,000, and in a few instances 10,000, to turn out to watch the local amateur and semiprofessional teams battle for supremacy."[35]

Daylight saving time had no direct impact on professional baseball in Massachusetts. Both the Braves and the Red Sox continued to play their games at 3:00, as did the Springfield and Worcester teams in the Eastern League. With no athletic competition after supper time, twilight leagues thrived and grew from strictly amatuer to semi-pro status in the early 1920s. With large crowds at Sunday games, twilight leagues also provided the foundation for crusaders to initiate action to expand the 1920 state law to apply not only to amatuers but also to professional players.

The Boston Twilight League, formed in 1922, was the percursor to the next revival of the New England League in 1926. When it came to demonstrating the twin impacts of daylight saving time and Sunday baseball — two legislative acts signed into law by then governor Calvin Coolidge, now vice president of the United States in the Harding administration — the Boston Twilight League had no peer.

In 1922, the Boston Twilight League consisted of eight teams. Half the teams were from the neighborhoods of Boston — Dorchester, Forest Hills, Roxbury, and South Boston — while the other four teams were from cities and towns in suburban Boston — Malden, Reading, Somerville, and North Cambridge.

It was the North Cambridge team, managed by Dan Leahy, a city councilman, that was the transformative catalyst for the league to springboard into bigger ventures. Attendance for weekday twilight games at Russell Field was typically several thousand, while on Sunday afternoons upwards of ten thousand spectators reportedly witnessed the games at Russell Field.

"Sunday Baseball Brings Out Thousands of Fans in the Greater Boston District," the *Boston Globe* headlined on May 29, 1922. The *Globe* reported that 15,000 spectators attended the ball game at Wood Island Park between teams from East Boston and Marblehead, while "more than 10,000 fans" saw the North Cambridge game against the Lafayette nine of Salem.[36]

Attendance was in the thousands for Sunday games because spectators came not just from Cambridge, but also from many other places since there was absolutely no high-level baseball competition on Sundays in 1922.

The Braves and Red Sox were prohibited by law from playing on Sunday at Braves Field and Fenway Park. On Sundays, the teams either took a one-game road trip to New York to play at the Polo Grounds or Ebbets Field, or played an exhibition game in Connecticut or Rhode Island. For instance, in July 1922, the Red Sox played in Windsor Locks, Connecticut, on July 9 against a team of college players and in Bristol, Connecticut, on July 16 against a semi-pro team, the New Departures.

With Providence no longer having a minor league team to stage Sunday baseball games, there were no minor league games within reasonable proximity of Boston. Worcester, the last former New England League city still in the Eastern League, was on the road every Sunday playing in either Albany, New York, where Sunday baseball was legal, or in the Connecticut cities of Bridgeport, New Haven, or Waterbury, where Sunday baseball was tolerated despite the law prohibiting it. Because four cities in the Eastern League could play Sunday baseball, the league could schedule a full slate of games on Sunday among its eight teams (Hartford, Springfield, and Pittsfield also played every Sunday on the road).

As a result, North Cambridge had a virtual monopoly in top-caliber baseball on Sunday. Because the Sunday games at Russell Field drew such huge crowds, the Lord's Day League not surprisingly looked into whether the North Cambridge team complied with the Sunday law. The Sabbatarian group found that the North Cambridge team skirted the Sunday law, as did many semi-pro teams, by taking up a collection during the game, either by a "pass the hat" approach or other informal process.

While the North Cambridge team did comply with the letter of the Sunday law by not charging an admission fee, the team did violate the spirit of the law by receiving "voluntary" contributions from spectators. Many, including the Lord's Day League, considered this to be a de facto admission fee. Some of these voluntary contributions could also find their way to the players, which would be a violation of the "no pecuniary reward" portion of the law, which clearly was written as "either directly or indirectly."

By mid–June, the Rev. Kneeland of the Lord's Day League was publicly criticizing the Sunday games in North Cambridge, saying "it was commonly known that from $1500 to $2000 was earned at Sunday baseball games in North Cambridge." At a meeting of Cambridge pastors, Kneeland also remarked:

The subject touching commercial baseball in Cambridge is part of a very large, important, up-to-date question. In my honest judgment of the spiritual over against the worldly, the battle must be fought out all over the country along the same line you are fighting it here in Cambridge — if America is to survive ... Jesus says the Sabbath was made for man and, of all the passages in the Bible, that passage has been the most distorted in its meaning by men who wish to break the Sabbath. I don't believe the physical and the mental sides of life should be developed at the expense of the moral and spiritual. I am a believer in the development of the physical in life, and it is better cared for today than ever before, but it must not be at the expense of the spiritual.[37]

The battle was fought over the Sunday, July 2, game at Russell Field in North Cambridge, when the Lord's Day League complained to the Cambridge Park Commission, which was responsible for issuing the license to play Sunday baseball.

At a hearing on July 6, the Rev. Kneeland testified about the conditions he observed that Sunday at Russell Field. According to the *Cambridge Chronicle*, Captain Henry of the police force testified that police at the game "saw three men at the gate who were receiving money from some of the people who passed in." Police inspector Neilan testified that "he saw men at the gate receiving money, but said he did not see the men say anything to any of the people passing in. He saw money in people's hands and saw men at the gate pick up money which had been dropped. Some went in without paying. He saw no demand for money." Patrolman Landrigan, in plain clothes, testified regarding solicitation, saying he "entered a gate and a man said to him, 'What do you say? Want to help the cause along?' When he asked, 'What's that?' the man replied, 'It's a fine day.'" The lawyer for the North Cambridge team "said his client would admit that money had been received but claimed that the men at the gate were not 'collecting.'"[38]

The Park Commission, sympathetic to Leahy's cause, referred the matter to the city solicitor to consider the matter of exactly what constituted a "collection," and approved a permit to play on Sunday, July 9. "More than 15,000 fans attended the game, which was played despite the agitation in regard to Sunday baseball at which spectators make contributions," the *Boston Globe* reported. "Two men stood at the gate of the field silently receiving voluntary contributions and most every fan of the thousands who attended made such a contribution."[39]

City Solicitor Nelligan reluctantly conceded that the money being taken at the Sunday games at Russell Field could be a violation of the Sunday law. The Park Commission then granted a permit for the Sunday, July 16, game with the "definite understanding that no money should be collected, received, or accepted on the grounds of the city." After the North Cambridge team disregarded that condition and took in voluntary contributions at the Sunday, July 16, game, the Lord's Day League elevated the matter to a higher legal authority.[40]

On July 20, Middlesex County District Attorney Endicott Saltonstall "threw down the gauntlet to the advocates of collections at the Sunday baseball games and told them flatly that the law would be enforced," after conditions in the permit for the July 16 game were "blazenly ignored." Saltonstall sent a letter to Cambridge Mayor Quinn, stating, "I understand it at these [Sunday] games one or more men received contributions from the spectators and this is absolutely prohibited by General Laws, chapter 136, section 24."[41]

"This decision of the district attorney sounds the death knell of the [Sunday] games for the North Cambridge Columbus club, as it has been generally understood that the players were not playing the game for exercise," the *Cambridge Chronicle* remarked. The game of Sunday, July 23, was expected to be the last for the North Cambridge team if collections could not be made. Only 5,000 fans attended the July 23 game, where an extensive police presence ensured that no contributions were made.[42]

Dan Leahy was not a man to be denied. He came up with the idea to charge a "subscription" to attend Sunday games, without collecting money at the games. On Sunday, August 6, North Cambridge resumed Sunday baseball before a crowd of 10,000. "No money was collected at the gates," the *Cambridge Chronicle* reported. "During the week, friends of the club contributed money in order that the Sunday games may continue."[43]

Close to 15,000 spectators attended the Sunday, August 20, game against Medford, a new entrant in the Boston Twilight League. A crowd of 25,000 packed Russell Field on Sunday, September 24, to see North Cambridge shut out the Lynn Cornets, 1–0, just a few days after North Cambridge had won the championship of the Boston Twilight League in a game at Lynn.

Attendance was spectacular for these late-season games, but "subscription" receipts likely were not, requiring Leahy to find another way around the Sunday law. In 1923, he came up with the idea to sell ice cream at inflated prices outside the ball grounds as a substitute for contributions. This was quickly exposed as a ruse to avert the Sunday law.

Middlesex Country District Attorney Arthur Reading wrote a letter to the Cambridge Park Commission that the Sunday law had been violated "by charging an admission fee indirectly under the pretext that ice cream was being sold." The *Cambridge Chronicle* reported that "spectators were directed by men at the gate to 'get your ice cream over there' pointing to a small stand located a short distance away. Those who accepted the invitation found that small bricks of ice cream were on sale, accompanied by a small red ticket.

The price for the ice cream/ticket combination was anything you want to give." Leahy's statement that his baseball team "is not connected with the private sale of refreshments outside of Russell Field" fell on deaf ears.[44]

Leahy next tried band concerts, for a fee, which preceded a free baseball game afterwards. Crowds of 12,000 showed up for the Sunday, June 17, game and 15,000 for the Sunday, July 8, game with Lawrence. By July, though, permits for the band concerts were being denied. Leahy's next tactic to finance Sunday baseball landed him in court. In August, "near the entrance to the field was a box, above which was a sign telling of the restrictions in regard to collections and asking the fans to deposit their opinions in the box. It is alleged that money was deposited in the box."[45]

In September, Leahy was found guilty of violating the Sunday baseball law and fined $5. But he never paid the fine. "I'll never pay that fine," Leahy shouted during an outburst at a Cambridge City Council meeting in November. "I'll go to jail first. Some day we'll find out whether the courts are above petty, bigoted ideas. Sunday baseball is going to be one of the big State issues." In December, the court set aside the fine when Leahy agreed not to appeal his case further.[46]

North Cambridge continued in the Boston Twilight League in 1924 and played Sunday games without taking up collections. "No attempt at collections was made [at the May 11 Sunday game]," the *Cambridge Chronicle* reported. "But it was announced that tickets for Tuesday's game could be secured at the club's headquarters after the game and the Sunday games could be continued without charge if the receipts for the week-day games were large enough to carry the expense."[47]

Sunday games continued through the 1924 season, but with weekday receipts probably insufficient to cover lost revenue on Sundays, North Cambridge dropped out of the league before the 1925 season. Dan Leahy's loss in the November 1924 election for U.S. Congress from the Eighth District may also have had a part in that decision.

By 1925, the now Greater Boston Twilight League contained few teams from the immediate Boston area. North Cambridge dropped out the league. There was a team from South Boston and a Dilboy team from nearby Somerville, but most of the remaining teams hailed from cities far to the north and northwest of Boston, including two from New Hampshire (Nashua and Manchester). In the Merrimack River Valley, Lawrence fielded a team as did Abbott Worsted, a textile mill in Westford. Closer to Boston were teams from Lynn, Malden, and Salem.

The inclusion of two New Hampshire teams in the Greater Boston Twilight League was interesting not just from its geographic stretching of the definition of "greater Boston." New Hampshire did not observe daylight saving time, by law operating on standard time all year long, thus stretching the boundaries of what constituted "twilight" baseball. Nashua and Manchester "officially kept standard time to avoid a $500 state fine," historian David Prevan wrote in his book, *Seize the Daylight: The Curious and Contentious Story of Daylight Saving Time*. "But many businesses advanced work time one hour to keep in step with Boston and other New England municipalities."[48]

Abbott Worsted took up the cudgel of Sunday baseball in the absence of North Cambridge, playing Lawrence in several games during July in a bucolic setting in Westford. "There is no place in the entire circuit like Abbott Park to see a ball game," the *Lowell Courier-Citizen* remarked. "The entire layout suggests big league stuff, except surrounding scenery, and the big leagues never did and never will have vistas like those at Westford."[49]

South Boston, which played a few Sunday games itself, had to drop out of the league in late July when its owner, Jim Newton, died in an automobile accident. The independent semi-pro team in Lowell was recruited to replace South Boston for the latter part of the season. Lowell, which played to audiences comprised of textile mill workers, joined Abbott Worsted in hosting Sunday games at its local ball park in defiance of the Sunday baseball law. On Sunday, August 16, Lowell hosted Nashua before 6,000 spectators at Alumni Field, "the biggest crowd that has been seen at Alumni Field since the palmy days of the old New England League."[50]

However, the large Sunday crowds began to draw attention from the authorities, much as had occurred in North Cambridge. Another 6,000 crammed into Alumni Field the following Sunday to see Lowell defeat Lynn, 7–4, which was the last Sunday game of the season for the Twilight League. "The minions of the law were present, and they objected to the collection at the gate," the *Lowell Courier-Citizen* reported. "It was optional with customers whether they paid or not, but the limbs of the law took exception to any cash changing hands.[51]

By August, the Greater Boston Twilight League had grander ambitions than simply pushing the geographic boundaries of the meaning "greater." The league had its sights set on becoming an official minor league. "While the various team owners are not saying much about it, there is reason to believe that the cities of this section now in the Greater Boston league will enter organized baseball next season. Also the name of the league will be changed to suit the territory. The Greater Boston league is a myth at the present time. Nearly all the original teams have dropped out, and the breadth of life is made possible in the outfit by teams quite apart from Boston."[52]

In August 1925, the legality of professional Sunday baseball in Massachusetts seemed just around the corner. In February 1925, the Legislative Committee on Legal Affairs held hearings on a proposed initiative petition to put the Sunday baseball question on the ballot for voters to decide. The Sunday baseball voter initiative began in 1923, when long-time New England minor league manager and owner Fred Doe, backed by the management of the Boston Braves, collected 26,000 signatures to force the legislature to act. If the legislature then failed to enact the Sunday baseball bill, and if another 5,000 signatures were collected, the question would be put to the voters at the next state-wide election.[53]

Even though it had been nearly five years since the amateur Sunday sports bill had been passed by the Massachusetts legislature, its opponents hadn't forgotten how that bill came to be. Horace Cole of the Massachusetts Civic League found himself now standing with the Lord's Day League. Cole said that he believed in Sunday sports as much as ever, "but there is a sharp distinction between legalizing amateur sports and encouraging our youth to sit on a board Sunday afternoon to watch hired players." Added the Rev. A.Z. Conrad, "I have been at hearings on amateur Sunday sports and heard these same men lift their hands and swear to Heaven they never would desecrate the Sabbath by charging admissions to a ball game. How they have the gall to come now and ask for admissions is beyond me."[54]

The proponents were outgunned at the committee meeting, as their arguments fell on deaf legislative ears. "Forty-one thousand New Bedford mill workers who now never get a chance to see a Boston ball game without taking a day off can have such a chance on Sunday," argued ex-Mayor Ashley of New Bedford. "There is nothing new in commercializing Sunday," said ex-Attorney General Herbert Parker, who said people will not tolerate the rigors of the New England Sabbath and that the concept of the Puritan Sabbath had passed. "The present law is based on subterfuge," Parker added, since money was being covertly paid to players for Sunday baseball.[55]

When the House defeated the bill, 152–51, and the Senate voted it down, 25–7, Doe and his troops (including the Boston Braves' management) charged on and looked toward the 1926 state election to get their initiative petition before the voters.

In August 1925, Doe filed 17,206 signatures — far more than the 5,000 required — with the Secretary of State to get the question on the November 1926 ballot. "The question of whether professional baseball games may be played on Sundays in Massachusetts will be on the ballot for approval or rejection by voters at the 1926 election," the *Boston Post* reported in its article "Sunday Ball on Ballot."[56]

The foundation for the next revival of the New England League, in 1926, had been laid.

9

Davidson Revives
League, 1926–1930

WITH MASSACHUSETTS VOTERS EXPECTED TO overwhelmingly approve the
Sunday baseball question to be contained on the ballot for the November
1926 state election, and thus legalize Sunday baseball, the New England
League restarted operations in 1926 in a fourth revival of the venerable minor
league.

Claude Davidson, a twenty-nine-year-old former ball player turned baseball promoter and administrator as president of the Boston Twilight League,
led the effort to revive the New England League, which had last successfully
completed a full season in 1915. Davidson anticipated that twilight games,
starting at 5:00 or 5:30 in the late afternoon, would fortify the New England
League ball clubs enough to survive the 1926 season. Then after the voters
approved a more liberal Sunday law for professional baseball games, the New
England League could play Sunday games during the 1927 season.

The basis for Davidson's plan to bring the league financial success was
to play its games at times more conducive to the average worker being able
to attend the games — in the evening and on Sunday. It was the first time in
the league's history that such an explicit campaign was targeted to have mill
workers be the lynchpin to financial success. "The later starting time for the
games which appealed to followers of the Twilight League is easily seen as the
biggest thing in favor of the success of the present league," noted a January
1926 newspaper article based on a Davidson interview. "The mill employees
of Lawrence, Manchester and Lowell and the shoe workers of Lynn will receive
the benefit of the later opening and they are the most loyal followers of the
game."[1]

With such an auspicious outlook for Sunday baseball, Davidson was able to line up local ownership for several cities such as Lowell and Lynn in Massachusetts and Manchester, New Hampshire, that had teams in the Twilight League during 1925 to elevate them to minor league status for the 1926 season. Other teams were located to suit influential backers, such as the team in Portland, Maine, that was owned by Fred Doe, the ardent proponent of the Sunday baseball initiative in Massachusetts.[2]

Who was Claude Davidson? And why was he so passionate to revive the New England League?

Davidson was born in the Dorchester section of Boston on October 13, 1896, the son of Mayberry and Mary (Boucher) Davidson. His father, a printer, worked his way up to an executive-level position as president of Wilkins Press. Davidson played baseball for two years at Dorchester High School before attending a prep school, the Volkmann School (now the Noble & Greenough School), where he played two more years of baseball. Upon graduation from Volkmann in 1915, Davidson enrolled at Brown University in Providence, Rhode Island.[3]

The left-handed hitting Davidson refined his baseball skills as a third baseman in two years of varsity play at Brown. He also likely gained an appreciation for the merits of Sunday games while in Providence since the local minor league team played Sunday games at the Rocky Point resort fifteen miles down Narragansett Bay from Providence. The raucous crowds at the Sunday games at Rocky Point were a stark contrast to the staid, quiet Sundays that Davidson remembered while growing up in Boston.

A rainy day on May 2, 1917, when Brown played at Boston College, provided the big break Davidson needed to advance into the professional ranks. "Davidson had at least two big league scouts giving him the 'up and down,'" the *Providence Journal* reported the next day. "Several members of the Philadelphia Athletics ball club, whose game with the Red Sox was called off on account of rain, watched the game with interest, centering their attention on the Brown infielders."[4]

Having gained the attention of Philadelphia manager Connie Mack, Davidson left Brown after his sophomore year to join the Athletics for the 1918 season. Davidson played in thirty-one games with Philadelphia, mostly as a second baseman and outfielder for the last-place Athletics, but was a weak hitter, batting just .185 in eighty-one at-bats. Philadelphia played Sunday games on the road in Chicago, Cleveland, Detroit, and St. Louis as well as in Washington, D.C., where the law was changed in 1918 to legally permit Sunday games. Davidson saw that Mack was not averse to sending his team on a train down to Washington to play just one game there on Sunday before returning to Philadelphia to play on Monday afternoon; such was the popularity of Sunday baseball.

Davidson played most of the 1919 season with the New Haven club of the Eastern League, where he gained an even greater appreciation for Sunday games. The New Haven team played home games on Sunday at its regular park, not in an isolated location like Providence had at Rocky Point, in the most blatant example he had observed of a ball club not observing the Sunday laws in New England.

In September 1919, he briefly joined the Washington Senators, where in two games he collected three hits in eight at-bats before badly injuring his foot. In an article entitled "Claude Davidson Laid Up With a Poisoned Foot," the *Boston Globe* reported, "He has been in bed for a week, and yesterday was the first time he had been able to stand on the foot. Davidson does not expect to go back to the Washington club this season, as his physician has advised him not to play again this year."[5]

Davidson's professional baseball career was over, partly due to the injured foot, but probably equally due to his fight to collect unpaid salary. In January 1920, the National Commission ruled that Washington had to pay Davidson through the end of the 1919 season since he hadn't "quit of his own accord" as the Washington club had contended. While his baseball playing career was over, Davidson's administrative career in baseball was just beginning to warm up.[6]

During his first year out of baseball in 1920, Davidson went back to Boston and worked mornings as a clerk at Commonwealth Trust Company. In the afternoons he pursued a baseball-related occupation as freshman baseball coach at Harvard University, a position he would hold for eleven years. As an ambitious person like his father, Davidson sought upward mobility. He also needed more income to support his growing family, as his son Robert was born in December 1920, the only child of his October 1917 marriage to his cousin, Abigail Ruth Davidson.

As a personable fellow who knew many people, Davidson in 1922 became president of the Boston Twilight League. After four years of successfully expanding the Twilight League, Davidson leveraged that success to bring the New England League back into the minor league fold. "The youngest minor league in Organized Baseball — the Class B New England circuit — also has the youngest president," the *Sporting News* touted Davidson, the budding baseball executive.[7]

Davidson thought there was a need for a professional league that would fill the void between the not-so-good Boston pro teams and the pretty-good semi-pro teams in the region like the ones in the Twilight League. In 1925, this market segment was occupied only by the Worcester team in the Eastern League, a faltering team that moved to Providence for the 1926 season.

It wasn't an easy task for Davidson, though. Sunday baseball was now legal in New York, Rhode Island, and Connecticut (as of July 1925). Most of the region's largest cities, outside of Boston, were either franchises in the Eastern League where Sunday baseball thrived or had suffered a major economic setback due to the decline of the textile industry. This left out of consideration such long-time New England League locations as Fall River and New Bedford.

Davidson focused on cities where the shoe industry was still dominant in order to recruit economically viable baseball fran-

Claude Davidson orchestrated three revivals of the New England League, in 1926, 1933, and 1946. He labored indefatigably in his quest to keep minor league baseball alive in New England (© The Sporting News/ZUMA).

chises for the rebirth of the league. The foundation of the 1926 league lineup was four cities with strong shoe economies — Lynn and Haverhill in Massachusetts, holdovers from the league's 1907–1912 heyday; Manchester, New Hampshire; and Lewiston, Maine — along with Portland, Maine, with its diversified economy.

But to create an eight-team league, Davidson was forced to accept teams in three old, textile-dominated cities suffering from the declining Merrimack River Valley economy — Lawrence and Lowell in Massachusetts and Nashua, New Hampshire.

Lowell almost immediately collapsed, lasting only a dozen games before the franchise was transferred to another city. Adding to the demise of the Lowell team was the unusual way that it lost its catcher just one week into the season:

Forrest Duncan, star backstop of the Lowell baseball team of the New England League, was held in $20,000 bail yesterday afternoon by Lawrence police following his arrest on a charge of robbery. The police accuse him of being the lone gunman who held up and robbed a paymaster of $12,000 at the Wood mill, October 3, 1925. Duncan was a millwright by trade and had worked at the Wood mill for 12 years, and was absent from work the morning of the robbery. Duncan asserted that he was in Fisherville on the day in question, in connection with his baseball activities, but this alibi, the police claim, has been exploded.[8]

Duncan was unfairly victimized by the legal system at the time. When questioned by the Lawrence police, Duncan "maintained his innocence throughout the severe grilling," which according to the *Lawrence Eagle* lasted twelve hours. Duncan pleaded not guilty at his arraignment, but because he couldn't post the bail amount, he spent the next four months in the Essex County Jail awaiting trial. Finally, on September 17, a grand jury rendered a "no bill" decision, indicating that the prosecution had insufficient evidence to prove the case, and Duncan was released from jail.[9]

Duncan joined the Lawrence fire department in 1928. He served the city as a fireman for thirty-two years, the last three years as fire chief, before retiring in 1960. He was also a champion blood donor. "The chief is Greater Lawrence's leading blood donor," the *Lawrence Eagle-Tribune* reported on the eve of his retirement. "Friday as he contemplated his retirement, he recalled that his first blood donation was made in Jersey City, New Jersey, in 1921 when a fellow player (the chief was a professional baseball player in his youth) broke his leg, complications set in, and donations of blood were needed." The retirement article briefly mentioned that he "played with the Lowell team in the New England League in 1926" along with his other baseball stops and his numerous promotions within the fire department. Duncan died in 1974, with his arrest and four-month jail term in 1926 long forgotten and left unnoted in either the retirement article or his obituary.[10]

While its catcher Duncan sat in jail, the Lowell franchise was transferred in early June to a once-vibrant New England League city, but one that hadn't witnessed a league contest since 1892 — Salem, Massachusetts.

Twilight baseball was "not a paying proposition" for Lowell. The *Lowell Courier-Citizen* blamed the team's failure on the half-dollar admission charge and lack of cooperation from the street car company to lower fares from ten cents to five cents from Kearney Square, in downtown Lowell, to remote Alumni Field, on the Lowell-Tewksbury line. It was simply inconvenient for spectators to go to a 5:45 ball game after finishing work while costing almost a dollar in transportation and admission for most people to attend. In comparison, there were two twilight leagues in the city that featured local players and no admission charge. As for Salem, since its team in the Greater Boston Twilight League had lost money the past two seasons, "Possibly the man down there is willing to assume a further loss in anticipation of Sunday baseball next year," the *Courier-Citizen* remarked.[11]

The usual bleak New England spring also chilled the evening game experiment. In the league's first twilight contest on May 10, at 5:45 at O'Sullivan Park in Lawrence, only 1,000 people showed up in cold and threatening weather to see Lewiston defeat Lawrence, 6–2. The local newspaper understatedly observed, "The New England League opened inauspiciously as far as Lawrence is concerned last night."[12]

Lawrence not only had the first twilight game in 1926, but also the inaugural Sunday game. Lawrence owner Bill McDonough jumped the gun on Sunday baseball when he "pre-arranged" with local authorities to play a game with Nashua on Sunday, July 4. The game was designed to be a prelude to the holiday doubleheader held on Monday, July 5, when Independence Day was officially observed that year because the Fourth fell on a Sunday. About 1,500 spectators showed up for the first Sunday game played in the New England League since 1909.[13]

The timing of McDonough's trial of Sunday baseball, coming some four months before the November election at which voters would pass judgment on the legality of Sunday baseball, was especially sticky because three weeks earlier a legal challenge to the voter initiative had been set in motion by the Lord's Day League, which cast doubt on the wording of the voter petitions.

"Two years ago when the initiative petitions were circulated to place the matter before the Legislature, some 26,000 signers affixed their names to a document calling for the legalizing of 'Sunday sports.' After the matter was defeated last year in the Legislature, it became necessary to obtain 5000 additional signatures in order to place the issue on the ballot, but this time the signers approved a petition which would authorize 'Sunday baseball' alone," reported the *Christian Science Monitor* on the apparent legal snafu. The Lord's Day League contended "because in one case voters favored Sunday sports, which is a much broader term, and in the other case approved only Sunday baseball ... the matter would be illegally placed on the ballot."[14]

The eight New England League teams feverishly fought red ink to finish out the 1926 season in expectation of financial redemption through Sunday baseball games in 1927 that could be authorized by Massachusetts voters in November. Manchester won the New England League title in 1926 after the Labor Day twin bills were rained out, and then played a postseason series with Scranton, the champion of the New York-Penn League. Scranton swept Manchester in four games to win the series, which concluded on September 17. Hours later on the morning of September 18, the highest court in Massachusetts ruled in favor of the Lord's Day League appeal and ordered the Secretary of State to strike from the November ballot the Sunday baseball question.

"It is manifest that there are substantial differences between the proposed law and the description of it contained in the initiative petition signed by not less than 20,000 voters, on the one hand, and the description of it contained in the additional petition, signed by 5000 voters, on the other hand," the *Boston Globe* reported on the court ruling in a front-page article headlined, "Sunday Sports Law Not to Appear on Ballot."[15]

Coming as it did in a Saturday morning session of the court following the completion of the New England League season, with athletic attention squarely focused on football, the court ruling certainly seemed to have been perfectly timed to inflict maximum damage with minimum public exposure. Since the next possible time to get on the ballot was November 1928, the league would have to endure two more years before it could schedule Sunday games.

A few weeks later, Davidson dodged what would have been a fatal bullet to the league when the U.S. Supreme Court upheld the legality of the daylight saving time law in Massachusetts (most states, and the federal government, operated on standard time during the entire year). The Massachusetts State Grange, a group of farmers, opposed the law as "unconstitutional because it deprived persons of property without compensation." The Supreme Court didn't agree with the grange. If daylight saving time were to be declared illegal, then twilight games would not be possible and the New England League would have to disband.[16]

"The little New England League finished the season of 1926 under anything but the best of conditions," the *Sporting News* reported in October. "Handicapped almost all season by unfavorable weather, the league certainly stormed a rough voyage and finished intact. It is said that most of the clubs were on the short end financially... The failure of Sunday baseball in Massachusetts to get on the ballot this fall hit the league hard. The owners were looking forward to next year with legalized Sunday baseball."[17]

Davidson eventually issued a statement saying "the league will positively function the coming season," which the *Sporting News* noted was issued after Davidson had done "a lot of missionary work with the owners." Davidson had to use the best sales skills he could possibly muster to convince eight owners to weather another two years before their financial ship would finally arrive.[18]

Without the availability of Sunday baseball, Davidson needed something to stimulate season-long interest in the New England League in order to help assure the league would survive the 1927 season. Davidson took the bold move of adopting a split-season schedule, a tactic only the lowest minor leagues used to keep fans coming to the games. But he knew once the first half ended, a competitive second half would kindle interest through most of the summer and keep paying customers coming to the ballpark.

The New England League had considered adopting a split-season arrangement for the 1915 season, when the Federal League was ravaging spectator interest in the minor leagues throughout the country. However, the league rejected the idea as overly detrimental to the process of determining the league champion. A few leagues did use the split-season format during the war years, among them the Class A Western League in 1917, but in the post-war years only leagues at the Class C and D levels, for the most part, used split seasons.

The one exception was the Texas League, then a Class B league. However, the experience of the Texas League with the split-season format caused the concept to fall into serious disrepute during the 1920s. Its inaugural use in 1919 worked fine, with Shreveport winning the first half and Fort Worth taking the second half, resulting in an exciting best-of-seven-games playoff series won by Shreveport, four games to two with one tie.

It was the last time for six seasons, however, that the Fort Worth Panthers would finish second in the Texas League to any team, as "Atz's Cats," managed by legendary Jake Atz, completely dominated the Texas League competition. Over the next three years, 1920 to 1922, Fort Worth won both halves of all three seasons to torpedo the purpose of the split-season format. After a return to a full-season pennant race in 1923 (which Fort Worth ran away with by thirteen games), the now Class A Texas League tried the split-season format again in 1924 and 1925 — with Fort Worth once again winning both halves.

Against this legacy of split-season play, Davidson convinced the New England League owners that the concept would work in their league. Davidson would either make the concept work or the New England League would go out of business trying. In 1927, the New England League was the highest classification minor league to use the split-season format. Although it was the only Class B organization to use a split-season schedule, the trend was firmly taking hold in lower classifications. Three of the four Class C leagues that year used the format as did six of the seven Class D leagues.

Davidson was a pioneer, as the split-season concept rapidly took hold among higher classification minor leagues during the remainder of the 1920s. One year later, in 1928, four of the six Class B leagues had adopted a split-season schedule as had three of the four Class A leagues. Of the three highest classification leagues, those in Class AA, the Pacific Coast League adopted the split season in 1929.

After being outfoxed on a technicality with the initiative petition targeted for the 1926 state ballot, Sunday baseball proponents worked harder for the next attempt to change the Sunday law. In March 1927, the professional Sunday sports bill was actually reported favorably out of the Legal Affairs Committee by a sliver of a margin, eight votes to seven. Proponents at the March 9 hearing emphasized the health of the youthful population who would benefit by attending games when they couldn't actually participate in them. They also strengthened their argument about under-the-table payments to players by showing that police were aware of the actions but did nothing to stop it. Thus, if the law was to be broken time after time, legislation should be enacted.[19]

By now, nearly seven years after the passage of the amateur Sunday sports bill in 1920, the arguments of opponents — that it was bad faith on the part of bill supporters to agitate further on the subject — were beginning to fall on deaf ears. A week after the hearing, the bill's margin of defeat in the House of Representatives narrowed, by a vote of 129 to 98.

The change in the nation's attitude toward Sunday was becoming evident in Massachusetts. What was once firmly believed by most to be a "day of rest" was being transformed into a "day of leisure."

"Rep. Spear of Everett spoke for the opposition, asserting that those who were in favor of the bill were largely those who are financially interested in Sunday sports; those opposed believe in the Sabbath," the *Boston Herald* reported. "Rep. Kirkpatrick of Holyoke spoke for the bill, saying that those opposing it sit in their motor cars on Sunday [while driving them] and say that this bill is a violation of the Sabbath. Sunday is already desecrated and this bill will not add to the desecration" that movies and Vaudeville already had by being permitted on Sunday.[20]

With the opponents of Sunday sports becoming more polarized, and the proponents appealing even more to the concerns of the general population, the outlook seemed favorable for the legality of Sunday professional sports.

Despite the disappointment over not being able to conduct Sunday games, all eight league cities in 1926 returned for the 1927 season. Davidson promoted the Chamber of Commerce aspects of having a New England League ball club in a city, pushing the concept that "representation in Organized Baseball is splendid publicity for a city." He lobbied various civic and service organizations in each city in the league to drum up support for the ball clubs, which "amounts to the sale of hundreds of season tickets ... that assures sufficient patronage to maintain a club." Baseball was no longer the only entertainment in town. Most movie theaters were air conditioned by the mid–1920s, a definite draw during the hot summer months; in 1927 the "talkies" began to replace the silent movies, which further drew people away from the ball park.[21]

Another concept that Davidson advanced that season was the idea of playing baseball games at night under artificial lighting. During the summer of 1927, Davidson arranged with engineers from General Electric to stage an exhibition baseball game under floodlights at the General Electric Employees Athletic Association field on Summer Street in Lynn. There they tested out the idea of playing professional baseball at night, when it was the most convenient time for workers to go to a ballpark without interfering with their work hours.

The exhibition game was initially set for June 23. The date coordinated with the getaway date of the New York Yankees leaving Boston after its series with the Red Sox at Fenway Park so that Babe Ruth could play in the exhibition game. Davidson believed that the Babe's appearance would provide an incentive for more spectators to come watch the newfangled concept of night baseball.

Weather fouled up Davidson's plan, though, as rain on the night of June 23 forced a postponement of the experimental game to the following evening, June 24. Ruth, though, had another commitment on June 24 that involved playing with the Yankees in an exhibition game in Springfield, Massachusetts, on the team's way back to New York City. Ruth hit two home runs in Springfield and helped attract 8,000 spectators to the ballpark, which the *Springfield Union* called "the largest crowd that ever witnessed a ball game in Springfield."[22]

With the weather cooperating on June 24, two New England League teams — Lynn and Salem — took their positions on the GE field "playing under an arrangement of projections that approximated daylight conditions" in the "first night game ever attempted by organized league teams." Lynn defeated Salem, 7–2, in a seven-inning contest, which the *Lynn Evening Item* headlined the next day as "Floodlight Baseball Game at G.E. Field Draws 5000 Fans."[23]

Members of the Boston Red Sox and the Washington Senators, who were in Boston for a series at Fenway Park, attended the June 24 game in Lynn. The managers of both teams issued encouraging remarks to the press after the experimental night game about playing major league exhibitions under lights. Washington outfielder Goose Goslin spoke very favorably about the night game. "I didn't believe they could do it," Goslin said. "It's just as good ball as they could play by daylight."[24]

Also attending the game was fifteen-year-old William "Chub" Fallon. "It was quite a thrill," Fallon, then ninety years old, remarked in the *Boston Globe* in 2002 in a seventy-fifth anniversary retrospective on the night game. "I couldn't figure out at first how they could see the ball. But the illumination was very good, and you could follow the ball quite well."[25]

The wizardry of the GE engineers had created what must have seemed like a surreal scene to the thousands of spectators at the experimental night game. "Four floodlight projectors lighted up the 'ceiling' of the General Electric field so that outfielders had no trouble with high flies," one account described the lighting technology. "These floodlights carried a volume of 500,000 mean candlepower. The field itself was lighted by seventy-two projectors which gave an estimated volume of 26,640,000 candlepower."[26]

In an article later that year in *Baseball Magazine*, F.W. Ralston, the GE engineer in charge of the lighting at the June 24 game, explained the background about how the GE engineers had created an outdoor lighting system sufficient to play a baseball game:

> For ten years or more, numerous attempts have been made to interest both players and spectators in night sports. It wasn't until 1923 that we took the matter seriously. At that time we were asked to illuminate the G.E. field in Lynn for a celebration. The lights were turned on for adjusting and focusing on the night preceding the affair, and we were surprised to see the boys of the neighborhood play a baseball game. That gave us the definite idea of lighting a baseball diamond.[27]

In August 1923, a night baseball game was played on the GE field between the Polish National Alliance and the Midnight Wanderers, which drew 5,000 curious persons to watch. "Baseball by floodlight was played last night at the new General Electric field, but the demonstration proved that Old Sol has no need to worry," the *Lynn Evening Item* reported. "The rays of light were centered on the diamond and balls hit to the infield were handled almost as well as in the daylight. High batted flies to the outfield proved hard to follow."[28]

Four years later after some engineering improvements in lighting, things looked more auspicious for baseball to be played at night on a regular basis. After the June 24 game, Davidson optimistically "predicted that within five years, night baseball would be played in all leagues."[29]

But the traditional-bound baseball world, run by conservative men, didn't latch onto the novel idea right away. The *Sporting News* called that night game "the stunt" in a brief note buried in agate type far from the front page. New England League owners, already hurting for profits, were not in a position to invest in the technology to use lights in the league's ballparks.[30]

The inaugural postseason playoff spawned by the split-season format pitted the winners of the first and second halves. The "Little World Series,"

The first baseball game played under artificial lights by professional league teams was played in the New England League in 1927. As noted in this headline from the *Lynn Evening Item*, 5,000 people witnessed the historic event.

as Davidson promoted the postseason clash, generated good crowds and bid well for the future. Lynn, the winner of the first half, trounced Portland, the second half winner, in four straight games to take the New England League championship. More than 3,000 spectators attended each game, with a league-record crowd of 4,461 attending the Saturday game in Lynn on September 10 when Lynn, managed by local hero Tom Whelan, won the fourth and final game of the series.

After the series, Lynn engaged in another exhibition night game, defeating a local semi-pro team, the Cornet Stars, at the GE field in front of 2,500 fans. "The lighting arrangement on the field was more efficient than in the previous game the Lynn club played three months ago and the spectators could follow the ball a mite closer," the *Evening Item* reported. "The G.E. engineers have made considerable improvement on the lighting effects and appear to have taken several strides in the direction for playing baseball under cover of darkness."[31]

While the experimental night games in Lynn posed some interesting possibilities, baseball played by daylight would remain the rule in the New England League for many years to come. Of more immediate concern to Davidson and the New England League magnates was the ability to play ball games on Sunday since the New England League was the last minor league in the country lacking the ability to play on Sunday.

At the 1928 hearings on that year's Sunday sports bill, proponents lined up clergymen to speak on behalf of the bill to solidify their position. "I think Christ would be in favor of anything that would give the youth of the country honest recreation," the Rev. Paul Sterling of Melrose said at the hearings. "If I can play golf on Sunday, if I can go to a movie theatre on Sunday, I don't see why I shouldn't be allowed to see a good game of baseball."[32]

Despite the growing wave of acceptance for the concept, the House once again voted down the measure. The 110 to 93 vote was an even closer margin than in 1927; a change of sentiment in only nine votes would have passed the bill.[33]

Proponents had no trouble obtaining the required 5,000 signatures to put the matter on the November 1928 ballot as a voter referendum question. Since it was a presidential election year, a large number of voters sympathetic to the cause of Sunday baseball were likely to vote. And this time, proponents ensured that the bureaucracy didn't do them in.

Despite Davidson's efforts to promote the New England League and entice spectators to its ballparks, without the ability to play Sunday games it remained a trying time for owners to make money playing twilight ball. Portland, under manager Duffy Lewis, was the only team to clear a profit in 1927. "All other clubs dropped a bit of money, but it is expected that they will come back for more next year," the *Sporting News* reported after the season concluded in an article entitled "New England League Hasn't Found Rainbow."[34]

Only six of the eight cities returned for the 1928 season, with the Lawrence team moving to Attleboro and the Haverhill club transferring to Brockton. Because Davidson believed the city of Haverhill remained a viable spot for New England League baseball, he arranged for the shift of the Nashua team to Haverhill.

Davidson helped convince the Attleboro Chamber of Commerce to support the move of the Lawrence team to the city. Attleboro, known for its jewelry business, was a small city in southeastern Massachusetts located on the state line adjacent to Pawtucket, Rhode Island. Davidson emphasized the civic pride that having a minor league baseball team would bring to the city and its inhabitants, as well as the benefits that Sunday baseball would have if it were legalized for the 1929 season.

If the Chamber could raise $5,000 by convincing local businessmen to purchase 200 season tickets (at $25 each), Bill McDonough, owner of the Lawrence team, would have enough money to pay off his Lawrence partners ($3,000) with enough left to start fresh in Attleboro. Davidson then estimated that 800 additional people per game, at a fifty-cent admission price, would carry the team through the season.[35]

The *Attleboro Sun* reported that Walter Kendall, president of the Chamber of Commerce, was suspicious that his city was being used as a way station for just one season "or until such time as a more favorable field opens." Left unsaid by the *Sun* was the concern that McDonough had selected Attleboro simply for its close proximity to Rhode Island, where Sunday baseball was legal, so that he could easily stage Sunday exhibition games in Rhode Island to gain additional revenue. Since there was no local ownership of the team, once Sunday baseball was legal in Massachusetts, as anticipated in 1929, McDonough would have no further use for Attleboro and would transfer the team to a larger, more lucrative, city.[36]

"I am glad that such a real baseball city as Attleboro will be in the New England League this season," Davidson announced with an extra-large dose of promotional spin. "It means original ball for Attleboro. Much faster than the ordinary semi-pro games; for the league it means the acquisition of a baseball community that will appreciate the heads up baseball that will be played there."[37]

The citizens of Attleboro did support the Burros, as the team was called. On opening day at Hayward Field, a crowd of 1,307 showed up to watch Portland defeat Attleboro. When Attleboro quickly moved into first place after twelve games with a 9–3 record, hundreds attended the team's games. Although Attleboro finished in first place during the first half of the season, fan support dwindled when evidence to support Kendall's skepticism about McDonough began to seep into public.

"Burros to Play at Fall River, Talk Transfer" blared the *Attleboro Sun* headline on June 29, referring to the scheduling of a league game against Salem on Sunday at Mark's Stadium in Tiverton, Rhode Island, just across the state line from Fall River. "McDonough has agreed to play league games at the Stadium every Sunday from now on," the *Sun* reprinted a report from the *Fall River Herald*. "If the patronage warrants it, he will transfer the team to this city."[38]

"McDonough, who despite the fact that his team is leading the circuit, does not believe it is receiving the support it deserves," the *Fall River Globe* reported. "For the remainder of the season, or until Attleboro transfers its franchise to this city, the Attleboro team will represent Fall River on Sundays."[39]

The Sunday exhibition game on July 1, which drew only 600 spectators, ended in a 5–5 tie when rain stopped play after ten innings. McDonough's Sunday experiment was a dismal failure financially, even though the game was staged at a "new park laid out by Sam Mark at considerable expense and with a diamond that has been carefully curried and put in shape."[40]

Tiverton, Rhode Island, was not conveniently located to attract numerous baseball fans, even for the novelty of a Sunday game played by professional ballplayers. Two weeks later on July 15, Mark enticed the Chicago White Sox of the American League to come to Tiverton on the Sunday off-day during the team's series with the Boston Red Sox. Even with major league competition as an attraction, "less than 1,200 made the trip to the Stadium" to see the White Sox defeat a Fall River team.[41]

By winning the first half and gaining a guaranteed spot in the New England League playoffs, Attleboro had little incentive to play hard during the second half. If the team won the second half, there would be no playoff and McDonough would forego the revenue he'd receive from the playoff games. By the end of July, Attleboro was in last place in the second half standings.

On July 22, McDonough tried out a Sunday exhibition game in Woonsocket, Rhode Island. With tepid attendance at that game, McDonough abandoned the Sunday game experiment and began cutting expenses to improve his bottom line. In August he released Bob Gill for the public reason that "age gets him," even though he was leading the New England League in hitting; the real reason, of course, was to avoid paying Gill his stipulated salary.[42]

Attleboro finished in seventh place in the second half and met Lynn, the second half winner, in the postseason.

Without outdoor lighting systems, the early sunsets in September were a problem for the twilight games in the playoff series, as every game played during the workweek ended before the regulation nine innings could be completed. Attleboro won the first game on September 11, which ended after seven innings due to darkness. Lynn won the next three games (including a 4–3 victory on Saturday, September 15, that did go nine innings). Attleboro took the next two games to tie the series, with the sixth game on Tuesday, September 18, having to be stopped after six innings.

Davidson then decided to postpone the seventh and deciding game of the series to Saturday, September 22, so that it could be played in the afternoon in Lynn with sufficient time to get in nine innings. Lynn defeated Attleboro, 14–7, in the seventh game to cop its second consecutive New England League championship.

Once the 1928 season was over, attention turned to the voter referendum question on Sunday sports that was on the November ballot. In its article entitled "New England Loop Holding Its Breath For Election Results," the *Sporting News* summed up the situation thusly:

> If passed, the New England League will prosper. The bill will make it optional in Massachusetts cities and towns to allow the playing of professional baseball on the Sabbath. Chances are that, if the Sunday baseball bill is defeated, the New England circuit will go the way of many other small circuits, entering oblivion.[43]

In August, with the Sunday sports initiative petition in the hands of the secretary of state to verify its eligibility for the November ballot, organized opposition sprung up again. The Rev. Conrad, pastor of the Park Street Church and staunch opponent from the Lord's Day League at the 1925 Sunday baseball hearings, formed a political organization called SOS Campaign Committee. The organization pledged "to work for the defeat of any initiative petition appearing on the ballot at the State election November 6 favoring commercialized or professional sports of any kind on the Lord's Day."[44]

The proponents countered by forming a branch of the Outdoor Recreation League, led by Davidson. Conrad's group, however, could not repel the changing attitudes of the majority of the Massachusetts electorate.

The year 1928 turned out to be a defining year for Massachusetts, as the state "witnessed a striking transformation in the political status ... from a rock-bound Republican stronghold to a Democratic state," Joseph Huthmacher wrote in *Massachusetts People and Politics*.[45]

Sunday baseball was a huge beneficiary of that change in political mood.

Al Smith, governor of New York and Democratic Party candidate for president, was a big impetus behind the political transformation in Massachusetts. Smith was also a Catholic, a fact that polarized opposition to him among the dry-Protestant-rural voters and generated huge support with the wet-Catholic-urban-immigrant affiliations.

While Smith lost the election in a landslide to Herbert Hoover, Smith did initiate a dramatic reversal in political power in Massachusetts. For the first time, a majority of the Massachusetts electorate voted for a Democratic candidate for president, as Smith carried the state by a slim margin. Republicans had badly misunderstood the voters in 1928.

"Because of the large scale unemployment in textile and shoes, the Massachusetts Republican party was in the difficult position of explaining why the Bay State was excluded from the apparent prosperity of the Coolidge era," historians Richard Brown and Jack Tager wrote of the times in *Massachusetts: A Concise History*.[46]

Between 1919 and 1929, Massachusetts lost more than 150,000 jobs in manufacturing, including 94,000 in the state's dominant industries of textiles and shoes, in an economy that was otherwise booming nationwide. In New Bedford, eighty-two percent of workers were in textiles; the percentage was seventy-eight percent in Fall River and seventy-six percent in Lawrence. In Haverhill, eighty-four percent of workers were in boots and shoes, with eighty-one percent similarly situated in Brockton. "The prosperity of these communities was dependent on the growth of industries that were, owing to external low-wage competition, on the verge of a long-term slide into oblivion," Brown and Tager observed.[47]

Republican support for Prohibition also "galled the French Canadians and Italians who usually voted Republican. That the national Republicans, supporting 'pure Americanism,' were nativistic and anti–Catholic was enough to create a new coalition of Democrats in 1928."[48]

While Republicans couldn't stop the Sunday baseball initiative petition from making the ballot in 1928, they certainly didn't make passage easy.

In order for the referendum to pass, "yes" votes had to number at least thirty percent of the total vote cast. Republicans were hoping that many voters, after choosing the candidates for offices, would bypass the two questions at the end of the ballot since the wording of the questions was extraordinarily complicated. The Sunday sports one was also very lengthy (a 243-word sentence, "probably the longest question, in a single sentence, ever appearing upon a ballot in this state" the *Boston Globe* reasoned the day before the election). Many voters — twenty-one percent of total ballots cast — did bypass the ballot questions, but not enough to offset the overwhelming preference of voters who did vote one way or the other.

There was also that menacing line near the bottom of the question, if one did read that far, that reminded voters that the legislature had disapproved of the proposed law.

The Outdoor Recreation League organized efforts to counter these obstacles. As the *Sporting News* noted, "The state has been placarded and covered with letters and workers." Sample ballots were also a big item to avert the necessity of voters having to actually attempt to read the ballot question and just have them mark the "yes" box.[49]

Sunday sports were overwhelmingly approved by Massachusetts voters in the election held on November 6. Question 2 on Sunday sports garnered 803,281 "yes" votes versus 467,550 "no" votes, for a resounding sixty-three percent of the tabulation of affirmative selections, excluding the 339,183 blanks among the 1,610,014 ballots cast. The "yes" vote nearly equaled a majority of all ballots — marked and blank — falling just one-tenth of a percent shy of the fifty percent mark.[50]

Massachusetts thus joined thirty-one other states and the District of Columbia that permitted professional Sunday baseball. The only New England states where professional Sunday baseball was not permitted were Maine, New Hampshire, and Vermont.[51]

With assurance that Sunday games could be played in the 1929 season, optimism reigned in the New England League.

> All eight clubs being in the red after three lean years, it can easily be seen that Sunday baseball is going to be the means of transforming the anemic circuit into a most healthy one. With an increase in revenue in sight, the owners are preparing to have their turnstiles overhauled.[52]

In an editorial, though, the *Sporting News* cautioned that Sunday baseball was not a certain ticket to financial success. "One is not likely to go [to the ballpark] unless there is a probability of seeing something which can offset a fine automobile ride, a trip to some beach, or a pleasant afternoon with a friend in the country. Sunday baseball is not an insurance of profit to any baseball club owner."[53]

At its November 15 league meeting, the New England League owners voted to re-elect Davidson as league president for another three years. They also voted to abolish the split-season format and revert back to the champion being determined by winning percentage over the entire playing season. "Expulsion from the rules of the split-season purges the game of the 'in the bag' chatter of cynical and suspecting fandom," the *Sporting News* commented. "In '27 and '28, the first-half winners failed to win the second half. This resulted in the voicing that there were teams that laid down and let some other club take the second-half honors." The passage of the new rule certainly seemed aimed to prevent another Attleboro situation, where the first-place team during the first half of 1928 descended to a next-to-last place finish in the second half.[54]

Scheduling was one of the first challenges the New England League had with the newly legal Sunday baseball in Massachusetts. Just five of the eight league teams were located in Massachusetts; the other three teams were based in Maine and New Hampshire, where Sunday baseball played by pros was still prohibited by law.

To try to optimize revenue for all eight teams, the league owners decided to schedule all four league games every Sunday in Massachusetts; on Saturday, three of the four league games would be held in Maine and New Hampshire. This meant that the three teams in Maine and New Hampshire would travel every Sunday to Massachusetts, where they could expect to gain the visitor's share of a lucrative gate. For the five Massachusetts-based teams, they'd have a home game on four of every five Sundays and a road game on four of every five Saturdays.

Then there was the jockeying for location in the commonwealth's most populous cities, where it was thought that Sunday crowds would be the largest. Worcester and Lowell were immediate targets. Jack Ryan, owner of the Haverhill team, moved his team to Worcester, while Bill Merritt, a former major leaguer, bought the bankrupt Salem team and moved it to Lowell. As expected, McDonough abandoned Attleboro and relocated his team to the vacancy in Haverhill.

The panacea of Sunday baseball in the New England League began to unravel in February when Ryan needed to relocate his team from Worcester to New Bedford. The Worcester City Council decided it didn't want professional Sunday baseball played within the city limits, as was its right under the local option provision of the new law. As the *Fitchburg Sentinel* later revealed, the Worcester City Council "declined to be a party to any scheme which enabled an out-of-town promoter to play Sundays and skim the cream of the patronage while industrial, shop and city leagues furnished baseball during the week and lost out on Sunday."[55]

"After an absence of close to 15 years from the ranks of league baseball, New Bedford is once more to return to the ranks of organized ball," the *New Bedford Morning Mercury* proclaimed. "The franchise held by the Worcester team has been transferred to this city and the season will open in May. The games will be played at Battery Park."[56]

Lowell and Haverhill were admitted to the league at a meeting on March 12 at the New American Hotel in Lowell, where the owners agreed to play a 126-game season, fourteen more games than in 1928, that would begin on May 1 and run through September 8. "Massachusetts has voted overwhelmingly for Sunday baseball. That means a lot to the baseball public; it means a lot to the New England League," Davidson remarked after the meeting. "The New England League is on a sound financial footing, more so than at any stage in its honorable career, and a season of unparalleled success awaits it."[57]

Five teams planned to play twilight ball during the week, starting their games between 5:00 and 6:00 P.M., while Portland, Lowell, and Brockton planned to play in the later afternoon, starting their games between 3:00 and 4:00 P.M. Wednesday games in Lynn and Manchester would start at 3:30 since many businesses in those cities observed a half-holiday on Wednesday.

Lousy spring weather also posed a challenge to New England League owners. Before the 1929 season even began, rain washed out preseason Sunday games. On Sunday, April 21, Brockton had planned to play two games, with New Bedford and Providence, after its exhibition game on Saturday with New Haven had been rained out. The *Brockton Enterprise* called the cancellations financial "body blows" by the weatherman. "The blows landed with telling effect, right on the purse strings. The games Saturday and Sunday were expected to net enough money to defray training expenses of the club."[58]

When there was no rain, there was often a brisk wind. On Sunday, April 28, Lowell played the first legal Sunday game in Lowell, defeating Haverhill before just 700 fans who "wore overcoats, ear flaps and mittens."[59]

One of the spectator-friendly policies that the league adopted for 1929 was to put numbers on the player uniforms so that spectators could more easily identify the players. At a league meeting in March, "It was voted to number the players of all clubs, an innovation in this section of the country," the *Haverhill Evening Gazette* reported. "In fact the New England League is the second to adopt the plan." The *Evening Gazette* reported that the Pacific Coast League in 1928 was the first league to number its players.[60]

The inaugural Sunday games in the New England League on May 5 were well attended. Brockton, Lynn, and New Bedford each hosted crowds of more than 3,000 fans, while Lowell attracted 2,000 spectators despite a cold, raw breeze that swept across Alumni Field. At Brockton, however, the *Brockton Enterprise* reported that "the box office receipts were not sufficient to arouse any enthusiasm on the part of the Brockton directors."[61]

In its article headlined "Sunday Baseball in State Viewed by 50,000 Persons," the *New Bedford Evening Standard* reported, "The question of whether Massachusetts wants Sunday baseball seemed today to have been settled. Virtually 50,000 persons saw professional games in the state yesterday afternoon."[62]

While ostensibly geared to a positive theme on the Sunday turnout, in reality the *Evening Standard* story highlighted a huge problem for the New England League owners — most of the Sunday attendance was in Boston to see major league baseball, not in the minor league ballparks of the New England League. Of the 50,000 number cited in the *Evening Standard* article, 35,000 were at Braves Field to see the National League game played there. Another 3,000 were at the Eastern League game in Springfield. Less than one-quarter of the total 50,000 figure — only 12,000 — was attributable to the four New England League games played within the state.

Sunday baseball at the major league level in Boston was drawing the fans. Because the two teams in Boston had interlocking schedules, when one team was home the other was on the road, every Sunday there was a baseball game in Boston. It was becoming obvious that Sunday baseball was not the lifesaver that Davidson expected it to be for the New England League. For example, at an exhibition game with the Philadelphia Athletics on Monday, May 28, New Bedford attracted 4,000 spectators to Battery Park, which was about double the attendance of the previous day, Sunday, May 27, that witnessed New Bedford's game with Portland.

Haverhill had its inaugural Sunday game on May 12 at Haverhill Stadium, where according to the *Haverhill Evening Gazette*, the spectators numbered about 1,500, "including boys admitted free."[63]

With rain canceling several weekday games, and attendance already on the wane, teams scheduled doubleheaders for Sunday, May 19, to induce as many spectators as possible to come to the ballpark. However, rain washed out three of the four scheduled matches that Sunday, as only New Bedford was able to use its field, but just for one game with Brockton.

Ironically, the Saturday games in Maine and New Hampshire, at Manchester, Lewiston, and Portland, may have been better attendance draws than the Sunday games in Massachusetts.

Many New England League owners resorted to scheduling doubleheaders on Sunday to try to solve their financial woes that spring of 1929. And the league soon reverted to a split-season format to shore up attendance over the summer.

Even when the weather cooperated, though, the law sometimes conspired to irk patrons at a Sunday doubleheader because both games had to be completed within four hours. The Sunday sports law called for play only between the hours of 2:00 and 6:00 P.M. The New England League created a rule that no inning would start after 5:40 to ensure that an even number of innings would be finished before the 6:00 curfew.

On Sunday, June 16, the first game of Lynn's doubleheader with Manchester went into extra innings before Lynn won, 9–8, in twelve innings. The second game had to be halted after four innings to comply with the Sunday curfew, which was half an inning short of counting as a completed game. Lynn's 7–2 lead at the time went for naught, as the team was denied a victory due to stalling tactics employed by the visiting Manchester team.

"The Manchester team 'stalled' throughout and disgusted nearly 3,000 fans in the stands," the *Lynn Evening Item* reported on the game. "There was sufficient time to have played four and one-half frames had the visitors showed any inclination to hustle."[64]

It turned out that Lynn didn't need that victory, as the team had a sufficient number of victories to cop first place in the first half standings. Manchester finished in second place.

With first place assured, Lynn tried to woo spectators to its games by playing some games at local fields rather than at Lynn Stadium before the second half of the season began on the Fourth of July holiday. On July 2, Lynn played a doubleheader with New Bedford at Curtin Park, a new athletic complex of the Lynn Gas & Electric Athletic Association on Broad Street. The following day, July 3, Lynn played an exhibition night game under the floodlights at the GE field against New Bedford.

Two years after the inaugural night game in Lynn, GE engineers continued to make improvements to their lighting system. At the 1929 game, more floodlights were added in the outfield area to increase the range of light there. Lynn defeated New Bedford, 14–9, in front of 1,000 spectators in a seven-inning game. "Spectators in the stands did not have any trouble following the balls, both grounders and high hoists, and the ball was in sight continually," said the *Evening Item* of the conditions, which led to twenty-seven hits and six errors between the two teams.[65]

When local fields and games under floodlights failed to attract spectators, Lynn reduced ticket prices, and even offered free admission to a few games at the stadium in hopes that people would gain interest and come back as a paying customer to a future game.

Lynn stayed on to finish out the 1929 season. However, Lowell did transfer to Nashua and Haverhill moved to Fitchburg.

Fitchburg wasn't very receptive to the transfer of the Haverhill team. "If the Lawrence-Attleboro-Haverhill team is wished on the fans, despite their lack of interest," the *Fitchburg Sentinel* commented, "it will merely be because the Haverhill team must go somewhere and the New England League feels it is time to give Fitchburg another middle-of-the-season chance to help out-of-town promoters."[66]

When the Fitchburg City Council granted a permit for Sunday baseball, Haverhill took up residence there to play at the Summer Street ball grounds. In the first game played in Fitchburg, on Sunday, July 28, the team lost, 17–7, to Manchester. Only about 700 fans showed up for the game.

McDonough canceled the scheduled Friday game in Fitchburg, and rescheduled it as part of a Sunday doubleheader, on the pretext that the grounds needed to be worked on. While there was no question that the Summer Street field was in rough condition, some people were suspicious about the motive. The *Fitchburg Sentinel* reported, "Some of the fans believe that the club owner realizes the fans are not turning out during the week and he is using Fitchburg as a Sunday filling station, confident that the fans will turn out on that day better than in Haverhill or other places he might go."[67]

Less than 200 people showed to watch the Sunday doubleheader on August 11 between Fitchburg and Portland. The *Sentinel* took to calling the Fitchburg team "McDonough's Tourists." After another meager crowd at the Sunday doubleheader on August 18 against Lewiston, Davidson helped orchestrate a transfer of the team from Fitchburg to Gloucester, where it was hoped the ocean-side location of the renowned fishing port would attract more fans to Sunday games than did inland Fitchburg.

Davidson was upfront about the ball club playing in Gloucester only on

Sundays and Labor Day, with its remaining games played on the road. Davidson put the best angle he could on his announcement: "The change was made partially due to the small attendance at games in Fitchburg and also because the New England League was desirous of getting the sentiments of the people of Gloucester with a view to playing the team in that city next year."[68]

The initial game in Gloucester on Sunday, August 25, attracted 2,000 people to the ball grounds at Centennial Avenue Park, according to a *Gloucester Times* report, as the down-trodden Haverhill-Fitchburg-Gloucester club defeated first-place Manchester, 6–1. The final game of the season there on Sunday, September 8, was an ignoble end for the transient team, with the rain-shortened game ending in a 0–0 tie.[69]

Despite the league's attendance challenges through the 1929 season, the playoff series between first-half winner Lynn and second-half winner Manchester was a financial coup. The third game, played at Manchester on Saturday, September 14, attracted a new league record of 4,698 spectators, as Manchester won its third consecutive game of the series. However, the fourth game played the following day, in Lynn on Sunday, September 15, topped that attendance record by more than a thousand people. "All New England League records for attendance were shattered, 5853 paid admissions being recorded at the portals," the *Evening Item* reported on the crowd at Lynn Stadium. Lynn won the fourth game to stay alive for the championship, but then lost the fifth game as Manchester claimed the 1929 league title.[70]

Each ball club in the postseason series realized about $3,000 from the series, while the league took in $1,400, based on the 16,634 people that attended the five games. However, any forward momentum generated by the 1929 postseason series was eviscerated when the stock market crashed a few weeks later on October 29, 1929, to usher in the Great Depression, a time of great economic crisis throughout the country, especially in New England.

Davidson, though, was already looking to parlay his success with the New England League into something bigger. His name was bandied by the *Sporting News* to become the president of the Eastern League ("Claude Davidson Mentioned as New Eastern League Head") when Herman Weisman resigned the presidency. But the Eastern League passed up the opportunity to employ Davidson, and instead chose long-time Springfield club owner William Carey to head the league. Based on the prior history between the New England League and the Eastern League, in which the latter basically absorbed the former after the 1916 merger between the two, it was highly unlikely that Davidson would get the nod to run the Eastern League.[71]

Embarking on the 1930 season with six clubs, down two from the eight-club circuit in 1929, Davidson had his work cut out for him to keep the New England League alive for another year.

Brockton and Gloucester were definitely out for 1930, the franchises ready to be turned back to the league if no takers were found. Davidson scoured the New England countryside seeking cities to take on the two floundering franchises. He even engaged in discussions with representatives from St. John, New Brunswick, Canada, about establishing a team there, but to no avail. Davidson surely would have renamed the league to be the New England-New Brunswick League if he had to in order to keep the league afloat.

The New Bedford franchise was transferred to Salem, although attendance had been fairly good in 1929 in the whaling city. With four of the six league teams now in New Hampshire and Maine, though, the club owners felt that the cost to travel to distant New Bedford in southeastern Massachusetts was too much of an expense for a depression economy.

With only two Massachusetts-based teams in 1930, Davidson did not have enough locations to produce a full card of Sunday games, which, despite the problems in 1929, was still a key to financial success in the league. He delayed the start of the 1930 season two weeks to May 21 so that he could find a suitable solution for a third Sunday site, preferably one that was not too proximate to Boston where fans flocked to the Sunday games played by the Red Sox and the Braves. The *New Bedford Evening Standard* suggested Battery Park in New Bedford as that third site.

> Lynn and Salem are the only clubs that can play Sunday baseball at home, as state laws in New Hampshire and Maine ban professional sporting activities on the Sabbath. With Sunday games at Lynn and Salem, only four of the league's six clubs would be occupied this summer. The answer appears to be to pit the remaining two clubs against each other in New Bedford, which has shown an inclination to give good support to Sunday baseball.[72]

New Bedford became the third site for Sunday games in 1930, even though the city had already been determined to be too distant from the majority of league cities to be economically viable. Davidson probably had few other choices, if any, of cities that would grant a permit for Sunday baseball if Sunday were the only day of the week that the league planned to play in that city. The use of Fitchburg and Gloucester as Sunday-only sites in 1929 only reinforced the Worcester rationale for declining a Sunday baseball permit.

The 1930 season started out as inauspiciously as the previous year. Crowds on opening day, May 21, were meager, with less than 1,000 people attending the season opener in Lynn. Rain canceled the three Sunday games scheduled for

May 25 in Lynn, Salem, and New Bedford (Portland vs. Manchester). For the Sunday game in New Bedford on June 1, only 400 spectators came to see Nashua play Lewiston; the game in New Bedford on June 8 was also rained out.

Nashua and Lewiston quickly fell behind in paying player salaries, as their players periodically threatened to strike. When Davidson went to Nashua to quell the angry players, the *Nashua Telegraph* complained that "the only thing he did toward paying the ball players was to take out $450 from the receipts of ball games, all of which amounted to about $30 a man."[73]

The 1930 season seemed doomed when less than 1,500 spectators went to see the three Sunday games slated for June 15. As the *Lynn Evening Item* reported, "Sunday a total of 1,409 witnessed the league games," with 756 at Lynn, 400 at Salem, and only 253 at New Bedford to see Portland defeat Lewiston.[74]

Nashua and Lewiston officially disbanded on June 17, shrinking the league to four teams, all of which were desperately trying to sell off their players to other leagues before the league collapsed and the players were off on their own.

Attendance plummeted as fans sensed the league was on its last legs. In Lewiston's last game of the 1930 season (and its New England League tenure) at Lynn, "attendance was about the poorest of the season, with only a dozen spectators in the grandstand when play was called." The official attendance was 56 people. A *Salem Evening News* headline on June 21 stated: "Turnstile Clicked 36 Times at Game Here Last Night."[75]

Salem, with a 21–9 record, was in first place when the New England League disbanded after the games on Sunday, June 22. Almost no one cared. Davidson was still working to keep the league alive at the eleventh hour, trying to interest businessmen in Brockton and New Bedford to take teams, but they understandably passed on the opportunity.

"New England League Magnates Give Up Ghost," stated a *Lynn Evening Item* headline on the league's demise. "It seems that the little old New England loop will now enjoy a long undisturbed sleep until the fans become hungry again and want to have baseball better than the grade as played by the amateur and semi-pro clubs," said the *Evening Item*, quite astutely painting the picture of the competitive situation in New England baseball.[76]

The *Evening Item* would have had an even more far-sighted perspective had it mentioned adding lighting systems to the ballparks to play night games, a concept that the GE engineers in Lynn had pioneered. Night baseball swept the minor league landscape during the spring of 1930, creating the economic salvation of minor league baseball.

On May 2, 1930, the first regular-season professional baseball game played under a permanent lighting system was staged in Des Moines, Iowa, in a Western League engagement, before 8,000 paying customers. Lee Keyser, owner of the Des Moines ball club, installed the lights after witnessing crowds flock to football games played at night during the fall of 1929.

"As the turnstiles whirled, believers were made — you could even say they saw the light," David Pietrusza wrote in his book *Lights On! The Wild Century-Long Saga of Night Baseball.* "Within weeks, such far-flung franchises as Joplin, Denver, Omaha, Lincoln, Buffalo, Rochester, Montreal, Indianapolis, and Fort Worth had installed lamps."[77]

While the minor leagues rapidly embraced night baseball in the early 1930s, major league ball club owners flogged the concept as a passing fad and focused on its downsides — the late hours (games typically started at 9:00 P.M.), wet grass, the glare of lights, and the disruption of eating times for the players. However, as F.C. Lane pointed out in 1930 in his *Baseball Magazine* article "The Romance of Night Baseball," there was no denying one huge positive attribute of night baseball:

> The main advantage is, of course, the fact that many more patrons can attend night baseball than can possibly attend day baseball. In short, night baseball multiplies the prospective customers greatly, perhaps, as William Veeck suggested, even twenty-fold.... Baseball does not belong to the owners nor to the players. It belongs to the public. And if the public want night baseball, you may rest assured they will get night baseball.[78]

As the Great Depression devastated the U.S. economy between 1930 and 1932, the New England League was by no means the only minor league to disband operations. Despite the inroads made by the popularity of night baseball, only thirteen minor leagues completed the 1932 season, in comparison to twenty-three leagues that had begun the 1930 season. There just weren't enough people with jobs that could afford to attend ball games, whether played during the daytime or at night.

By September 1932, while it was bad enough that there was no New England League, there also was no minor league baseball anywhere in New England — not even in the larger cities of Hartford, Providence, or Springfield — due to the disbanding of the Eastern League in July 1932. At that time, the closest minor league ball club to Boston was in Jersey City, New Jersey, in the International League.

During March 1933, as President Franklin Roosevelt entered the White House after sweeping to an election victory the previous November over incumbent Herbert Hoover, the country was on the precipice of economic disaster. In the Boston area, unemployment surged to thirty percent of the workforce, a rate not uncommon in other large cities across the country.

At this ebb of the Great Depression, Davidson took action to fill that baseball void in New England.

10

Great Depression
Revival, 1933

ON MARCH 8, 1933, IN THE MIDST OF a nationwide banking crisis when money essentially stopped circulating among citizens, the ever-optimistic Claude Davidson scheduled an organizing meeting in his attempt to revive the New England League.

Davidson expected nineteen potential team owners to attend the meeting, but instead found a meager audience. Memories of the 1930 meltdown of the New England League were still fresh in the minds of such long-standing league cities as Lynn, Manchester, and Portland. Potential team organizers from those cities were highly resistant to the siren song of Davidson's pitch for a 1933 revival of the league.

The "bank holiday" then in effect no doubt also kept attendance down. Since Monday, March 6, two days following the inauguration of President Franklin Roosevelt, all the nation's banks had been closed, as FDR moved to quell fears about people losing their money in the bank failures that pervaded the country in those pre–FDIC days.

"A great fear about the security of the nation's banks surged through the nation during February and early March 1933," Ronald Edsforth wrote in *The New Deal: America's Response to the Great Depression*. "With financial institutions failing in record numbers, more and more people decided to turn their accounts into cash ... a genuine stampede to liquidity developed. This financial panic swept away one-fourth of all the nation's banks before it was tamed during the early days of the New Deal."[1]

Many potential organizers of baseball clubs had much larger issues on their minds in Depression-ridden New England than the challenges associ-

212

ated with starting a baseball team in a league that had a demonstrable difficulty staying in business.

"Claude Davidson was visibly disappointed last night," the *Lowell Evening Leader* reported on Davidson's reaction to the small number of attendees at the organizing meeting. "But his voice was husky. There was something about the scene that suggested the sepulchral. Claude finally pulled himself together and turned on his best promotional countenance, and the effort found response in several bosoms, though there were no wild scenes of optimism."[2]

One of the attendees at the March 8 meeting was Vic Lecourt, from Lowell, who the *Evening Leader* described as "in a hopeful spirit." Lecourt also had land on Aiken Street, near the city center, where he could build a ballpark. "Mr. Davidson accepted the information as progress, a glad gleam possessing his eyes as he noted possibilities, if not robust realities."[3]

The word "revival" had a double meaning when related to Davidson. In one sense, he was driven to revive, or restart, the league to complete the unfinished work left when the league disbanded in 1930. But in another sense, his approach to restarting the league had the evangelical feel of a revivalist preacher in the sense of Aimee Semple McPherson.

"Claude B. Davidson is on the job as only Claude can be when there is occasion for a baseball revival. With Lowell a prospect, Claude finds baseball fertility in the places where he spotted merely a barren surface a few weeks ago," said the *Evening Leader* in describing Davidson. "Claude is the true baseball revivalist, a crusader inspired."[4]

In a lengthy depiction of Davidson, the *Evening Leader* wrote:

Organizing a league is no sinecure, even when conditions are normal, and it is one of the toughest assignments conceivable when depression stalks the land. But we have faith in Claude Davidson, who has faith in Massachusetts, Rhode Island, New Hampshire and Connecticut as baseball territory; and Claude is still traveling about, his pockets full of franchises and his future full of hope. Claude is the original optimist. Where he journeys the sun is always shining.[5]

"Claude is a born organizer," the *Evening Leader* wrote on another occasion. "While he may drop a word or two about financial obligations to the league, he will do so in a perfectly friendly way, so friendly the assembled guests will hardly sense their prospective liability."[6]

It took an evangelical tact to persuade businessmen to invest in a minor league baseball team during a period when unemployment was high, the future very uncertain, and money frugally spent by those people who did have jobs.

"Investing in a baseball team had never been a highly profitable venture," Charles Alexander wrote in *Breaking the Slump: Baseball in the Depression Era*.

"The modest return (if any) from operating a franchise had its rewards in high civic visibility, the sense of providing wholesome recreation for the general public, and — for most of the entrepreneurs who put their money into baseball — the satisfaction of being close to players, fans, and something most of them genuinely loved."[7]

Davidson finally convinced six men to operate teams in the 1933 revival of the New England League. All six teams were located in Massachusetts to reap the benefits of Sunday baseball permitted in the state. Three of the six cities were old hands from past New England League seasons (Lowell, New Bedford, and Worcester), two cities had sporadically fielded teams (Attleboro and Taunton), and one city was a complete newcomer (Quincy).

While Davidson tried hard to entice supporters in the New Hampshire cities of Nashua and Manchester to field teams, and had even tentatively announced that clubs would be located in both cities, Davidson was forced to steer clear of New Hampshire in establishing the makeup of the 1933 New England League.

Although Sunday baseball was legal in New Hampshire by 1933, a bill was passed by the New Hampshire legislature that March, and became law in April, to permit parimutuel betting on horse racing at Rockingham Park in Salem, a town located just across the Massachusetts border near the city of Lawrence. The novelty of legalized betting at the race track was sure to attract spectators that might otherwise pay to see a minor league baseball game.

Even though Davidson was able to roust up six teams to revive the New England League once again, the league still faced considerable challenges to fill seats in the ballparks, despite its inexpensive twenty-five cent admission policy. The New England League went against the grain of the majority of minor leagues still operating in 1933 by neither playing night games nor affiliating as farm clubs of major league teams.

Nearly all minor leagues by 1933 had adopted night baseball as essential to their survival. With the rise of modern corporations that eliminated many small businesses, there were fewer people with the type of jobs that enabled them to take the afternoon off to see a ball game. Additionally, the expansion of radio broadcasts of major league games in the afternoon provided an alternative (and free) way for people to enjoy baseball, which further reduced attendance at minor league games staged in the afternoon. Radio station WNAC in Boston broadcast every home game of the Braves and Red Sox. Twilight games in the New England League were barely a step up from mid-afternoon games compared to the attendance possibilities of night baseball.

Money was still in short supply in New England during the Great Depression, preventing the team owners from making a capital expenditure for outdoor lighting. While Davidson was a proponent of night games, the club owners may have harbored sentiment (shared by major league club owners) that night baseball just wasn't "real." As Lou Gehrig once said in regard to night baseball, "As far as being a true exhibition of baseball, I don't think I can say it is. It's very hard and very difficult on the ballplayers themselves. It's not real baseball. Real baseball should be played in the daytime, in the sunshine."[8]

After one very well-attended evening exhibition game played by a New England League team that was conducted under portable lighting equipment, one writer defended the "fake" nature of night baseball.

> One would be inclined to believe that more leagues would go in for night games. The one outstanding catch is that bona fide fans do not relish seeing baseball at night as a regular menu. Primarily a game to be played under the rays of Old Sol, the national pastime may flourish in certain parts of the country under electric lights, but as a whole the sport will meet with real success only when played under ordinary conditions.[9]

The New England League team owners in 1933 definitely clung to their independent ways, honed over decades of regional iconoclastic mentality, by shunning affiliation as farm clubs of the major league teams. Not forging farm-system arrangements with major league clubs was perhaps Davidson's biggest mistake in the 1933 revival of the league. But the "chain store" mentality of the farm club system probably struck a chord with the club owners, who had seen numerous small businesses put out of business by the expansion of nationwide firms such as Woolworth's and A&P. However, being a farm club provided quality players and money (some of which could have been used to purchase or rent lighting systems) and was virtually essential in 1933 for a minor league team to remain solvent.

"Under the presidency of Claude Davidson, its former head, the loop returns with the unique distinction of having no major league tie-ups," the *Sporting News* noted in an editorial at the beginning of the 1933 season. "Thus the New England is coming back to the game under the same principals that brought about the original organization of the [minor league] National Association — freedom from major league entanglements. In view of the present day tendency to the contrary, it will be interesting to note the progress the circuit makes the coming season."[10]

Said in a nice way, the editors at the *Sporting News* thought the New England League had no hope of making it.

One of those independent-minded owners was Lowell's Lecourt. Not only did he organize a team to play in the moribund Lowell market — the last two attempts at minor league ball in Lowell had been dismal failures — but Lecourt also built a new ballpark for the team to play in.

Davidson understood the reasons why the previous Lowell clubs had failed, which included an out-of-the-way playing site and lack of local interest to compete with twilight league games in the city. Lecourt, president of the Laurier Club, a local social organization, addressed both weaknesses in forming the 1933 Lowell entry in the New England League.

Lecourt built Laurier Park on the fringe of downtown Lowell, at the corner of Aiken and Pawtucket streets, a site that was more convenient for spectators to get to in the early evening after work. With its cozy dimensions, Laurier Park was despised by pitchers, but the friendly confines were a delight for both hitters and spectators:

> In 1933 Laurier Park was 297 feet down the left-field line but only 275 feet down the right-field line and a mere 310 feet to straightaway center field. The fences were 10 feet high, and a 10-foot-high screen was added to the fence from center field to the right-field foul pole. Balls hitting the screen were in play, but it was only marginally successful in cutting down the number of home runs that would be hit there that summer.[11]

Lecourt added additional spectator interest by using a number of local players on the Laurier team. Among the locals he signed were Rusty Yarnall, the baseball coach at Lowell Textile Institute, to manage the team and Aimee "Jerry" Savard, a right-handed power hitter at Lowell Textile, to play the outfield.

Savard loved the close proximity of the left-field wall at Laurier Park and frequently stroked home runs there. In his first ten days as a Laurier, Savard hit three home runs and by the Fourth of July he had eleven home runs. Savard and teammate Larry Donovan waged a duel for the New England League home run crown over the summer of 1933. Donovan, a left-handed hitter, took advantage of the short distance to the right-field fence and clubbed twenty home runs at Laurier Park — and none anywhere else in the league. Savard overtook Donovan for the home run lead by cracking five home runs in the last week of the season, to post a total of twenty-four home runs to lead the New England League. Following the 1933 season, after a few more years of minor league and semi-pro baseball, Savard used his college degree to work as a chemist for the U.S. Finishing Company, a cloth printing firm in Norwich, Connecticut, and later for General Dynamics, the submarine boatyard in Groton, Connecticut. He died in 1981 at age seventy-one.[12]

Two other new owners that Davidson interested in investing in a revived New England League were John Saunders, a Quincy dentist, and Joe Ford.

Jerry Savard, shown here in the middle of the back row, led the New England League in home runs in 1933. His output was helped by playing his home games at Laurier Park in Lowell, with its short distance to the left field fence that was hemmed in by its proximity to the Merrimack River (courtesy of Harry Savard).

Originally, the two men were to co-own a Quincy team, but Ford split off to run his own team, somewhat inexplicitly, in Attleboro. Since neither location was ready to support a minor league team in 1933, both soon perished as New England League sites.

Attleboro lasted barely one week. Even though owner Ford had fashioned a working relationship with the New York Giants to secure three ball players for the Attleboro squad (catcher Point and pitchers Madden and Mulcahy), Attleboro residents were reluctant to support the team after their jilted experience with the city's 1928 team in the New England League.

Less than five hundred fans showed up for the team's home opener on May 18 at Haywood Field, as the *Attleboro Sun* gave greater coverage in the next day's sports pages to the Attleboro High School track meet. Three days later on Sunday, May 21, "a handful of fans estimated at under 200 braved the cold weather" to watch Taunton shut out Attleboro, 4–0. Attendance at Haywood Field hit a nadir on May 24 when "the smallest crowd of the season, numbering a few under 100" saw Quincy crush Attleboro, 13–4.[13]

In desperation, Davidson reluctantly arranged to transfer the Attleboro franchise to Lawrence. The city in the past had been a hotbed for New England League baseball, but in 1933 the city was crumbling under the demise of its one-industry economy based on the textile industry. Even worse, Lawrence was just five miles from Salem, New Hampshire, so the ball club competed head-to-head with Rockingham Park, which was set to begin its legalized gambling operation on June 21.

Quincy survived a little longer than Attleboro did, but not much. Quincy played its home games at Fore River Field, which unfortunately lacked a fenced enclosure and thus prevented the team from charging admission. The team was forced to take up a collection among the spectators at each game, hardly the soundest financial arrangement for running a team. After 2,500 people attended Quincy's home opener on May 18, Fore River Field also lacked ample spectators at Quincy's games. The competition from semi-pro leagues like the Old Colony League that used local players was just too strong.

Eighteen games into the 1933 season, Saunders abandoned the Quincy experiment, even though his team was in first place in the New England League standings. "The few dollars which were collected from the few persons who attended the games in this city were wholly inadequate to keep the organization in bats, let alone balls and pay the expenses of the outfit," said the *Quincy Patriot Ledger*.[14]

Davidson stepped in to find the Quincy team a new home in Nashua, New Hampshire, which had expressed some interest in March of housing a New England League team. Nashua was no panacea for the former Quincy franchise; the city's small population and proximate location to Rockingham Park did not bode well for the ball club. The team's first game in Nashua versus Taunton at the North Common baseball diamond on June 6 drew just two hundred paid customers. "The team was practically doomed from the start," the *Nashua Telegraph* reported just a few weeks later.[15]

Competition from Rockingham Park was just too overwhelming for both Nashua and Lawrence. In the midst of the Great Depression, those people that did have a job or money in their pocket were more inspired to drive their automobile to the race track in bucolic Salem, New Hampshire, than to attend a New England League baseball game at a ballpark located in a gritty, urban area.

While Rockingham Park had an adverse effect on the fortunes of the New England League, the race track did have a beneficial impact on the state finances of New Hampshire, which in 1933 experienced a thirty-three percent unemployment rate.

"Although it could hardly be imagined at the time, an abandoned horse track in a quiet community would save the state from fiscal collapse and dramatically change New Hampshire's social, political, and economic environment," Paul Peter Jesep wrote in *Rockingham Park, 1933–1969*. The state received a percentage of the betting handle, which in 1933 generated $400,000, equal to about twenty percent of total state spending appropriation.[16]

Even a holiday doubleheader on the Fourth of July, which traditionally attracted huge crowds, couldn't draw spectators to O'Sullivan Park in Lawrence. The ball club didn't even try to compete with horse racing, instead canceling the scheduled holiday doubleheader with Nashua. Attendance at Rockingham Park on the holiday was 35,000, the highest of the season, as Brass Monkey won the Independence Day Handicap to capture the $1,200 pursue. A $2 wager on Brass Monkey to win, who went off at 5–2 odds, paid bettors $7 to win. The pre-race favorite, Dark Hope, finished in second place, and seemed to symbolize the fate of not only the Lawrence and Nashua ball clubs but also the New England League as a whole.[17]

The holiday doubleheader in Worcester, far removed from Rockingham Park, drew only 1,800 fans to see first-place Worcester clash with Lowell, which sported a local favorite in former Holy Cross star Pete Cote at shortstop. With the ease of automobile transportation, it was just as easy for baseball fans to head into Boston to see a major league baseball game as it was to journey to the local ballpark to view a New England League contest. Many did go to Boston, as the holiday doubleheader at Braves Field between the Boston Braves and the New York Giants drew 20,000 people.[18]

The wooden O'Sullivan Park on the west side of Lawrence during the 1930s. The New England League briefly located a ball club in Lawrence in 1933, before attendance at O'Sullivan Park was decimated by competition from Rockingham Park, a nearby racetrack where parimutuel betting was legalized in 1933 (Lawrence Public Library, Special Collections).

Another attendance draw at Braves Field, as well as Fenway Park, was the ability to purchase a beer at the game, a beverage seemingly not available at ballparks in the New England League. With Prohibition ending in 1933, the federal government authorized the sale of 3.2 beer just before the start of the 1933 major league baseball season. Both the Braves and Red Sox eagerly opted to sell beer at their games to attract more spectators. If beer was sold at New England League ballparks, the newspapers didn't highlight the beverage's availability.

Worcester was one of the few bright spots in New England League attendance. Sunday baseball finally debuted in Worcester in 1933, after the city had rejected the idea in 1929 and caused its ball club to move to another city. The first Sunday game in Worcester was played on June 4, 1933, against New Bedford at League Park, as the *Worcester Telegram* reported that "a heartening crowd of 2,400 paying customers roared loudly." Worcester owner Charles Murphy, who "was all smiles," said, "If we get support like this, we'll build new stands immediately."[19]

The first Sunday game in Worcester was a doubleheader, so the 2,400 spectators got to see two games for the price of one (actually they saw about one and two-thirds games, since the second game was stopped after six innings due to the Massachusetts Sunday law that required no play to occur after 6 P.M.). Sunday doubleheaders were now a staple of the New England League schedule, since the major league team owners in Boston felt compelled to offer doubleheaders on Sunday as a way to entice spectators to the ballpark with the lure of the second "free" game.

"Since fewer people could afford to attend baseball games in the early 1930s due to hard times, doubleheaders on Sunday helped to attract spectators on the day that people who did continue to hold jobs could get to the ballpark," one historian wrote of the Sunday doubleheader craze. The second "free" game encouraged urban residents to go to the ballpark; people in rural areas were enticed to travel to the ballpark where they would be reluctant to go to see just one game.[20]

With lukewarm attendance at holiday and Sunday games, downright weak attendance at weekday games, and two teams ready to fold up, Davidson knew he needed to do something to jumpstart the New England League or the league wouldn't last through the summer. An article in the *Lowell Courier-Citizen* entitled "N.E. League on the Verge of Collapse" had a dismal outlook: "If reports coming from within the league are true, the 'little old' is having a rocky time after an apparently fine start. It is more than a Fourth of July league, its strongest backers are insisting, yet appearances show that Nashua, Lawrence and possibly Taunton are not too well situated as regards the financial angle."[21]

At a league meeting on July 7, the league decided to convert to a split-season format. The games on Saturday, July 8, ended the first half of the season, and a second half began on Sunday, July 9. The split-season format had helped to spark attendance in the New England League when used during the three years of 1927 through 1929. Davidson, who was earning every penny of his $1,500 annual salary as league president, hoped the split-season format would help save the 1933 season.

The change in regular-season format, though, created an issue about the determination of the league champion. Originally, Davidson had planned to crown the champion via a three-team playoff format, a variation of the playoff concept that several minor leagues were experimenting with in 1933. The New England League playoffs were going to be patterned after the professional hockey playoffs conducted in the Canadian-American League, where the top three teams entered a postseason playoff for the league championship. The baseball playoff format wouldn't have been an exact replica, since the Canadian-American League format called for an opening round between the second- and third-place teams as a two-game competition decided by total goals scored. The winner of that initial series advanced to a best-of-five-games series against the first-place team.

Davidson was swayed by his friend and former New England League team owner Jean Dubuc, who also happened to run the Rhode Island Reds hockey team in the Canadian-American League where such a playoff format was standard fare.[22]

While the playoff concept today is an accepted part of not only minor league baseball but also all major league sports, the playoff was just in its infancy in 1933. The American Association was the first league to vote for a playoff system when it opted in December 1932 to split into East and West divisions for the 1933 season and stage a two-team playoff between the division winners.

In February 1933, Frank Shaughnessy, general manager of the Montreal club in the International League, convinced the International League to divide into North and South divisions for the 1933 season and institute a four-team playoff. Shaughnessy's playoff system was patterned after the National Hockey League's Stanley Cup playoff format, established in 1927. Shaughnessy's basic concept was to have the top four teams in the eight-team league enter into a playoff to determine the champion. The International League playoff format matched the two first-place teams in each division in one series and the two second-place teams in the other series; the winners squared off for the pennant.[23]

Besides additional postseason revenue from the playoff games, the Shaughnessy system was also designed to stimulate interest in regular season games during the second half of the season as teams vied for the final playoff spots without the negative element associated with the split-season format (i.e., the results of the first half were tossed out once the second half of the season began). The most significant downside to the playoff system was that it made a first-place finish in the regular season less meaningful. While Shaughnessy became known as the father of the playoffs, it was the Texas League format in 1933 that eventually became the standard playoff format in the minor leagues. The Texas League used a four-team approach without the divisional setup, pairing the first- and fourth-place teams in one series and the second- and third-place teams in the other series.

The revised playoff format for the New England League was described in a July 7 article entitled "New England League Votes Split Season" in the *New Bedford Evening Standard*:

> This automatically assures Worcester of the first half pennant, but New Bedford and Taunton, in second and third places, respectively, will be in the playoff at the end of the second half on Labor Day. It was agreed at the meeting [in Boston on July 7] that the three leading teams in the first half would play a round-robin series with the three leading clubs of the second half at the end of the regular schedule.[24]

The switch to the first half/second half format, along with the modified playoff scheme, was intended to stimulate interest not only in the three cities likely to qualify for the playoffs under the original idea but also in the two new cities where the Nashua and Lawrence franchises were transferred. The modified playoff format — the "round robin" — seemed to presume that three different teams would qualify for the playoffs in the second half than the three that qualified in the first half. The vaguely defined playoff structure became a problem once Labor Day rolled around.

"The New England League is going to finish out the season," Davidson told a reporter on July 17 while, ironically, attending the races at Rockingham Park (it was a Monday afternoon, an open date for all league teams). Davidson was said to be confident and "beaming good will in all directions."[25]

Of the two shaky franchises, Davidson found a home first for the Lawrence team when he was able to arrange for a transfer of the team to Woonsocket, Rhode Island, to finish out the season. It took Davidson several more weeks to persuade a group in Brockton to take on the remaining schedule of the Nashua team.

Davidson convinced a semi-pro team in Woonsocket, Standard Cab, to absorb the Lawrence team and finish out its schedule, with the team to be known as Woonsocket-Standard Cab. "The best players on the Standard Cab nine, which has been playing Sunday ball at St. Ann's Park, will be used with the best players of the old Lawrence club," the *Woonsocket Call* reported about the newest team in the New England League.[26]

One of the players that transferred from Lawrence to Woonsocket and had started out on the original Attleboro squad was pitcher Hugh Mulcahy. He hurled Woonsocket to a 7–2 victory over Lowell on Sunday, July 23, in the first game of a doubleheader before a crowd of 1,800 at St. Ann's Park. In two years, Mulcahy would be in the major leagues, pitching for the Philadelphia Phillies of the National League. Mulcahy returned to pitch in the New England League in 1941 during its semi-pro years after he was one of the first major leaguers drafted into the military. He may be the only player to have played in both the 1933 and 1941 seasons of the New England League.

Davidson had more trouble finding a home for the Nashua team. Rumors began flying that the Nashua team was disbanding when both Nashua and the visiting Lowell team failed to show up for the scheduled game on July 6 at the North Common grounds in Nashua. "The New England League did not play in this city last night and another chapter in the crazy quilt pattern that is making up the present season history was written in the books," the *Nashua Telegraph* commented.[27]

On Saturday, July 8, the headline in the sports page of the *Nashua Telegraph* gave a semi-pro game top billing and the New England League team secondary billing: "Independents Play Colored Team Sunday — N.E.L. Game Today." On Monday, July 10, the *Nashua Telegraph* printed only the line scores of the New England League team's games on Saturday and Sunday, while providing full coverage and a box score of the 15–3 victory by the Nashua Independents over a black team comprised of Pullman Porters (in which young Freddie Dobens, a future newspaperman and key person in the post-war 1946 league revival, played first base in the late innings for the Independents). Clearly, the image of the New England League in Nashua had severely sagged.[28]

Dr. Saunders, the Quincy dentist who was the team owner, threw in the towel on July 10 and offered the team to anyone that would take it. There were no takers and the team was turned over to the league. Nashua became a road team, playing only the away games on its schedule and no home games. "Nashua's New England League baseball team is still barnstorming, playing league dates every other day," the *Nashua Telegraph* reported in mid–July. "On days that it is scheduled to show here, the players lay off."[29]

By early August, Davidson found a home for the orphaned ball club in Brockton, where the team played games on Saturday and Sunday at Walkover Park.

The league limped through the summer of 1933 with meager attendance at many ballparks. The biggest crowds were for exhibition games under portable floodlights played at night against barnstorming teams.

The House of David team played in Woonsocket on Saturday night, July 29, and drew 1,500 for a game with the Woonsocket team that had been in the New England League just two weeks (the team drew just 500 spectators to its first league game on July 19). Besides the bearded men that made the House of David famous, the baseball team also sported a female participant. "Miss Jackie Mitchell, the only girl under contract in organized baseball, pitched the first inning against Standard Cab and retired the side in 1–2–3 order," the *Woonsocket Call* reported of the male/female competition.[30]

On September 5, Taunton played the House of David team before more than 2,000 spectators in a night game at Hopewell Park. Two days later, according to the *Taunton Gazette*, Taunton drew "a paid crowd of a few over 50" for its league game against Lowell played in the twilight at Hopewell Park.[31]

Barnstorming teams like the famously bearded House of David team used a fleet of trucks to transport a portable lighting system between cities. The novelty of night games in small cities attracted sizeable crowds that supported the cost of transporting the lighting equipment, which was quite a production to set up before the game.

> It consisted of telescoping poles, which could be raised to a height of forty-five to fifty feet. Two poles, raised parallel to one another about five feet apart, supported six floodlights, themselves about four feet across. The poles were fastened to the beds of trucks, and raised by a derrick. Each truck bearing the poles and lights was placed along the outfield foul lines, protected by a six-foot canvas fence that stretched the circumference of the outfield. Another truck with poles and lights was parked behind home plate. The entire system was powered by a generator, set up in distant center field, which had a 250-horsepower motor and was as large as a car, ran continuously throughout games, making a great deal of noise. The system took about two hours to assemble before each game, and some time to be dissembled and packed on trucks after it had been used.[32]

Playing the actual ball game with the portable lighting system created its own obstacles. Players could trip over the wires strung between the generator and the poles. If the generator sputtered and dimmed the lights on the field when the ball was hit, players could lose sight of the ball. Players often did lose sight of high fly balls that were hit into the darkness above the light poles.

Despite its challenges and shortcomings, artificial lighting would have come in handy in August for several New England League twilight games that ended prematurely due to darkness and left spectators frustrated in the outcome of the game. For instance, on August 1, Woonsocket was credited with a 10–8 victory over Lowell in a darkness-shortened, seven-inning game. Lowell was rallying in the eighth inning and had loaded the bases with one out when the game was stopped and the outcome reverted to the score at the last completed inning.

Surprisingly, other than exhibitions against the House of David or black teams, there were few promotions to try to stimulate interest in attending the games. Baseball owners clung to the belief that the game on the field was enough to attract spectators, and steadfastly refused to indulge in what was then called the fine art of ballyhoo. Promotions were viewed derisively as hippodroming, and were frowned upon. A free game as part of a Sunday doubleheader and perhaps an occasional ladies night was about as far as New England League owners went with promotional activity.

Owners of many minor league teams across the country in 1933, however, orchestrated whatever promotions would attract paying customers to
the ballpark, which according to one historian involved "resorting to such
attractions as raffles, beauty pageants, chicken chases, and cow-milking contests."[33]

While the promotions brought fans into the minor league ballparks, the
baseball establishment lampooned the blatant salesmanship, such as in this
fictional exchange published in *Baseball Magazine*:

> "Have you noticed," inquired Jorkins, unfolding his sports-extra in Schimmel's
> restaurant, "what some minor league ball clubs have been doing this last season?"
> "Uh-huh," replied Hickey, the Fan, as he sampled the cheese on his friend's
> apple-pie. "They have been folding up on their owners like a busted accordion."
> "I mean in the way of adding outside attractions at ball games," Jorkins explained.
> "In Dayton, Ohio, for example, at a night game, they held a pajama parade for
> women. It greatly increased the attendance."
> "It would," said Hickey. "A lot of them dames must be in better shape then the
> ballpayers themselves. And they certainly showed the fans some new curves. But
> so long as it was a night baseball game, why didn't they add a nightshirt parade for
> men?"
> "And in Huntington, W. Va., they turned fifty chickens loose on the ball field
> and invited the fans to go after them. That," said Jorkins, "brought out a large
> crowd also."
> "It would of brang out a even larger crowd," thought Hickey, "if they had turned
> the umpires loose on the ball field and then invited the fans to go after *them*. But
> if these minor league owners are gonna have circus stuff added to their ball games
> to keep their clubs from explodin' like a bootlegger's home in a gang war, why don't
> they think up some real stuff to bring out the baseball fans?"[34]

The staunchly independent New England League owners were very much
akin to the conservative major league owners, who, with few exceptions such
as the All-Star Game inaugurated in 1933, refused to change their operating
ways. "Baseball has been a laggard in up-to-date promotion," Fred Lieb wrote
in his "What's Wrong with Baseball?" series of articles in 1933. "Its general
attitude has been we are the great national pastime and are own advertisement and publicity. Boys always will play baseball, if only to emulate Ruth,
Cobb, Mathewson and the great men of the diamond."[35]

As teams neared the Labor Day end of the second half of the season with
New Bedford in first place, there was some confusion about the playoff format. In late July, the *Lowell Evening Leader* announced that "the original plan
of conducting a postseason series along the lines of the hockey championship
playoffs has been abandoned and will make way for a 'little world series' for
the league title." Some people thought that meant the second-half winner
would play Worcester, the winner of the first half.[36]

Davidson announced that New Bedford, Lowell, and Worcester had qualified for the round-robin playoff as the top three teams during the second half. Since New Bedford and Worcester had already qualified based on their first-half record, the third team from first-half qualifiers, Taunton, was added to the round-robin format. New Bedford, the winner of the second half of the season, balked at participating in the round-robin playoff format.

"New Bedford's players were packing their clothes and preparing to leave the city today, following the announcement yesterday by President Marty Madden of the local club that he would not enter the team in the proposed round-robin with Worcester, Lowell, and Taunton to determine the league championship," the *New Bedford Evening Standard* reported. Madden wanted to have New Bedford play Worcester, the first-half winner, in a seven-game series to determine the championship. "Madden pointed out that the round-robin is against all baseball precedent for determining a league champion after a split season and the logical play-off system in any league is for the winners of the two halves to meet for the championship, as he suggested."[37]

Madden may have just wished to avoid further losses and embarrassment since few paying customers would likely go to twilight games played in the cold nights of September when the game probably would be shortened by darkness well before the requisite nine innings were played. The *Evening Standard* did concede the next day that "perhaps he [Davidson] was right," but went on to summarize the feelings of many that "the round-robin idea from the start has been a rather hazy one which nobody understood until it was outlined recently by President Davidson."[38]

With New Bedford out of the playoffs, Davidson proceeded forward with a three-team round-robin series among Worcester, Lowell, and Taunton. The format proved quite awkward to implement on a day-to-day basis since one team would be idle while the other two teams played. For example, Lowell played Taunton on the first day of the round robin while Worcester was idle. Davidson finally latched onto three-team doubleheaders to expedite matters, with the home team playing two games, one each against the other two teams. At Lowell on September 9, Lowell defeated Taunton in the first game and beat Worcester in the second game. At Worcester on September 10, Worcester defeated both Lowell and Taunton in the two games there.

While Lowell and Worcester advanced to the finals of the playoff series, few people were happy with the format. "President Davidson of the New England League agrees that the round robin series was a first-class flop," the *Lowell Evening Leader* told its readers. "It will never be tried in the New England League again, and probably not in baseball leagues of any kind. Eventually, it will be dropped in ice hockey, we predict."[39]

The New England League playoffs turned from merely a "first-class flop" into a total embarrassment when the final series between Lowell and Worcester couldn't be completed. As a result, no New England League champion was crowned for the 1933 season.

The first game on September 12 ended in a 5–5 tie when darkness stopped play after seven innings. Worcester defeated Lowell, 5–0, the next day, but the September 14 game was canceled by rain. On September 15, Lowell defeated Worcester, 8–7, in a game that lasted only five innings before darkness halted play. After four days with just two completed games (barely) and meager attendance, Davidson called for a doubleheader to take place on Saturday, September 16, hoping that the "bargain bill" would draw spectators away from high school and college football games played that day. Rain from the remnants of a hurricane washed out doubleheaders on both Saturday and Sunday, the two most lucrative days for attendance, to wipe out the playoffs and end the baseball season.

"It's not exactly a satisfactory termination of the New England League season, for the reason that it leaves no champion," said the *Lowell Evening Leader*. "What is a baseball season without a pennant winner? In all the rest of the country you will look in vain to find a league that has no glad emblem possessor."[40]

In its article entitled "Call Off N.E. League Series," the *Worcester Telegram* wrote that the first three games were "a financial disappointment, small crowds attending both here and Lowell." The players were playing for a percentage of the gate, not a fixed payment. "We did it out of justice to the players," said Worcester manager Raymond Weare about abandoning the series. "They haven't made even enough money to pay their expenses since the league season closed and with Saturday and Sunday dates lost and the prospects of the next game being still further delayed by the rain, we believed it was unfair to keep them here."[41]

As for the playoffs themselves, the *Lowell Evening Leader* continued to express its dissatisfaction with the format, adding it was contrary to the principles of fair play. "Such arrangement wasn't sound. It was a bit too commercial. It gave to inferior teams the opportunity to profit by the element of luck in a brief series and come through a champion."[42]

That attitude was not confined just to the New England League's troubles with its playoff system. Across the nation after the 1933 playoffs concluded, the Shaughnessy Plan, as employed in several minor leagues, was roundly criticized because "inferior teams" did indeed become champions. Galveston in the Texas League and Buffalo in the International League were both crowned champions despite each having the fourth-best record in regular-season play. In other words, the worst team among the four teams in the playoffs was crowned champion.[43]

Compounding the problem was that the team with the best record in each league, Houston and Newark, had lost in the first round of the playoffs. This was particularly galling to Newark, which had a 102–62 regular season record and was by far the best team in the International League. In contrast, Buffalo, the declared champion of the league via its playoff victory, had a sub–.500 mark.

In spite of its flaws, the playoff system continued to be employed in the minor leagues because of its beneficial effects on the bottom line — the system increased interest and kept spectators coming to the ballpark late in the season. In 1934 the International League modified its playoff system to lengthen the first series from five games to seven games to minimize the possibility that an inferior team would become champion. In 1936, the Pacific Coast League adopted a playoff system, using the now-standard format of having the first- and fourth-place teams meet in one series and the second- and third-place teams in the other, to further minimize the chance that an inferior team would become champion. By 1937, most minor leagues had instituted a Shaughnessy Plan playoff arrangement for determining champions.

Given the playoff debacle and Depression-induced low attendance levels in 1933, even the evangelical Davidson could not keep the New England League alive for the 1934 season. Further thwarting a return of the league for the 1934 season was the legalization of parimutuel betting in Rhode Island, which extended the detrimental influence that New Hampshire's Rockingham Park had on New England League operations in 1933.

Narragansett Park in Pawtucket, Rhode Island, opened on August 1, 1934, in a coordinated racing calendar with Rockingham Park to provide New England residents with summer-long wagering opportunities. Narragansett Park basically extinguished hopes of New England League teams in southeastern Massachusetts — such as New Bedford, Taunton, and Brockton — to draw sufficient crowds to baseball games.

Lowell and Worcester, two of the league's strongest franchises in 1933, did join forces with remnants from the Eastern League that had disbanded during the 1932 season to form the Northeastern League for the 1934 season. The six-team circuit linked up Lowell and Worcester with Springfield, Massachusetts, and Hartford, Connecticut, to form a core of populous New England cities that would be least affected by parimutuel horse racing in New Hampshire and Rhode Island.

Although team owners still lacked the capital to install lights in ballparks, the league did devise an arrangement to use a portable lighting system to conduct night games on a rotating basis among the cities in the league. In this way, teams would be able to attract workers to their games in the evening at least once each week (and maybe some afternoon race track enthusiasts as well).

On Friday, June 7, the first official minor league night game played in New England was held in Springfield, where Hartford defeated Springfield, 7–4, at League Park. Night baseball didn't get off to an auspicious start, though, as Springfield outfielder Ken Malstrom was knocked unconscious by a ball thrown by Hartford pitcher Henry Capolla and was rushed to a local hospital.

By most accounts, the lighting provided by the portable system was not very good. "The light equipment was reported as only fair by players who have played under the lights in other cities," the *Springfield Union* reported. "There were shadows in many spots and the outfield was so dark that balls that got away from outfielders were limited to two bases. From the grandstand, the outfielders appeared misty, semi-obscured figures." There were also twenty-one strikeouts in the game, an unusually high number for the league, as batters had a hard time picking up the pitches.[44]

Night baseball in the Northeastern League didn't prove popular with fans. Only 400 showed up at the inaugural night game in Springfield. The night game in Lowell the following evening drew an undocumented audience count, but the lateness of the game no doubt kept attendance down. "The game ended only 25 minutes before midnight, a rather late hour," the *Lowell Evening Leader* reported. For people needing to get up early the next day, the timing of the ball games was sub-optimal.[45]

The low attendance at the night games, compounded by the injury to Malstrom, resulted in the jettisoning of the experiment by July. When the Northeastern League disbanded after the 1934 season, there not only was no New England League, but there also was not one minor league baseball team left within New England.

The ultimate knock-out punch for the New England League was the adoption of parimutuel betting in Massachusetts in 1935. Whereas trainloads of horse racing enthusiasts had left Boston daily in 1934 for Rockingham and Narragansett, they now only needed to go to East Boston to watch the races at Suffolk Downs. Massachusetts voters in November 1934 had ratified legislative action to allow parimutuel betting on both horse and dog races. Because no minor league baseball team could compete with conveniently located legalized betting, Davidson had to put his New England League dream in abeyance.

An unexpected outgrowth of the new racing law surfaced in January

1935 when the Boston Kennel Club applied for a license to operate a dog track at Braves Field, where the National League team played its games. Braves owner Emil Fuchs, in desperate financial straights, saw more projected revenue from dog races at Braves Field than from baseball fans watching the putrid Braves team. Reaction from National League officials was swift and negative — there would be no dog racing at Braves Field.

Preston Marshall, owner of the pro football Boston Redskins, sought to buy the Braves from Fuchs. In a move that might have ignited interest in a New England League revival, Marshall planned to stage night games at Braves Field to attract workers who couldn't get away from the job during the afternoon to see the Braves play.[46]

While night games in the minor leagues were the norm by 1935, the National League only grudgingly allowed the financially strapped Cincinnati Reds to play night games in 1935, the only major league baseball team to do so. Even then, the National League owners only permitted Cincinnati to play seven night games a season, one with each team. The Boston Braves made their night baseball debut on July 24, 1935, at Crosley Field in Cincinnati.

Marshall didn't get the Braves; instead, Charles Adams, who owned Suffolk Downs as well as the Boston Bruins hockey team, gained majority control of the team. Marshall moved the Redskins to his native Washington, D.C. after the 1936 season, when he claimed non-support from fans and the media in Boston after the Redskins had won the Eastern Division title in the National Football League.

Professional sports played under the lights in New England took another step forward in 1936 when the Boston Shamrocks of the American Football League played their home opener at Braves Field on Wednesday night, September 30. "The lights were pretty good, the play being clearly visible from all points in the grandstand," the *Boston Globe* reported. "The rain didn't help any, and all in all, the artificial illumination received a good test." Despite the ability to draw large crowds at night, the cold weather kept crowds down and the Shamrocks, and the AFL, lasted only two seasons, disbanding after the 1937 season.[47]

While Davidson's 1927 experiment with professional sports played at night had yet to materialize ten years later in 1936 as an everyday occurrence in New England and only at an occasional football game, night games were on the horizon for minor league baseball in New England.

By 1939, Davidson was one of the oldest surviving links to the legacy of the New England League. During the late 1930s, three of the league's pioneers died, leaving Davidson with far fewer human connections to the league's roots. Jake Morse, the long-time league secretary, died in April 1937. Walter Burnham, manager of the 1885 league champions and local mogul within minor league baseball, died in October 1937. Fred Doe, who was a player, manager, and owner over several decades, died in October 1938.[48]

Doe was lionized after his death as the "Father of Sunday Baseball," based on his efforts back in the 1920s to change the law forbidding Sunday baseball in Massachusetts. On July 6, 1939, the Boston club of the National League played an exhibition game in Quincy to honor Doe. The Boston Bees, as they were known then, defeated the South Shore All-Stars, 11–2, on Fred Doe Day at Adams Field before an afternoon crowd of 3,500 spectators. Bob Quinn, president of the Bees, was there to give a speech along with many other luminaries, including the mayor of Quincy. Before the game, a drinking fountain behind the backstop was dedicated in memory of Doe.[49]

Eugene Fraser was now the league's elder statesman. The treasurer of the Lynn Gas & Electric Company continued to promote baseball in Lynn following the disbanding of Fraser's Lynn team when the New England League discontinued operations in 1930. Fraser-sponsored teams copped two national titles during the 1930s. A Lynn Gas & Electric team won the National Amateur Baseball Tournament in September 1933. Three years later in 1936, the Fraser All-Stars won the American Baseball Congress national semi-pro tournament in Louisville, Kentucky.[50]

Spectator interest in semi-pro and high school baseball kept minor league baseball at bay for the remainder of the 1930s. Davidson maintained vigilant hopes for another New England League revival, though, despite the two disbandings of the New England League that he was forced to implement in 1930 and 1933 and the unfavorable conditions facing minor league baseball in New England.

"For 25 years, he has remained a baseball addict until today he stands as the ranking crusader for minor league baseball in New England," Joe Nutter described Davidson in an extensive profile in the *Providence Journal* in 1941. "Through feast and famine, war and peace, depression and recession, he, more than any other individual, has worked untiringly to keep alive the minor league idea in New England."[51]

Part of what motivated Davidson to keep the New England League alive was a desire to avoid being labeled a failure. This was a holdover of the general attitude in the nineteenth century toward identity. "Failures that arise from inevitable misfortune alone are not so numerous as they are generally supposed to be. In most cases, insolvency is caused by mistakes that originate in personal character," Scott Sandage quoted a Boston merchant's observation in *Born Losers: A History of Failure in America*.[52]

During the interlude following the failure of the 1933 revival, Davidson worked for the U.S. Forest Service, overseeing construction projects and waiting for the right time to forge another comeback of the New England League. He probably monitored the experiment with night games in professional football. There was no doubt that he closely watched the construction of new baseball stadiums in New England.

In many ways, the federal government fueled Davidson's dream to revive the New England League one more time. As part of FDR's New Deal legislation, the Works Progress Administration was formed in 1935 to put unemployed Americans back to work. The WPA built a half-million miles of roads, thousands of bridges, and hundreds of schools, hospitals, and government buildings. Also among the many WPA projects were "3,300 stadiums, 5,000 athletic fields, [and] 12,800 playgrounds," according to Ronald Edsworth, author of *The New Deal: America's Response to the Great Depression.*[53]

"Sport and recreation projects fit well with the WPA's aims of promoting labor-intensive projects without imposing upon work traditionally undertaken by private industry," explained historian Robert Kossuth. Another reason advanced by Kossuth for the building of athletic facilities was to dispel the public's perception that WPA projects were "boondoggling," or a waste of public money. "Those individuals in positions of authority with respect to the provision of relief funding believed that people wanted to support sport and recreation initiatives, which in the end justified the expenditures in these areas," Kossuth concluded. FDR himself said at the dedication of one baseball stadium, "My friends, if this stadium can be called boondoggling, then I am for boondoggling, and so are you."[54]

One of the first WPA-built ballparks to open in New England was Fraser Field in Lynn, named after long-time New England League benefactor Eugene Fraser. In 1940, Fraser Field quickly demonstrated how popular baseball could be with local residents, many of whom worked for General Electric, as the city's economy converted from shoe factories to electrical works.

Eventually, other WPA-built stadiums in Pawtucket and Nashua would lead to the final revival of the New England League in 1946. It's unclear what role, if any, Davidson played in influencing the location of WPA projects by serving as matchmaker between local governments and WPA administrators. He may well have exercised a degree of influence.

In 1940, the Fraser Club of Lynn was a member of the Suburban League, a semi-pro circuit that included other suburban Boston towns, such as Lexington, Woburn, and Medford. On June 18, the Frasers hosted the Pittsburgh Pirates of the National League in the inaugural game played at newly-built Fraser Field. Even though Pittsburgh defeated the Frasers, 10–1, fans packed the new ballpark, as 6,500 people came to see Vince DiMaggio, Lloyd Waner, and Arky Vaughn play for the Pirates in Lynn.

Although Fraser Field didn't yet have lights, the plan was to eventually install them in the new stadium. But the potential was already evident. "New England League ball would pay with night games under the arcs, according to one who has been looking intently into the baseball situation in several cities that formerly made up that circuit," the *Lynn Evening Item* reported from an unspecified source that no doubt was Davidson. "If handled correctly and with proper backing it could pay, for this is fertile field for the right promotion for nocturnal league ball."[55]

The Fraser Club played several exhibition games at Fraser Field under portable lighting systems during the summer of 1940, which produced adequate attendance numbers (several thousands of spectators at each game) to justify Davidson's optimism for night baseball. These night games also introduced eastern Massachusetts baseball fans to another side of professional baseball that they had little exposure to in the past — Negro League teams. While barnstorming black semi-pro teams had toured New England, Boston had never hosted a team in the professional Negro Leagues, leaving many baseball fans unaccustomed to seeing black players on the baseball diamond.

In 1940, Negro League teams came to Lynn not due to a groundswell of demand to see them play baseball, but for the simple reason that the Negro League teams had portable lighting systems. By booking exhibition games under the lights with these teams, Lynn could gauge just how popular night games would be at Fraser Field when it was outfitted with a permanent lighting system. By having portable lights, Negro League teams could book more exhibition games with semi-pro teams.

"These exhibition games [with semi-pro teams] were more lucrative than league games because black teams could play two games a day, could command a larger portion of the gate, and did not have to pay booking agents for a large stadium rental fee," one Negro League historian wrote. "Thus, even at the height of the popularity of the Negro Leagues, teams such as the [Homestead] Grays played 50 to 80 league games but 100 to 120 exhibition games a season against white and black semi-pro teams."[56]

On July 2, the Frasers defeated the Cuban Giants, 2–1, before 2,000 spectators at Fraser Field under portable lights brought to Lynn by the Cuban Giants. "If they continue to card nocturnal classics like that of last evening they'll have to build additional stands," the *Lynn Evening Item* remarked. "It was by far the best night game played here where night baseball was born through the efforts of illumination engineers and experts of the G.E." Two weeks later on July 16, the Homestead Grays, "the champions of their race," defeated the Frasers, 10–3, under portable lights as 3,000 people went through the turnstiles at Fraser Field.[57]

Seeing how successful the Fraser team was at attracting spectators to its exhibition night games played at the newly-built Fraser Field, Davidson envisioned the nascent vestiges of yet another New England League revival. He began to solicit new owners to re-launch a minor league operation in 1941. This time, though, he de-emphasized the emotional aspects and focused on the business aspects, as he solicited the savvy businessmen that had survived the rigors of the Great Depression days. He also began to target city officials and newspapermen, who would still be susceptible to an emotional pitch about how a minor league baseball team could benefit their city.

To encourage new ownership of teams in the New England League, Davidson detailed all expenses and potential revenues associated with a league franchise. Total estimated expenses were $18,529, which included such items as player salaries ($8,500), park rental ($2,000, at 10 percent of expected 40,000-person gate at 50 cents per ticket), hotel ($1,350, or $3 per day per player), meals ($324, or 60 cents per day per player), and baseballs ($500 for 600 balls). "Revenue, Davidson promised prospective owners, would come from crowds, expected to average 750 per game (more on weekends, less on weeknights), at 50 cents per ticket, for $22,000," one author chronicled. "That gave each owner a profit of $3,471— plus, Davidson emphasized, profits from concession stands, exhibition games, radio, and the lucrative outfield fence billboards. Revenue would come in weekly and be used to pay the bills. The only up-front money an owner would have to put up was the franchise fee, which was just $250."[58]

It wasn't just baseball-related issues that fueled Davidson's enthusiasm for another New England League revival. In September 1940, Congress passed the Selective Service Act, which provided for mandatory conscription of men into the military service.

By instituting a peace-time draft, the United States was clearly preparing for the possibility of entering the ongoing military conflict in Europe that would ultimately become World War II. The possibility of war meant the possibility of economic boom for those areas of New England housing shipyards and aircraft factories, which would need to increase production to meet an expanded military need. Such an economic boom could support minor league baseball in selected cities.

In October 1940, men aged 21 to 35 were required to register for the draft. A lottery was held on October 29 to determine the first men to enter military service, and on November 18 the first draft inductees were processed.

Davidson issued a press release on November 20 to announce that the New England League would operate once again in the 1941 season. When President Roosevelt proposed the Lend-Lease Act in December to produce military equipment for other countries to use in fighting the Axis powers of Germany, Italy, and Japan, the economic foundation for minor league baseball in New England was definitely on the horizon.

11

Semi-Pro Years, 1941–1945

"DAVIDSON TO REVIVE N. E. LEAGUE," the *Lynn Evening Item* declared in a headline on November 20, 1940, atop an Associated Press report that stated "plans were underway to revive the circuit in 1941."[1]

Davidson had issued the revival announcement from New Haven, Connecticut, which was picked up by the Associated Press and carried in numerous newspapers across New England. Davidson still held out hope to draw in Connecticut-based teams to truly live up to the circuit's "New England" moniker. He toured the state, which had a thriving economy based on numerous defense contracts awarded to plants there, but Davidson had to be satisfied with teams located in the eastern sectors of the New England region.

With night baseball as the driving force for this New England League revival, Davidson knew he had a unique product and a competitive advantage over the two major league teams located in Boston. While eleven major league teams began to play night games on their home grounds during the period of 1938–1941 to join Cincinnati as night-playing denizens, neither the Braves nor the Red Sox were yet ready for night baseball to be played in Boston. The Braves were the last National League team to play under the lights at home, beginning in 1946; the Red Sox were the next-to-last American League team, in 1947.

Davidson's confidence was somewhat awkwardly stated in the AP article: "He expressed the opinion that night baseball would avoid the competition factors of horse racing and major league baseball radio broadcasts, which he blamed for the collapse of the organized baseball in this district."[2]

"The future of his New England League, he tells you, is bound up in

night baseball," Nutter wrote in his 1941 *Providence Journal* profile of Davidson.[3]

Davidson had to be content with a semi-pro circuit in 1941, even though
he had alleged in the November 1940 announcement that the president of the
minor leagues supported his effort to operate as a minor league and that one
major league owner wanted to have a franchise in the league.

Eight teams joined the New England League for the 1941 season to play
a forty-two-game schedule from late May to Labor Day, with games on Sunday and one or two during the week. Many of the teams were located in cities
with economies now based on national defense contracts rather than textile
or footwear or were actually sponsored by a manufacturer, such as the Worcester team under the auspices of the Norton Company.

The Fraser Stars of Lynn were a foundation for the 1941 revival, joined
by four other Massachusetts-based teams in Worcester, Fall River, New Bedford, and Quincy. Rhode Island was represented by Pawtucket and
Woonsocket, and New Hampshire by Manchester. Before the season concluded, Cranston, Rhode Island, replaced New Bedford.

The first New England League games in nearly eight years were played
on Sunday, May 25, 1941, with 10,000 fans attending the four openers. Lynn
and Pawtucket drew the largest crowds, with 5,000 jamming Fraser Field to
see Lynn defeat Manchester, 4–2, and 4,500 at Armistice Boulevard Field in
Pawtucket to see the Slaters defeat Fall River, 8–2. In Worcester, 1,000 saw
the Nortons defeat New Bedford, 10–2, while 500 saw Woonsocket defeat
Quincy, 10–4, in a game played at Woonsocket's home field, located across
the Rhode Island state line in Blackstone, Massachusetts.

"Davidson was naturally elated at the attendance," the *Lynn Evening Item*
reported, "and predicted that New England League baseball was due for a big
season and that all the hard work he has undergone since last fall has been worth
his efforts as well as those who have aided him." Gene Fraser received the number one pass from Davidson at the Fraser Field opener. "Mr. Fraser has done
more for baseball in New England than any other man I know of," Davidson
said. "The first man to be given a pass was Gene — he's entitled to it."[4]

In a twist that would become a New England League hallmark during
its semi-pro war years, Lynn had a serviceman in its lineup on opening day.
Many New England League teams would use professional ballplayers, both
major leaguers and minor leaguers, who were serving in the military and stationed in New England. In 1941, the pros played under their real names, but
later during the war most professional players used assumed names to disguise their professional status and avoid contract disputes with their previous civilian employers.

The Lynn pitcher on opening day was Hugh Mulcahy, a draftee stationed at Camp Edwards, who had pitched the previous season for the Philadelphia Phillies in the National League. Mulcahy had been a workhorse pitcher for the Phillies, a dreadful team that had lost 100 games every season since 1938. He started at least thirty games for the Phillies in each of those 100-loss seasons, producing an average pitching record of 11–19 over those three seasons.

Mulcahy was sanguine about his military service time that denied him several prime years of pitching in the major leagues. "Bad luck? I might have got hit with a line drive if I spent six more months with the Phillies," Mulcahy jokingly said in his later years. "Seriously, I never felt really bad about it. It never shook me up; I never think back on what might have been. I'm very thankful that I came back."[5]

In the May 25 game with Lynn, Mulcahy pitched three innings and gave up one run and two hits. His pitching opponent that day for Manchester was John Broaca, who had formerly pitched for the New York Yankees.

Another new twist for baseball fans in 1941 was night baseball. The first regular-season night game in New England League history was played on May 27, when Woonsocket, known locally as the Club Marquette-Roosevelt Park team, hosted Pawtucket. "Floodlight Baseball To Be Started at Roosevelt Park Tonight," read a *Woonsocket Call* headline for the game slated to start at 8:45 P.M. that Tuesday evening at Roosevelt Park in Blackstone. Pawtucket defeated Woonsocket, 9–4, "before approximately 600 fans" that attended "the first New England baseball league floodlight game of the season."[6]

While permanent lighting was installed at Fraser Field in Lynn, where night baseball debuted on June 16, some teams still played under portable lights, which could cause havoc in the middle of the game. For instance, in the August 10 game at Pawtucket, the generator for the floodlights along the first base line failed, causing the lights to go out. Play resumed after a twenty-five minute delay to fix the generator.

Night baseball was a definite hit with New England League fans. Thousands attended night games in Lynn and Pawtucket, many of whom could not get away from work during the day to see a ball game, but could attend the evening contests. The New England League had finally reached its natural audience, the average worker.

Lynn, with the new lighting system at Fraser Field, played numerous exhibition games outside of its New England League schedule, including several against Negro League competition. After taking on the House of David team on July 3, Lynn defeated the Black Yankees, 8–1, in a Tuesday night game before 6,000 fans at Fraser Field.

On July 23, Lynn defeated the Newark Eagles of the Negro National

NEW ENGLAND LEAGUE BASEBALL PAWTUCKET vs. MARQUETTE

Tonight at 8:45 P.M.
Roosevelt Park, Blackstone

Admission:
Male Adults .....50¢
Women ....20¢
Children ....20¢

Service men in uniform
admitted free

Free Parking on Grounds

Reproduction of a 1941 advertisement in the *Woonsocket Call* newspaper for the first night game in the New England League during its semipro years. Roosevelt Park was just over the Rhode Island state line in neighboring Blackstone, Massachusetts.

League before a crowd of 4,000 at Fraser Field. The headline in the next day's *Lynn Evening Item* was "Fraser Stars Batter Newark Eagles, 7–0; Forys Allows Senegambians Three Blows; Con Creedon Socks Homer." Reflecting the decidedly un-politically-correct Caucasian perspectives of the 1940s, the Lynn newspaper often referred to the Negro League players as "senegambians" or "blackamoors" in addition to simply "colored boys."[7]

The *Evening Item* also offered a sanitized version of the game account, not only focusing on the exploits of the Caucasian players but also ignoring any controversial on-field incidents. For instance, in the July 23 game with Newark, the Lynn paper failed to mention a confrontation between home run hitter Creedon and the Newark pitcher. According to the *Boston Chronicle*, a weekly newspaper in the black community, "Hill almost started a riot when he tried to dust off Creedon, the big batter of the Lynn team. Creedon started for Hill and Hill started from the mound both angry, but the players from both teams stepped in and stopped the boys before blows were passed."[8]

After a game against the Black Yankees on August 8, which drew several thousands of spectators, Lynn booked a marquee match with the top-drawing team from the Negro Leagues. On August 26, Lynn took on the Kansas City Monarchs, a team that featured star pitcher Satchel Paige, who, alone among Negro League players, had gained national prominence in the Caucasian press during 1941. Feature stories on Paige appeared in *Life* and *Time* magazines in early June, with an extensive story in the *Saturday Evening Post* in July.

"While the [black baseball] industry typically attracted only sporadic coverage from the white media, Paige became a national celebrity after his outstanding pitching, various eccentricities, and uncertain age attracted the attention of white journalists," historian Neil Lanctot wrote in his book *Negro League Baseball: The Rise and Ruin of a Black Institution*. "Paige's rural background, colorful antics, and lanky appearance jibed more comfortably with white perceptions of African Americans and offered ample opportunities to reinforce existing stereotypes."[9]

The popularity of Paige in exhibition matches magnified one of the big economic concerns of Negro League teams. "Despite the growing profitability of [Negro] league ball in the 1940s, games with white semipros remained an unavoidable part of each team's schedule," Lanctot wrote. "The problem that confronts us," Newark Eagles owner Effa Manley explained, "is we can get a guarantee to go to a park and play a semipro club, where we are gambling when we go to a strange park to play each other."[10]

Caucasian spectators, especially those in New England, did heavily patronize the exhibition games with the Negro League teams. The reasons why are somewhat elusive, but likely centered on the novelty of inter-racial competition in the region. Whatever the reason, people in Lynn turned out in droves to see Paige pitch against the local semi-pro club.

"Satchel Paige, greatest of black ball players and baseball's No. 1 Nomad, will be here tonight," the *Evening Item* reported before the August 26 game. "He is more famous than Uncle Tom in *Uncle Tom's Cabin* and he is a pitcher who mows 'em down, even those big leaguers he has faced in the South on various occasions."[11]

"Satchel Paige Draws 7,000 Fans at Fraser Field," was the headline in the following day's *Evening Item*, as the Monarchs defeated Lynn, 3–1. Paige "pitched deliberately with plenty of deception, fanning nine batters in five innings, passing three, with one hit, and one run scored off him."[12]

While the *Evening Item* downplayed Paige's pitching performance against the Caucasian batters of Lynn, the *Boston Chronicle* accentuated Paige's pitching prowess for its black readers:

> The great Satchel pitched a one-hit game for five innings out of eight, striking out nine men, three of whom he struck out in the third inning with the bases filled. Naturally, such pitching evoked enthusiastic applause from the fans. Irving Burns of the Fraser outfit, who formerly played with the St. Louis Browns and Detroit of the American League, was struck out twice; he praised the stellar pitching of Paige in the following words: "Satchel Paige, without a doubt, is the greatest pitcher whom I have ever faced." All the spectators interviewed were of the same opinion that Paige is unquestionably of Big League caliber.[13]

Toughened by its exhibition games with Negro League teams, Lynn finished in first place during the 1941 regular season. With the minor leagues now universally using a Shaughnessy playoff system to determine league champions, the semi-pro New England League also adopted a postseason playoff format in 1941. The first round matched first-place Lynn with third-place Manchester and second-place Worcester with fourth-place Pawtucket, as the New England League used the Eastern League format for playoff matchups (rather than the alternate format increasingly used by minor leagues in 1941 of first versus fourth and second versus third).

Regular-season records and lineups meant little in the 1941 New England League playoffs, though, as teams packed their playoff lineups with as many ringers as possible by picking up minor league and college players that were no longer playing for their regular teams. The use of ringers was especially prevalent in the final round, best-of-seven-games series between Lynn and Pawtucket.

"With the implied benediction of President Claude Davidson of the New England League, playoff participants have been busily engaged in changing lineups and recruiting added strength," the *Pawtucket Times* reported. "Fans have found it hard to recognize the teams they watched battle through a regular season."[14]

Pawtucket, which finished in fourth place during the regular season, just squeaked into the final round of the playoffs. The opening round, best-of-five-games series with Worcester went its full five games before Pawtucket won the fifth game, 8–0. Pawtucket then bulked up for the final-round series with Lynn. "Pawtucket strengthened its playoff lineup with the addition of outfielder Dave Goodman and pitcher Alex Muskaitas from the Williamsport, Pennsylvania farm club of the Red Sox," the *Pawtucket Times* reported. "Lynn has also secured the loan of at least one player from the Red Sox."[15]

Muskaitas pitched Pawtucket to a 15–3 victory on September 17 in the second game of the best-of-seven-games series, as left fielder Goodman garnered one hit in four at-bats. It was a local ballplayer, though, not a professional ringer, that kept Lynn in the playoff battle with Pawtucket. Charlie Bird, a pitcher who threw submarine style, won three games for Lynn to force a seventh game showdown with Pawtucket.

The location of the seventh game sparked a disagreement, as both Lynn and Pawtucket vied for the game to be held in their city. Lynn's argument was that in mid–September the league had scheduled the seventh game, if needed, to be in Lynn. But Pawtucket argued that attendance — always a paramount consideration in the finances of semi-pro baseball — would be better in Pawtucket than in Lynn. Davidson upheld the Lynn view. Pawtucket appealed the decision, asking for a coin toss to determine the site. Davidson, ever the diplomat, convinced Lynn to agree to the coin toss — which Lynn won. The seventh game was scheduled for 2:00 P.M. on Sunday, September 28, at Fraser Field in Lynn, providing ample time to finish the game before 6:00 P.M. when, by Massachusetts law, the game would need to be stopped (the so-called "Sunday curfew" law).

Seven thousand people packed Fraser Field that Sunday, the largest crowd ever to watch a baseball game there. Lynn used a ringer to start the game on the mound. Bump Hadley, a pitcher with the Philadelphia Athletics of the American League, started the game for Lynn, which cruised to a 6–1 lead by the top of the eighth inning. When Hadley faltered, Bird came in to relieve him. But Bird couldn't hold the lead, as he "saw six consecutive hits bounce into all fields as his magic failed to hold true." Pawtucket scored eight runs in the inning to take a 9–6 lead. Lynn scored two runs in the bottom of the ninth inning to close the gap to 9–8. However, with the tying run on third base with two outs, pinch hitter Larry Kennedy popped out to end the game and make Pawtucket the 1941 New England League champion.[16]

Davidson later contended that he couldn't stop the roster shenanigans in the playoffs. More likely, though, is that Davidson wanted to use those maneuvers to bolster his efforts to get the New England League back into minor league baseball, where such action wouldn't be tolerated.

In early December 1941, Davidson attended the minor league meetings held in Jacksonville, Florida, and left with assurances that the New England League would re-enter Organized Baseball.

On December 2, 1941, the *Evening Item* reported in an article entitled "Lynn Sure to Return to Organized Ball in 1942" that Davidson "has been assured that organized ball will welcome the Little Old New England League back to the fold." The article went on to note that "Davidson is seeking to bring the New England League under the jurisdiction of organized baseball as a result of the farcical playoffs of late last fall when Pawtucket won the title from Lynn."[17]

The timing for Davidson, however, could not have been worse. Just when the New England League was on the verge of returning to minor league baseball, world events conspired to extinguish Davidson's hopes. On December 7, Japan attacked the U.S. Navy at Pearl Harbor, an action that forced the United States to enter World War II. With democracy at stake, the future of the New England League plummeted in importance.

Davidson "is going ahead on plans to bring his circuit under the jurisdiction of organized ball despite the war," the *Evening Item* reported soon after Pearl Harbor. "However, our first consideration in this country is to beat the Japs and give them a real good licking."[18]

At age forty-five, Davidson was too old to serve in the military, but he soon left civilian life to work for the War Department. His first assignment was in Newfoundland, where he served as "construction engineer in charge of construction of fortifications, including gun mounts, fire control stations, revetments, ammunition dumps (all reinforced concrete)." Later during the war, Davidson was redeployed to Alaska, where he was "Area Engineer in charge of construction of civilian and troop war housing, airports, construction of the Alaska Highway (500 miles), telephone lines, Canol pipe line." His final wartime assignment was in Brazil, where he was "Post Engineer in charge of Repair and Utilities program."[19]

While Davidson was away during the war, the New England League continued its semi-pro operations. For the 1942 season, Lynn's Gene Fraser served as president of a seven-team league. Six of the eight teams in 1941 returned (all except Cranston and Fall River), with a new team located in Fitchburg, Massachusetts. The eighth team was slated to be Nashua, New Hampshire, but it dropped out before the season began. One of the organizers of the ill-fated Nashua entry was newspaperman Fred Dobens, who would four years later play an important role in perpetuating Davidson's dream of reviving the New England League as a minor league.

Fostering the continuation of the semi-pro New England League in 1942 was the so-called "green light letter" that President Roosevelt sent baseball Commissioner Landis in January 1942, providing his stamp of approval to continue professional baseball during the war. "The outlines of Roosevelt's note to Landis would constitute the federal government's stance on baseball throughout the war years — sanction for the game itself but no favoritism toward individual players," Richard Goldstein wrote in *Spartan Seasons: How Baseball Survived the Second World War.* FDR also advocated night baseball to reduce absenteeism at war plants that day games might induce.[20]

Military-imposed restrictions on civilian life in 1942 made it challenging to attract spectators to ball games in the New England League. Tire rationing began in January, since the Japanese military operation controlled more than ninety-five percent of the U.S. crude rubber supply (tires were then made from real rubber, not today's synthetic forms). Tire rationing was a forerunner to the institution of gasoline rationing in May. The limit of four gallons of gasoline per week for a car with an "A" sticker got people to and from work, but didn't leave much in the gas tank for trips to the ballpark.

"Driving to baseball games was out in the East. Most families could not afford to squander their meager gasoline ration on trips to the ball park," William Mead wrote in *Even the Browns: The Zany, True Story of Baseball in the Early Forties.* "The basic gasoline ration was enough to drive about 240 miles a month, less than one-third of the average norm for most families."[21]

Automobile travel was now a primary mode of getting to the new ballparks of the New England League. The WPA-built ballparks were generally in areas not easily reached by public transportation, which consisted mostly of buses in the 1940s since many trolley systems went out of business in the 1930s. Walking, while an option for some fans, came with its own inhibition in 1943 when shoes began to be rationed.

Blackout restrictions imposed along the East Coast, though, were the biggest blow to New England League operations in 1942. One could hardly fashion a series of blackout curtains to mask the floodlights for night games at the ballpark. Lynn and Quincy carried an extra burden of not being able to play night games due to the government-imposed blackout restrictions. There were fears that lights at ballparks near the ocean "might aid enemy submarines ... if shined out to sea."[22]

"Blacking out the coast and calling off night games was a blow to the hopes of Pip and Leo Kennedy, but Sunday and Saturday games and a few twilight clashes [at 6:00 p.m.] will help out," the *Evening Item* reported. "Games are arranged for nights in New England League parks which do not come under the blackout regulations."[23]

One new venue for night games in 1942 was Hammond Pond Stadium in Pawtucket. The new ballpark opened in July 1942 after years of controversy over the expense, and even the efficacy, of the WPA-funded project advocated by Mayor Thomas McCoy and built on soil that had filled a drained swamp. "'McCoy's Folly' was either the vision of a great mayor with bullheaded tenacity or the work of a corrupt political machine bilking the City of Pawtucket out of hundreds of thousands of dollars for a baseball field built in a swamp," described one writer of the situation.[24]

Pawtucket Stadium, as it was commonly referred to by the *Pawtucket Times*, created another facility with modern lighting for New England League teams to use to attract large crowds for night games. While several thousands could watch night games under the floodlights at Armistice Boulevard Field, Hammond Pond Stadium could hold up to 10,000 spectators.

In the inaugural game on July 4, Pawtucket defeated Lynn, 4–2, in a night game witnessed by 6,000 spectators. In his dedication speech before the game, Mayor McCoy "criticized the press, praised those who worked to make the stadium a reality and declared the stadium is 'the concrete contribution of Pawtucket to the nation's war effort in a crisis.'" Reflecting the wartime conditions, admission to the game was the purchase of defense stamps. Fans were also assured that any ball hit into the stands, if given to an usher, would be donated to army and navy camps for use in their athletic programs.[25]

With restrictions on automobile travel and prohibition of night games in several cities, the New England League struggled through the 1942 season. To augment the gloomy financial picture of the regular season, the league opted for a six-team playoff format. However, when Worcester, which finished in first place during the regular season, refused to participate in the playoffs, the league reluctantly reverted back to a four-team format.

Playoff squabbles continued to hound the New England League in 1942. Despite President Fraser's decree that "the league insists that players from the ranks of organized baseball under contract will not be allowed to horn in, as a year ago, when the championship series became a farce," teams still proceeded to use ringers in the playoffs. Lynn skirted the pronouncement by adding former college players, not pros, in its first-round series with Manchester.[26]

Scheduling complications played havoc with the Lynn-Manchester series, leading Lynn to forfeit the series to Manchester. The fifth and deciding game slated for Sunday, September 20, was rained out. The game couldn't be played during the week in either city since Lynn was precluded from conducting night games by federal government decree and the lights at Manchester's Textile Field were being dismantled after a Tuesday exhibition game with the Red Sox. At that time of the year, there was not enough daylight to play a twilight game. Compounding the situation was that the game couldn't be played in Lynn the following Saturday or Sunday. Lynn was scheduled for its own exhibition game with the Red Sox on Saturday, and a scheduled high school football game on Sunday would significantly undercut attendance at a baseball game (10,000 did, in fact, attend the football game).

Lynn made the decision to forego an opportunity to win the New England League championship in order to reap the financial reward of the Red Sox exhibition game on Saturday, September 26. The Fraser Stars defeated the Red Sox, 4–3, as 3,500 fans saw Ted Williams get two hits and Tony Lupien hit a home run for the Sox.

In the playoff finals, Pawtucket, which had defeated Quincy in the other first-round series, polished off Manchester in early October to win the championship in a series shortened by the cold weather. In an extensive, and quite obvious, display of ringers, Pawtucket packed its lineup with professional players in the fourth game played on September 30 at Pawtucket Stadium. In the lineup for the Slaters that evening were pitcher Al Javery on "loan" from the Boston Braves and Red Sox sluggers Lupien and Jim Tabor. The pitcher for Manchester was former Yankee minor leaguer Bill Fallon.

"Tabor gave the shivering 2,100 fans a chance to clap their hands and thereby keep the blood circulating in the third when he blasted out a prodigious 415-foot triple to left that did not fall short of the distant left-field fence," the *Pawtucket Times* reported in an article headlined "Slaters Wallop Manchester, 9–1, With Big Leaguers in Feature Roles."[27]

Although Pawtucket lost the next game to Manchester on October 2, Pawtucket was declared the 1942 New England League champion. "Just when it was beginning to look as though the teams would battle up to Thanksgiving Day, league officials stepped in and halted the proceedings by announcing immediately after the Manchester victory that the rest of the series games were called off because of the cold weather," the *Pawtucket Times* reported. "Then they decided that the Slaters had won the New England League crown, three games to two. Now the football season can continue here in Pawtucket without baseball as a competitor."[28]

The 1942 New England League postseason was a calamity, and certainly was not conduct befitting a potential minor league circuit. "The New England League with so many handicaps presented wasn't so much and the sooner the circuit comes under organized ball the better for club owners, players and fans," the *Evening Item* scolded.[29]

Obtaining ballplayers, whether for professional teams or for the semi-pro New England League teams, became increasingly challenging when it was announced in January 1943 that "baseball players could not expect an occupational deferment" from the military draft, since being a baseball player was not considered to be an "essential" job. "The usefulness of the sport [to national morale] is a separate question from the 'essentiality' of individuals who play it," Manpower Commissioner Paul McNutt explained. "Thus it may well be that it is desirable that Blankville have a ball team. But Blankville may lose certain members of that team to higher priority industries — even members that might be 'essential' to winning the pennant. The pennant is not 'essential.'"[30]

Business prospects for baseball dwindled further in January 1943 when it was announced that the Office of Price Administration had banned all pleasure driving. "Of course, such a ban was difficult to enforce," Richard Lingeman wrote in *Don't You Know There's a War On? The American Home Front 1941–1945*. "OPA men took to hanging around race tracks and athletic stadiums, copying down license numbers of out-of-county cars on the theory that just getting to the athletic spectacle was per se pleasure driving."[31]

Many minor leagues that had operated in 1942 folded before the 1943 season began, as many professional ballplayers either enlisted or got a job that contributed to the war effort, which was the primary source of draft deferment in 1943.

With gas rationing curtailed to three gallons per week and pleasure travel completely prohibited, the New England League cut back to just four teams. Like the ubiquitous victory garden in war-time back yards, the league also renamed itself to be the New England Victory League to convey a spirit of patriotism, with its teams relying exclusively on players who were war workers by day. Some called the league the New England War Workers League.

All four teams in 1943 were associated with defense facilities located in Pawtucket, Woonsocket, Quincy, and Providence (Walsh-Kaiser). Lynn dropped out of the league for the 1943 season. With Fraser's connection lost to the league, Bob McGarigle took over as interim president in Davidson's absence.

The league almost didn't get off the ground in 1943 when the Woonsocket Civics nearly backed out of the league on the eve of opening day due to concerns about shortages of ballplayers and spectators. McGarigle organized a meeting with the Woonsocket club and invited Mayor McCoy from Pawtucket along with representatives from the Walsh-Kaiser shipyard to convince Woonsocket to stay in the league. After only 600 fans attended the home opener at Roosevelt Park, five miles outside the city center in Blackstone, the team switched its home games to St. Ann's Park near downtown. Even then, only 800 to 900 fans attended Sunday games.

Besides the transportation challenge for spectators in 1943, ball clubs also experienced their own inconvenience in traveling to away games. Travel was not too burdensome for the three teams located in Rhode Island, but the Quincy team in Massachusetts had to overcome considerable adversity to get to road games. War-worker status may have been helpful, as these employees received "B" stickers that permitted them eight gallons of gasoline per week, twice the normal ration. Friendly patrons of the team with "C" or "X" stickers that afforded unlimited gasoline use could have covertly made their vehicles available for team travel. After-hours visits to the infamous Mr. Black, for black-market refueling, also were not unheard of in 1943.

Fuel of another sort was also in short supply for ball players, as rationing began in early 1943 to equitably distribute the limited supply of meat and cheese; sugar and coffee had already begun to be rationed in 1942. "Food shortages caused perhaps the most pervasive rationing nuisance. Traveling baseball teams often encountered beefless menus; athletes accustomed to their nightly steak settled for fish instead," Mead wrote in *Even the Browns*.[32]

Walsh-Kaiser, which played its home games at Cranston Stadium, won the championship despite finishing in last place during the regular season. The Frigates won the 1943 New England Victory League championship on Sunday, September 12, by sweeping a doubleheader from the Pawtucket Slaters before 5,000 spectators at Pawtucket Stadium. Walsh-Kaiser edged Pawtucket, 3–2, in the first game, which was a completion of Thursday's game that was stopped after seven and a half innings due to dimout regulations. In the second game, Walsh-Kaiser thrashed the Slaters, 14–8, to win the best-of-seven-games series in six games.

Five teams participated in the 1944 season, when the league restored its New England League name. Three teams returned from the previous year — Pawtucket, Woonsocket, and Quincy. Since there was no longer a requirement that teams be comprised of war workers, Lynn returned while 1943 champion Walsh-Kaiser dropped out. Central Falls, Rhode Island, fielded a team for the 1944 season to maintain the league's nucleus in Rhode Island.

With the significant transportation challenges still in place, teams played less than two dozen games over the course of late spring and summer.

In 1944, with decreasing deferments allowed and a larger number of draftees, having a full allotment of ballplayers at the semi-pro level became ever more challenging, even as gas rationing lightened up and war wages burned a hole in people's pockets. The good news for the New England League was its proximity to military installations and defense facilities, which could supply baseball talent for more than an occasional ball game. While Organized Baseball frowned on this practice, spectators flocked to see professional players play for New England League teams, especially for Sunday games. Night games became less popular among fans due to the long workdays.

Lawrence "Crash" Davis, who played with the Philadelphia Athletics for three years from 1940 through 1942 before joining the navy, played for Lynn in 1944. Davis was stationed in Boston at Harvard University, where he was involved in the ROTC program and helped coach the baseball teams. In his first New England League game on May 25, Davis got three hits in Lynn's 11–3 victory at Adams Field in Quincy. However, in early June the navy notified Davis and other former major league ballplayers that it did not want them playing semi-pro games in their off-duty hours.

Bill Boyce replaced Davis at second base for Lynn. "Of course, I am not a Crash Davis," said Boyce, "but I will do the very best I can if I continue in that position." Less than two weeks later, Boyce had shipped out to Fort Devens to serve in the army and turned the second base position for Lynn into a merry-go-round for the season.[33]

Exhibition games with Negro League teams dwindled in number during 1943 and 1944, as gasoline rationing and other transportation challenges precluded the Negro League teams from traveling to New England. In 1944, Lynn did get in games with the Black Yankees on July 12 (in which Crash Davis did play, although going hitless in four at-bats) and the Homestead Grays on August 16.

Lynn also engaged in a three-game series with a local black semi-pro team, the Boston Colored Giants, which featured legendary pitcher Will "Cannonball" Jackman.

"Jackman has been one of the 'big name' pitchers in the senegambian ranks for lo these many years, and some have often referred to him as the 'Satchel Paige of New England,'" said the *Evening Item* about Jackman. "Old Pa Time has been reaching out for Cannonball Jackman for a long time, but the 46-year-old pitcher with the underhanded magic is not yet ready to enter the portals of Hasbeenville from which there is no return once you get inside."[34]

Jackman and the Colored Giants defeated Lynn, 4–3, on July 9 at Fraser Field. Jackman struck out nine and allowed only five hits. In the rematch on July 25, Lynn edged the Colored Giants, 3–2, reaching Jackman for eight hits. In the rubber game on August 10 before a crowd of 4,000 people, the Colored Giants defeated Lynn, 4–1, as Jackman repeated his nine-strikeout, five-hit performance of July 9.

Talent level in the New England League in 1944 was fairly good, especially on Sunday when the pros often played. Many of the New England League players were older men not eligible for the draft, or younger men declared 4-F (not draftable). Charlie Bird, a submarine-ball pitcher, was a thirty-something player at the time.

Lynn began to use high school players. In a night game on June 18 at Fraser Field, the team's first night game since the war started, seventeen-year-old Bobby Friberg played shortstop. In an exhibition game on July 16 against Camp Thomas, Lynn used fifteen-year-old Jack Campbell as a pitcher.

Night game attendance actually declined in 1944, and the league essentially turned into a Sunday-only league during the summer by playing home-and-home doubleheaders on Sunday. Massachusetts-based teams would play a home game on Sunday afternoon, then travel to Rhode Island for a Sunday night game in either Pawtucket or Central Falls. It was necessary to play the Sunday night games in Rhode Island because of the Sunday law in Massachusetts that prohibited the playing of professional baseball after 6:30 P.M. (a loosening of the original Sunday law that stopped games at 6:00 p.m.; limitations were finally eliminated in 1946).

"It may be from the fact that so many young men who have the yen of watching baseball are in the service," said the *Evening Item*, offering an explanation for the small crowds at night games. "Also many G.E. workers are so tired when they reach home at night that they figure that ball games starting around 9 o'clock and ending generally no earlier than 11 o'clock give them no chance to recuperate from the toil of the day."[35]

Spectators were men who were defense workers, but a new breed of minor league fan developed during the war. Housewives, pressed into service as war workers, attended games as did many youths of high school age that were also pressed into service to help out with family finances. With automobile travel restricted, there weren't many entertainment options available besides a ball game.

"Pres. Bob McGarigle has done well to keep even a five-club league going this summer, when ball players are scarce and hard to find with many youths in war service who otherwise would be performing on the diamond," said the *Evening Item*, summing up the 1944 season on the eve of the playoffs, which began in mid–August rather than after Labor Day as in previous years.[36]

Lynn, the first-place finisher with a 19–3 record, easily ousted Quincy in three games. Quincy was "having trouble fielding teams for away games due to the long trips and lack of sleep for its war worker team." Pawtucket, the second-place finisher with a 14–8 record, also dispatched Woonsocket in three games.[37]

For the fourth year in a row, Pawtucket advanced to the final series of the New England League playoffs. The best-of-seven-games series against Lynn went the full seven games in 1944 and stretched over two weeks by playing three doubleheaders and one game on a Friday night.

On Labor Day, September 4, Lynn and Pawtucket split two games, Lynn winning at Fraser Field in an afternoon contest and Pawtucket winning in an evening game in Rhode Island. On Friday night, September 8, Lynn edged Pawtucket, 5–4. On Sunday, September 10, Pawtucket took two from Lynn, including a thrilling thirteen-inning game at Pawtucket Stadium in the evening that the Slaters won, 2–1.

In the series finale on Sunday, September 17, Lynn swept both games from Pawtucket by the score of 2–0 to win the 1944 New England League championship. In the first game in Lynn, Johnny Fallon pitched Lynn to victory over Jim Reynolds, a former St. Louis Browns pitcher pitching under an assumed name for Pawtucket. In the second game at Pawtucket, Steve Kodis pitched Lynn to victory over New England League veteran Charlie Bird, who twirled for Pawtucket, despite later protests from Pawtucket that Lynn had illegally used Kodis, who had played all season for the Woonsocket team.

Davidson no doubt kept in mail contact with interim president McGarigle from Davidson's far-flung outposts in the Americas to use his engineering knowledge to help with the war effort. By the time the 1945 season began, the nation had celebrated V-E Day when hostilities ceased in Europe. Davidson had likely already begun plotting a return to minor league status for the 1946 season.

With the end of the war seemingly in sight, four new teams joined the New England League for the 1945 season. Pawtucket and Lynn were the only returning clubs. Cranston, Rhode Island, and New London, Connecticut, were able to make use of nearby war plants to stock their teams. There were two new teams from Massachusetts, Lawrence and Worcester.

"Cranston is spending plenty of money in the effort to win a New England League pennant," the *Evening Item* reported in mid–May. "The entire batting order is star-studded with players who have been in very fast company at some time or other, but are now working in Rhode Island war plants."[38]

In 1945, there was rampant use of professional ball players who used assumed names to participate in New England League games. The two most famous ball players to use an alias were Crash Davis and Yogi Berra.

Davis, who played briefly under his own name for Lynn in 1944, adopted the alias "Chuck Leary" to play for Lawrence in 1945. "I started playing under the name Chuck Leary in the New England Semi-Pro League," Davis recalled years later. "I played under an assumed name because I guess it was against the rules to play even though it didn't hurt anything. I chose the name Leary because there are a lot of Irish in that area. Later I played in Woonsocket, Rhode Island. I played as Bob Palliteria, a French name since there were a lot of French people there."[39]

Leary was listed at second base in the Lawrence box score in its May 20 game with Pawtucket, when, as the *Pawtucket Times* reported, "Ralph Wilson, ex-major leaguer, twirled a masterful no-hit, no-run game." Wilson, another player using an assumed name, faced the minimum twenty-seven batters in the game as the one batter he walked was erased on a double play.[40]

Berra played under his real name for the baseball team fielded by the New London, Connecticut, submarine base, where Berra was stationed in 1945. On Friday night, July 27, the sub base defeated Pawtucket, 4–1, before a crowd of 2,300 at Hammond Pond Stadium. "The Sub Base got its first tally in the second [inning]. Gleeson, leading off, was passed. 'Yogi' Berra singled to left putting Gleeson on second, and a single to right by Gryska scored Gleeson," the *Pawtucket Times* reported.[41]

But according to Davis, Berra also played some games under an assumed name in the New England League, perhaps in a Sunday game on Berra's day off from military duty.

> I also managed at Lawrence that same year. I remember one game when we were playing in Providence, Rhode Island, and all those players were using assumed names. Jimmy Gleeson, who had been with the Cubs and the Reds, was playing in that league and first base was open so I elected to walk him. I didn't know that little guy that was hitting next but I knew Gleeson. That short little guy looked about 18 or 19 years old and it turned out he hit a home run with the bases loaded. His real name was Lawrence "Yogi" Berra. Yogi was at New London in the Merchant Marine.[42]

Newspapers covering the New England League games universally participated in stifling the truth about the real names of the major league ball players playing in the league. The degree of truth suppression varied among the newspapers.

"Two former big leaguers, Johnny Steel and Jim Duffy, will be the battery for the Lawrence Millionaires when they open the New England League season of the Slaters at the Stadium tomorrow night at 8:30," the *Pawtucket Times* reported. Neither Steel nor Duffy has an entry in the *Baseball Encyclopedia*. Occasionally, the *Times* would provide a hint about who the player was, such as its report that "Tom Moylan, former National League star who faced the Yankees in the World Series a few years ago, is expected to pitch tonight for Pawtucket."[43]

The *Lynn Evening Item* was a little more above board. "One week from tomorrow, three former major league ball players who are in the service will join the Fraser Stars. Of course, they will have to play under fictitious names, but as soon as they are in uniform, the Lynn club expects to roll on victory road and be able to compete with the best in the circuit."[44]

"The New England is a league of aliases and fictitious names. No scribe desires to prevent any young man from earning a dollar by using his right name," the *Evening Item* rationalized.[45]

The use of major league players, even under assumed names, sparked interest in the New England League and attracted crowds to the ballpark. Pawtucket routinely played before crowds numbering several thousands for its night games. However, the use of players whose primary job was serving in the military caused chaos in scheduling games due to numerous rainouts that needed to be rescheduled. "Managers do not know who can play the next night due to so many of them using men in the service who often cannot figure what nights they are able to get away from their bases," the *Lynn Evening Item* reported.[46]

Teams in the semi-pro New England League, using healthy former major leaguers now in the military, were often just as good as the major league teams, which struggled to field decent squads. Major league rosters were replete with draft-ineligible players, such as Pete Gray, a one-armed outfielder, and Bert Shepherd, a pitcher with an artificial leg.

Sometimes, a stellar performance in an exhibition game would earn a semi-pro player a promotion to the major leagues. On July 9, the Lynn Frasers defeated the Boston Braves, 9–5, in an exhibition game behind the pitching of Bob Whitcher. A month later, after Whitcher threw a two-hit shutout victory over New London, the Braves added Whitcher to their National League roster. Whitcher first appeared in a major league game on August 20 as a pinch runner, before taking the mound for the Braves on September 4. In his six-game major league career that spanned six weeks in 1945, Whitcher started three games, pitched fifteen innings, and recorded a lifetime 0–2 won-lost record.

On July 30, Pawtucket nearly defeated the New York Yankees in an exhibition game, narrowly losing, 4–3, before a crowd of 14,000 at Pawtucket Stadium. The exhibition game with the Yankees was a chance for New England League veteran Charlie Bird to show the major leaguers that he had the potential to pitch at that level.

With Pawtucket leading the Yankees, 3–2, Bird entered the game as a relief pitcher in the seventh inning. Bird promptly struck out the side by whiffing Hershel Martin, Don Savage, and Oscar Grimes. He wasn't as fortunate in the eighth inning, though. "Although he displayed plenty of stuff working in a relief role, Charlie Bird was the victim of some real tough luck in the eighth when he gave up the two runs which enabled the Yankees to win and was charged with the defeat," the *Pawtucket Times* reported. Snuffy

Stirnweiss reached Bird for a single to tie the game and then Russ Derry drove in Joe Page with the winning run.[47]

Bird never did pitch in the major leagues. He did go on to play semi-pro baseball for twenty more years and was inducted into the Boston Park League Hall of Fame in 1982.[48]

After Japan surrendered in early August to end World War II, Davidson began planning a return of the New England League to Organized Baseball. There was one potential hitch in his plans — the Boston Braves announced on July 19 that the team planned to erect lights in order to play night games in 1946. "The new departure in Boston big league ball will have an effect on nocturnal games in the New England League, but more especially to the Fraser Stars," said the *Lynn Evening Item*.[49]

Cranston, with the best regular-season record at 22–8, captured the 1945 New England League championship by downing Pawtucket four games to one in the playoffs. In the fifth and final game, Cranston, behind the pitching of Arne Ericcson, defeated Pawtucket, 6–1, in front of 5,600 fans in Cranston Stadium. Bird suffered the loss for Pawtucket, as he left the game after pitching just two and two-thirds innings.

In late October 1945, Branch Rickey of the Brooklyn Dodgers announced that Jackie Robinson, a black, had signed a contract to play professional baseball in the Dodgers organization.

Robinson, in a "charade" tryout with the Boston Red Sox in April 1945 along with Marvin Williams and Sam Jethroe, had helped to paint Boston, and by extension the New England region, as an unfriendly environment for black players. "The audition of the three players took a little over one year to arrange and lasted only ninety minutes," Glenn Stout wrote in "Tryout and Fallout: Race, Jackie Robinson, and the Red Sox" in the *Massachusetts Historical Review*. "Yet the fallout from that day echoes through Red Sox history almost to the present as an example of the institutional racism practiced by the ballclub under the tenure of Red Sox owner Tom Yawkey."[50]

Davidson knew otherwise, though. Lynn had staged numerous, well-attended exhibition games with Negro League teams, which demonstrated Caucasian spectator tolerance for black players in that city. He also knew that newspapers, in a self-imposed gag order, suppressed any negative actions at the exhibitions with Negro League teams and also withheld information regarding professional players using aliases to play for New England League teams. These actions showed the length the media would go to hide news to protect a fragile local economy.

Davidson used these two attributes to revive the New England League one more time in 1946.

12

Final Years, 1946–1949

ON MAY 8, 1946, THE NASHUA DODGERS played their season-opening game against the Lynn Red Sox. New England League president Claude Davidson must have been beaming. He had done it again — the New England League was back in business as a minor league.

"Those identified with Organized Baseball say he pulled the present league out of a hat, a la Blackstone, the magician," said the *Lynn Evening Item* about Davidson that May. "He certainly is an organizer, when a year or so ago back they said resurrecting a New England League in this section couldn't be done."[1]

In this revival of the New England League, two black ball players played for the Nashua Dodgers and broke new ground in Organized Baseball. Roy Campanella and Don Newcombe were the first black players to play for a U.S.-based minor league team since the nineteenth century. Although Jackie Robinson, playing that year for the Brooklyn organization at Montreal, Canada, in the International League, gained far more attention than Newcombe and Campanella did playing in Nashua, New Hampshire, the New England League's embracing of black players during the 1946 season was an historical occasion in itself.

Exactly how Nashua came to be the site of the first black players on a Caucasian professional baseball team since the 1890s has remained shrouded in legend and lore, for the most part. Having black players in the New England League in 1946 was not only an historical event; the presence of Campanella and Newcombe was also an essential ingredient in Davidson's conquest to revive the New England League. Without the black players, it is not likely that the New England League could have been revived for its sixth and final time.

256

Brooklyn president Branch Rickey and historians portrayed the arrival of Campanella and Newcombe in Nashua as a combination of desperation on Rickey's part and benevolence by Nashua business manager Buzzy Bavasi. In reality, though, the selection of Nashua very likely was part of a well-planned maneuver orchestrated by Rickey to serve as the base for the newly signed black players in 1946. Rickey seems to have collaborated with Davidson during the autumn of 1945 to revive the New England League as an out-of-the-way sanctuary to develop black players for the Brooklyn Dodgers. Bavasi did play an important role, performing the yeoman work to maximize the chances that the black players would succeed in the all-Caucasian world of professional baseball.

Early on, Nashua was most assuredly Plan B in Rickey's post–Robinson, black-player strategy. By December 1945, three months before the signing of Campanella and Newcombe, Nashua became Plan A for the location where Rickey could most effectively develop the black ball players.

The conventional explanation posited for Campanella and Newcombe playing in Nashua was detailed in Campanella's autobiography, *It's Good to Be Alive*, published in 1959.

Campanella met in early March 1946 with Bob Finch, Rickey's assistant, at the Dodgers' offices in Brooklyn, to discuss signing his contract. Because of some concerns at Brooklyn's spring training site due to Robinson's appearance there, "Mr. Rickey feels it would not be wise to have you join the Montreal club at this time," Campanella quoted Finch about the possibility of going to Brooklyn's top farm club, at the AAA level. "He suggested I try to place you with our Danville club," which was in the Three-I League, a Class B league, the same level as the New England League. After Finch called Danville, Campanella quoted Finch as saying, "They don't want you." After reassuring Campanella that they'd find a place for him, Finch then said without making any intervening phone calls, "Mr. Rickey told me to try Nashua. He thinks Bavasi will take you." After a phone call to Bavasi, Finch turned to Campanella and said, "It's all set. Bavasi will take you."[2]

Newcombe echoed the story sketched by Campanella with comments made in 1997 during the celebration of the fiftieth anniversary of Jackie Robinson's major league debut. "[Rickey] told us they wouldn't let us down South for spring training, and they wouldn't let us play in Danville," Newcombe said. "He told us the Dodgers had only one farm club left to put us, and that it was up in Nashua."[3]

It's a great story about how Nashua unintentionally came to be the home site for the first U.S.-based black players in Organized Baseball in more than a half century. It is arguably a tall tale, though. A strong case can be made that the selection of Nashua was no accident, in that Rickey had already determined months earlier that Nashua would be the location for the next group of blacks signed after Robinson. Therefore, the story about Danville refusing to take the black players was simply a ruse.

Campanella wasn't untruthful in his retelling of the story — he just didn't have all the facts at his disposal. As he admitted in his book, Campanella didn't hear the conversation at the other end of the telephone; he only heard what Finch said. Newcombe wasn't in the room at all, so neither person actually talked to Rickey at that time, nor did they have any idea what Rickey told Finch, nor what Finch heard from the Danville owner or Bavasi. Campanella said Finch did more listening than talking on the line with Rickey, who was in Florida attending to the situation surrounding Jackie Robinson's arrival at Brooklyn's spring training camp.

Therefore, Rickey and Finch could have easily executed the Danville-Nashua ruse to mask Rickey's true intent for having the Nashua franchise in the Brooklyn farm system. Why all the secrecy? Rickey did not want to arouse suspicion that he had a plan for minimizing the distractions so that black players could develop within the all-Caucasian system of Organized Baseball.

As early as 1950, the Danville-Nashua story was in the public domain, published in a *Saturday Evening Post* article about Newcombe. "Originally, the Dodgers tried to farm him out to Danville, Illinois, but the Three-Eye League's president made it rather plain that Newcombe wouldn't be welcome. Nashua proved to be the perfect choice. A mill town in New Hampshire with a black population of exactly one dozen souls, it was a spot virtually free of race prejudice."[4]

The incorporation of the Danville-Nashua story in Campanella's autobiography published in 1959 gave the explanation an imprimatur of credibility.

The spurned-by-Danville-accepted-in-desperation-by-Nashua explanation gained added momentum in 1983 when historian Jules Tygiel recounted the story in his seminal book on baseball integration, *Baseball's Great Experiment.* "They don't want me?" Tygiel quotes Campanella from his autobiography about the telephone call orchestrated by Finch, which in turn became the title of that chapter of the book.[5]

With Tygiel's validation of the Danville-Nashua tale, the story was perpetuated in the *Boston Globe* article in 1997 and by historians Steve and Stephanie Roper in a 1998 article in the journal *Historical New Hampshire,* which was partially based on 1994 correspondence with Bavasi. "By the middle of March 1946 ... [Rickey] planned to assign Campanella and Newcombe to the class-B Danville Dodgers in Illinois," the Ropers wrote. "But that

Mural depicting Don Newcombe and Roy Campanella, two Nashua Dodger players in 1946, who were the first black players to play for a U.S.-based minor league team in the twentieth century. The mural is painted on the side of a building on West Hollis Street in downtown Nashua, New Hampshire.

month, experience with racism in Florida and Illinois led the Dodgers to assign Don Newcombe and Roy Campanella to Nashua."[6]

However, nobody asked Bavasi the right questions to get at the true story of how Nashua came to play the role that it did in baseball integration. Bavasi was not untruthful in his remarks, only tantalizingly incomplete in his statements.

For instance, in the 1997 *Boston Globe* article, Bavasi was quoted as saying, "One of the first things we did was to make sure that the city of Nashua would be behind us. What we did was hire the editor of the *Nashua Telegraph*, Fred Dobens, to be president of the team. That way we knew the city's newspapers would back us." Everyone presumed that Bavasi meant after the players were signed in March 1946. The Ropers even explicitly interpreted Bavasi's similar comments by injecting an explanatory parenthetical in their 1998 article: "One of the first things we did [after the players were assigned to Nashua] was to make sure that the city of Nashua would be behind us."[7]

However, Bavasi really did mean the *first* thing, i.e., in December 1945, not after the players were signed in March 1946. While nearly everyone admits that Dobens was brought on board to ensure proper publicity concerning the black players, few have mentioned when newspaperman Dobens signed on with the Nashua Dodgers — Dobens was recruited long before Campanella's meeting with Finch in March.

The Danville-Nashua tale is an excellent example of President Kennedy's remark about truth, which he mentioned in his commencement address at Yale University in 1962. Kennedy said: "The great enemy of the truth is very often not the lie — deliberate, contrived, and dishonest — but the myth — persistent, persuasive, and unrealistic."[8]

To replace the Danville-Nashua "myth," here is a more plausible account of the "truth" about how Nashua became the home base for Brooklyn's black players in 1946.

In the fall of 1945, Davidson, upon his return to civilian life from his military construction duties during the war, campaigned with minor league officials to bring the New England League back into Organized Baseball. Although the league had a successful run as a semi-pro circuit during the war years, Davidson encountered resistance in trying to elevate the league back to minor league status.

The *Lynn Evening Item* reported in November 1945 that there was a "movement afoot to operate a minor league in New England, although an informant says the group 'will never get to first base' with the national association" in charge of the minor leagues. The *Evening Item* quoted the informant as saying, "What we are after is a league as good as the Eastern and which will play Class A ball."[9]

Davidson, never one to be deterred in his quest to revive the New England League, attended the annual minor league meeting held that December in Columbus, Ohio. Branch Rickey, looking to expand his farm system and talk with executives of his existing farm clubs, was at the Columbus meeting before heading to Chicago for the National League meeting the following week. The affable Davidson met up with the cunning Rickey at some point during the Columbus meetings. Desperate for any way to revive the New England League, Davidson could easily have extolled Rickey on the virtues of several New England cities that had large French-Canadian populations, which could mirror Montreal as a U.S. base for black players in the Brooklyn minor league system. New England League cities, particularly Lynn, also had an excellent record in supporting exhibition games with Negro League teams during the war.

Davidson may have even talked with Rickey in the intervening weeks following the Robinson signing and before the Columbus meetings. Curiously, the *Nashua Telegraph* ran a story on November 27 with the headline "See Possibility of Organized Baseball Here Next Year." Davidson had obviously talked with someone at the *Telegraph*, probably Dobens, to plant that story.[10]

If Davidson hadn't already talked to Rickey before November 27, why would the *Telegraph* speculate on the city having a minor league team? Nashua was a poor candidate for minor league baseball. Its last attempt at supporting a team was in 1933, when the Quincy team shifted to Nashua. The shift was a miserable failure, as citizens of the Great Depression-weary city didn't support the team, and it became an orphan team within weeks, playing all its games on the road. During the war years, with better prosperity and a brand new WPA-financed ball park in Holman Stadium, the city failed to field a team in the semi-pro New England League. The *Telegraph* later even volunteered that since that 1933 team, "baseball has slowly withered away in this city."[11]

Rickey bought the pitch of super-salesman Davidson and struck a deal to help revive the New England League by owning a team to serve as an out-of-the-way incubator for black minor leaguers in the Brooklyn farm system. With Rickey's support as a willing accomplice to the quest of dream-chaser Davidson to revive the New England League, minor league officials at the Columbus meeting ratified the return of the league to Organized Baseball.

A deal between Davidson and Rickey as well as the established Davidson-Dobens connection was evident when the *Nashua Telegraph* provided the first public pronouncement of the revival of the New England League. In a December 8 article headlined "Nashua Set For Spot in Proposed N.E. Baseball League," the *Nashua Telegraph* heralded Davidson's expectations that minor league baseball would come to Nashua. "Nashua may be represented in a newly organized baseball circuit if the efforts of Claude B. Davidson, one time president of the old New England League, now attending the baseball meeting at Columbus, Ohio, achieve the results hoped for."[12]

Three days later, in an article headlined "Nashua May Be Home of Brooklyn Farm Team in 1946," the *Telegraph* confirmed that Rickey would place a team in Nashua. "Nashua may well be the home of a Brooklyn Dodger farm team when the 1946 baseball season rolls around as the result of a visit of Branch Rickey's personal representative to the city last night," reported the *Telegraph* of Bavasi's initial visit to the city. "No money is expected from the city to run the team, in as much as the Brooklyn outfit will finance and run its own club."[13]

Davidson, upon his return to Boston, was ebullient about the chances of the New England League once again becoming a minor league. "He said that major league clubs are anxious to back teams in this section and three of them have gone on record as willing to operate franchises outright," said the *Lynn Evening Item*, reporting Davidson's mild exaggeration in mid–December. In actuality, only the Brooklyn Dodgers had advanced such a claim.[14]

Rickey prevailed upon Bavasi to assume the task of selecting a minor league site for the future black players Rickey expected to sign. Bavasi, having arrived home in November 1945 from three years in the service and intending to take some time off before rejoining the Dodgers' front office, was Rickey's foot soldier to evaluate potential sites for the black players to play. Rickey had indeed desired that site to be Danville, located as it was in an out-of-the-way location 100 miles south of Chicago on the Illinois-Indiana border. New England seemed to be the second choice.

"After a week [of vacation], Mr. Rickey called and asked me to come to New York as he was having a problem," Bavasi recalled in 2004. "I flew to New York and then was asked to go to Danville, Illinois. The purpose of the Danville trip was to ascertain whether or not Mr. Rickey's friend Book Kishwalter, owner of the club, would entertain the idea of playing two black boys. The answer was definitely no, by the club and the league. The [Three-I] League was not ready for such action."[15]

While Danville did indeed reject Rickey's entreaty to use black players, that rejection occurred in December 1945, not March 1946. Rickey knew that Danville was not a viable candidate three months before Campanella signed a contract with Brooklyn in the aftermath of the myth-making Finch-Rickey phone call that Campanella witnessed.

Bavasi's next stop that December was Nashua, New Hampshire, to see officials at the *Nashua Telegraph* newspaper at the suggestion of Davidson, the New England League president. After Danville, "I then proceeded to Nashua and a meeting with Fred Dobens," Bavasi recollected in 2004. "After meeting with Fred, the Dodgers now had a club in Nashua," with assurances that the newspaper, and by extension the city itself, would be accepting of the black players.[16]

Based on the *Nashua Telegraph* reports, Bavasi was most likely in Danville on December 8 (when the newspaper speculated on having a team, since Danville was Rickey's first choice) and almost definitely in Nashua on December 10 (for the "visit of Branch Rickey's personal representative to the city last night").

With the New England League locked in by December 11 as the base for the black players, Rickey immediately began a misinformation campaign to mask the true nature of his farm club in the New England League. Rickey was already getting some heat about not compensating Negro League teams for the two black players he had already signed (Robinson and John Wright), and he knew matters would escalate further once he signed Campanella and Newcombe. If it were known that Rickey had explicitly planned a minor league base for these "poached" players from the Negro Leagues, he would be in a far more untenable position to defend his actions than if everyone believed the development of the black players was merely being done on an ad hoc basis.

On December 12, Rickey gave an interview to an Associated Press sportswriter to help create a cover story for his New England League team. "The Brooklyn Dodgers will have the second-largest farm system in the Major Leagues in 1946, President Branch Rickey said today," the AP story began. "When arrangements are completed for a team in the Class B New England League, which is being organized, Brooklyn will have 18 farm teams," second only to the 26 farm teams of the St. Louis Cardinals.[17]

Rickey created an excuse for expanding the farm system into the Class B New England League, claiming "the chain was too 'top heavy,' having too many clubs in the higher classifications for the number of Class C and Class D teams which serve as feeders." The article went on to note, "Rickey said he believed about 24 teams was the right number to balance out this upper bracket," which consisted of two AAA teams and two AA teams.[18]

Back in New England, Davidson told the *Lawrence Evening Tribune* that he already had six cities lined up for the 1946 New England League season — Cranston, Providence, Lynn, Lawrence, Nashua, and Manchester — and that several major league teams were interested in having farm clubs in the league. "The Boston Braves are interested in Cranston, the Red Sox in Providence, and the Dodgers have already had a man looking over Nashua," the *Evening Tribune* reported of Bavasi's travels in the region.[19]

"The Brooklyn Dodgers will sponsor a New England League team in Nashua instead of Manchester, it has been learned from a reliable source," the *Lawrence Evening Tribune* reported on January 5. "E.J. Bavasi, Dodgers official, who will be business manager of the Gate City team, informed Eddie Bourassa that Branch Rickey had decided to settle on Nashua since that community had offered them the use of Holman Stadium, inside the park advertising, outright concessions, and other inducements."[20]

While the *Evening Tribune* didn't elaborate on what the "other inducements" might be, they certainly included a very favorable public perspective that Dobens could virtually guarantee through his twin roles as newspaper editor at the *Nashua Telegraph* and president of the Nashua Dodgers team.

With the strategy set and the main players in place, the official January 14 announcement of the formation of the Nashua Dodgers was strictly routine. "The Brooklyn Dodgers will own Nashua outright with E.J. 'Buzz' Bavasi as general manager," the *Telegraph* reported. All the elaborate behind-the-scenes moves were completely transparent at the time. There was no public hint of why Nashua was in the New England League.[21]

Newcombe always credited Bavasi with not being a bigot with his acceptance into Organized Baseball. While Bavasi definitely felt "the color of a man's skin was immaterial as long as they could play the game as well or better than the white player," he acted on that belief in December 1945, not March 1946.[22]

When viewed within the context of other facts of the time and retrospective statements, it should have been more apparent that Nashua was part of a pre-meditated plan to be a staging area for Brooklyn's black players.

Why would Brooklyn initiate a report on December 12 that it was sponsoring a farm team in an unspecified location in a league being revived after it had experienced so many failures over the previous thirty years? Nashua itself was a poor candidate for minor league baseball, with its last successful attempt at supporting a team coming in 1929 before its aborted attempt to support a team in 1933. There had to be an ulterior motive, not simply another team to stock with surplus returning post-war players.

Why would Brooklyn want to directly own the Nashua franchise? All the other teams in the New England League were owned and operated by local people, many of whom were associated with the semi-pro New England League during the war years. The answer had to be to have total control of the team's operations and minimize adverse publicity over the black players.

Davidson no doubt saw the potential for the black players to infuse some new life into the league by attracting crowds to the games and helping to ease the economic challenges that had always beset league franchises. Having Brooklyn backing a club would also provide a solid foundation for the league to temper any hard times. Davidson could settle for less than top billing to achieve his goal of having minor league baseball in New England once again.

In Davidson's quest to revive the New England League, Rickey had a dedicated ally to support his goals for the black players.

Interestingly, Davidson reached out to the black community in January 1946, a full two months before the signings of Campanella and Newcombe were announced. According to the *Boston Guardian*, a black newspaper, Davidson spoke at the Boston City Club on January 26 about "the use of colored ball players." While Davidson toed the line of Organized Baseball in saying "there was no rule barring colored players," the *Boston Guardian* commented in February, "We shall watch developments in the New England League and we expect to see colored players therein."[23]

While this is by no means a smoking gun that Davidson was paving the way for the arrival of the to-be-signed black players, it is an interesting development, especially the overt optimism of the black newspaper. It is entirely possible that Davidson dropped some broad hints to the *Guardian* sportswriter.

Davidson had the public relations savvy to smooth over any difficulties with the black players and the motivation to keep the owners of the other teams in line if there were difficulties. The fact that there were several racial incidents in 1946 that only came to light years later and were never publicized in the newspapers at the time they occurred is testament to Davidson's ability to effectively control the public posture of the league.

Davidson also understood the dynamics of New England cities and could pinpoint exactly how Nashua, with its French-Canadian heritage, would be accepting of blacks. Nashua was a fabulous place for black players to re-enter Organized Baseball. The city had a history of ethnic tolerance, as many nationalities lived there to work in the textile mills. French-Canadians were especially prevalent in the 1940s, and proved to be exceptionally conducive to the black players. Located forty miles northwest of Boston, Nashua was certainly off the beaten path baseball-wise, and in a Class B league outside of the media specter as well.

On April 4, 1946, the signings of Campanella and Newcombe were announced. A short article in the *New York Times*, entitled "Nashua Acquires 2 Negro Players," focused on Dobens and mentioned Rickey only in the context of having earlier signed Robinson:

> The Brooklyn Dodgers of the National League have assigned two black players to their Nashua farm club, Fred H. Dobens, president of the New England League

team, said today.... The Brooklyn club "is carrying [out] its plan to give deserving black players a chance to make good in organized baseball down through its farm clubs," Dobens said.[24]

The story in the *Nashua Telegraph*, entitled "Nashua Dodgers Sign Two Negro Baseball Players," focused on Rickey, although it was buried on page 19.

Branch Rickey of the Brooklyn Dodgers will test New England fandom's democratic attitude toward the racial question this spring it was revealed today with the announcement that the Brooklyn baseball club has signed two more black players and will place them in organized ball with their New England League farm team here in Nashua.[25]

In the other New England League cities, the signings were blandly reported. "The Brooklyn Dodgers have signed two Negro ball players to play for their Nashua farm club, Donald Newcombe, a right-handed pitcher, and Roy Campanella, a catcher," the *Lawrence Evening Tribune* reported as an item in its "N.E. League Briefs" column. The *Lynn Evening Item* wrote, "Two Negro recruits have been assigned to the Nashua, N.H., club of the New England League, by the Brooklyn Dodgers, Pres. Fred Dobens of the Nashua farm announced last night."[26]

Just about the only Caucasian newspaper interested in the story was the *Daily Worker*, a Communist publication in New York City. Writer Bill Mardo closely followed the story of how Jackie Robinson broke down racial barriers in baseball as an extension of the paper's socialist editorial focus. In reporting the signings of Campanella and Newcombe, Mardo wrote, "Thus was another body-blow ripped into the heart of Jimcrow in America's National Pastime." Mardo also reported comments from Effa Manley, owner of the Newark Eagles in the Negro National League, which had lost pitcher Newcombe from its roster. Manley was sanguine about the impact of the signings of the black players by major league teams. "When Negroes make good in big-league baseball, it will have the same effect upon Negro-white unity that has been created as a result of the fine records established by Negroes in other sports," Manley said. "There's no reason why Negroes can't be included among the finest baseball players in the country — just as they have proven themselves in boxing, football, and on the cinder paths [in track]."[27]

Black newspapers naturally hailed the signings. The *Boston Chronicle* wrote, "You can mark down in your memory book that the spring of 1946 marked the end of the talking about and experimenting with Negro players in organized baseball, and heralded the advent of full democracy in the big leagues."[28]

The *Boston Chronicle* also noted an advantage for Campanella and Newcombe, one that perhaps Rickey had carefully considered, but didn't articulate publicly, in selecting Nashua:

> Both Newcombe and Campanella have a decided advantage that is denied to Robinson and Wright, their predecessors on the Dodgers farm roster. They will be able to limber up mentally with greater ease because the thought of carrying a whole race on their shoulders will not be original enough to bother them too much.[29]

However, baseball writer Sam Lacy of the *Baltimore Afro-American* didn't congratulate the signings. "The departure of Roy Campanella from the ranks of the Negro National League leaves colored baseball in this neck of the woods in a bad way for catchers," Lacy wrote.[30]

Lacy may have been still steamed about being misled by an apparent misinformation campaign initiated by Rickey in early April. Lacy heard from some source that the next black players signed by Rickey would play for the Danville farm club. This appears to be an early indication that Rickey made a conscious effort to foster the Danville-Nashua ruse as a cover story for why Rickey chose Nashua as the site for the next wave of black players:

> Unconfirmed rumors that Roy Campanella, hustling 26-year-old Baltimore Elite Giants catcher, was destined to join the Danville club of the Brooklyn Dodgers, were denied by Pres. Branch Rickey on Monday.... Rickey told the *Afro-American* that he knew of no plan to send Campanella, who batted .365 in Negro National League play last year, to the Danville club ... and emphatically denied that any of the colored boys will be sent there as a start.[31]

That was most of the publicity that Nashua garnered during 1946 and for the next five decades for being a pioneer in the racial desegregation of baseball.

The Rickey version of how Nashua gained its place in the history of baseball's racial desegregation went unchallenged for many years, as Nashua was viewed simply as a footnote to the focus on Jackie Robinson.

In his 1970 history of black baseball, Robert Peterson, author of *Only the Ball Was White*, devoted just one paragraph to the signing of Campanella and Newcombe. Peterson simply stated, "Both were assigned to Nashua in the Class B New England League."[32]

While a more extensive analysis of Nashua's role was undertaken by Jules Tygiel in his 1983 book *Baseball's Great Experiment*, his wrap-up paragraph highlighted but still understated Nashua's role. "The national press largely ignored the events at Nashua," Tygiel wrote. "The spotlight in 1946 justifiably belonged to Jackie Robinson. But Rickey's 'second front' in the integration battle was as successful as the primary staging ground in Montreal."[33]

Rickey's biographers barely mentioned the "second front" of integration, focusing entirely on the signing of Jackie Robinson and his early days with

Montreal. In the years before his death in 1965, Rickey seemed to have left no amplification of how the Nashua franchise came into existence; his biographers also avoided the issue.[34]

We will never have documented truth about how Nashua was selected to be the site of the first U.S.-based black players in a Caucasian professional baseball league in the twentieth century. Bavasi, whose recollection in 2004 does provide clarity to illuminate the situation, was an octogenarian at the time, and thus his remarks do need to be viewed in that context, as possibly revisionist or even inaccurate. (Note: The author believes those remarks to be accurate.)

Beyond some tidbits about the Robinson signing, the Rickey papers at the Library of Congress "add surprisingly little to the familiar contours of the integration saga," according to one historian, and "are strangely silent about the critical 1944–1948 period." In its summary of the Rickey papers, the Library of Congress notes bluntly, "Items relating to the Brooklyn Dodgers relate primarily to the sale of Rickey's stock in the Dodgers and contain no material relating to Robinson's integration of baseball."[35]

Davidson died in 1956, leaving no surviving record of his thoughts on Nashua's role in the racial integration of baseball.

By combining the Brooklyn-owned Nashua club with several clubs from the wartime semi-pro New England League (Lynn, Pawtucket, Lawrence, and Cranston), Davidson had a solid foundation for the league revival. Old standbys Manchester, Fall River, and Portland filled out the eight-team circuit for 1946.

Forsaking independent status, a hallmark of the league since its beginning in 1885, was a key element of the 1946 revival. In addition to Nashua's direct ownership by Brooklyn, three other clubs operated as farm teams of major league clubs — Manchester with the New York Giants, Lynn with the Boston Red Sox, and Pawtucket with the Boston Braves. These four clubs prospered not only from the financial support (especially provision of players), but also from the rivalries cultivated among them.

While geographic rivalries had been a key component of previous New England League seasons, the post-war rivalries within the league were based much more on major league affiliation. The Dodgers-Giants rivalry in New York fostered the Nashua-Manchester rivalry in 1946, while the natural Boston connection between the Red Sox and the Braves supported the Lynn-Pawtucket rivalry. Manchester and Nashua also developed a rivalry with Pawtucket through their common National League parentage. Lynn and Nashua also became rivals in 1946, helped along by the pennant runs of their parent clubs. The Boston Red Sox cruised to the American League pennant and the Brook-

Plaque at Holman Stadium in Nashua, New Hampshire, describing how racial barriers were broken in 1946 when Don Newcombe and Roy Campanella played for the Nashua Dodgers.

lyn Dodgers tied for first place in the National League (losing the pennant in a playoff with St. Louis).

Due to the legacy of wartime baseball, the 1946 version of the New England League was perhaps the league's healthiest in its entire history. Seven of the eight teams played night games under lights, with only Portland steadfastly maintaining a daytime schedule. Attendance swelled as returning servicemen and war-weary workers craved entertainment as a refuge from the hassles of the post-war economy.

Night baseball in 1946 was still a rarity in Boston. Red Sox owner Tom Yawkey continued his policy of all day games at Fenway Park in 1946. Although the new management of the Braves installed lights at Braves Field, the Braves had just twenty night games on the 1946 National League schedule released on March 31.

The limited number of night games at Braves Field created little overlap to the schedule of night games played by New England League teams.

Baseball aficionados in Lynn could easily watch games of both the Boston Red Sox and the Lynn Red Sox on the same day. Fans could take the train (or drive a car) to Fenway Park for the 3:00 P.M. afternoon game in Boston and return to Lynn for the evening game at 8:30 P.M. (night games typically started this late in 1946 so that the entire game could be played under the lights). For Braves fans in Rhode Island, it was slightly more difficult, but not impossible, to see an afternoon game at Braves Field in Boston and an evening game at McCoy Stadium in Pawtucket (renamed from Hammond Pond Stadium in June 1946 to honor the deceased Mayor McCoy).

But the handwriting was on the wall for the New England League regarding the impact of night baseball in Boston.

The Braves drew 37,407 fans for the first night game at Braves Field on May 11, when the team routinely attracted just a few thousand for day games played during the week. "The first night game in Boston major league history at Braves Field last night did about everything but produce a victory for the Tribesmen who were beaten, 5 to 1, by the Giants in their first nocturnal appearance at the beautifully-lighted Wigwam," the *Boston Herald* reported on that first night game.[36]

Ironically, night baseball, which Davidson had tried to popularize via an exhibition game between New England League teams in Lynn in 1927, was destined to help destroy the New England League rather than help it prosper. At that first night game at Braves Field, the *Boston Herald* reported, "Included in the crowd were 30 chartered bus loads of fans from outlying towns and cities." Potential fans of New England League baseball were already expressing a decided interest in attending major league night games rather than local minor league contests.[37]

With the Red Sox rolling to an American League pennant in 1946, fans also streamed to the day games at Fenway Park on the strength of the team's first-place cachet. While Yawkey had once been vehemently against night baseball — "I certainly hope I will never live to see the time when I shall see a major league night baseball game at Fenway Park," he declared in 1935 — the Red Sox announced on May 3 that the team would install lights at Fenway Park to play night games during the 1947 season.[38]

Even Sunday doubleheaders in 1946 at Fenway Park and Braves Field were enticing New England League fans to forsake their local games. On May 17, Governor Maurice Tobin signed a bill eliminating the former 6:30 curfew that halted Sunday baseball. The new law permitted Sunday baseball "until dark," so the doubleheaders could proceed at a more leisurely pace since they no longer needed to be completed in a rush within the legal time frame of four and a half hours.[39]

Despite the attraction of the major league teams in Boston, the New England League did reasonably well at the gate in 1946 due to the strong economy in the first post-war year.

While Davidson kept a watchful eye to ensure that no negative publicity was associated with the black players in Nashua, racial conflict between the black and Caucasian players was inevitable in 1946.

Campanella took it more in stride than Newcombe did. "The bench jockeys gave us a pretty hard time but it didn't bother me," Campanella wrote in his autobiography. He was victimized by subtle actions, like Manchester catcher Sal Yvars tossing dirt in his face while rubbing his hands at home plate and getting ready to bat. Campy reported that he responded to the action by telling Yvars, "Try that again and I'll beat you to a pulp."[40]

Newcombe was far more expressive about the racism in his comments in later years:

> Campy was more relaxed and mature than I was. I remember playing against the Lynn Red Sox when this guy, who was standing 10 feet away from Campy and myself, yelled out, "Get the niggers off the field." I started to charge him, but Campy put me in a bear hug and wouldn't let go until this guy, realizing I was going to kill him if I caught him, sprinted away. There were many other times that we were tested by racist comments. Looking back, and knowing my own personality, it's a miracle I kept my temper in check. There were times Campy and I couldn't get served in diners or restaurants. It was difficult to ignore how we were being treated by not only the fans but other ballplayers and even some coaches and managers. Still, as Mr. Rickey had told us, if we wanted to get to the majors and stay there, we had to keep our emotions under control, both on and off the field.[41]

Newcombe did not have found memories of the Lynn Red Sox. "They had this catcher, this redneck from the South, Matt Batts," Newcombe recalled in 1997. "And they had this pitcher, Walker Cress, he could pitch, but he was a bigot, too." Cress, a native of Louisiana, pitched a no-hitter against Nashua on May 26 at Fraser Field.[42]

Campanella, Newcombe, and Bavasi have talked most explicitly about an incident involving Lynn manager Tom "Pip" Kennedy (whom Newcombe may have been referring to in the lengthy quotation above). Their recalls are conflicting on many details, including whether the game was played in Nashua or Lynn, but all three men agree that Lynn personnel hurled explicit racial taunts at the black players in Nashua uniforms.

"One night in Lynn, I hit a couple of home runs and Newk pitched good," Campanella recalled in Roger Kahn's classic book about the Brooklyn Dodgers, *The Boys of Summer*. "After the game Buzzy went in to get his money and the manager of Lynn said, 'If it wasn't for them niggers, you wouldn't have beat us.' Buzzy jumped him. And they were swinging [fists] and all the players came running in. Buzzy was fighting him for what he said. It was always some sly thing. I never let it peeve me."[43]

"Lynn had this manager and he had been using the n-word the whole game. I was mad and I had them come to get their share of the gate receipts," Bavasi remembered in 1997. "The whole Red Sox team was there behind Kennedy, the bus was right there with all of them. And I said to him, 'Why don't you say to me right now what you said to them and I'll kick your ass. Go ahead and say that to me.'"[44]

To be sure, Lynn and Nashua had a number of on-field battles, including a night game on June 17 at Fraser Field in Lynn when the next day's headline on the sports page of the *Lynn Evening Item* read, "Lynn Wins Tempestuous Battle From Nashua." Lynn defeated Nashua, 11–10, in ten innings. Kennedy was ejected in the fourth inning of the game after a heated discussion to protest the ejection of batter Bill Boyce for complaining about a called third strike. In the sixth inning, there was a controversial play at the plate, when Campanella was thought to have juggled the ball as he tagged out a Lynn runner trying to score. "This caused another jostling session," the *Evening Item* reported, but "no blows were struck." The home plate umpire needed police protection after the game.[45]

Since Kennedy had managed numerous exhibition games for Lynn against Negro League teams during the New England League's semi-pro years during the war, his alleged actions in 1946 may have been a carryover from "accepted" taunting action that took place in those games.

With Newcombe compiling a 14–4 pitching record and Campanella clouting thirteen home runs, Nashua manager Walter Alston piloted the team to a second-place finish behind Lynn when the regular season concluded in early September.

By 1946, the Shaughnessy playoffs were conducted in every minor league. Only a dozen years after their birth, the playoffs were a natural part of the operation of a minor league. Unlike the 1933 round-robin fiasco and the chaotic, ringer-filled wartime playoffs during the league's semi-pro years, the 1946 playoffs proceeded smoothly. Nashua and Lynn won their first-round matchups against Pawtucket and Manchester, respectively. Nashua then took the title, defeating Lynn in six games, to help validate Rickey's Nashua strategy. It was the first of three consecutive New England League titles for the Nashua Dodgers.

As Davidson prepared for the 1947 season, the economies of several New England League cities posed a concern. Fall River and Lawrence, two cities dependent on textile mills, had seen better days. Even worse, the ball teams in those two cities played in crumbling facilities near downtown areas. With no major league backing, the two teams were comprised of mediocre players that produced poor playing records. The combination deterred spectators from attending games, since potential fans were now located more in the suburban towns than within the inner city. Fall River won only thirty of its 124 games played in 1946 to finish in seventh place in the standings; Lawrence finished in fifth place.

Providence and Portland — the other two clubs without working agreements with major league teams — played in more modern facilities, but also suffered from a lack of playing talent. Portland finished dead last in 1946, with a 20–99 record, while Providence eked out a sixth-place finish.

Of the four clubs that did qualify for the playoffs in 1946, three played in cities that were dependent on the textile industry and thus posed a long-term threat to the health of the New England League. Manchester, with the shutdown of the Amoskeag Mills in the 1930s, and Nashua were the most vulnerable. In Nashua, Textron had purchased the Nashua Manufacturing Corporation in December 1945, but the conglomerate was seeking significant efficiencies to keep the plant operating. Pawtucket had augmented its textile mills with defense industries, but the wind down of the war made the future of defense uncertain.

Lynn was the only one of the eight league cities with an auspicious economic base. The General Electric plant had permitted the city to successfully convert from its prior economic foundation based on the shoe industry.

Nevertheless, the ever-confident Davidson plunged ahead in December to organize a second minor league in the New England region, a Class A league to begin operation in 1948. "The new loop, known as the Atlantic Coast League, will operate along with the present New England League, which has a Class B rating," the *New York Times* reported. The proposed franchises were Worcester, Springfield, and Holyoke in Massachusetts; Providence and Pawtucket in Rhode Island; and Waterbury, Bridgeport, and New Haven in Connecticut. "All the clubs will either be owned outright by major league teams or have working agreements with them."[46]

Rickey seemed to be behind the formation of the Atlantic Coast League. Fresco Thompson represented Brooklyn at a second meeting held in January in New Haven, joining executives from several other major league teams and representatives from New Haven, Waterbury, Springfield, Holyoke, and Worcester. "In addition, Davidson said that Pawtucket, Fall River, and Bridgeport were being considered as potential franchise holders, the latter as a Brooklyn Dodger farm."[47]

Without Rickey's backing for the venture, it seems doubtful that Davidson would have proposed such an alignment, given the previous history of trying to combine the largest eastern and southern New England cities into a broader-based New England League. The experiments at such a combination in 1889, 1916, and 1934 had all been distinct failures. When it turned out that Davidson had enough challenges on his hands with just the New England League in 1947, the Atlantic Coast League never came to fruition.

The Boston Red Sox, American League champions in 1946, adopted night baseball in 1947, playing their first night game on June 13, adding further pressure on attendance at New England League games that initially began in 1946 when the Braves adopted night baseball. The Red Sox scheduled fourteen night games in 1947, which in combination with the twenty-nine night games of the Braves provided ample opportunity for working people in New England League cities within fifty miles of Boston to see professional baseball during the week.

With a doubleheader virtually every Sunday at either Fenway Park or Braves Field, the New England League had stiff competition for spectator dollars in 1947. Further diverting fans from New England League ball parks were numerous bus excursions from the outlying cities into Boston, making it all that much easier to attend a major league game instead of settling for a minor league one. Both Boston teams established new attendance records in 1947, as each team drew over a million spectators for their home games. Combined attendance for New England League games was less than half a million.

Six of the eight clubs for the 1947 season had major league affiliations, with Providence and Fall River picking up support from Cincinnati and the Chicago White Sox, respectively. However, Portland and Lawrence were still entirely independent.

The first chink in the 1947 New England League lineup was exposed in July when the Lawrence club folded a week after the Fourth of July holiday. The reason, according to the *Lawrence Evening Tribune*, was the "failure of Lawrence officials to fulfill contractual obligations both to the league and the players." The short explanation was the fans stopped going to O'Sullivan Park to see the games, even though the Lawrence team was not that bad. At the time of its disbanding, Lawrence had a 29–38 record and was in fourth place in the league standings.[48]

The timing of the demise of the Lawrence team rekindled memories of earlier New England League years when critics called the circuit a "Fourth of July league," since many teams disbanded after the holiday due to poor finances. Desperate to keep an eight-team league operating, Davidson transferred the team to Lowell, another textile industry victim.

Lowell was an unworthy candidate for a New England League franchise in 1947, as local baseball allegiances in Lowell were strongly bonded with amateur ball clubs. On July 17, the opening night game in Lowell was rained out. The next night, the home opener drew only 1,000 fans. Within a week, the American Legion team, comprised of teenagers, got top billing on the sports pages of the *Lowell Sun*, with the New England League team relegated to the second page.[49]

In August, there was scant attendance at the Lowell games. On August 11, only 200 fans showed up to Alumni Field. For a Sunday doubleheader on August 17, the official attendance was 101 people, just 85 of whom paid. After the doubleheader loss on August 17, the team was in last place with a 35–70 record, which translated to an abysmal 6–32 record after transferring from Lawrence. Lowell owner Tom Sellers then gave up and the team became an orphan for the remainder of the season, playing all its games on the road.[50]

The geographic rivalries between cities that had once kept the New England League together had been transferred to high school baseball teams in the spring and amateur teams in the summer, such as those sponsored by the American Legion. Organized leagues for children also infringed upon old-time New England League rivalries. Little League baseball became a focus of potential adult spectators for New England League games, as they increasingly chose to attend twilight games played by their ten-year-old children rather than New England League games played at night under the lights.

New England League attendance was propped up in 1947 by the return of pitcher Don Newcombe for a second year with the Nashua Dodgers. The black pitcher continued to attract good crowds at New England League games, even though he was displeased to return to a Class B team while Campanella was promoted to the AAA level to play with St. Paul of the American Association for the 1947 season.

However, the status of blacks in Organized Baseball underwent a distinct change in 1947, which started to negatively impact the New England League. Jackie Robinson debuted in the major leagues with the Brooklyn Dodgers in April 1947. Several months later, Larry Doby debuted in the majors with the Cleveland Indians. Baseball fans in the New England region could now see black players at Braves Field and Fenway Park when the Dodgers and Indians played there, not just in New England League ball parks.

Rickey may have kept Newcombe at Nashua for the 1947 season to maintain attendance levels in Nashua. Rickey was still awaiting the initial outcome of the Great Experiment with Robinson at the major league level, and had been reluctant to sign additional black players with which to stock the Nashua club in 1947. What started out as a haven for black players to develop quickly turned into just another minor league farm team, as the novelty of black players in a Caucasian league evaporated almost overnight. Even with Newcombe pitching Nashua to another championship in 1947, attendance declined in Nashua from its 1946 level.

When Brooklyn won the National League pennant in 1947, Robinson played in the World Series. That fall, for the first time, the World Series games were transmitted across the country through a new communication medium — television. Watching moving pictures of a ball game in a box was a novel concept in 1947. Few people actually watched the World Series games on TV in 1947 due to lack of access and picture quality, but the idea had great promise.

"He'd watched some of the World Series games on the TV at Jimmy's, a bar around the corner from his apartment," one commentator described how most people in the late 1940s would have seen the ball games on television. "But the picture was small, fuzzy, and a lot of the time you'd get a better idea of what was going on listening to the radio."[51]

While television is the oft-cited explanation for the demise of the New England League, the league's ultimate doom was the proximity to Boston of the majority of the league's franchises. Television would have surely killed off the New England League in the 1950s, as it did many minor leagues across the country. But in the late 1940s, television was just one contributing factor.

The 1948 season was very challenging for Davidson to keep the New England League alive. Both the Braves and the Red Sox made pennant charges that year. The two teams combined to attract more than three million spectators to their games, which included nearly fifty night games and two dozen Sunday doubleheaders. There was almost a subway World Series in Boston in 1948, as the Braves won the National League pennant and the Red Sox tied for first place in the American League (losing the pennant in a one-game playoff with Cleveland). Without the success of the Braves and Red Sox in 1948, the end of the New England League simply would have been postponed a few years.

Besides their on-field success in 1948, the Braves and Red Sox also attracted fans off the field by beginning to televise their games in the spring of 1948. Harold Kaese of the *Boston Globe* captured the direct impact on baseball spectatorship as well as the indirect impact on the New England League:

In a fortnight, Boston's first big league game will be telecast by WBZ-TV, 40-odd miles North beyond Newburyport, Northeast to Gloucester, South to Plymouth, Southeast to Central Falls, R.I., and West through Worcester.... Some 3,500 television sets have been sold in Greater Boston, about a third to restaurants, taverns, and hotels. Most people will see their first Braves and Red Sox games telecast on such a set, the only price of admission being a spot of refreshment.[52]

Even without the success of the local major league teams and the advent of televised baseball on WBZ-TV, the underpinning of the New England League showed signs of failure. For the 1948 New England League season, Davidson had to deal with an economic recession that began that year when the region's textile and footwear industries went into a nosedive that they never recovered from.

Springfield had replaced the failed Lawrence/Lowell franchise, as Davidson convinced the Chicago Cubs to place a farm team in the western Massachusetts city. The addition of Springfield, five miles from the Connecticut border, was the closest the New England League would come to having a Connecticut-based club over the course of its Organized Baseball existence.

Springfield added a favorable dimension to the league. At ninety miles from Boston, Springfield was less influenced by the Braves and Red Sox than were Lynn, Nashua, and Pawtucket, which were within forty miles of Boston. Springfield and Portland became the cornerstone of the New England League for its final two seasons, leading the league in attendance both years. Springfield had Pynchon Park, with a seating capacity of 4,500 spectators. Portland was aided by the installation of lights so that the team could finally play night games.

Both clubs affiliated with National League franchises, Springfield with the Cubs and Portland with the Philadelphia Phillies. Since the two clubs had finished in sixth and seventh place during the 1947 season, the Cubs and Phillies sent lots of prospects to Springfield and Portland. A bolstered talent level and ample distance from Boston boosted attendance in both cities in comparison to the other six cities.

Lynn seemed to suffer the most. Just ten miles north of Boston, the city was within easy travel to Braves and Red Sox games and completely within range of Boston television station signals. Further hindering attendance at Fraser Field in 1948 was a change in ownership, resulting from the death of Gene Fraser in January. Fraser, a New England League icon, was a true community spirit rather than bottom line-oriented owner. The specter of new ownership turned off fans.[53]

Rickey demoted black pitcher Dan Bankhead from the Brooklyn club to Nashua to replace Newcombe, who had finally received his promotion to a higher classification league. Rickey must have thought having at least one black on the Nashua team was essential to maintaining the team's proving-ground genesis, as Bankhead was much too good for the New England League competition.

"Crack Negro Star Assigned to Nashua," read a *Nashua Telegraph* headline in late April, announcing the transfer of Bankhead from Montreal to the

Dodgers' New England League team. The *Telegraph* reported that Montreal manager Clay Hopper "predicts he'll win 30 games for Nashua." Bankhead did overwhelm his New England League opponents, winning twenty games for Nashua and registering 240 strikeouts in just 202 innings pitched.[54]

Even with Bankhead's spectacular pitching, attendance in Nashua plummeted in 1948.

On August 20, Nashua pitcher Bob Ludwick married Dorothy Bickings at home plate in Holman Stadium. The couple's wedding attracted 3,500 spectators to see the nuptials and the Nashua-Portland ball game following the wedding. The club denied that the wedding was a publicity stunt to attract paying customers. "The Dodgers haven't got to the point where they are running weddings as come-ons to attract crowds to our ball games," team president Dobens announced. But it surely didn't hurt the club's finances. Fifty years later, Ludwick admitted, "As we look back, my wife doesn't really think that highly of it," saying she would have preferred a traditional ceremony rather than one that concluded with the bride and groom walking under an arch of baseball bats held up by the Nashua players. "She still doesn't look at the wedding album."[55]

Promotions were becoming increasingly necessary to attract fans to the minor league ballparks of the New England League. Kids loved the games; the challenge was getting paying adults to come.

Former Rhode Island governor Lincoln Almond remembered going to New England League games in Pawtucket as a child. "We used to sit for the most part in the second tier on the third base side," Almond recalled nearly fifty years later, in 1995. "You would try and get a front-row seat where the railings are, and I can remember one day trying to catch a foul ball, and I had it right in my hands, and it hit the railing—pshew!—it went over my head. I remember that because it scared the hell out of me!"[56]

After the New England League teams struggled through the 1948 season as their fans followed the exploits of the Boston Braves and Boston Red Sox toward their first-place finishes, attendance was lackluster for the playoff series between Nashua and Lynn to determine the New England League champion. The New England League faced a new competitive threat — football — especially high school football games.

Only 1,366 fans showed up for the fourth game on Thursday night, September 16, as New England League veteran pitcher Charlie Bird won his third game of the playoffs for Nashua. "Tonight's tilt may set a record for the smallest attendance at a New England League finals playoff game," said the *Nashua Telegraph*. "Schoolboy grid games at Lynn and here in Nashua are expected to draw heavily from the playoff gate." Additionally, a National Football

League game was telecast that evening on WNAC, Channel 7, between the Boston Yanks and the Green Bay Packers at Fenway Park.[57]

Nashua blasted Lynn, 11–0, in the fifth and deciding game on Friday, September 17, at Fraser Field to win the Governor's Cup, with the football game between Lynn English and Lowell taking place next door in the Manning Bowl. The *Nashua Telegraph* did not note the attendance at the baseball game in its newspaper coverage.

Things started to look bleak for the New England League as Davidson planned for the 1949 season.

"Rumor is that the New England League may turn up as a six-team loop in 1949," the *Lynn Evening Item* speculated in October 1948. "The likelihood of anyone replacing the Red Sox in Lynn looks slim. Providence is still searching vainly for an angel. Fall River may also go under. Manchester is listed as a doubtful starter." On the bright side, the *Evening Item* noted, "But Lewiston, Me., and Augusta, Me., are reportedly interested in establishing franchises in the circuit. Six teams, all located far enough from Boston to escape the major leagues' distracting influence, might survive."[58]

The minor leagues as a group tried to ward off the intrusion of televised major league games, but to no avail. In early December, a minor league committee recommended to both major leagues "to keep telecasting and broadcasting within a fifty-mile radius of major league cities so as not to interfere with attendance at neighboring minor league towns." At the major league meetings on December 13, "both leagues made short shrift of the minor leagues' amendment curtailing television and radio in major league cities."[59]

A final blow to the New England League was the broader acceptance of black players in the major leagues. After three years of using Nashua as a haven for its black minor leaguers, Rickey no longer needed the services of Nashua, beginning in 1949.

After Satchel Paige was signed by the Cleveland Indians during the summer of 1948, there was a "rapidly growing interest of Organized Baseball in black athletes" in 1949, according to historian Neil Lanctot in his book *Negro League Baseball*. "Responding to a combination of public pressure, evidence of [Jackie] Robinson's gate appeal, and competitive concerns, several previously uninterested clubs began to recruit black players for the first time. The Boston Braves, for example, began integrating their minor league clubs, signing Walden Williams, a non–NAL player, in January 1949. In the next six months, the Giants, Yankees, Cubs, and Red Sox followed suit, albeit with varying degrees of actual commitment to major league integration."[60]

The Negro National League collapsed after the 1948 season, when the Newark Eagles club, one of its cornerstone franchises, was sold and relocated to Houston. The remaining teams merged into the Negro American League, but the future of black-only baseball was in serious doubt. This provided further fuel for the major leagues to recruit black players for seasoning in the minor leagues, thus expanding the need for the minor leagues in the Midwest and the South to be more accepting of black players. This further lessened the need for safe havens like Nashua to develop black players.

The first black player to play in the New England League outside of Nashua was George Crowe, with Pawtucket. The Boston Braves signed the stocky first baseman, who had played professional basketball with the all-black New York Renaissance and baseball with the New York Black Yankees of the Negro National League. After just a few years in the Braves' farm system, Crowe advanced in 1952 to the major leagues, where he played nine seasons.

Developing black players was no longer a unique Brooklyn venture and thus the special nature of the Nashua franchise was lost. Instead of veteran players, Rickey stocked the Nashua team in 1949 with very young players like outfielder Gino Cimoli, pitcher Billy Loes, and infielder Wayne Belardi.

Davidson cobbled together the same eight teams that ended the 1948 season to begin the 1949 season. Manchester and Lynn had different major league affiliations, Manchester with the New York Yankees and Lynn with the Detroit Tigers.

Almost immediately, the league was beset with attendance problems. To spur attendance, New England League club owners used various promotions. Unlike their Depression-era counterparts that were reluctant to engage in promotional activities during the dark days of the 1933 season, owners in 1949 tried many approaches.

Lynn's new owner, Larry Kelly, immediately cut admission at Fraser Field to sixty cents. The lowest price in the league still didn't attract spectators in droves; at one point Kelly even dispensed with an admission fee, just to get people to come to the ballpark.[61]

In Fall River, owner Joe Madowsky scheduled many promotions to try to attract people to the ballpark. On July 5, he held Knot Hole Gang Night, when children under age twelve were admitted for nine cents, and on July 6 he held Father and Son Night, where children under age twelve were admitted free if accompanied by their dad.[62]

Giveaways were a popular promotion. "The Slaters management tried again last night to lure some fans to McCoy Stadium, but threatening weather and the usual indifference made 'Television Night' something of a failure," the *Pawtucket Times* reported in August. "Except for Marilyn Lodge of 100 Maynard Street, who took home the TV set. Business manager Bill Cousins was none too happy because only 991 showed up."[63]

Around the Fourth of July holiday, matters started to look bleak for the league, now with only seven clubs when Providence disbanded in June.

Rickey started to move his best prospects out of Nashua, which was in first place in the league, to other farm clubs in the Brooklyn system. Cimoli was the first to go, being pulled off the team bus headed for Portland on July 2 to be reassigned to Montreal.

"With attendance dropping off, and one club out from the league and another on the verge, there is some question whether or not this is the final season for the New England Class B baseball league," said the *Nashua Telegraph* upon Cimoli's departure. Loes, who had compiled a 11–3 pitching record, was moved to Ft. Worth in the Class AA Texas League and Belardi, who had hit fifteen home runs, was promoted to Greenville in the Class A South Atlantic League.[64]

Despite Davidson's best efforts to try to keep the remaining seven teams afloat financially, the Manchester, Lynn, and Fall River clubs disbanded in July. (See Chapter One for more details).

"With only a handful of mourners in the stands, organized baseball in Lynn was given a decent burial last night by the Lynn Tigers," the *Lynn Evening Item* eulogized, "as they edged the Manchester Yankees, 9–8, in the final game of the local season."[65]

In his article, "New England Loop Woe Laid to TV," Harold Kaese recounted the factors that doomed the league:

> Television was blamed above all else by the surviving magnates for the demise of the Lynn, Manchester, Fall River, and Providence clubs. According to the business managers of Portland, Nashua, Springfield, and Pawtucket, most fans in New England League's larger cities are more interested in the Braves and the Red Sox than in their local Class B teams.... The New England League might have prospered, except for 1, The automobile; 2, Good transportation facilities to Boston; 3, Radio broadcasting; 4, Big league night games; 5, High pressure salesmanship of bus-and-meal ticket packages in outlying communities for Braves and Red Sox games.[66]

Nashua stumbled to a last-place finish during the artificially created second half of the New England League season and missed the playoffs. "Slightly more than 600 paid admissions" saw Nashua lose a doubleheader to Springfield on Sunday, September 5, as "the curtain came ringing down on the Gate City's final professional showing for, perhaps, many years to come." In the opinion of the *Nashua Telegraph*'s sports staff, "You can blame it on television, bad times, indifference or simply a matter of reaching the financial saturation point."[67]

Portland claimed the 1949 New England League championship by defeating Springfield for the Governor's Cup. Due to that "indifference" factor, almost no one noticed. Minor league baseball in New England was defunct; nearly every baseball fan's attention was riveted on the major league teams.

On October 5, Don Newcombe, just two years removed from pitching for the Nashua Dodgers, was the starting pitcher for the Brooklyn Dodgers in the first game of the 1949 World Series. His catcher was Roy Campanella, three years removed from catching in Holman Stadium for the Nashua Dodgers.

Branch Rickey's experiment with nurturing his black minor leaguers in the contained environment of Nashua and the New England League had clearly paid big dividends. As a side benefit, Claude Davidson got the opportunity to revive the New England League one more time, this time for a four-year run before the league ran aground once again, this time for good.

Newcombe pitched well in that World Series game, but the Dodgers lost, 1–0, as New York Yankees pitcher Allie Reynolds pitched a two-hitter to shut down the Brooklyn bats.

Nashua residents hadn't forgotten the two black players. "Nashua's working man went to his job this morning with a portable radio set under his arms. Television set owners were making room for expected company and scatter-

Retired numbers of three black players displayed on the left field wall of Holman Stadium in Nashua, New Hampshire. From left to right, #36 Don Newcombe, #39 Roy Campanella, and #42 Jackie Robinson (although he never played in Nashua).

ing ash trays profusely over their premises," the *Nashua Telegraph* reported on the opening day of the World Series. "One of the biggest crowds was expected to be at the *Nashua Telegraph* where a television set had been erected in one of the newspaper's spacious front windows and amplifiers had been placed in front of the building to carry the voices of commentators working the series to fans watching the game."[68]

Baseball fans that were gathered in front of the *Nashua Telegraph* building that afternoon cheered the actions of Newcombe and Campanella. The New England League had played an unheralded part in helping to establish racial integration in Organized Baseball. After 1949, those baseball fans could only cheer for their diamond heroes while watching a television set or traveling to Boston.

Epilogue

THERE WERE NO MORE REVIVALS OF THE New England League following the league's demise in 1949. Davidson's 1946 effort to restart the league, the sixth such revival over the course of the league's thirty-nine seasons of play, was the last one.

Davidson, the Don Quixote of New England minor league baseball, passed away in 1956 at the age of fifty-nine, never fully realizing his dream to establish an economically viable minor league among the smaller cities of New England.

At his death, Davidson was remembered in obituaries printed in many newspapers of cities that had once fielded teams in the New England League. Nearly all of the obituaries, though, were simply a standard recitation of the facts of his life and his survivors without further elaboration. There were few eloquently crafted goodbyes or passionate words penned about Davidson and his effort for more than twenty years to try to keep minor league baseball alive in New England.

One exception was a eulogistic obituary published in the *Lynn Evening Item*, which a sharp-eyed clerk at the New England Newsclip Agency spotted and mailed to Providence, Rhode Island, for inclusion in Davidson's alumni biographical file at Brown University.

> Claude B. Davidson, who weathered the violent storms of both the Boston Twilight League and two cycles of the New England League as president of those circuits, passed away at this home in Braintree, aged 59 years. He was a consulting engineer and worked with the late George A. Cornet of Lynn in Newfoundland during World War II. Davidson saw the ups and downs of both sandlot and organized baseball as an efficient official.[1]

At the time of Davidson's death in the spring of 1956, minor league baseball was extinct in New England. Seven years after Bob Pugatch made the final bat swing in New England League history on September 18, 1949, there was not one New England city represented in all of minor league baseball. Indeed, there was only one major league team in the region by that point, the Red Sox, since the Braves had fled Boston to play in Milwaukee beginning with the 1953 season. The Springfield Cubs, a team that had survived beyond the demise of the 1949 New England League, continued to play in the International League for four years. But by 1954, the city of Springfield was also bereft of a minor league team.

There was sporadic resurgence of interest in minor league baseball in the 1960s. The Eastern League took on several hopeful New England cities during the course of three decades, but none of these efforts panned out. Springfield tried again the year following Davidson's death, but that club died after the 1965 season. Pawtucket, Rhode Island, and Manchester, New Hampshire, took shots at fielding teams in the late 1960s, but neither lasted more than three years before folding. Nashua, New Hampshire, and Lynn, Massachusetts, tried in the 1980s, but also to no avail.

After the serious decline in the textile and shoe industries within the New England region in the post-war period, the region slowly rebounded. "Periodic challenges to major employers were followed by the emergence of replacement activities with higher skill and technology content," Lynne Browne and Steven Sass wrote in *Engines of Enterprise*. "Textiles was succeeded by aircraft engines and electronics. When defense cutbacks in the early 1970s caused these industries to falter, the minicomputer and instruments industries emerged to provide a powerful impetus to growth. And when these, too, began to encounter difficulty, nonmanufacturing industries such as computer services, financial services, and health care helped sustain the economy."[2]

Minor league baseball finally found some sustained traction in New England after the Pawtucket team in the International League went bankrupt after the 1976 season. What saved the Pawtucket franchise, and Davidson's minor league dream, was a gentleman by the name of Ben Mondor, who bought the bankrupt ball club in 1977. Through some savvy promotion and community relations, Mondor, a bankruptcy specialist rather than a baseball man, established the Pawtucket ball club as a solid player development facility for the Boston Red Sox.

"I thought I'd stay three, four, maybe five years, and get out," Mondor told the *Providence Journal* in 2004 during his twenty-eighth year of owing the ball club. "I figured I'd have it going by then, making money. I'd made a living buying bankruptcies, restoring them and then selling them. But then I fell in love with this job. It's like there is no end to it. No end to bettering the team, bettering the building."[3]

Textile mills in Lowell have been converted into condominiums and apartment buildings, such as the Massachusetts Mills complex. Another part of the renewal of the city of Lowell is the highly successful Lowell Spinners minor league ball club.

By the 1990s, Davidson's dream really took hold throughout New England, as minor league teams in Portland, Maine, and Lowell, Massachusetts, turned into overnight successes. Soon independent minor leagues, unaffiliated with major league baseball, sprung up in New England to provide a professional baseball outlet for fans in Nashua and Lynn. Soon, Brockton and Worcester jumped on the bandwagon.

Minor league baseball flourished in New England during the first decade of the twenty-first century because the market for minor league baseball had fundamentally changed. It was no longer baseball for baseball's sake that drew spectators to the ballpark — it was the entertainment factor.

"Our philosophy is, you're coming out to the ballpark to be entertained and during that entertainment, there happens to be a game that's on the field," Lowell general manager Tim Bawmann told the *Lowell Sun* in 2006. "We feel like we're in the entertainment business more so than in the baseball business. I'd like to think our fans get entertained literally from the moment they get out of their car to the moment they get back into their car at the end of the night."[4]

"If there's a better entertainment value than minor league baseball, I haven't found it," Brian Mooney wrote in a Travel Section article in the *Boston*

Globe in 2006. "For less than the price of a movie ticket, you get a great seat in a charming park, watching professional ballplayers, some of whom will play in Fenway Park one day. Parking is inexpensive and there's a carnival atmosphere, especially in Lowell and Portland, with non-stop contests and entertainment between innings."[5]

Minor league baseball is now thriving in New England. Claude Davidson would be proud, as would Walter Burnham, Tim Murnane, Jake Morse, John Donnelly, and a host of others who spent so many years of their lives trying to make the New England League a success.

Chapter Notes

Chapter 1

1. Letter from Bob Pugatch to author, dated June 4, 1999.
2. *Portland Press-Herald*, September 19, 1949.
3. Letter from Hank Nasternak to author, dated June 21, 1999.
4. *Providence Journal*, June 22, 1949.
5. *Manchester Union*, July 20, 1949.
6. *Lynn Evening Item*, July 20, 1949.
7. *Fall River Herald*, July 16, 1949.
8. *Pawtucket Times*, August 30, 1949.
9. Letter from Bob Pugatch to author, dated June 4, 1999.
10. Letter from Barbara Watson to author, dated April 30, 2000.
11. Ibid.
12. Obojski, *Bush League*, p. 27.

Chapter 2

1. Obojski, *Bush League*, p. 4; *Sporting News*, February 18, 1905.
2. Sullivan, *The Minors*, p. 14.
3. *Spalding's Official Base Ball Guide*, 1878, p. 31.
4. Seymour, *Baseball: The Early Years*, pp. 26–30.
5. Soos, *Before the Curse*, p. 6; Phil Bergen, "Lovett of the Lowells," *The National Pastime*, 1996.
6. *Lowell Courier*, June 9, 1870; *Boston Herald*, June 10, 1870.
7. Soos, *Before the Curse*, p. 20.
8. *Boston Globe*, October 21, 1877.
9. Seymour, *Baseball: The Early Years*, p. 94.
10. *Spalding's Official Base Ball Guide*, 1878, p. 36.
11. *Lowell Courier*, June 21, 1877.

12. *New York Clipper*, June 7, 1877.
13. *Louisville Courier-Journal*, November 3, 1877; *New York Clipper*, November 10, 1877.
14. *Lowell Courier*, August 30, 1877.
15. *Providence Journal*, June 20, 1877; *Fall River Herald*, June 23, 1877; *Lynn City Item*, July 21, 1877.
16. *Lowell Courier*, August 11, 1877; *Lynn City Item*, August 25, 1877.
17. Brown and Tager, *Massachusetts: A Concise History*, p. 122.
18. Danzell, *Enterprising Elite*, p. 5–7.
19. Eno, *Cotton Was King*, pp. 70–73.
20. Hareven and Langenbach, *Amoskeag*, p. 22.
21. Blewitt, *Constant Turmoil*, pp. 23–38.
22. Yafa, *Big Cotton*, p. 182.
23. McLoughlin, *Rhode Island*, p. 125.
24. Melder, *Life and Times in Shoe City*, p. 3.
25. Dawley, *Class and Community*, p. 8.
26. Danzell, *Enterprising Elite*, p. 110.
27. Eno, *Cotton Was King*, p. 124.
28. Joshua Rosenbloom, "The Challenges of Economic Maturity: New England, 1880–1940," in Temin, *Engines of Enterprise*, p. 161.
29. Ibid.
30. *Lowell Courier*, July 5, 1877; *Manchester Union*, July 6, 1877.
31. *Lowell Courier*, October 17, 1877.
32. *New York Clipper*, February 16, 1878.
33. Melville, *Early Baseball*, p. 98.
34. *Lowell Courier*, January 29, 1878.
35. *Lowell Courier*, August 24 and September 3, 1878.
36. Bevis, "Rocky Point."

Chapter 3

1. Roth, *Connecticut: A History*, pp. 23–30.
2. Hardy, "Long Before Orr," pp. 246–247.

3. *Boston Globe*, July 8, 1917; *Haverhill Evening Gazette*, July 2, 1917.

4. *American National Biography*, "William Henry Moody."

5. *Boston Globe*, July 8, 1917.

6. *Eastern Argus*, June 16, 1884.

7. Anderson, *Was Baseball Really Invented in Maine?* p. 6.

8. *Brockton Enterprise*, August 3, 1896; *Boston Globe*, October 19, 1885.

9. Hudon, *Lower Merrimack*, pp. 55–56.

10. Judd, *Maine: The Pine Tree State*, p. 334.

11. Lomax, *Black Baseball Entrepreneurs*, p. 56.

12. *Boston Herald*, May 12, 1885.

13. *Sporting Life*, April 22, 1885.

14. *Boston Globe*, January 21, 1886.

15. *Lewiston Evening Journal*, May 24, 1919.

16. *Biddeford Journal*, May 5, 1885.

17. *Biddeford Journal*, June 16, 1885.

18. *Boston Globe*, October 19, 1885.

19. *Brockton Enterprise*, May 31, 1885.

20. *Brockton Enterprise*, May 1, 1885.

21. Stilgoe, *Borderland: Origins of the American Suburb*, p. 107.

22. *Brockton Enterprise*, May 2, 1885; *Lawrence Eagle*, May 9, 1885; *Eastern Argus*, April 30, 1885.

23. Cialdini, "Basking in Reflected Glory."

24. *Lawrence Eagle*, July 27, 1885.

25. *Newburyport Herald*, September 17, 1885.

26. *Brockton Weekly Gazette*, October 10, 1885.

27. *Eastern Argus*, October 5, 1885.

28. *Lawrence Eagle*, October 9, 1885.

29. *Lawrence Eagle*, October 16, 1885.

30. *Boston Globe*, October 29, 1885.

31. *Brockton Enterprise*, August 3, 1896.

32. *Washington Post*, December 19, 1885.

33. *Boston Globe*, March 28, 1886.

34. *Boston Globe*, May 11, 1886.

35. Ibid.

36. *Boston Globe*, June 2, 1886.

37. *Boston Globe*, July 1, 1886.

38. *Lawrence Eagle*, July 13, 1886.

39. *Lawrence Eagle*, July 19, 1886.

40. *Boston Globe*, July 18, 1886.

41. Ibid.

42. Ibid.

43. *Lawrence Eagle*, July 19, 1886.

44. *Lawrence Eagle*, July 23, 1886.

45. *Lawrence Daily American*, July 23, 1886.

46. *Brooklyn Eagle*, August 30, 1886.

47. Robert Kane, "Billy McGunnigle: Baseball's Forgotten Pioneer," *Baseball Research Journal*, 1999.

48. *Brockton Enterprise*, October 16, 1886.

49. *Biographical Directory of the United States Congress*, "William Shadrach Knox."

50. *Lowell Courier*, May 6, 1887.

51. *Lowell Daily News*, May 16, 1887.

52. *Haverhill Evening Gazette*, April 30, 1886.

53. *Brockton Enterprise*, May 31, 1885.

54. *Brooklyn Eagle*, April 11, 1887.

55. *Lynn Bee*, September 6, 1887.

56. *Boston Globe*, September 6, 1887.

57. *Boston Globe*, June 25, 1887.

58. *Salem Evening News*, July 2, 1887.

59. *Salem Evening News*, July 7 and 12, 1887.

60. *Salem Evening News*, July 12, 1887.

61. Scoggins, *Bricks and Bats*, p. 222.

62. *Lowell Courier*, July 13, 1887.

63. Lomax, *Black Baseball Entrepreneurs*, p. 63.

64. *Boston Globe*, September 12, 1887.

65. Lomax, *Black Baseball Entrepreneurs*, p. 87.

66. *Lowell Courier*, September 27 and 29, 1887.

67. *Lowell Courier*, September 28, 1887.

68. *Boston Globe*, September 28, 1887.

69. *Boston Globe*, October 6, 1887.

70. Dick Thompson, "Cudworth Was a Local 19th Century Baseball Pioneer," *Middleboro Gazette*, April 26, 1990.

71. *Lowell Courier*, October 8, 1887.

72. *Boston Globe*, March 18, 1889.

73. *Lowell Courier-Citizen*, January 10, 1916.

74. Brown and Tager, *Massachusetts: A Concise History*, p. 214.

75. *Eastern Argus*, March 13, 1885.

76. *Eastern Argus*, June 11, 1888.

77. Lou Hunsinger, Jr., "George W. Stovey," *National Pastime*, 1994.

78. Malloy, "Out at Home."

79. Jerry Malloy, "George Washington Stovey," in Ivor-Campbell, *Baseball's First Stars*.

80. Ibid.

81. *Worcester Telegram*, June 9, 1888.

82. *Worcester Spy*, June 11, 1888.

83. *Worcester Spy*, July 16, 1888.

84. *Lowell Daily News*, July 18, 1888.

85. *Worcester Spy*, July 21, 1888.

86. *Boston Herald*, July 25, 1888; *Lynn Bee*, July 26, 1888.

87. *Portsmouth Chronicle*, July 22, 1888.

88. *Worcester Spy*, September 11, 1888.

89. *Lowell Courier*, September 11, 1888.

90. *Worcester Spy*, August 9, 1888.

91. *Boston Herald*, May 23, 1887.

92. *Boston Globe*, November 10, 1888.

93. *Boston Globe*, November 27, 1888.

Chapter 4

1. *Brooklyn Eagle*, April 8 and 15, 1889.

2. *Brooklyn Eagle*, June 7, 1889.

3. *Lowell Courier*, June 10, 1889.

4. *Worcester Spy*, June 15, 1889.

5. *Lowell Morning Mail*, July 15, 1889.

6. *Lowell Daily News*, July 16, 1889.

7. *Boston Globe*, July 22, 1889.
8. *New York Tribune*, July 22, 1889.
9. Ibid.
10. Bevis, "Rocky Point."
11. Irving Sanborn, "The Pros and Cons of Sunday Baseball," *Baseball Magazine*, October 1926.
12. *New Bedford Evening Standard*, July 29, 1889.
13. *Worcester Spy*, July 23 and August 4, 1889.
14. *Boston Globe*, August 19, 1889.
15. *Worcester Spy*, January 19, 1890.
16. *Boston Globe*, December 27, 1889.
17. *Lowell Courier*, December 28, 1889.
18. *Boston Globe*, January 12, 1890.
19. *Providence Journal*, January 15, 1890.
20. *Worcester Spy*, January 17, 1890.
21. *Worcester Spy*, January 18, 1890.
22. *Boston Globe*, January 18, 1890.
23. *Providence Journal*, January 23, 1890.
24. *Boston Globe*, January 30, 1890.
25. Ibid.
26. *Worcester Spy*, January 30, 1890.
27. *Worcester Spy*, February 1, 1890.
28. *Worcester Spy*, February 2, 1890.
29. *Lowell Daily News*, February 5, 1890.
30. *Worcester Spy*, February 10, 1890.
31. *Worcester Spy*, February 13, 1890.
32. *Boston Globe*, December 7, 1890.
33. *Providence Journal*, March 29, 1891.
34. *Lowell Daily News*, April 4, 1891.
35. *Lowell Daily News*, April 10, 1891.
36. *Lowell Daily News*, April 13, 1891.
37. *Lowell Daily News*, March 9, 1891.
38. Bevis, "Rocky Point."
39. *Eastern Argus*, March 26, 1891.
40. *Lowell Daily News*, March 28, 1891.
41. *Eastern Argus*, March 28, 1891.
42. Jerry Malloy, "The Cubans' Last Stand," *The National Pastime*, 1992.
43. *Boston Globe*, March 22, 1891.
44. *Sporting Life*, April 4, 1891.
45. *Lowell Daily News*, March 24, 1891.
46. *Eastern Argus*, April 30, 1891.
47. Cox, *A Century of Light*, p. 38; *Sporting Life*, May 30, 1891.
48. *Woonsocket Evening Reporter*, June 24, 1891.
49. *Lowell Morning Mail*, July 1, 1891.
50. *Worcester Spy*, July 11, 1891.
51. *Lowell Morning Mail*, July 16, 1891.
52. *Sporting Life*, July 25, 1891.
53. *Lewiston Evening Journal*, July 24, 1891.
54. *Worcester Spy*, July 27, 1891.
55. *Worcester Spy*, August 2, 1891.
56. *Sporting Life*, August 15, 1891.
57. *Boston Globe*, April 9 and December 27, 1899.
58. *Providence Evening Bulletin*, August 10, 1891.
59. *Sporting Life*, April 2, 1892.
60. Ibid.

Chapter 5

1. *Boston Globe*, March 31, 1892.
2. *Lowell Courier-Citizen*, March 8, 1913.
3. *Boston Globe*, November 25, 1894.
4. Sullivan, *The Minors*, p. 15.
5. Kenny, *Newspaper Row*, p. 11.
6. *Boston Globe*, March 31, 1892.
7. *Sporting Life*, July 23, 1892.
8. Judd, *Maine: The Pine Tree State*, p. 459.
9. Rivard, *A New Order of Things*, p. 9.
10. *Woonsocket Call*, July 11, 1892.
11. Ibid.
12. Mason, *The Street Railway*, p. 6.
13. *Sporting Life*, April 1, 1893.
14. *Boston Globe*, April 6, 1893.
15. *Fall River Globe*, September 5, 1893.
16. *Fall River Globe*, August 1, 1893.
17. Latham, *The Panic of 1893*, p. 3; Hoffman, *The Depression of the Nineties*, p. 63.
18. Dunwell, *The Run of the Mills*, p. 110.
19. *Fall River Globe*, August 3, 1893.
20. Judd, *Maine: The Pine Tree State*, p. 271.
21. Ibid, p. 427
22. *Haverhill Evening Gazette*, May 2 and 7, 1894.
23. *Fall River Globe*, April 30, 1894.
24. *Boston Globe*, July 19, 1894.
25. *Boston Globe*, January 13, 1895.
26. Ibid.
27. *Boston Globe*, January 16, 1895.
28. *Boston Globe*, March 17, 1895.
29. *Boston Globe*, March 24, 1895.
30. *Kennebec Journal*, April 4, 1895.
31. *Kennebec Journal*, April 30, 1895.
32. *Kennebec Journal*, June 15, 1895.
33. *New Bedford Morning Mercury*, March 27, 1895.
34. *Pawtucket Times*, July 15 and 29, 1895.
35. *Chicago Tribune*, March 18, 1896.
36. J.M. Murphy, "Napoleon Lajoie: Modern Baseball's First Superstar," *National Pastime*, 1988.
37. *Providence Journal*, May 2, 1996.
38. *Bangor Whig and Courier*, July 16, 1896.
39. *Bangor Whig and Courier*, September 9, 1896.
40. *Fall River Globe*, September 12, 1896.
41. *Eastern Argus*, September 14, 1896.
42. *Bangor Whig and Courier*, September 25, 1896.
43. *Bangor Whig and Courier*, January 14, 1897.
44. Judd, *The Pine Tree State*, pp. 427–429.
45. McLoughlin, *Rhode Island*, p. 169.
46. Jackson, *Crabgrass Frontier*, p. 136.
47. Fogelson, *Downtown*, pp. 28–29.
48. Warner, *Streetcar Suburbs*, p. 53.

49. Morris, *The Tycoons*, p. 168.
50. *Pawtucket Times*, June 14, 1897.
51. *Pawtucket Times*, August 2, 1897.
52. *Pawtucket Times*, August 9, 1897.
53. *Brockton Enterprise*, September 10, 1897.
54. *Brockton Enterprise*, September 11, 1897.
55. *Brockton Enterprise*, January 13, 1898.
56. Blewitt, *Constant Turmoil*, p. 356.
57. *New Bedford Morning Mercury*, June 15, 1898.
58. *Sporting Life*, July 16, 1898.
59. *Pawtucket Times*, August 14, 1899.
60. *Pawtucket Times*, July 24, 1899.
61. Dick Thompson, "Matty and His Fadeaway," *Baseball Research Journal*, 1996.
62. *Eastern Argus*, September 6, 1899.
63. *Boston Globe*, September 6, 1899.

Chapter 6

1. *Sporting News*, December 8, 1900.
2. *Bangor Daily News*, June 29, 1901.
3. *Boston Globe*, June 29, 1901.
4. *Lowell Courier*, July 11, 1901.
5. *Haverhill Evening Gazette*, March 21, 1902.
6. Land, "Organizing the Boys of Summer."
7. Ibid.
8. *Boston Globe*, September 13, 1903.
9. *Lewiston Evening Journal*, May 21, 1901.
10. *Lowell Courier-Citizen*, April 11, 1906.
11. *Concord Evening Monitor*, May 16, 1903.
12. Hilton and Due, *The Electric Interurban Railways*, p. 3.
13. *Foster's Daily Democrat*, April 18, 1902.
14. *Holyoke Transcript*, September 8, 1903.
15. *Lowell Sun*, September 15, 1903.
16. *Holyoke Transcript*, September 21, 1903.
17. *Fall River Globe*, August 22, 1904.
18. *Boston Globe*, January 30, 1905.
19. *Boston Globe*, April 24, 1905.
20. *Boston Globe*, January 30, 1905.
21. David Pietrusza, "Sliding Billy Hamilton," *Baseball Research Journal*, 1991.
22. *Haverhill Evening Gazette*, September 4, 1904.
23. *Concord Evening Monitor*, February 5, 1906.
24. *Lowell Courier*, June 27, 1904.
25. *Concord Daily Patriot*, June 27, 1904.
26. *Concord Evening Monitor*, June 27, 1904.
27. Scoggins, "Youngest Ever To Play Professional Baseball."
28. *Concord Evening Monitor*, September 20, 1905.
29. William Akin, "Jesse Cail Burkett," in Ivor-Campbell, *Baseball's First Stars*.
30. *Worcester Telegram*, May 28, 1953.
31. Patrick Dowd, "A Successful Manager," *Baseball Magazine*, December 1909.

32. Jacob Morse, "The Skirmish," *Baseball Magazine*, July 1909.
33. *Fall River Globe*, May 18, 1906.
34. *Worcester Telegram*, July 24, 1908.
35. *Providence Journal*, July 30 and August 6, 1906.
36. *Worcester Telegram*, June 24, 1907.
37. *Worcester Telegram*, August 12 and 19, 1907.
38. *Worcester Telegram*, September 6, 1907.
39. *Worcester Telegram*, September 14, 1907.
40. *Worcester Telegram*, September 16, 1907.
41. *Worcester Telegram*, September 10, 1907.
42. *Boston Globe*, September 12, 1907.
43. *Worcester Telegram*, September 10, 1907.
44. *Worcester Telegram*, August 24, 1908.
45. *Fall River Globe*, July 19, 1909.
46. *Brockton Enterprise*, May 15, 1909.
47. *Fall River Globe*, May 17, 1909.
48. *Fall River Globe*, August 2, 1909.
49. Alumni biographical file of Jacob Morse in Harvard University Archives, Pusey Library, Harvard University; Harvard Class of 1881 anniversary report published in 1931.
50. Jacob Morse, "Editorial Comment," *Baseball Magazine*, May 1908.
51. Charles Fleischer, "Sunday Baseball the Crying Need," *Baseball Magazine*, August 1908.
52. *Sporting Life*, August 15, 1908.
53. *Boston Globe*, February 3, 1908.
54. *Sporting Life*, July 21, 1906.
55. *Brockton Enterprise*, March 5, 1907.
56. *Woonsocket Call*, May 4, 1908.
57. *Boston Globe*, February 16, 1911.
58. *Boston Globe*, January 23, 1912.
59. *Haverhill Evening Gazette*, August 30, 1911.
60. Ibid.
61. Ibid.
62. *Haverhill Evening Gazette*, September 19, 1911.
63. F.C. Lane, "The Greatest Problem in the National Game: The Critical Situation in Sunday Baseball," *Baseball Magazine*, October 1911.
64. *Boston Globe*, May 21, 1911.
65. Watson, *Bread & Roses*, p. 12–13.
66. *Lawrence Evening Tribune*, January 15, 1912.
67. Cahn, *Lawrence 1912: The Bread and Roses Strike*, p. 10.
68. Brown and Tager, *A Concise History*, p. 255.
69. *Lawrence Evening Tribune*, May 11 and 13, 1912.
70. *Lawrence Evening Tribune*, June 21, 1912.
71. *New York Times*, July 22, 1921.
72. *Brockton Enterprise*, September 30, 1990.

Chapter 7

1. *Lowell Courier-Citizen*, September 9, 1912.
2. Ibid.

3. *Boston Globe*, November 8, 1912.
4. *Lowell Courier-Citizen*, November 9, 1912.
5. *Lowell Courier-Citizen*, November 11, 1912.
6. *Eastern Argus*, January 29, 1913.
7. *Boston Globe*, January 29, 1913.
8. *Boston Globe*, February 1, 1913.
9. *Lowell Courier-Citizen*, February 2, 1913.
10. *Lynn Evening Item*, February 1, 1913.
11. *Eastern Argus*, May 9, 1913.
12. *Lowell Courier-Citizen*, March 8, 1913.
13. *Lynn Evening Item*, March 8, 1913.
14. *Lowell Courier-Citizen*, January 8, 1916; alumni biographical file of Morse in Harvard University Archives.
15. *New York Times*, December 10, 1912.
16. *Lowell Courier-Citizen*, November 13, 1912.
17. *Haverhill Evening Gazette*, March 8, 1913.
18. *Lowell Courier-Citizen*, March 8, 1913.
19. *Lewiston Evening Journal*, January 9, 1914.
20. *Haverhill Evening Gazette*, April 23, 1914.
21. *Fitchburg Sentinel*, January 2, 1914.
22. *New Bedford Morning Mercury*, January 10, 1914.
23. *Boston Globe*, July 31, 1914.
24. *Lynn Evening Item*, July 9, 1914.
25. *Boston Globe*, April 9, 1914.
26. *New York Times*, January 24, 1915.
27. *Springfield Republican*, January 10, 1915.
28. *Springfield Republican*, January 16, 1915.
29. *Washington Post*, January 31, 1915.
30. *Boston Globe*, February 1, 1915.
31. *Boston Globe*, February 3, 1915.
32. *Boston Globe*, February 5, 1915.
33. *Lowell Courier-Citizen*, February 2, 1915.
34. *Sporting Life*, May 22, 1915.
35. *Sporting Life*, May 29, 1915.
36. *Greenfield Recorder*, June 23, 1915.
37. *Greenfield Recorder*, June 30, 1915.
38. *Manchester Union*, July 1, 1915.
39. *Boston Globe*, August 24, 1915.
40. *Boston Globe*, August 15, 1915.
41. Ibid.
42. *Lowell Courier-Citizen*, August 18, 1915.
43. *Boston Globe*, August 15, 1915.
44. *Manchester Union*, August 25, 1915.
45. *Manchester Union*, September 7, 1915.
46. *Lawrence Evening Tribune*, September 8, 1915.
47. *Lawrence Evening Tribune*, September 7, 1915.
48. *Springfield Republican*, September 8, 1915.
49. *Lowell Courier-Citizen*, October 28, 1915.
50. *Springfield Republican*, October 19, 1915.
51. *Lynn Evening Item*, October 29, 1915; *Lowell Courier-Citizen*, November 2, 1915.
52. *Lowell Courier-Citizen*, November 6, 1915.
53. *Lowell Courier-Citizen*, November 2, 1915.
54. John Farrell, "Merger Allowed."
55. *Lowell Courier-Citizen*, December 11, 1915.
56. *Boston Globe*, January 9, 1916.
57. *Boston Globe*, January 25, 1916.
58. *Boston Globe*, August 20, 1916.
59. Farrell, "Merger Allowed."
60. *Lowell Courier-Citizen*, December 17, 1915.
61. *Lowell Courier-Citizen*, December 31, 1915.
62. Farrell, "Merger Allowed."
63. *Lowell Courier-Citizen*, February 1, 1916.
64. Farrell, "Merger Allowed."
65. *Lowell Courier-Citizen*, February 28, 1916.
66. *Lowell Courier-Citizen*, February 25, 1916.
67. *Worcester Evening Post*, May 2, 1916.
68. *Lawrence Evening Tribune*, July 5, 1916.
69. *Lowell Courier-Citizen*, September 5, 1916.

Chapter 8

1. *Boston Globe*, February 8, 1917.
2. Ibid.
3. Welsh, "Tim Murnane."
4. *Boston Globe*, September 28, 1917.
5. Welsh, "Tim Murnane."
6. *Boston Globe*, July 20, 1918.
7. *Boston Globe*, April 29, 1918.
8. *Boston Globe*, May 6, 1918.
9. Bevis, "Rocky Point."
10. *Providence Journal*, April 11, 1919.
11. *Providence Journal*, May 18, 1919.
12. Bevis, "Rocky Point."
13. *Lawrence Evening Tribune*, March 28, 1919.
14. *Lewiston Evening Journal*, May 1, 1919.
15. *Lewiston Evening Journal*, May 9, 1919.
16. *Lowell Courier-Citizen*, May 23, 1919.
17. *Lewiston Evening Journal*, May 1, 1919.
18. Ibid.
19. *Lewiston Evening Journal*, May 5, 1919.
20. *Lewiston Evening Journal*, May 9, 1919.
21. *Lowell Courier-Citizen*, July 11, 1919.
22. *Lewiston Evening Journal*, July 5, 1919.
23. *Lewiston Evening Journal*, August 4, 1919.
24. *Lowell Courier-Citizen*, August 4, 1919.
25. *Lewiston Evening Journal*, August 5, 1919.
26. *Boston Globe*, May 15, 1919.
27. *Lowell Courier-Citizen*, July 11, 1919.
28. Charles Murphy, "The Pros and Cons of Sunday Baseball," *Baseball Magazine*, June 1919.
29. *Boston Globe*, January 26, 1920.
30. Ibid.
31. *Boston Globe*, March 12 and April 3, 1920.
32. *Boston Globe*, April 3, 1920.

33. Ibid.
34. *Boston Globe*, April 10, 1920.
35. *Boston Globe*, September 4, 1921.
36. *Boston Globe*, May 29, 1922.
37. *Boston Globe*, June 19, 1922.
38. *Cambridge Chronicle*, July 8, 1922.
39. *Boston Globe*, July 10, 1922.
40. *Cambridge Chronicle*, July 15, 1922.
41. *Cambridge Chronicle*, July 22, 1922.
42. Ibid.
43. *Cambridge Chronicle*, August 12, 1922.
44. *Cambridge Chronicle*, May 12, 1923.
45. *Boston Globe*, August 16, 1923.
46. *Boston Globe*, November 28, 1923.
47. *Cambridge Chronicle*, May 17, 1924.
48. Prevan, *Seize the Daylight*, p. 119.
49. *Lowell Courier-Citizen*, August 10, 1925.
50. *Lowell Courier-Citizen*, August 17, 1925.
51. *Lowell Courier-Citizen*, August 24, 1925.
52. *Lowell Courier-Citizen*, August 1, 1925.
53. *Boston Post*, October 27, 1923.
54. *Boston Globe*, February 6, 1925.
55. Ibid.
56. *Boston Post*, August 4, 1925.

Chapter 9

1. *Christian Science Monitor*, January 30, 1926.
2. "An Old Favorite Comes Back," *Baseball Magazine*, June 1926.
3. Davidson's alumni biographical file in the archives of Hay Library at Brown University; *Boston City Directory*, 1913.
4. *Providence Journal*, May 3, 1917.
5. *Boston Globe*, September 14, 1919.
6. *Washington Post*, January 11, 1920.
7. *Sporting News*, May 20, 1926.
8. *Lowell Courier-Citizen*, May 20, 1926, p. 1.
9. *Lawrence Eagle*, May 20 and September 18, 1926.
10. *Lawrence Eagle-Tribune*, May 21, 1960, and June 10, 1974.
11. *Lowell Courier-Citizen*, June 2, 1926.
12. *Lawrence Eagle*, May 11, 1926.
13. *Lawrence Eagle*, July 3 and July 5, 1926.
14. *Christian Science Monitor*, June 8, 1926.
15. *Boston Globe*, evening edition, September 18, 1926.
16. *Washington Post*, October 14, 1926.
17. *Sporting News*, October 28, 1926.
18. *Sporting News*, November 11, 1926.
19. *Boston Herald*, March 10, 1927.
20. *Boston Herald*, March 17, 1927.
21. *Sporting News*, April 14, 1917.
22. *Springfield Union*, June 25, 1927.
23. *Lynn Evening Item*, June 25, 1927; *New York Times*, June 25, 1927.
24. *New York Times*, June 25, 1927.
25. *Boston Globe*, North section, August 18, 2002.
26. *New York Times*, June 25, 1927.
27. Guy Bartlett, "Baseball at Night," *Baseball Magazine*, September 1927.
28. *Lynn Evening Item*, August 28, 1923.
29. *Lynn Evening Item*, June 25, 1927.
30. *Sporting News*, June 30, 1927.
31. *Lynn Evening Item*, September 15, 1927.
32. *New York Times*, February 1, 1928.
33. *Boston Globe*, April 5, 1928.
34. *Sporting News*, October 4, 1927.
35. *Attleboro Sun*, April 11 and April 19, 1928.
36. *Attleboro Sun*, April 21, 1928.
37. Ibid.
38. *Attleboro Sun*, June 29, 1928.
39. *Fall River Globe*, June 30, 1928.
40. *Fall River Globe*, June 28, 1928.
41. *Fall River Globe*, July 16, 1928.
42. *Attleboro Sun*, August 11, 1928.
43. *Sporting News*, November 1, 1928.
44. *Boston Globe*, August 13, 1928.
45. Huthmacher, *Massachusetts People and Politics*, p. 260.
46. Brown and Tager, *Massachusetts: A Concise History*, p. 272.
47. Ibid., pp. 242–246.
48. Ibid., p. 272.
49. *Sporting News*, November 1, 1928.
50. Bevis, *Sunday Baseball*, p. 226.
51. *Sporting News*, November 15, 1928.
52. *Sporting News*, November 22, 1928.
53. *Sporting News*, November 15, 1928.
54. *Sporting News*, November 22, 1928.
55. *Fitchburg Sentinel*, August 5, 1929.
56. *New Bedford Morning Mercury*, February 23, 1929.
57. *Lowell Courier-Citizen*, March 13, 1929.
58. *Brockton Enterprise*, April 22, 1929.
59. *Lowell Courier-Citizen*, April 29, 1929.
60. *Haverhill Evening Gazette*, March 20, 1929.
61. *Brockton Enterprise*, May 3, 1929.
62. *New Bedford Evening Standard*, May 6, 1929.
63. *Haverhill Evening Gazette*, May 13, 1929.
64. *Lynn Evening Item*, June 18, 1929.
65. *Lynn Evening Item*, July 5, 1929.
66. *Fitchburg Sentinel*, July 25, 1929.
67. *Fitchburg Sentinel*, August 5, 1929.
68. *Fitchburg Sentinel*, August 22, 1929.
69. *Gloucester Times*, August 26, 1929.
70. *Lynn Evening Item*, September 16, 1929.
71. *Sporting News*, November 7, 1929.
72. *New Bedford Evening Standard*, May 11, 1930.
73. *Nashua Telegraph*, June 5, 1930.
74. *Lynn Evening Item*, June 18, 1930.
75. *Lynn Evening Item*, June 18, 1930; *Salem Evening News*, June 21, 1930.
76. *Lynn Evening Item*, June 23, 1930.
77. Pietrusza, *Lights On!* p. 71.
78. F.C. Lane, "The Romance of Night Baseball," *Baseball Magazine*, October 1930.

Chapter 10

1. Edsforth, *The New Deal*, p. 114.
2. *Lowell Evening Leader*, March 9, 1933.
3. Ibid.
4. *Lowell Evening Leader*, March 17 and 10, 1933.
5. *Lowell Evening Leader*, March 28, 1933.
6. *Lowell Evening Leader*, March 18, 1933.
7. Alexander, *Baseball in the Depression Era*, p. 2.
8. Jonathon Eig, *Luckiest Man: The Life and Death of Lou Gehrig* (New York: Simon & Schuster, 2005), p. 198.
9. *Lowell Evening Leader*, July 29, 1933.
10. *Sporting News*, March 13, 1933.
11. Scoggins, *Bricks and Bats*, p. 146.
12. Ibid, pp. 152–153.
13. *Attleboro Sun*, May 19, 22, and 25, 1933.
14. *Quincy Patriot Ledger*, June 6, 1933.
15. *Nashua Telegraph*, July 11, 1933.
16. Jesep, *Rockingham Park*, pp. 6–7, 98.
17. *Lawrence Evening Tribune*, July 5, 1933.
18. *Worcester Telegram*, July 5, 1933.
19. *Worcester Telegram*, June 5, 1933.
20. Bevis, "Evolution of the Sunday Doubleheader."
21. *Lowell Courier-Citizen*, July 6, 1933.
22. *Lowell Evening Leader*, September 12, 1933.
23. In the winter of 1933, the National Hockey League conducted a six-team playoff similar to that of the Canadian-American League (two divisions with three teams each), with an additional round with the division winners facing each other for the Stanley Cup.
24. *New Bedford Evening Standard*, July 7, 1933.
25. *Lowell Evening Leader*, July 18, 1933.
26. *Woonsocket Call*, July 17, 1933.
27. *Nashua Telegraph*, July 7, 1933.
28. *Nashua Telegraph*, July 8 and 10, 1933.
29. *Nashua Telegraph*, July 15, 1933.
30. *Woonsocket Call*, July 31, 1933.
31. *Taunton Gazette*, September 6 and 8, 1933.
32. White, *Creating the National Pastime*, pp. 144–145.
33. Alexander, *Baseball in the Depression Era*, p. 62.
34. W.R. Hoefer, "Hickey, the Fan," *Baseball Magazine*, November 1932.
35. Lieb, "What's Wrong with Baseball?"
36. *Lowell Evening Leader*, July 21, 1933.
37. *New Bedford Evening Standard*, September 5, 1933.
38. *New Bedford Evening Standard*, September 6, 1933.
39. *Lowell Evening Leader*, September 12, 1933.
40. *Lowell Evening Leader*, September 18, 1933.
41. *Worcester Telegram*, September 18, 1933.
42. *Lowell Evening Leader*, September 18, 1933.
43. "Inferior teams" also won the professional hockey playoffs during the winter of 1933, when the New York Rangers won the National Hockey League's Stanley Cup with the third-best record in the league and the Boston Cubs won the Canadian-American League's Fontaine Cup with the third-best record in the league.
44. *Springfield Union*, June 8, 1934.
45. *Lowell Evening Leader*, June 9, 1934.
46. *New York Times*, August 8, 1935.
47. *Boston Globe*, October 1, 1936.
48. Morse death in *Boston Herald*, April 13, 1937; Burnham death in *Los Angeles Times*, October 3, 1937; Doe death in *Quincy Patriot Ledger*, October 6, 1938.
49. *Quincy Patriot Ledger*, July 7, 1939.
50. *Lynn Evening Item*, September 11, 1933, and September 28, 1936.
51. Nutter, "Claude Davidson's League."
52. Sandage, *Born Losers*, p. 46.
53. Edsworth, *The New Deal*, p. 226.
54. Kossuth, "Boondoggling, Baseball, and the WPA."
55. *Lynn Evening Item*, June 20, 1940.
56. Snyder, *Beyond the Shadows of the Senators*, p. 34.
57. *Lynn Evening Item*, July 3 and 17, 1940.
58. Chadwick, *Baseball's Hometown Teams*, p. 116.

Chapter 11

1. *Lynn Evening Item*, November 20, 1940.
2. Ibid.
3. Nutter, "Claude Davidson's League."
4. *Lynn Evening Item*, May 26, 1941.
5. Mead, *Even the Browns*, p. 29.
6. *Woonsocket Call*, May 27 and 28, 1941.
7. *Lynn Evening Item*, July 24, 1941.
8. *Boston Chronicle*, August 2, 1941.
9. Lanctot, *Negro League Baseball*, pp. 104–105, 227.
10. Ibid. p. 186.
11. *Lynn Evening Item*, August 26, 1941.
12. *Lynn Evening Item*, August 27, 1941.
13. *Boston Chronicle*, August 30, 1941.
14. *Pawtucket Times*, September 16, 1941.
15. Ibid.
16. *Pawtucket Times*, September 29, 1941.
17. *Lynn Evening Item*, December 2, 1941.
18. *Lynn Evening Item*, December 9, 1941.
19. Alumni questionnaire completed by Davidson in January 1950, contained in Davidson's alumni biographical file in the archives of Hay Library at Brown University.
20. Goldstein, *Spartan Seasons*, p. 20.
21. Mead, *Even the Browns*, p. 82.
22. *Lynn Evening Item*, May 1, 1942.

23. *Lynn Evening Item*, May 22, 1942.
24. Arning and Klyberg, "McCoy Stadium: Legacy or Folly?"
25. *Pawtucket Times*, July 6, 1942.
26. *Lynn Evening Item*, September 4, 1942.
27. *Pawtucket Times*, October 1, 1942.
28. *Pawtucket Times*, October 3, 1942.
29. *Lynn Evening Item*, September 28, 1942.
30. *New York Times*, January 7, 1943.
31. Lingeman, *Don't You Know There's a War On?* p. 235.
32. Mead, *Even the Browns*, p. 77.
33. *Lynn Evening Item*, June 13, 1944.
34. *Lynn Evening Item*, July 9 and 10, 1944.
35. *Lynn Evening Item*, July 1, 1944.
36. *Lynn Evening Item*, August 19, 1944.
37. *Lynn Evening Item*, August 26, 1944.
38. *Lynn Evening Item*, May 19, 1945.
39. Utley, "The Legend of the Real Crash Davis."
40. *Pawtucket Times*, May 21, 1945.
41. *Pawtucket Times*, July 28, 1945.
42. Utley, "The Legend of the Real Crash Davis."
43. *Pawtucket Times*, May 19 and July 30, 1945.
44. *Lynn Evening Item*, June 2, 1945.
45. *Lynn Evening Item*, July 9, 1945.
46. *Lynn Evening Item*, July 9, 1945.
47. *Pawtucket Times*, July 31, 1945.
48. Bird's obituary in *Quincy Patriot Ledger*, February 4, 1994.
49. *Lynn Evening Item*, July 20, 1945.
50. Stout, "Race, Jackie Robinson, and the Red Sox."

Chapter 12

1. *Lynn Evening Item*, May 11, 1946.
2. Campanella, *It's Good to Be Alive*, pp. 118–119.
3. Madden, "Nashua, N.H., Was Safe Haven."
4. Harold Rosenthal, "He Made a Difference for the Dodgers," *Saturday Evening Post*, April 8, 1950.
5. Tygiel, *Baseball's Great Experiment*, p. 146.
6. Roper, "Baseball Integration."
7. Madden, "Nashua, N.H., Was Safe Haven"; Roper, "Baseball Integration."
8. *Los Angeles Times*, June 20, 1962.
9. *Lynn Evening Item*, November 29, 1945.
10. *Nashua Telegraph*, November 27, 1945.
11. *Nashua Telegraph*, December 11, 1945.
12. *Nashua Telegraph*, December 8, 1945.
13. *Nashua Telegraph*, December 11, 1945.
14. *Lynn Evening Item*, December 10, 1945.
15. Letter from Buzzy Bavasi to author, dated November 18, 2004.
16. Ibid.
17. *Washington Post*, December 13, 1945.
18. Ibid.
19. *Lawrence Evening Tribune*, December 13, 1945.
20. *Lawrence Evening Tribune*, January 5, 1945.
21. *Nashua Telegraph*, January 15, 1946.
22. Letter from Buzzy Bavasi to author, dated November 18, 2004.
23. *Boston Guardian*, February 9 and April 20, 1946.
24. *New York Times*, April 5, 1946.
25. *Nashua Telegraph*, April 4, 1946.
26. *Lawrence Evening Tribune*, April 6, 1946; *Lynn Evening Item*, April 5, 1946.
27. *Daily Worker*, April 6, 1946.
28. *Boston Chronicle*, April 20, 1946.
29. Ibid.
30. *Baltimore Afro-American*, April 13, 1946.
31. *Baltimore Afro-American*, April 6, 1946.
32. Robert Peterson, *Only the Ball Was White* (New York: McGraw-Hill, 1970 [paperback edition, 1984]), p. 197.
33. Tygiel, *Baseball's Great Experiment*, p. 152.
34. Arthur Mann, *Branch Rickey: American in Action* (Boston: Houghton Mifflin, 1957); Murray Polner, *Branch Rickey* (New York: Atheneum, 1982); Harvey Frommer, *Rickey & Robinson: The Men Who Broke Baseball's Color Barrier* (New York: Macmillan, 1982).
35. Jules Tygiel and John Thorn, "Jackie Robinson's Signing: The Untold Story," *Sport*, June 1988, pp. 65–70; "Branch Rickey: A Register of His Papers in the Library of Congress," 1998, p. 5.
36. *Boston Herald*, May 12, 1946.
37. Ibid.
38. F.C. Lane, "Will the Major Leagues Adopt Night Baseball?" *Baseball Magazine*, October 1935; *Boston Herald*, May 4, 1946.
39. *Boston Herald*, May 18, 1946.
40. Campanella, *It's Good to Be Alive*, pp. 123–124.
41. Mike Carey and Jamie Most, *High Above Courtside: The Lost Memoirs of Johnny Most* (Champaign, Ill.: Sports Publishing, 2003), pp. 25–26.
42. Madden, "Nashua, N.H., Was Safe Haven."
43. Roger Kahn, *The Boys of Summer* (New York: Harper & Row, 1973 [paperbook edition]), p. 339.
44. Madden, "Nashua, N.H., Was Safe Haven."
45. *Lynn Evening Item*, June 18, 1946.
46. *New York Times*, December 24, 1946.
47. *New York Times*, January 27, 1947.
48. *Lawrence Evening Tribune*, July 15, 1947.
49. *Lowell Sun*, July 19 and 24, 1947.
50. *Lawrence Evening Tribune*, August 12 and 18, 1947.

51. Eric Stone, *Wrong Side of the Wall: The Life of Blackie Schwamb, the Greatest Prison Baseball Player of All Time* (Guilford, Conn.: Lyons Press, 2004), p. 161.
52. *Boston Globe*, May 12, 1948.
53. *Lynn Evening Item*, January 15, 1948.
54. *Nashua Telegraph*, April 24, 1948.
55. Associated Press, August 31, 1998.
56. *Providence Journal-Bulletin*, August 3, 1995.
57. *Nashua Telegraph*, September 17, 1948.
58. *Lynn Evening Item*, October 21, 1948.
59. *New York Times*, December 14, 1948.
60. Lanctot, *Negro League Baseball*, pp. 344–345.
61. *Lynn Evening Item*, May 9, 1949.
62. *Fall River Herald*, July 5, 1949.
63. *Pawtucket Times*, August 25, 1949.
64. *Nashua Telegraph*, July 3 and 11, 1949.
65. *Lynn Evening Item*, July 20, 1949.
66. *Sporting News*, August 3, 1949.
67. *Nashua Telegraph*, September 6 and 7, 1949.
68. *Nashua Telegraph*, October 5, 1949.

Epilogue

1. *Lynn Evening Item*, April 19, 1956, contained in Davidson's alumni file at Brown University.
2. Lynne Browne and Steven Sass, "From Mill-Based to Knowledge-Based Economy," in Temin, *Engines of Enterprise*, pp. 205–206.
3. *Providence Journal*, May 12, 2004.
4. *Lowell Sun*, June 9, 2006.
5. *Boston Globe*, July 30, 2006.

Bibliography

Alexander, Charles. *Breaking the Slump: Baseball in the Depression Era.* New York: Columbia University Press, 2002.

Anderson, Will. *Was Baseball Really Invented in Maine?* Portland: Will Anderson, 1992.

Arning, Chuck, and Kevin Klyberg. "McCoy Stadium: Legacy or Folly?" *Cultural Resource Management,* November 2000.

Bevis, Charlie. "Evolution of the Sunday Doubleheader and Its Role in Elevating the Popularity of Baseball." In *The Cooperstown Symposium on Baseball and American Culture, 2003–2004,* ed. William Simons. Jefferson, N.C.: McFarland, 2003.

_____. "Rocky Point: A Lone Outpost of Sunday Baseball Within Sabbatarian New England." *NINE: A Journal of Baseball History & Culture,* Fall 2005.

_____. *Sunday Baseball: The Major Leagues' Struggle to Play Baseball on the Lord's Day, 1876–1934.* Jefferson, N.C.: McFarland, 2003.

Blewitt, Mary. *Constant Turmoil: The Politics of Industrial Life in Nineteenth-Century New England.* Amherst: University of Massachusetts Press, 2000.

Brown, Richard, and Jack Tager. *Massachusetts: A Concise History.* Amherst: University of Massachusetts Press, 2000.

Cahn, William. *Lawrence 1912: The Bread and Roses Strike.* New York: Pilgrim, 1982.

Campanella, Roy. *It's Good To Be Alive.* Boston: Little, Brown, 1959.

Chadwick, Bruce. *Baseball's Hometown Teams: The Story of the Minor Leagues.* New York: Abbeyville, 1994.

Cialdini, R.B. "Basking in Reflected Glory." *Journal of Personality and Social Psychology,* 34 (1976).

Cox, James. *A Century of Light.* New York: Benjamin, 1979.

Cremins, Dave. "The Evolution of the Trolley." www.railroadinfo.com.

Danzell, Robert, Jr. *Enterprising Elite: The Boston Associates and the World They Made.* Cambridge, Mass.: Harvard University Press, 1987.

Dawley, Alan. *Class and Community: The Industrial Revolution in Lynn.* Cambridge, Mass.: Harvard University Press, 1976.

Dunwell, Steve. *The Run of the Mills.* Boston: David R. Godine, 1978.

Edsforth, Ronald. *The New Deal: America's Response to the Great Depression.* Malden, Mass.: Blackwell, 2000.

Eisenmenger, Robert. *The Dynamics of Growth in New England's Economy.* Middletown, Conn.: Wesleyan University Press, 1967.

Eno, Arthur Jr., ed. *Cotton Was King: A History of Lowell, Massachusetts.* Lowell: Lowell Historical Society, 1976.

Farrell, John. "All-New England League Merger Allowed." *Sporting Life,* February 19, 1916.

Fogelson, Robert. *Downtown: Its Rise and Fall, 1880–1950.* New Haven, Conn.: Yale University Press, 2001.

Goldstein, Richard. *Spartan Seasons: How Baseball Survived the Second World War.* New York: Macmillan, 1980.

Hardy, Stephen. "Long Before Orr: Playing Hockey in Boston, 1897–1929." In *The Rock, The Curse and The Hub: A Random History of Boston Sports,* ed. Randy Roberts. Cambridge, Mass.: Harvard University Press, 2005.

Hareven, Tamara, and Ralph Langenbach. *Amoskeag: Life and Work in an American Factory City.* New York: Pantheon, 1978.

Hilton, George, and John Due. *The Electric Interurban Railways in America.* Stanford, Calif.: Stanford University Press, 1960.

Hoffman, Charles. *The Depression of the Nineties: An Economic History.* Westport, Conn.: Greenwood, 1970.

Hudon, Paul. *Lower Merrimack: The Valley and Its Peoples.* Sun Valley, Calif.: American Historical, 2004.

Huthmacher, Joseph. *Massachusetts People and Politics.* Cambridge, Mass.: Harvard University Press, 1959.

Ivor-Campbell, Frederick, ed. *Baseball's First Stars.* Cleveland: Society for American Baseball Research, 1996.

Jackson, Kenneth. *Crabgrass Frontier: The Suburbanization of the United States.* New York: Oxford University Press, 1985.

Jesep, Paul Peter. *Rockingham Park, 1933–1969.* Portsmouth, N.H.: Peter E. Randall, 1998.

Johnson, Lloyd, and Miles Wolff, eds. *The Encyclopedia of Minor League Baseball,* 2nd ed. Durham, N.C.: Baseball America, 1997.

Judd, Richard, *Maine: The Pine Tree State from Prehistory to the Present.* Orono, Maine: University of Maine Press, 1995.

Kenny, Herbert. *Newspaper Row: Journalism in the Pre-Television Era.* Chester, Conn.: Globe Pequot, 1987.

Kossuth, Robert. "Boondoggling, Baseball, and the WPA." *NINE: A Journal of Baseball History and Culture,* Fall 2000.

Lanctot, Neil. *Negro League Baseball: The Rise and Ruin of a Black Institution.* Philadelphia: University of Pennsylvania Press, 2004.

Land, Kenneth. "Organizing the Boys of Summer: The Evolution of Minor-League Baseball, 1883–1990." *American Journal of Sociology,* November 1994.

Latham, Frank. *The Panic of 1893.* New York: Franklin Watts, 1971.

Lieb, Fred. "What's Wrong with Baseball?" *Los Angeles Times,* January 29–February 10, 1933.

Lingeman, Richard. *Don't You Know There's a War On? The American Home Front 1941–1945.* New York: Nation, 2003.

Lomax, Michael. *Black Baseball Entrepreneurs, 1860–1901.* Syracuse, N.Y.: Syracuse University Press, 2003.

Madden, Michael. "Nashua, N.H., Was Safe Haven." *Boston Globe,* March 28, 1997.

Malloy, Jerry. "Out at Home." In *The Armchair Book of Baseball II.* New York: Scribner's, 1987.

Mandlebaum, Michael. *The Meaning of Sports.* New York: Public Affairs, 2004.

Mason, Edward Sagendorph. *The Street Railway in Massachusetts: The Rise and Decline of an Industry.* Cambridge, Mass.: Harvard University Press, 1932.

McLoughlin, William. *Rhode Island: A History.* New York: W.W. Norton, 1978.

Mead, William. *Even the Browns: The Zany, True Story of Baseball in the Early Forties.* Chicago: Contemporary, 1978.

Melville, Tom. *Early Baseball and the Rise of the National League.* Jefferson, N.C.: McFarland, 2001.

Melder, Keith. *Life and Times in Shoe City: The Shoe Workers of Lynn.* Salem, Mass.: Essex Institute, 1979.

Morris. Charles. *The Tycoons: How Andrew Carnegie, John D. Rockefeller, Jay Gould, and J.P. Morgan Invented the American Supereconomy.* New York: Times, 2005.

Nutter, Joe. "Claude Davidson's League Battles For Its Foothold." *Providence Journal* (Section VI), August 10, 1941.

Obojski, Robert. *Bush League: A History of Minor League Baseball.* New York: Macmillan, 1975.

Okkonen, Marc. *The Federal League of 1914–1915: Baseball's Third Major League.* Garrett Park, Md.: Society for American Baseball Research, 1989.

Peterson, Robert. *Only the Ball Was White.* New York: McGraw-Hill, 1970 (paperback edition, 1984).

Pietrusza, David. *Lights On! The Wild Century-Long Saga of Night Baseball.* Lanham, Md.: Scarecrow, 1997.

Prevan, David. *Seize the Daylight: The Curious and Contentious Story of Daylight Saving Time.* New York: Thunder's Mouth, 2005.

Ribowsky, Mark. *Don't Look Back: Satchel Paige in the Shadows of Baseball.* New York: Simon & Schuster, 1994.

Rivard, Paul. *A New Order of Things: How the Textile Industry Transformed New England.* Hanover, N.H.: University of New England Press, 2002.

Roper, Scott, and Stephanie Abbott Roper. "Baseball Integration and the 1946 Nashua Dodgers." *Historical New Hampshire,* Spring/Summer 1998.

Roth, David. *Connecticut: A History.* New York: W.W. Norton, 1979.

Sandage, Scott. *Born Losers: A History of Failure in America.* Cambridge, Mass.: Harvard University Press, 2005.

Scoggins, Chaz. *Bricks and Bats.* Lowell, Mass.: Lowell Historical Society, 2002.

_____. "Lowell's Baseball History Rich in Pennants, Stars." *Lowell Sun,* November 27–30, 1994.

_____. "Youngest Ever to Play Professional Baseball." *Lowell Sun* (*SUN/day* magazine section), May 11, 1975.

Seymour, Harold. *Baseball: The Early Years.* New York: Oxford University, 1960.

Snyder, Brad. *Beyond the Shadows of the Senators: The Untold Story of the Homestead Grays and the Integration of Baseball.* Chicago: Contemporary, 2003.

Soos, Troy. *Before the Curse: The Glory Days of New England Baseball, 1858–1918.* Hyannis, Mass.: Parnassus, 1997.

Stilgoe, John. *Borderland: Origins of the American Suburb, 1820–1939.* New Haven, Conn.: Yale University Press, 1988.

Stout, Glenn. "Tryout and Fallout: Race, Jackie Robinson, and the Red Sox." *Massachusetts Historical Review,* Volume 6, 2004.

Sullivan, Neil. *The Minors: The Struggles and the Triumph of Baseball's Poor Relations from 1876 to the Present.* New York: St. Martin's, 1990.

Temin, Peter, ed. *Engines of Enterprise: An Economic History of New England.* Cambridge, Mass.: Harvard University Press, 2000.

Tygiel, Jules. *Baseball's Great Experiment: Jackie Robinson and His Legacy.* New York: Oxford University, 1983.

Utley, Hank. "The Legend of the Real Crash Davis." www.philadelphiaathletics.org.

Voigt, David. *American Baseball: From Gentleman's Sport to the Commissioner System.* Norman: University of Oklahoma Press, 1966.

Warner, Sam Bass, Jr. *Streetcar Suburbs: The Process of Growth in Boston (1870–1900)*. Cambridge, Mass.: Harvard University Press, 1978.

Watson, Bruce. *Bread & Roses: Mills, Migrants, and the Struggle for the American Dream*. New York: Viking, 2005.

Welsh, Norman. "Tim Murnane: Champion of Baseball's Integrity." *The Pilot*, November 1, 1985.

White, G. Edward. *Creating the National Pastime: Baseball Transforms Itself 1903–1953*. Princeton, N.J.: Princeton University Press, 1996.

Yafa, Stephen. *Big Cotton: How a Humble Fiber Created Fortunes*. New York: Viking Penguin, 2005.

Baseball Periodicals

Baseball Magazine

Baseball Research Journal

National Pastime

New York Clipper

Spalding Guide

Sporting Life

Sporting News

General Newspapers

Attleboro Sun

Baltimore Afro-American

Bangor Daily News

Bangor Whig and Courier

Biddeford Journal

Boston Chronicle

Boston Globe

Boston Guardian

Boston Herald

Boston Post

Brockton Enterprise

Brockton Times

Cambridge Chronicle

Christian Science Monitor

Concord Daily Patriot

Concord Evening Monitor

Dover Republican

Eastern Argus

Fall River Globe

Fall River Herald

Fitchburg Sentinel

Foster's Daily Democrat

Gloucester Times

Greenfield Recorder

Hartford Courant

Haverhill Evening Gazette

Holyoke Transcript

Kennebec Journal

Lawrence Daily American

Lawrence Eagle

Lawrence Evening Tribune

Lewiston Evening Journal

Lowell Courier

Lowell Courier-Citizen

Lowell Daily News

Lowell Evening Leader

Lowell Morning Mail

Lowell Sun

Lynn Bee

Lynn Evening Item

Manchester Union

Nashua Telegraph

New Bedford Evening Standard

New Bedford Morning Mercury

Newburyport Herald

New York Times

Pawtucket Times

Portland Press-Herald

Portsmouth Chronicle

Providence Evening Bulletin

Providence Journal

Quincy Patriot Ledger

Salem Evening News

Springfield Republican

Springfield Union

Taunton Gazette

Woonsocket Call

Woonsocket Evening Reporter

Worcester Evening Post

Worcester Spy

Worcester Telegram

Index

Numbers in **_bold italics_** indicate pages with photographs